The 'do-it-yourself' artwork

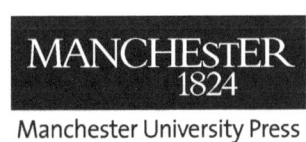
MANCHESTER
1824

Manchester University Press

rethinking
art's histories

SERIES EDITORS
Amelia G. Jones, Marsha Meskimmon

Rethinking Art's Histories aims to open out art history from its most basic structures by foregrounding work that challenges the conventional periodisation and geographical subfields of traditional art history, and addressing a wide range of visual cultural forms from the early modern period to the present.

These books will acknowledge the impact of recent scholarship on our understanding of the complex temporalities and cartographies that have emerged through centuries of world-wide trade, political colonisation and the diasporic movement of people and ideas across national and continental borders.

The 'do-it-yourself' artwork

Participation from Fluxus to new media

Edited by
Anna Dezeuze

Manchester University Press

Manchester and New York

distributed in the United States exclusively by Palgrave Macmillan

Published by Manchester University Press
Oxford Road, Manchester M13 9NR, UK
and Room 400, 175 Fifth Avenue, New York, NY 10010, USA
www.manchesteruniversitypress.co.uk

Distributed in the United States exclusively by
Palgrave Macmillan, 175 Fifth Avenue,
New York, NY 10010, USA

Distributed in Canada exclusively by
UBC Press, University of British Columbia, 2029 West Mall,
Vancouver, BC, Canada V6T 1Z2

British Library Cataloguing-in-Publication Data is available

Library of Congress Cataloging-in-Publication Data is available

ISBN 978 0 7190 8747 9 paperback

First published by Manchester University Press in hardback 2010

This paperback edition first published 2012

Printed by Lightning Source

Contents

List of figures

List of contributors

ANNA DEZEUZE completed a Leverhulme Trust Early Career Postdoctoral Fellowship at the University of Manchester in 2009, and will be a Terra Foundation for American Art Postdoctoral Fellow at the Smithsonian American Art Museum, Washington DC (October 2009–July 2010). In addition to articles on contemporary art for magazines, she has published a number of essays, in journals and edited books, about 1960s art practices including Neo-dada, Fluxus, kinetic art, and the work of Lygia Clark and Hélio Oiticica. She has co-edited, with Julia Kelly and Jo Applin, a special cluster on 'Assemblage/ Bricolage' for the *Art Journal* (Spring 2008), and is currently editing, with Julia Kelly, an edited volume on *Found Sculpture and Photography from Surrealism to Contemporary Art* (forthcoming with Ashgate). With David Lomas, she curated the touring exhibition *Subversive Spaces: Surrealism and Contemporary Art* (Whitworth Art Gallery, Manchester, 2009).

CLAIRE BISHOP is Associate Professor in the Art History department at CUNY Graduate Center, at the City University of New York. In addition to articles in art magazines such as *Artforum* and *Flash Art*, she has published *Installation Art: A Critical History* (Tate Publishing, 2005) and edited the anthology *Participation* (Whitechapel Art Gallery and MIT Press, 2006). She recently curated, with Mark Sladen, the touring exhibition *Double Agents* (ICA, London, 2008) and edited the accompanying catalogue.

GUY BRETT is an independent curator and critic based in London. His interest in spectator participation started in the 1960s when he was an art critic for the *Times* and met Lygia Clark and Hélio Oiticica in Brazil. Since that period, he has written on a wide range of art and artists and published two books – *Through Our Own Eyes: Popular Art and Modern History* (GMP/Heretic and New Society Publishers 1986) and *David Medalla: Exploding Galaxies* (Kala Press, 1995). He co-curated the first major retrospective of Hélio Oiticica's work in London in 1969, and staged thematic exhibitions including *Transcontinental: 9 Latin American Artists* (Ikon Gallery, Birmingham, 1990) and *Force Fields: Phases of the Kinetic* (MACBA, Barcelona and Hayward Gallery,

London, 2000). A selection of his critical writings has been collected in *Carnival of Perception* (Iniva, 2004). He recently edited the volume on *Hélio Oiticica in London* (Tate Publishing, 2007) and co-curated the exhibition of *Cildo Meireles* at Tate Modern in 2008.

BERYL GRAHAM is Professor of New Media Art at the University of Sunderland. She has curated exhibitions of new media art, including *Serious Games* (Barbican Art Gallery, London, 1996), and published widely on this topic, including a co-edited book (with Sarah Cook and Sarah Martin), *Curating New Media* (Baltic Centre for Contemporary Art, 2002), and essays in edited volumes such as Sarah Kenderdine (ed.) *Theorizing Digital Cultural Heritage* (MIT Press, 2007), Christiane Paul (ed.) *Curating New Media* (University of California Press, 2006) and Paul Brown, Charlie Gere, Nick Lambert, Catherine Mason (eds) *White Heat and Cold Logic: British Computer Arts 1960–1980* (MIT Press, 2009). Her book *Digital Media* was published in 2003 (Heinemann), and she has co-authored with Sarah Cook, *Rethinking Curating: Art After New Media* (MIT Press, 2010).

JENNIFER A. GONZÁLEZ is Associate Professor in the History of Art and Visual Culture Department at the University of California, Santa Cruz. She has written a number of essays and articles on contemporary artists (*Christian Marclay*, Phaidon, 2005), as well as on race and cyberspace for edited volumes including C.H. Gray (ed.) *The Cyborg Handbook* (Routledge, 1995), Lisa Bloom (ed.) *With Other Eyes: Looking at Race and Gender in Visual Culture* (University of Minnesota Press, 1999), and Beth Kolko, Lisa Nakamura, Gil Rodman (eds) *Race in Cyberspace* (Routledge, 2000). In 2008, she published *Subject to Display: Reframing Race in Contemporary Installation Art* (MIT Press).

AMELIA JONES is Professor and Pilkington Chair in Art History and Visual Studies at the University of Manchester; she will be moving to McGill University in Montreal in 2010, as the Grierson Chair in Visual Culture. She has organised exhibitions on contemporary art and on feminist, queer, and anti-racist approaches to visual culture. Her recent publications include the edited volumes *Feminism and Visual Culture* (Routledge, 2003, new edition forthcoming 2010) and *A Companion to Contemporary Art since 1945* (Blackwells, 2006). Following on *Body Art/Performing the Subject* (Minnesota University Press, 1998), Jones's recent books include *Irrational Modernism: A Neurasthenic History of New York Dada* (MIT Press, 2004), and most recently *Self/Image: Technology, Representation and the Contemporary Subject* (Routledge, 2006). Her current projects are an edited volume *Perform, Repeat, Record: Live Art in History* (with co-editor Adrian Heathfield), and a book tentatively entitled *Seeing Differently: Identification and the Visual Arts.*

CHRISTIAN KRAVAGNA is an art historian, critic and curator. He is Professor of Postcolonial Studies at the Academy of Fine Arts in Vienna. He has edited *Privileg Blick: Kritik der visuellen Kultur* (ID-Verlag, 1997), *Agenda: Perspektiven kritischer Kunst* (Folio Verlag, 2000), *The Museum as Arena: Artists on Institutional Critique* (Verlag der Buchhandlung Walther König, 2001) and *Routes: Imaging Travel and Migration* (Revolver Verlag, 2007). He is also the curator (with Hedwig Saxenhuber) at the Kunstraum Lakeside in Klagenfurt, and curated in 2008 *Planetary Consciousness* at Kunstraum der Leuphana, Universität Lüneburg.

JANET KRAYNAK is Assistant Professor of Contemporary Art at the New School University in New York, with a joint appointment at Parsons, the New School for Design, and Eugene Lang College, the New School for Liberal Arts. She has published essays on a number of artists, including Nan Goldin (in Rhea Anastas with Michael Brenson (eds) *A Witness to Her Art*, Bard College, 2006), and such topics as the relationship between art history and criticism, in Elizabeth Mansfield (ed.) *Making Art History: A Changing Discipline and its Institutions*, Routledge, 2007). As the editor of *Please Pay Attention Please: Bruce Nauman's Words: Writings and Interviews* (MIT Press, 2003), she is currently completing a book entitled *Reiterating Nauman*, which critically re-evaluates the artist's early work.

MIWON KWON is Professor of Contemporary Art History at the University of California, Los Angeles (UCLA). In addition to her book, *One Place After Another: Site-Specific art and Locational Identity* (MIT Press, 2002), she is the author of many texts on the art of Francis Alÿs, Michael Asher, Cai Guo-Qiang, Jimmie Durham, Felix Gonzales-Torres, Christian Marclay, Ana Mendieta, Christian Philipp Müller and Do Ho Suh, among others. She was founding editor of *Documents*, a journal of art, culture and criticism (1992–2004), and serves on the advisory board of *October*. She is currently preparing an essay on the public projects of Barbara Kruger for Rizzoli Publications and is co-organising a historical exhibition entitled *Ends of the Earth: Land Art to 1977*, with co-curator Philipp Kaiser, to be presented at Los Angeles Museum of Contemporary Art in 2012.

ARNAULD PIERRE lectures in Art History at the Université Paris-Sorbonne (Paris IV). He has published monographs about Frank Kupka (Liverpool University Press, 1998), Francis Picabia (Gallimard, 2002), Bernar Venet (Marval, 2000), Julije Knifer (Adam Biro, 2001), and Tania Mouraud (Flammarion, 2004), and is working on a monograph about Alexander Calder (Hazan, 2009). He has written articles and catalogue essays about abstract and kinetic artists such as Calder, Lygia Clark, Jesús Rafael Soto, Carlos Cruz-Diez, Nicolas Schöffer, Victor Vasarely, François Morellet and the Groupe de

Recherche d'Art Visuel. In 2003, he co-curated the exhibition *Aux Origines de l'abstraction* (Musée d'Orsay, Paris); other curated exhibitions include *L'Œil moteur* (Musée d'art moderne et contemporain, Strasbourg, 2005) and *Maternidades cosmicas: En busca de los orígenes, de Kupka a Kubrick* (Tenerife Espacio de las Artes, Santa Cruz de Tenerife, 2008).

JUDITH RODENBECK holds the Noble Foundation Chair in Art and Cultural History at Sarah Lawrence College. She has published articles on happenings (*Grey Room*, 13, Fall 2003) and co-curated with Benjamin Buchloh the exhibition *Experiments in the Everyday: Allan Kaprow and Robert Watts – Events, Objects, Documents* at Columbia University in 2000. She served as editor-in-chief of the *Art Journal* from 2007 through 2009. Her book *Radical Prototypes: Allan Kaprow and the Invention of Happenings* is forthcoming in 2010.

FRAZER WARD teaches the History of Contemporary Art and Architecture at Smith College (Mass.). He has written extensively on art since the 1960s, and his work appears in catalogues, essay collections and journals, including *Art + Text*, *Documents*, *Frieze*, *October* and *Art Journal*.

CATHERINE WOOD is Curator of Contemporary Art/Performance at Tate Modern. She was co-curator of *Pop Life: Art in a Material World* at Tate Modern in September 2009. Wood programmes Tate Live and is co-producer of the Tate's annual performance and film event, *The Long Weekend*, which featured in 2009 a re-staging of the 1971 participatory exhibition by Robert Morris, which she discusses in this volume. In 2007, she co-curated, with Jessica Morgan, the exhibition *The World as a Stage* at Tate Modern. Wood has regularly published articles in *Afterall*, *Artforum*, *Frieze*, *Art Monthly* and *Untitled*, as well as catalogue essays on many artists including Mark Leckey, Marc Camille Chaimowicz, Daria Martin, Sharon Lockhart and Gerard Byrne. Her book on Yvonne Rainer's *The Mind is a Muscle* was published by Afterall/MIT Press in 2007. She is on the board for *Afterall* and for the exhibition and studio space, Studio Voltaire, London.

Acknowledgements

This volume has been in the making for a long time, and my thanks go above all to the contributors for their patience, support and hard work. Many thanks to Guy Brett, Judith Rodenbeck, Catherine Wood, Frazer Ward, Amelia Jones and Beryl Graham for their original contributions to the volume. Thanks to Arnauld Pierre, Janet Kraynak, Jennifer González, Miwon Kwon, Christian Kravagna and Claire Bishop, for letting me reprint, as well as intervene in their essays, whether through translation or re-translation, and/or cuts and edits. I would also like to thank, on behalf of all the authors, the small number of artists, artist families and galleries who generously agreed to waive reproduction and copyright fees. Finally, I would like to extend my thanks to the anonymous peer reviewers of the manuscript, and to the series editors Amelia Jones and Marsha Merskimmon.

An introduction to the 'do-it-yourself' artwork

Anna Dezeuze

Defining the 'do-it-yourself' artwork

Lygia Clark's *Air and Stone* (1966) (figure 1.1) and Yoko Ono's *Painting to Hammer a Nail* (1961) (figure 1.2) are works that mobilise spectator participation. *Air and Stone* only exists as a work when the participant takes a plastic bag, fills it with air, closes it with an elastic band, places a stone on one of its corners, and holds it in his or her hands. Similarly, Ono's work exists as an instruction to be performed. 'I think painting can be instructionalized', Ono wrote in 1965. 'The artist, in this case, will only give instructions or diagrams for painting – and the painting will be more or less a do-it-yourself kit according to the instructions.'[1] In a letter to a friend, Clark echoed Ono, simply stating a propos of one of her works: 'I want people to do it themselves.'[2]

Following Ono's and Clark's suggestions, I will be defining as 'do-it-yourself' artworks a range of artistic practices that require an active physical and/or conceptual participation on the part of the spectator. This category of works, which has been developed since the 1960s and is particularly prominent in contemporary art today, is not unified by formal characteristics. A participatory practice can take many forms: it can be an object to be worn or to be touched, a score to be performed, a collective performance in which the artist may or may not participate, an environment to be entered or a sequence of spaces to be traversed, a digital image to be clicked on, or a combination of one or more of these features. Because of this variety of forms, participatory practices are often included in established categories of twentieth-century visual art such as performance, conceptual, installation or new media art, which tend to emphasise discussions of new types of practices over an analysis of the spectator's role. While some studies have addressed the role of spectator participation in specific installation and sculptural practices,[3] mainstream histories of art often fail to take into account the specificity of do-it-yourself artworks. The inclusion of works by Yoko Ono, Lygia Clark and Hélio Oiticica in a survey of performance art edited by Tracey Warr, for example, is misleading, since the very title of this book, *The Artist's Body*, quite simply obscures the fact that their works involve the *spectator's* rather than

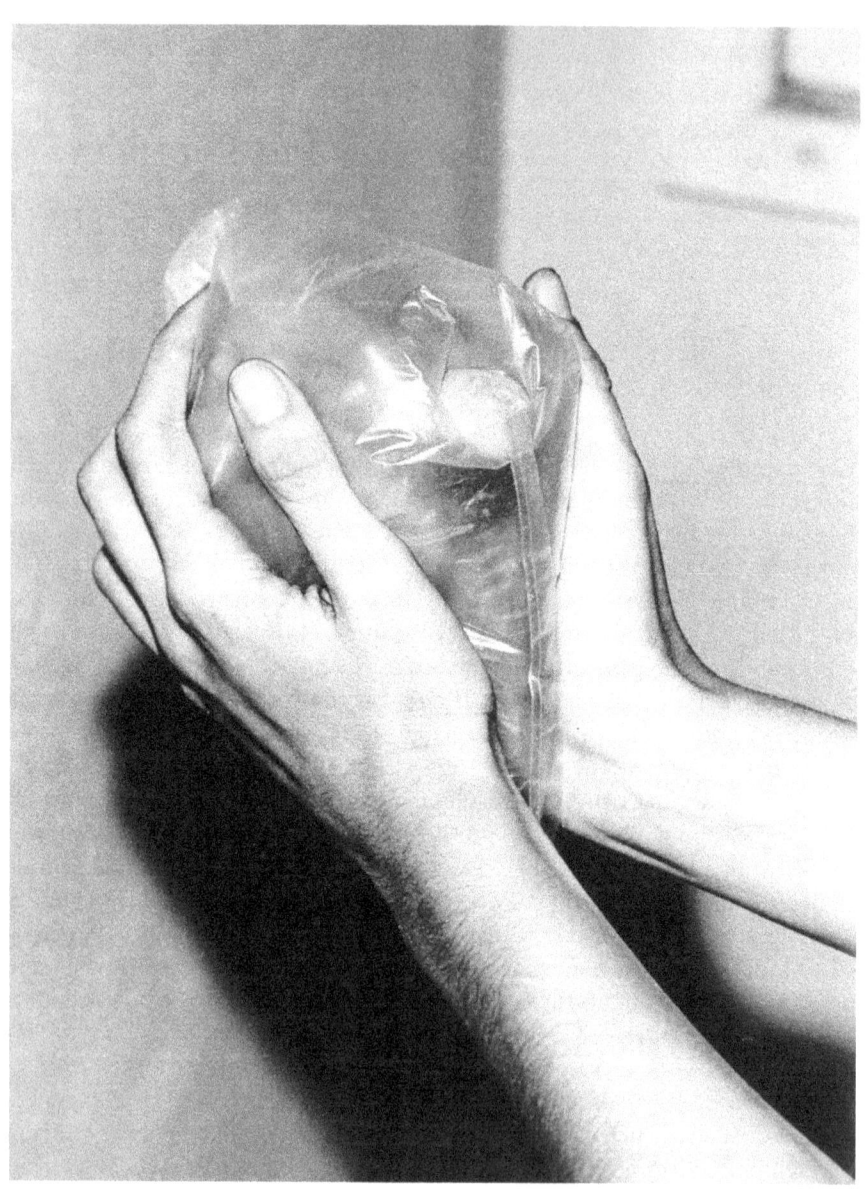

1.1   Lygia Clark, *Air and Stone*, 1966

the artist's body, unlike most performance art.[4] These misunderstandings may explain why, as Guy Brett complained in 1998, 'There is no twentieth-century art history which gives … participatory experiments their due.'[5] Along with the exhibition *The Art of Participation: from 1950 to Now*, and Claire Bishop's anthology of primary sources,[6] this book seeks to redress this situation. Most

```
PAINTING TO HAMMER A NAIL

Hammer a nail into a mirror, a piece of
glass, a canvas, wood or metal every
morning. Also, pick up a hair that came
off when you combed in the morning and
tie, it around the hammered nail. The
painting ends when the surface is covered
with nails.

                  .

1961  winter
```

Yoko Ono, *Painting to Hammer a Nail*, Winter 1961

importantly, it also aims to demonstrate the theoretical relevance of do-it-yourself artworks for our wider understanding of art since the 1950s.

Unlike the past participle ' made' in 'ready-made', the imperative form 'do' and the indexical pronouns 'it' and 'yourself' are, grammatically speaking, performative; they are contingent on the specific situation in which they are used. In the same way as the reader of Yoko Ono's scores can slip into the text by responding to the imperatives ('hammer a nail', 'tie'...), the hands visible in photographs of Clark's *Air and Stone* could be yours or mine. The invitation comes from the artist, and the 'yourself' becomes anyone willing to participate. When such participatory work is exhibited as a traditional form of painting or sculpture that cannot be touched, or presented as a performance to be watched by an audience, it is deprived of its central defining feature: the do-it-yourself artwork is a practice that exists *only* through a potential participation. The verb 'do' suggests an emphasis on process and actions to be performed by an active spectator in real time and space, while the pronoun 'it' remains open, as the result of this process will be determined by each individual's unique personal experience. The conjunction of a task suggested by the work, the result of this action, and the pronoun 'yourself', sets up a new triangular relation between the artist, the artwork and the spectator/participant, which lies at the centre of this book.

It was precisely this 'overall change in the relations between artist, work of art and spectator' that Frank Popper highlighted in his 1975 book on *Art, Action and Participation*. As he summarised it:

> The 'work of art' itself has more or less disappeared by gradual stages. The artist has taken upon himself new functions which are more like those of an intermediary than a creator, and has begun to enunciate open-ended environmental propositions and hypotheses. Finally the spectator has been impelled to intervene in the aesthetic process in an unprecedented way.[7]

While articles in the Paris-based periodical *Robho* highlighted the importance of spectator participation in 1960s art, and Adrian Henri's 1974 book on *Environments and Happenings* contained a short section on 'spectator involvement',[8] Popper was certainly the first to register the full extent of participatory practices in Europe, North and South America. Like Popper's account, this volume locates the development of participation in the 1960s. Precursors can be found in the early twentieth-century experiments of Dada, Futurism and Constructivism, which often sought to shock or disorient their spectators, through physical involvement and/or direct provocations. Boris Groys has suggested that the drive to involve spectators can be traced even further back to Romanticism and the Wagnerian *Gesamtkunstwerk*, and argues that it should be read as a response to the secularisation of art, and the subsequent isolation of artists from their audiences.[9] Though original, Groys's general focus on the artist's ritual self-sacrifice does not account for the significant development and expansion of participatory artworks in the 1960s. This present volume seeks to shed light on this historical phenomenon by revisiting and providing more in-depth analyses of the seminal 1960s and early 1970s practices first mentioned by Popper and Henri, whether the performances of Allan Kaprow and Fluxus, kinetically oriented works by David Medalla, Lygia Clark and Hélio Oiticica or the Groupe de Recherche d'Art Visuel (GRAV), or the sculpture of Minimalists and post-Minimalists such as Robert Morris and Bruce Nauman.

The second wave of do-it-yourself practices in twentieth-century art, I would argue, occurred in the 1990s, and was made most visible through the curatorial and critical activities of two important figures in the international art world at that time – Nicolas Bourriaud and Hans-Ulrich Obrist. Obrist's

Do It project, started in 1994, focused on the do-it-yourself artwork as a mode of production, using the format of the instruction piece or score (exemplified by Ono's *Painting to Hammer a Nail*) to bring together artists of different generations who shared an interest in spectator participation. The thematic focus was the relations between the 'actualization and virtualization', and between 'repetition and difference', at the heart of this body of instructions – which have been carried out by different museums in a travelling exhibition, and by individuals reading the two *Do It* books or logging on to the website, which encourages participants to post images of their performances.[10] In his 1998 collection of essays on *Relational Aesthetics*, Bourriaud similarly sought to highlight the connections between contemporary art and 'the spectator "participation" theorised' in 1960s practices, but he focused on another aspect of the do-it-yourself artwork – the fact that it 'takes as its starting point human relations and their social context, as opposed to autonomous and exclusive art'.[11] In addition to his active role as curator and as director of the Palais de Tokyo in Paris, Bourriaud has stimulated through his writings debates about the political potential of participation in contemporary art – Claire Bishop's essay on contemporary participatory practices is a direct response to his position (see Chapter 14), as was Jessica Morgan's introduction to her own exhibition *Common Wealth* (at Tate Modern in 2003), which included do-it-yourself works by Thomas Hirschhorn, Gabriel Orozco and Carsten Höller among others.[12]

In parallel to this 1990s turn to 'relational' art, other forms of participatory practices emerged in the developing field of new media. Most recently, the concept of spectator participation has been associated to the exponential rise of user-generated content on the web – the 2008 *Art of Participation* exhibition was originally titled *MyMuseum*, in reference to the social networking website MySpace. The complex relations between such new media practices, 'relational aesthetics' and participation are mapped out by Beryl Graham (Chapter 15), while Jennifer González focuses on the performance of race in 1990s digital do-it-yourself artworks (Chapter 10).

This book includes discussions of a range of artists who have developed participatory works during the period from the late 1950s to the present. Artists such as the GRAV, Lygia Clark or Rirkrit Tiravanija have made spectator participation their central theoretical concern; others, such as Bruce Nauman, Marina Abramović, or Thomas Hirschhorn have created do-it-yourself artworks in the context of other artistic preoccupations. While many recent texts and exhibitions acknowledge the importance of 1960s do-it-yourself artworks, the relations between contemporary practices and their precedents remain largely unmapped. One of this book's aims, then, is to trace the emergence and evolution of spectator participation from the 1960s onwards in historical terms, but unlike Popper's survey, or the more recent *Art of Participation* exhibition, this book does not seek to provide an inventory of participatory practices. Rather, by focusing on case studies situated within their specific historical contexts, and by adopting a thematic approach, this anthology develops critical tools with which to distinguish different forms of spectator participation, and with which to analyse the new relations between artist, object and participant set up by the do-it-yourself artwork.

The very definition of participation itself is, of course, open to debate. Both Beryl Graham and Christian Kravagna distinguish, in their chapters (Chapters 13 and 15), between the terms interactive, participative and collaborative. Both agree that collaboration, which aims at erasing altogether the difference between producers and recipients (or artists and spectators), raises a set of issues that is qualitatively different from that of interactivity and participation, which hinge on this distinction, even as they seek to frame it in terms departing from traditional modes of viewing art in the modern era. According to these distinctions, the do-it-yourself artworks discussed in this volume tend to be either interactive, participative, or hybrids of both, depending on the level at (and degree to) which the participant can intervene in the work's conception, progression and ultimate form and content.

Let us take two examples that are included here. In Bruce Nauman's 1969 *Live-Taped Video Corridor* (included in the *Corridor Installation* discussed in Chapter 8), we walk down a narrow enclosed corridor, at the end of which stand two television monitors. On one of the monitors is relayed an image of an empty corridor, while on the other we can see someone walking away from the monitor (this someone, we realise after a brief lapse of time, is ourselves, seen from behind). David Medalla's 1968 *A Stitch in Time* (mentioned in Chapter 2) offers a very different kind participation. In this work, the artist invited participants to sit on stools and stitch their own motifs onto a common fabric stretched across the exhibition room, using spools of coloured threads hanging above them. If we follow Kravagna's definitions, we would say that the *Live-Taped Video Corridor* is interactive, because the structure of work is not affected by the participant's actions, whereas *A Stitch in Time*, which is transformed in the course of the exhibition, could be called participative. Similarly, Graham's discussion of participation and interactivity in the new media opposes scenarios in which content is generated by an artist and arranged by participants (interactive) to situations in which content is generated by participants and curated by the artist or a group of participants (participative).

The separation between content on the one hand, and form or structure on the other, on which these distinctions rely is not, however, always clear cut in do-it-yourself artworks, which specifically set out to challenge the differences between object and process, between the work in itself and the experience of the work. The content or visual aspect of Medalla's *A Stitch in Time* may indeed be generated by the work's 'users' (to use a new media term), but the artist seems more interested in the experience of the work than in the actual resulting stitched piece of fabric, and this emphasis on experience is precisely what relates it to Nauman's *Live-Taped Video Corridor*, which will also be experienced differently by each single participant. Perhaps more useful for our purposes, then, could be an analysis of the *experience* of each do-it-yourself artwork, and in particular its temporality. I would suggest that some do-it-yourself artworks privilege an experience of the here and now (whether very short or very long, individual or collective, reversible or not), whereas others privilege a cumulative experience over a fixed duration that requires more than one step in a longer process, and/or which involves more than one participant maintaining or transforming the material existence of the work (whether a specific space, an object or a project). If the former is exemplified by Lygia Clark's *Air and Stone* as well as Nauman's *Corridor*, Medalla's *Stitch in Time* could be considered as an instance of the latter. Even if experienced collectively, the former tends to privilege individual experiences, while the latter conjures temporary communities through a process that exceeds individual experiences. Although all the participants in *A Stitch in Time* may never meet in the same room, the final object visualises their collective labour.

Ontologically, the durational dimension of do-it-yourself artworks bears strong affinities with those at play in what Grant Kester has described as 'dialogical practices' – community-based art projects which aim at facilitating discussions about, and suggesting solutions to, specific political and social issues.[13] For Kester, as for artists promoting what Suzanne Lacy has called 'New Genre Public Art' (discussed in Chapter 13), such dialogical practices are the only truly participatory practices today, because they focus on the very definition of the audience. In addition to the temporal, durational engagement required from the participants, both dialogical practices and do-it-yourself artworks also share a tendency towards relational models of directness, intimacy and empathy. Kester eloquently demonstrates that both features challenge some of the crucial foundations of avant-garde art, with its privileged moment of epiphany or shock, and its rhetoric of critical distance and resistance. Unlike the dialogical practices discussed by Kester, however, do-it-yourself artworks remain largely embedded within the discursive and institutional frameworks of contemporary art, and do not purport to provide direct, concrete solutions to specific issues. In this sense, I would argue that do-it-yourself artworks exist in an intermediate position between the two extremes of self-reflexive autonomous practices and collaborative community projects, and thus operate strategically within the history of art since 1950 to disturb and unhinge models of art making and art viewing.

It is within this framework that the political connotations of the very term 'do-it-yourself' can be considered. Some of the do-it-yourself artworks discussed in this book share common features with the 'do-it-yourself ethic'

characterising certain forms of political activism since the late 1970s. Origi-
nating in punk counterculture, this 'DIY' approach has been mobilised by a
range of groups including Reclaim the Streets and Food Not Bombs.[14] It is
based on non-violent action and non-hierarchical organisation, and, like the
do-it-yourself artwork, relies on the direct participation of its volunteers. Other
significant crossovers between DIY activism and the do-it-yourself artwork
occur in the field of distribution and dissemination. It will become apparent
that many do-it-yourself artworks have sought to bypass both commercial and
institutional modes of display and exchange, in the same way as DIY activists have developed independent media such as zines, as well as self-sufficient
networks of production and communication. This critique of commodity
fetishism, paired with a discourse of individual empowerment through participation, is as central to DIY activism and recent activist theory as it is to many
do-it-yourself artworks in the 1960s (see Chapter 11) or in new media art (see
Chapter 15). The utopian opposition between commodity fetishism and *doing*
as a 'total movement of practical negativity, of the practical projection beyond
the world that exists towards a radically different world' continues to play a
central role in certain trends of contemporary political thought, as in John
Holloway's highly influential *Change the World Without Taking Power* (2002).[15]

Experimental protocols

'"The participation of the spectator", like all other labels in art, has the cold ring
of an easily traded phrase', wrote Guy Brett in 1969.[16] Brett was alerting readers
to a kind of participatory practice, which used participation as a fashion-
able gimmick: 'the spectator's contribution' was either 'merely mechanical'
– because it only involved the enactment of 'some pre-conceived effect' – or
entirely 'arbitrary' –because 'there is no potential for making relationships'.
Some thirty-five years later, Jessica Morgan would similarly warn readers of
the *Common Wealth* catalogue that 'the mere involvement of the actions of
audience members is not enough to assume a vital or direct relationship to
the work of art'.[17]

It may seem paradoxical that two figures involved in promoting participatory practices would seem so keen to emphasise that spectator participation
should not constitute an aim in itself, but this apparent paradox points to one
of the central features of the do-it-yourself artwork. If, as Clark explained in
1965, the do-it-yourself artist's aim is '[t]o give the participant an object that
has no importance in itself and that will only take on [importance] to the
extent that the participant will act',[18] then spectator participation is, indeed,
always conceived as a means within a wider process, rather than an end in
itself. This kind of process, which seeks to involve 'vital' relations to the work
of art (as Morgan hopes), and often sets up 'relationships' between participants

(in Brett's words), lies at the heart of this volume. Spectator participation, it will emerge, is always caught up between two opposing threats: the risk of being used as a superficial gimmick, and that of being invested with unattainable hopes of social change or personal transformation.

These two related issues can be usefully discussed by describing do-it-yourself artworks as experimental practices, which share with scientific experimental protocols a concern with maintaining a balance between limited variables and an openness to a range of results, including unexpected ones. If the variables are too restrictive, the experiment will not prove anything new – just as a constrained participation becomes 'merely mechanical'. If, on the other hand, they are too open, then the experiment risks being as 'arbitrary' as a do-it-yourself artwork with no meaningful result. When John Cage, a crucial influence for many do-it-yourself artists, defined his conception of experimental music in 1955, he emphasised that the term 'experimental' should be understood 'not as descriptive of an act to be later judged in terms of success and failure, but simply as an act the outcome of which is unknown'.[19] Around the same time in Europe, the term 'experiment' was also being used by the Situationists to describe activities that set up 'situations' in which participants could discover new types of experiences within their everyday lives (one such experimental activity was the *dérive*, an aimless drifting through the streets of Paris). While Cage's description accounts for the appeal of spectator participation as a means to introduce 'unknown outcomes' within the structure of the artwork, the Situationist conception of the experiment highlights another crucial feature of the do-it-yourself artwork: the intrinsic relation between such open 'situations' and the participant's everyday, lived experience.

This broad experimental tendency operates in a variety of ways. Some do-it-yourself practices follow scientific protocols by exploring the points at which the habitual landmarks of perception break down. Just as Nauman's *Live-Taped Video Corridor*, mentioned earlier, focused on the point at which two kinds of information – the visual and the kinaesthetic – do not add up, the participatory environments of the Groupe de Recherche d'Art Visuel (discussed in Chapter 5) set up unfamiliar disjunctions between visual perception and the bodily experience of gravity and verticality. Both the GRAV and Nauman aimed at disorienting the spectator through experimental situations.

Contemporary artist Carsten Höller, who trained as a scientist himself, has also been exploring the relation between physiological and psychological states in his works. His *Upside-Down Glasses* (1993/2001) to be worn by participants echo a range of late 1960s works involving modified glasses (mentioned in both Chapters 2 and 5), and were in fact inspired by an actual nineteenth-century experiment by psychologist George Stratton. Höller's giant slides, most recently displayed in the Turbine Hall at Tate Modern under the title *Test Site* (figure 1.3), stimulate an 'emotional state that is a unique condition

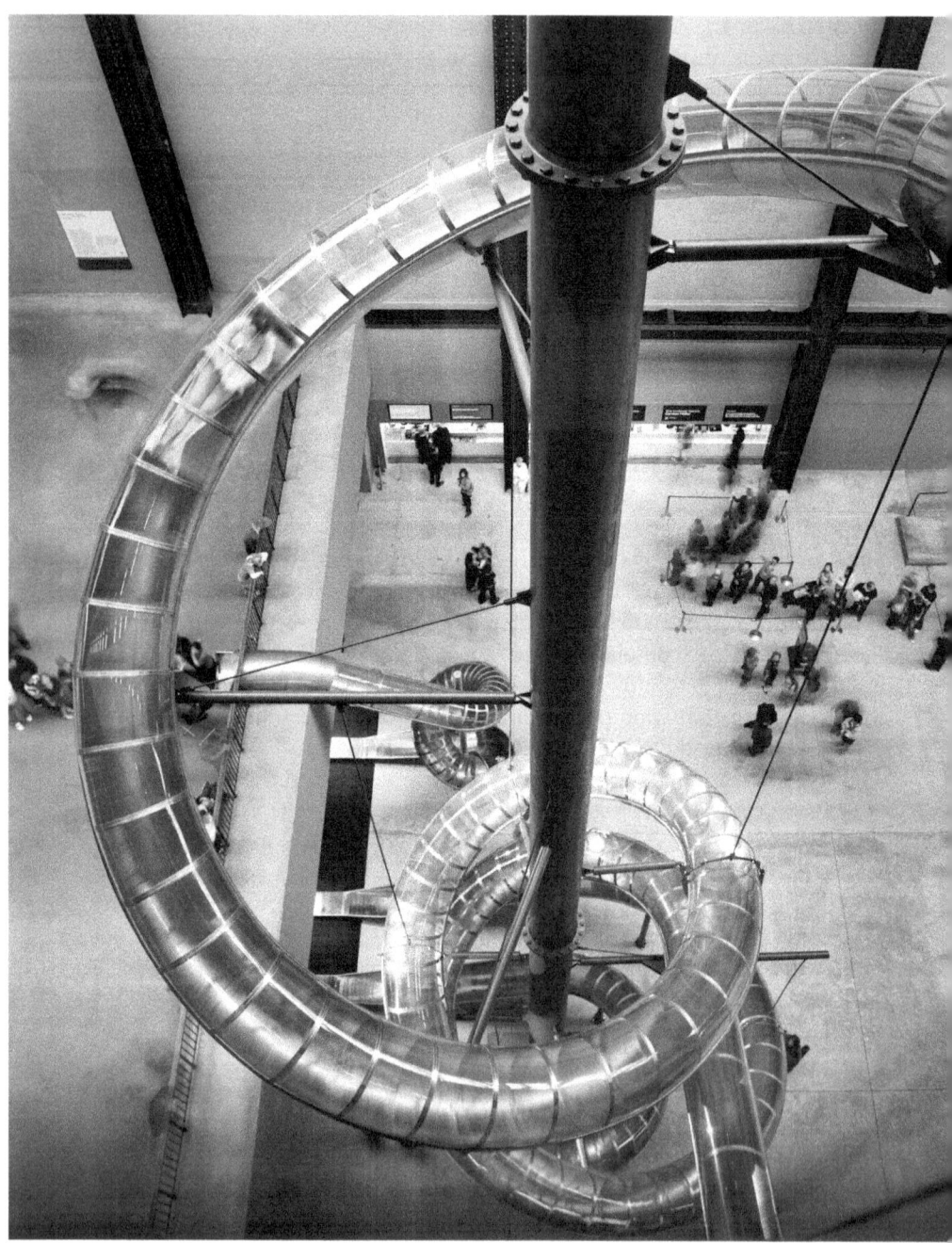

1.3   Carsten Höller, *Test Site*, 2006. Tate Modern, London, 2006.

somewhere between delight and madness' – the pleasurable equivalent of the sensations of discomfort in the GRAV's or Nauman's environments. 'The tests are conducted by visitors themselves, there is no "objective" authority taking measurements. It's all personal experience.'[20] Höller's description of *Test Site*, which invokes the scientific protocol of the 'test' as well as the Cagean and Situationist definitions of experimentalism, clearly locates the unknown variable in the spectator's very physical engagement with the work.

Where the participatory 'test sites' of Höller, Nauman or the GRAV conjure images of the behaviourist psychologist's laboratory environments, other participatory practices discussed in this volume are more akin to experiments by social psychologists. One can imagine a psychologist or anthropologist being interested in the behavioural patterns that led to the confrontation, in Marina Abramović's *Rhythm 0*, between one section of the audience bent on harming – and even killing – the artist, and another faction who sought to save her from such aggression (see Chapter 7). Even in less extreme scenarios, questions relating to collective behaviours, and the relations between personal and collective actions, are relevant. Discussing the reception of do-it-yourself artworks, one often finds oneself reaching for generalisations found in statistical, cultural, sociological or anthropological studies. All do-it-yourself artworks, it seems, can be considered as 'test sites' of some kind in that they operate as probes into a set of givens, as seismographs taking the measure of ethnic, social, or gender differences, as well as pointing to patterns of behaviour that bind human beings. And highlighting such differences and similarities, as Amelia Jones and Jennifer González argue, allows us to access the mechanisms through which the very concepts of the self, and the other, are constructed (see Chapters 8 and 10).

The definition of the do-it-yourself artwork as a tool, probe, seismograph, or simply a platform, implies its transportability from one context to another. Whether, and how, a do-it-yourself artwork can successfully be transposed to a new temporal, geographical or institutional context reveals the extent to which it engages with the world outside art. Both Nauman and Höller are particularly interested in the phenomenon of a 'repeatable surprise'[21] (in Höller's words): 'Something happens that you didn't expect and it happens every time' (as Nauman put it).[22] Nauman's and Höller's participatory works may be among the do-it-yourself artworks that are the most easily transportable, and the closest to scientific protocols, but I would like to argue that all do-it-yourself artwork rely on more or less predictable forms of 'repeatable surprise'. To borrow from another scientific terminology, one could say that 'windows of order' appear regularly within the most chaotic situations (in which the 'relationship between what goes into a system and what comes out' appears to be 'random').[23] This would imply that an ideal spectator, with an unlimited access to the total sum of a do-it-yourself artwork's outcomes, could potentially be able to demarcate a probable field of participatory behaviours for each work. The very form of the objects, spaces or instructions offered to the participant certainly constitutes a minimal framework for the range of participatory activities that they invite. Without such frameworks, do-it-yourself artworks would, indeed, be entirely arbitrary, and truly chaotic.

Consequently, the differences between various do-it-yourself experiments lie perhaps in the degrees of unpredictability allowed by each framework. Broadly, do-it-yourself protocols can be classified along an axis spanning the two extremes of constraint and openness. This axis could be described in terms of play, which constitutes a recurrent theme in debates about spectator participation. Play as an activity can include games (performances) and toys (objects), but can more generally be conceived as a psychological state or a symbolic space (see Chapter 11). Play initially emerged for many artists as an alternative to traditional forms of 'serious culture', as Fluxus leader George Maciunas explained in relation to his conception of 'art amusement'.[24] It was also used strategically by the Situationists, as well as Fluxus, as a means to challenge the very foundations of a capitalist society that seeks to control the division between work and leisure.[25] Just as Allan Kaprow believed that artists, redefined as 'players', needed to teach people how to play outside the repressive frameworks of competition, authoritarianism and a Protestant work ethic,[26] Lygia Clark and Hélio Oiticica celebrated play as an avenue to individual liberation and self-discovery (see Chapters 2 and 11). Oiticica defined his *Eden* (1969) (figure 1.4), discussed in Chapter 2, as an environment 'where all human experiments will be allowed'.[27] In contrast, Bruce Nauman perceived 'game-playing', as he called it, as a trivial and superficial activity.[28] Janet Kraynak has suggested elsewhere that Nauman's stated 'mistrust of audience participation' is related to the broader context of an emerging 'programmed society' in which participation is coerced by social, political and cultural manipulation, and choice is an illusion.[29] Rather than a rhetoric of freedom and creativity, Nauman's environments mobilise devices of confinement, oppression and control, in order to comment precisely on a new kind of capitalist society in which ideas of efficiency and management have permeated every sphere of experience – including leisure – thus constantly renewing an endless series of 'repeatable surprises'.

The very definitions of play, order and disorder, freedom and control, within the do-it-yourself artwork, are thus contextually specific. The notion of chaos that came to the fore in late-1950s participatory works, for example, was related to both new forms of neo-capitalist urban life reflected in the multi-sensory form of happenings (see Chapter 4), and a newly popularised scientific worldview influenced by quantum physics (see Chapter 3). Moreover, the same devices can be used for diverging aims. As Beryl Graham points out (in Chapter 15), many forms used in new media art, such as global positioning systems, virtual reality and the internet, were initially developed by the military as 'command and control' systems; similarly, Nauman's *Live Live-Taped Corridor* mobilised the emerging video surveillance technology with which we are now more familiar than ever.

Within the do-it-yourself work itself, the dynamics of control and freedom can also operate at different levels. Lygia Clark's work appealed to the subconscious of viewers as well as their conscious thinking selves, and many do-it-yourself artworks mobilise a range of unconscious desires and fears as well as more easily definable conscious acts and decisions. As well as being physical, as in the case of Nauman's environments, control can also be covert. Claire Bishop effectively argues (in Chapter 14) that the audience present at Tiravanija's meals, for example, will tend to be self-selected members of the art world, and hence their behaviour is largely predictable. Ultimately, as Janet Kraynak and Miwon Kwon suggest (in Chapters 9 and 12), all forms of spectator participation can potentially be read as affirmations of authorial control under the cover of gift giving. Just as the gift giver, according to anthropologist Marcel Mauss, sets up a situation of reciprocity with which the receiver needs to comply, the artist defining him- or herself as an educator or therapist seems to be reaffirming his or her superiority, by implying that we need to be educated, cured, liberated, or transformed – perhaps even against our will.

Power relations between the experimenter and the experimental subject have also been an issue in the history of psychology experimentation, as

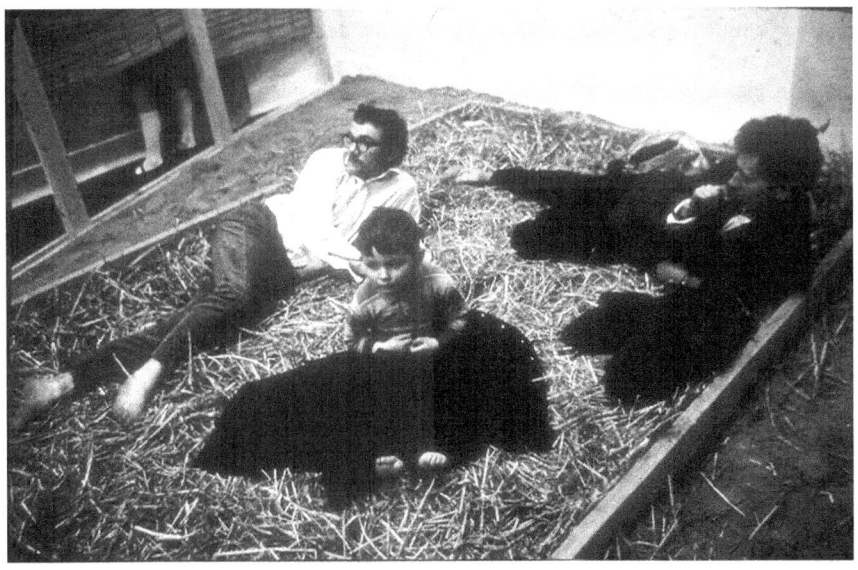

Hélio Oiticica, *B55 Area Bolide* in *Eden*, Whitechapel Gallery, London, 1967–69.   **1.4**

scientists have been accused of abusing their power and even harming their subjects in order to obtain results. Debates in the 1960s led to a call for ethical regulations and for contracts between experimenter and experimentees, and I would like to suggest here that such contracts lie implicitly at the heart of all participatory works. Abramović went so far as to claim 'full responsibility' for the actions of participants in her *Rhythm 0*, and the legal implications of this contract would no doubt be scrutinised by an art gallery today more fully than they were at the time. (In our contemporary compensation culture, the assessment of potential risks to participants by lawyers and insurers can determine whether, and how, a do-it-yourself artwork is presented.) *Rhythm 0* is actually a rare instance of a contract between the artist and the participant being made explicit, and what happened to Abramović during the performance, however extreme, had been envisaged by the artist as a possible outcome of the experiment (she had, after all, included the loaded gun amongst the objects that could be used by the participants).

The history of spectator participation is haunted by other cases in which implicit contractual agreements were misinterpreted or altogether breached. Both Robert Rauschenberg's attempt to involve spectator participation in his combine *Black Market* (1961), and George Brecht's 1959 exhibition *Toward Events* (see Chapter 3), suffered from the fact that participants stole and destroyed objects rather than handling or exchanging them with other objects as they were instructed. As a consequence, Brecht moved away from this mode of participation, and Rauschenberg's work, on display at the Ludwig Museum in Cologne, is no longer available for spectator participation.[30] 'I had hoped that people would enter the game with a certain gentleness', remembered Brecht with disappointment.[31] Robert Morris had, in all evidence, also presumed 'a certain gentleness' from visitors to his 1971 retrospective at the Tate Gallery, which is mentioned in Chapters 2 and 15, and discussed at length by Catherine Wood in Chapter 6. Morris's exhibition has become a landmark in discussions of spectator participation because participants engaged with the do-it-yourself artworks presented by the artist so enthusiastically that they destroyed the objects and injured themselves, and the Tate decided to shut down the display only a few days after the opening. Like Morris, Thomas Hirschhorn was not able to predict that one of his works, his *Deleuze Monument* (2000) in Avignon, would be vandalised shortly after it was constructed. Retrospectively, however, he concluded: 'I accepted its early dismantling because it was my error. It was neither a success nor a failure, it was just what it was.'[32]

Of course, as Kwon points out in Chapter 12, the refusal to participate also constitutes a breach in the implicit contract between artist and audience. The image, brought up by Beryl Graham in Chapter 15, of Joseph Beuys sitting by himself in his empty Bureau for Democracy, waiting for days on end for people to come and start a discussion with him, represents the counterpart to the chaotic mess of destructive exuberance and silly stunts that led to the closure of Morris's exhibition. The participatory situation requiring the presence of the spectator, which Kwon likens to a gift offered by the artist, is inherently threatened by such a breach of the artist-participant contract. This ultimate impossibility of predicting the act of participation itself is precisely where, I want to argue, the experimental nature of the do-it-yourself artwork can be located. It is at this point that the do-it-yourself artist, however controlling, remains vulnerable. In this sense, Hirschhorn's refusal to brand the destruction of his *Deleuze Monument* as either a success or a failure directly echoes Cage's definition of the term 'experimental': 'not as descriptive of an act to be later judged in terms of success and failure, but simply as an act the outcome of which is unknown'.

Participation then and now

The complex dynamics between order and disorder, control and play, organisation and risk, which lie at the heart of the do-it-yourself artwork as an experimental practice, have not precluded artists from conceiving specific objectives, or at least possible outcomes, for their participatory works. The do-it-yourself artwork, in general, is designed by artists to be more than a measuring tool; as a tool or platform, it can also serve as a catalyst for change, whether through self-consciousness and self-transformation, or through social interactions and exchanges. Participatory works are often premised on the belief that participation will encourage individuals and groups to take control of their own social and political existence. This can be effected in two ways in the do-it-yourself artwork: by offering alternative models for social or political interaction, and by acting as means to empower participants. In *A Stitch in a Time*, mentioned earlier, Medalla brought to life a non-hierarchical symbolic community of creative collaborators. As the artist explained: 'By a method of freely linking one person with another, and by linking people together to form a united and mobile whole, I seek to increase the awareness of voluntary cooperation between one person and another … without the possibility of one individual dominating another.'[33] In addition, the work tries to encourage people 'to trust their own capacities to be creators' – to empower them through the act of participation.[34]

Significant social and political changes have occurred, however, which have cast doubts on utopian projects such as Medalla's. In a 1977 project bid to the National Endowment for the Arts, Kaprow demonstrated his awareness that the self-consciousness and understanding of human behaviour achieved in his experimental group 'activities' could find applications in the commercial field as 'sales training'.[35] In addition to training, participation in today's workplaces takes a number of different forms, from improving staff efficiency through feedback and teambuilding exercises, to group activities designed to boost workforce morale. Meanwhile, museums since the 1960s have welcomed and encouraged participatory practices to complement the explosion of so-called 'interactive' displays and the increasing drive to create enjoyable and memorable museum 'experiences'. Clark's concern, in 1975, that artists would be hired by governments to create new 'leisure' activities was well founded: when Tiravanija is invited by a museum or by a collector to set up a participatory situation, he could be seen as providing such a service. Indeed, the emphasis on situations rather than objects simply replicates the shift from commodities to 'decentred networks and ephemeral flows of communication' in our globalised information economy (as Janet Kraynak points out in Chapter 9). Thus, the do-it-yourself artist today is caught between a new type of management ready-to-use participation as a tool for higher productivity, and a leisure industry always thirsty for new forms of entertainment. In addition to the roles of healer or educator adopted by many 1960s artists, then, the contemporary artist is increasingly cast as a service provider – whether as a creative source of new ideas for business training, or as a kind of party planner. If, as Kravagna points out (Chapter 13), 1960s artists such as Franz Erhard Walther still sought to offer participants genuine forms of non-alienated experience, such an option no longer seems relevant today, as experience itself has become an economic commodity.

The liberatory potential of participation, on which many political claims for the do-it-yourself artwork are premised, was already being contested on the walls of Paris during the May 1968 uprisings. One graffiti asked 'Êtes-vous des consommateurs ou des participants?' (are you consumers or participants?), while a poster recited a glum refrain: 'Je participe, tu participes, il participe, nous participons, vous participez, ils profitent' (I participate, you participate, he participates, we participate, you participate, they profit). The graffiti echoes Situationist Guy Debord's influential idea, in his 1967 *Société du spectacle*, that the passive modes of engagement encouraged by late-capitalist, consumer-driven economies can be countered with action and lived experience (see Chapter 11). The satirical refrain of the poster, on the other hand, suggests that participation itself can be appropriated by institutional and economic dominant powers. The poster was most likely a specific response to a speech by President de Gaulle at the time, who tried to pacify striking workers in France by promising them a new 'participation' in the decision-making processes in their factories. Like de Gaulle, the different forms of authority against which students and workers were protesting in Europe and America very quickly sought to mobilise such notions of participation to reaffirm their power in new guises. It is no coincidence that the May 1968 poster about participation was used one year later as an illustration for one of the earliest indictments of the ways 'citizen participation' was being mobilised in city planning in the

United States. For Sherry Arnstein, this new form of citizen participation was an exercise in 'manipulation' and 'tokenism' rather than true 'citizen power', as no real 'partnerships', 'delegated power' or genuine 'citizen control' were being offered.[36]

In addition to the new 'them' and 'us' division foregrounded by such critiques (*nous participons/ils profitent*), the 'us' itself became subjected to fragmentation as the united front of the late-1960s New Left started to break down, in the 1970s, into interest groups focusing on issues of class, gender, sexuality or race. The rise of identity politics, which would irreversibly affect perceptions of the human body, had crucial repercussions on do-it-yourself artworks, which invited, from the start, embodied participation. When do-it-yourself artist Felix Gonzalez-Torres concluded, in 1994, that 'the body at this time in our history, at this time in culture, is defined not just by the flesh but also by the law, by legislations, and by language first of all',[37] he was in fact summarising the successive waves of debates emerging from feminism, gay and lesbian activism in the 1970s, as well as post-colonial discourse and the 1980s Aids crisis. As Catherine Wood highlights (Chapter 6), Robert Morris's 1971 Tate retrospective was largely predicated on a universalised conception of the body developed by do-it-yourself artists in the 1960s. The shift to new relations between body and space, and between bodies, as inherently marked by discursive and institutional structures – the language and legislations described by Gonzalez-Torres – was occurring at the very moment of Morris's exhibition, in works by artists such as Bruce Nauman or Marina Abramović (see Chapters 7 and 8).

The other crux in the history of contemporary culture to which Morris's exhibition also pointed (as Wood convincingly argues) was the major shift from direct experience to a field in which experience is always already mediated by the spectacle of images and video. While Morris was still struggling with the discrepancy between direct and mediated experience in his work, artists such as Nauman or Dan Graham both deliberately used live feedback within their do-it-yourself works in order to explore this relation in a more systematic and self-conscious way. As Amelia Jones demonstrates in Chapter 7, the split between direct and mediated self-images in Nauman's work challenges our very self-perception as present and coherent subjects. Today, in a context when reality television has successfully highjacked participation and turned it into the very spectacle that it had hoped to counter in the 1960s, it becomes clear that an unmediated experience has become a distant dream.

In parallel with this fragmentation of the subject through the rampant spectacularisation of society, and the politics of identity mapped onto the body, the notion of community has also become a contested site. Medalla had referred to Lenin's belief in 'the presence of democratic and socialist elements in every national culture' as his motivation for using sewing in *A*

Stitch in Time: here was an activity that could exceed national and cultural boundaries and be shared by everyone. A few years later, Marina Abramović's *Rhythm o* would question this universal ideal by demonstrating, as Frazer Ward explains in Chapter 8, what happens when the very notion of community breaks down. Body artists such as Abramović introduced, in the 1970s, a new form of 'masochistic contract' with the audience, as Kathy O'Dell has described it.[38] This new contract dramatised a wider breakdown of relationships of trust among individuals in society: by allowing extreme behaviours to emerge, Abramović's *Rhythm o* certainly demonstrated that no trust and respect could be taken for granted. This marked a move away from earlier 1960s do-it-yourself artworks which had set up a network of trust as a precondition for new conceptions of community and activism (see chapter 11).

Notions of community and democracy are central to contemporary debates about participation. The spectre of totalitarianism has led philosophers like Jean-Luc Nancy (cited by Frazer Ward) and Giorgio Agamben (cited by both Ward and Jennifer González) to criticise the notion of a coherent community, while Ernesto Laclau and Chantal Mouffe's 1985 *Hegemony and Socialist Strategy* suggests that democracy can only exist through the antagonist relations between multiple communities. Consensus thus emerges as the enemy of both community and democracy. Just as Kravagna considers the New Genre Public Art's 'pastoral' attempts to heal social wounds to be misled (Chapter 13), Bishop draws on Laclau and Mouffe's writings to criticise the ways in which relational aesthetics use participation to iron out any frictions (Chapter 14). Both Bishop and Kravagna hold up counter-examples of participatory practices which, like Abramović's *Rhythm o*, deliberately avoid any preconception or idealisation of what a 'community' is. When Adrian Piper invites participants to respond to her discussion of funk as a 'black working-class idiom' in her *Notes on Funk* (1982–84), argues Kravagna, 'Community emerges, if at all, in the course of the event' – through dance, discussions and confrontations. Similarly, according to Bishop, Thomas Hirschhorn's and Santiago Sierra's participatory practices create a space for antagonism because they make us aware of differences, tensions and oppositions between, and within, communities. Pointing to a legacy of Piper's work in contemporary art, Jennifer González's discussion of race in digital art practice (Chapter 10) directly addresses the renewed ideal of a 'community beyond identity' that has accompanied the internet revolution. González draws a crucial distinction, following the writings of Jodi Dean, between 'a consensus model addressing universal subjects' and a 'neo-democracy, with its emphasis on contestation and conflict centred on political issues'. Only the neo-democracy model, according to González, can reveal the ways in which race discourse operates 'as an oppressive regime' through visual signs. González's provocative description of race as a 'radically participatory discourse' suggests new ways of thinking about do-it-yourself artworks in terms of gender, racial and social difference.

The chapters in this volume address the central defining features of do-it-yourself artworks, while situating them within their historical and discursive contexts. Part I focuses on the historical emergence of the do-it-yourself artwork in the 1960s, while Part II brings together in-depth case studies of specific participatory practices in the 1960s, 1970s and 1990s, analysing the issues that they raise in their very modes of operation. The more general critical chapters in Part III map out a range of theoretical approaches to the do-it-yourself artwork. The history, practice and theory of the do-it-yourself artwork are, of course, too closely intertwined to be set apart in such clear-cut categories. There are intersections and dialogues among the chapters across all three parts, as some practices central to the development of the do-it-yourself artwork, certain critical discourses surrounding this type of work, as well as some methodological approaches, are discussed by more than one author in this volume. At the same time, a plurality of voices can be heard. The book starts with a chapter by Guy Brett, who has written about participation since the 1960s (Chapter 2), includes reprints of contemporary responses to the emergence of 1990s participatory practices (Chapters 9 and 13), and offers a varied sample of more recent reflections on do-it-yourself works from the 1950s to the present. Crucial topics for discussion emerge from the juxtaposition of such diverse, and at times conflicting, perspectives. As a critical anthology, this volume seeks to carve out a space for frictions and debates, as much as it aims to serve as a user's manual for do-it-yourself artworks.

Notes

1 Yoko Ono, 'Letter to Ivan Karp, 4 January 1965', in *Grapefruit: A Book of Instructions and Drawings* (New York: Simon & Schuster, 2nd edn, 2000), n. p.
2 Lygia Clark, 'Letter to Guy Brett, 10 November 1968', quoted by Guy Brett, 'Lygia Clark: six cells', in Guy Brett et al., *Lygia Clark* (Barcelona: Fundació Antoni Tàpies, 1997), p. 23.
3 Julie Reiss (*From Margin to Center: The Spaces of Installation Art*, Cambridge: MIT Press, 1999) and Claire Bishop (*Installation Art: a Critical History*, London: Tate Publishing, 2005) have addressed elements of a history and analysis of environments requiring spectator participation. Similarly, Alex Potts's excellent analysis of the role of the spectator in Minimalist sculpture in *The Sculptural Imagination: Figurative, Modernist, Minimalist* (New Haven: Yale University Press, 2000) provides invaluable tools for our understanding of those forms of interaction, but it remains framed within the history of sculpture, and Minimalism in particular. Like Reiss's study, Lars Blunck's *Between Object and Event: Partizipationskunst Zwischen Mythos und Teilhabe* (Bonn: VG Kunst, 2001) focuses on the theme of spectator participation in the works of a specific set of artists (George Brecht, Allan

Kaprow, Robert Rauschenberg, Jasper Johns and Edward Kienholz).

4 Tracey Warr (ed.), *The Artist's Body* (London: Phaidon, 2002).

5 Guy Brett, 'Life strategies: overview and selection, Buenos Aires / London / Rio de Janeiro / Santiago de Chile, 1960–1980', in Paul Schimmel (ed.), *Out of Actions: Between Performance and the Object, 1949–1979* (Los Angeles and London: Museum of Contemporary Art and Thames & Hudson, 1998), p. 216.

6 Rudolf Frieling (ed.), *The Art of Participation: 1950 to Now* (San Francisco and London: Museum of Modern Art and Thames & Hudson, 2008); Claire Bishop (ed.), *Participation* (London and Cambridge: Whitechapel Art Gallery and MIT Press, 2006).

7 Frank Popper, *Art, Action and Participation* (London: Studio Vista, 1975), p. 11.

8 Six numbers of *Robho* were edited by Jean Clay and Julien Blaine in Paris between 1967 and 1971. Adrian Henri, *Environments and Happenings* (London: Thames & Hudson, 1974).

9 Boris Groys, 'A genealogy of participatory art' in Frieling (ed.), *The Art of Participation*, pp. 18–31.

10 Hans-Ulrich Obrist (ed.), *Do It* (New York: Independent Curators Incorporated, 1997), p. 13. See www.e-flux.com/projects/do_it/homepage/do_it_home.html (accessed 5 May 2009). Obrist also conducted a range of interviews with many of the artists included in *Do It*. See Hans-Ulrich Obrist, *Interviews*, vol. 1 (Milan: Charta, 2003).

11 Nicolas Bourriaud, *Esthétique relationnelle* (Dijon: Presses du réel, 1998), p. 117 (my translation). An English translation by Simon Pleasance and Fronza Woods was published in 2002 (*Relational Aesthetics*, Dijon: Presses du réel).

12 Orozco's work is referred to in Chapter 12, and Hirschhorn's discussed extensively in Chapter 14 of this volume.

13 Grant Kester, *Conversation Pieces: Community and Communication in Modern Art* (Berkeley and London: University of California Press, 2004).

14 See Ben Holtzman, Craig Hughes and Kevin Van Meter, 'Do It Yourself ... and the movement beyond capitalism', in Stevphen Shukaitis and David Graeber (eds), *Constituent Imagination: Militant Investigation/Collective Theorization* (Edinburgh: AK Press, 2001), pp. 44–61.

15 John Holloway, *Change the World Without Taking Power: The Meaning of Revolution Today* (Ann Arbor: Pluto Press, 2nd edition, 2005), pp. 24, 43.

16 Guy Brett, [untitled text], in Brett (ed.), *Hélio Oiticica* (London: Whitechapel Gallery, 1969), n. p.

17 Jessica Morgan, 'Introduction', in Jessica Morgan (ed.), *Common Wealth* (London: Tate Modern, 2003), p. 24.

18 Lygia Clark, 'A propósito da magia do objeto', in Brett et al., *Lygia Clark*, p. 152 (my translation).

19 John Cage, 'Experimental music: a doctrine' (1955), in *Silence: The Lectures and Writings of John Cage* (London: Marion Boyars, 1978, reprinted 1999), p. 13.

20 'Carsten Höller in conversation with Vincent Honoré', 2006, www.tate.org.uk/modern/exhibitions/carstenholler/interview.shtm (accessed 17 January 2007).

21 'Carsten Höller interviewed by German Celant', in Celant (ed.), *Carsten Höller: Register* (Milan, Fondazione Prada, 2000), n. p.

22 Willoughby Sharp, 'Interview with Bruce Nauman, 1971 (May 1970)', in Janet Kraynak (ed.), *Please Pay Attention Please: Bruce Nauman's Words: Writings and Interviews* (Cambridge and London: MIT Press, 2002), p. 151.

23 James Gleick, *Chaos: The Amazing Science of the Unpredictable* (London: Vintage, 1997), pp. 74, 8. My thanks to Aris Sarafianos for bringing this theory to my attention.

24 George Maciunas, 'Fluxus broadside manifesto' (1965), in Achille Bonito Oliva (ed.), *Ubi Fluxus ibi Motus, 1990–1962* (Venice: Biennale, 1990), p. 219.

25 See 'Situationist manifesto', *Internationale Situationniste*, 4 (June 1960), trans. F. Thompsett, www.cddc.vt.edu/sionline/si/manifesto.html (accessed 17 February 2009).

26 See Allan Kaprow, 'The education of the un-artist, Part II' (1972), in *Essays on the Blurring of Art and Life*, ed. Jeff Kelley (Berkeley, Los Angeles, London: University of California Press, 1993), pp. 110–26.

27 Hélio Oiticica, in Brett (ed.), *Hélio Oiticica*, n. p.

28 Joan Simon, 'Breaking the silence: an interview with Bruce Nauman, 1988 (January, 1987)', in Kraynak (ed.), *Please Pay Attention Please*, p. 327.

29 See Janet Kraynak, 'Dependent participation: Bruce Nauman's environments', *Grey Room*, 10 (Winter 2003), 22–45.

30 The *Black Market* file at the Ludwig Museum in Cologne suggests that items were stolen from the case as early as 1962, and again in 1968. In 1969, Rauschenberg provided a new set of objects and drawings which are currently stored in a safe at the Ludwig Museum. The now empty case in *Black Market* is permanently closed when the combine is on display.

31 George Brecht, 'Interview with Irmeline Lebeer' (1973), in Henry Martin (ed.), *An Introduction to George Brecht's Book of the Tumbler on Fire* (Milan: Multhipla Edizioni, 1978), p. 88.

32 'Alison Gingeras in conversation with Thomas Hirschhorn', in Carlos Basualdo et al., *Thomas Hirschhorn* (London: Phaidon, 2004), p. 38.

33 David Medalla, quoted in Guy Brett, *Exploding Galaxies: The Art of David Medalla* (London: Kala Press, 1995), p. 95.

34 Steve Thorn, interview with David Medalla, May 1977, quoted by Guy Brett in Chapter 2.

35 Allan Kaprow, 'The Use of Art Performance as a Model for Personal and Social Awareness', unpublished proposal to the National Endowment for the Arts, 1977, p. 8. Allan Kaprow Papers, Getty Research Library Archives.

36 Sherry R. Arnstein, 'A ladder of citizen participation', *Journal of the American Planning Association*, 35:4 (July 1969), 216–24. This article is also mentioned by Beryl Graham in Chapter 15.

37 'Felix Gonzalez-Torres' (1994) in Obrist, *Interviews*, p. 309.

38 Kathy O'Dell, *Contract with the Skin: Masochism, Performance Art and the 1970s* (Minneapolis and London: University of Minnesota Press, 1998). See Chapter 7.

Part   I

Situating participation

Three pioneers 2

Guy Brett

If I knew what these things were, they would no longer be an invention.
(Hélio Oiticica)

All art is interactive. All art is a potentiality. Rose English wrote in one of her performance scripts, 'Being looked at with engagement and love is more potent, more energising than being stared at blankly and uncomprehendingly.'[1] She may have been speaking of human encounters but her words can be taken as a metaphor for the experience of an artistic exchange, for example, between a viewer and a painting. The key connection is the quickening, energising process, a reciprocal phenomenon which can come into being in any number of ways. It so happened, however, that in the visual arts, in the mid-twentieth century, the three familiar agents of the aesthetic communication – the artist, the spectator and the mediating object – began to be deeply questioned in their singularity and their interrelations. New models began to be proposed, which gave a new dynamic to the notion of artist–spectator dialogue.

This chapter seeks to examine the birth and development of the idea of 'the participation of the spectator' as it occurs in the work of three artists: Lygia Clark (born Belo Horizonte, Brazil, 1920; died Rio de Janeiro, 1988), Hélio Oiticica (born Rio de Janeiro, 1937; died in the same city, 1980); David Medalla (born Manila, Philippines, 1942; lives in London).[2]

Outside the writings of artists themselves, 'participation' was barely recognised as a subject for discussion in art history or art criticism until recently. The radical nature of some of the proposals being made by artists was such that they could not be assimilated to traditional frameworks of artistic production and exhibition, or to art historical discourse. Even today, when the subject and some of its key innovators are being widely discussed, there is a tendency to relate notions of participation back to the established categories of artistic expression, such as 'theatre', or 'sculpture', from which these radical artists had decisively broken away. Excitement that bodies of work, which some of us have long believed in and defended, are recognised internationally is mixed with fear that fame and the institutionalising process will rob them of their vitality and raison d'être.

Documenta X of 1997, curated by Catherine David, was the main instrument of introducing Clark's and Oiticica's work to the widest international art public. But it was also the instrument of that work's distortion. Lygia Clark's work was exhibited as a conventional display of objects. Nothing could be touched or put on the body. Such a travesty was only possible posthumously since if Lygia Clark had been alive she would never have allowed it. Perhaps, nevertheless, certain important things about the work could be surmised by visitors despite the static presentation. Jean-Christophe Royoux, in his review of the exhibition, contrasted the notion of participation in work such as Clark's with 'the minimal and largely pointless form of interactivity that now serves as the basic principle of the new communications technologies, [which] has done so much to trivialise the participatory model of the neo-avant-garde, eroding its initial effectiveness'.[3] There was irony here because, at *Documenta*, there seemed to be a limitless number of computer terminals one could sit down and interact with, but one was not allowed to touch the Lygia Clarks.

The contradiction which stood out so clearly in the *Documenta* ambience had been present from the inception of the idea of participation in the 1960s. Then, as now, it seemed important to distinguish between a deep and complex understanding of the possibilities of artist/spectator interaction and one that was relatively superficial and limited. Depth/complexity here is measured in the capacity of the work to touch upon – no less deep if it touches playfully and lightly – crucial philosophical, political and psychological dilemmas of contemporary culture. This is exactly where the experiments of Lygia Clark, Hélio Oiticica and David Medalla should be placed.

These three artists are linked by a number of circumstantial connections. All were born in what for convenience may be called the developing world, and in any case, outside the 'cultures of plenty'. All have at one time or other been described as 'marginal', either to the art world of their countries of origin, to the mainstream international art community, or to both. The Brazilian critic Harry Laus called Oiticica the 'marginal man of art',[4] and the French critic Pierre Restany once described David Medalla as 'the marginal artist par excellence'.[5] Lygia Clark saw her exclusion in dramatic terms:

> I realise that if this were the middle-ages I would be burnt alive, such is the concept which I am proposing, so opposite to everything which has been proposed up to now in that which is called art![6]

In each case this was a description less of their origins on the geographical-cultural periphery, than of the dissenting, experimental, unclassifiable nature of the positions they took up vis-à-vis the conventional notions of a professional artistic career. Oiticica and Medalla have made prolific work without a relationship to a commercial art gallery, and only the earlier work of Clark, up to the mid-1960s, offers an object which can be readily merchandised.

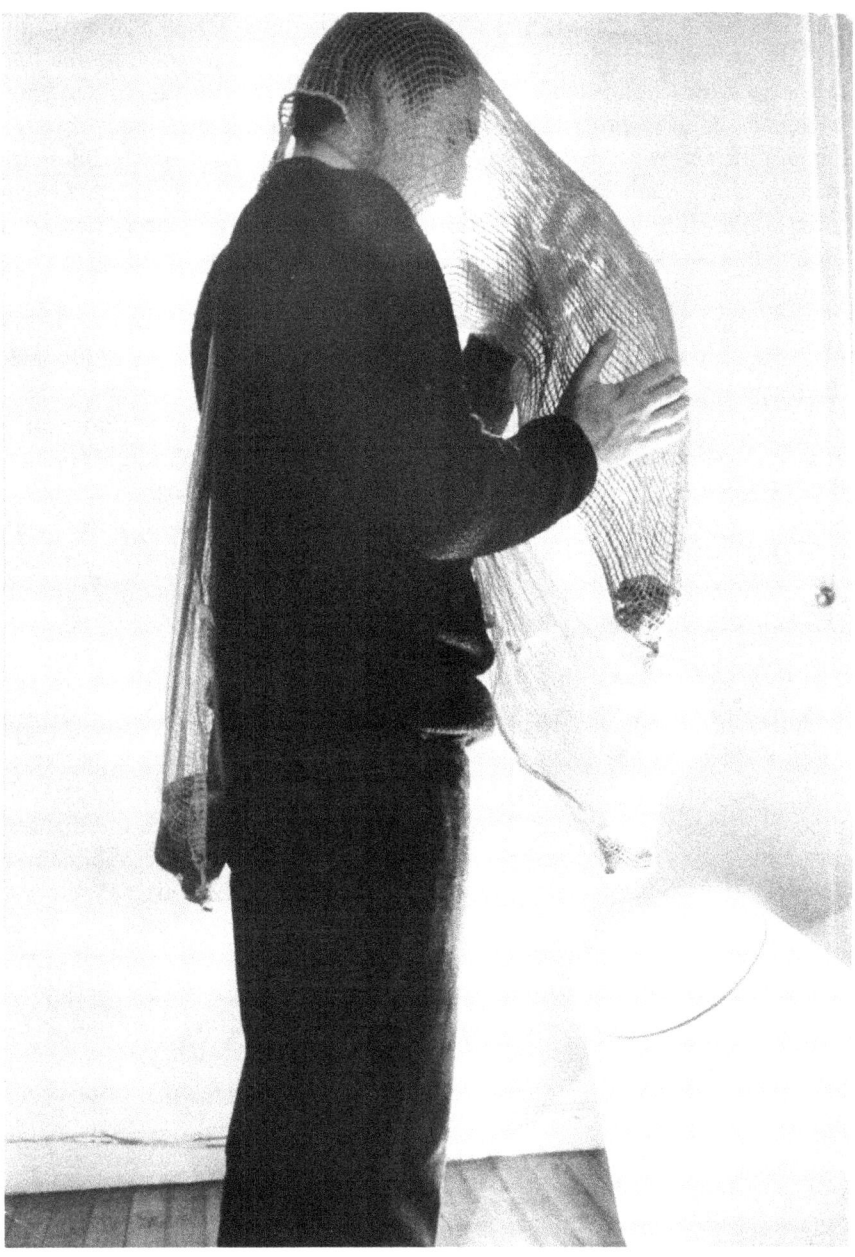

Lygia Clark, *Abyss Mask*, 1968. Cloth, netting, plastic, elastic bands, stones, air.　**2.1**

Clark and Oiticica entered into a life-long dialogue in terms of their work, not always free of rivalry, but of the deepest mutual respect. Medalla had meetings with Clark, exchanged letters with Oiticica, and was instrumental in introducing the work of both artists to Britain in the mid-1960s through Signals, the art space he ran with Paul Keeler in London. A notable difference distinguishing Medalla from Oiticica and Clark is that the former has spent most of his adult life outside his native country, whereas the other two, even though they worked abroad for periods of their lives, seemed to need periodic re-immersions in the Brazilian reality.

This combination of factors is significant in many ways, I believe. In fact the formation of a sensitive artist in a country like Brazil or the Philippines in the period after the war could be influenced by an extraordinary clash or cross-fertilisation of contradictory experiences. On the one hand, young artists were fired with the ambition to be 'absolutely modern', to take further the advanced positions reached by the European and North American avant-gardes and to claim the right to speak in universal terms. On the other hand, they grew up in a tradition of popular cultures of a collective and participatory kind that were fast disappearing in the West under the onslaught of corporate and technological media. Nor did these popular cultures have the static character of a corpus of folklore – they were full of the vitality of a 'culture in formation', to use Oiticica's words.[7]

Much has been made of Oiticica's relationship with the Afro-Brazilian carnival. Here we may note only the mass-participatory, creative nature of what he called 'the greatest public improvisation in the world'.[8] An appreciation of the ephemeral was no doubt also instilled: carnival dance and carnival costumes were prepared over the entire year to be shown and evaporate in a few days of celebration. And in the material practice of these artists there was what could be called an ethic of scarcity, closely linked to a poetic of wit and transformation: Lygia Clark made her *Relational Objects* and clothings out of onion-sacks, plastic bags, stones, shells, air, water and rubber bands (figures 1.1 and 2.1); Oiticica used earth, liquid, cloth, gauze, plastic, straw and so on in his *Parangolé Capes* (figures 2.2 and 3.3); Medalla's Exploding Galaxy (see below) and *Eskimo Carver* (figures 2.3 and 2.4) appropriated the waste-debris of London streets.

All these factors inflect the particular quality of each individual's work. At the same time they all play a part in what can only be described as a profound perceptual shift, which took place in the art of the 1950s and 1960s. In a nutshell: a movement away from a static and towards a dynamic interpretation of reality. This shift may be identified with Kinetic Art, but only if kineticism is interpreted in the broadest sense of an outlook on the universe, a vision of cosmological scope, and not a narrow stylistic phenomenon in the history of art. I believe this perceptual shift is intimately related to the emergence of participatory models of art, and is a process that can be traced in the youthful development work of Clark, Oiticica and Medalla.

Already, there are intimations of it in early twentieth-century kineticism, for example in the work of László Moholy-Nagy ('work', in his case, encompasses his painting, sculptures, machines, photography and pedagogical texts), and Alexander Calder. Moholy-Nagy's and Alfred Kemeny's manifesto 'Dynamic-Constructive Energy-System' (1922) clearly identifies an art making use of real forces with an enhanced interaction between work and spectator. Moholy-Nagy and Kemeny speak of 'material employed only as a carrier of forces', leading to the attainment of 'a dynamic constructive system of energy' where the beholder, 'hitherto merely receptive in his observation of works of art, experiences a heightening of his own faculties, and becomes himself an active partner in the forces unfolding themselves'.[9] Calder's *Mobiles* are systems of intricate balance between two types of intervention in the structure and expression of the work: human touch and currents of air. Although 'conservation' considerations have made it an increasingly rare experience today, a person has only to push one of the wire rods or discs which make up a Calder sculpture to see the way a small injection of energy is reflected in the complex dance of the interconnected masses in space. In seeing the aesthetic effect of their small charge of energy the person really does feel 'a heightening of their own faculties'.

The kinetic work of David Medalla from the 1960s, in an important sense, clearly takes off from the possibilities imagined by Moholy-Nagy and Kemeny and is epitomised by his *Bubble Machines* (first version 1963) and *Sand Machine* (first version 1964). The *Bubble Machines* are highly sophisticated meditations on form (as well as being a delight to come upon in the rather solemn spaces of contemporary museums). They produce, out of soap, water and pumped air, biomorphic sculptural shapes with no hierarchy or finality, delicately balanced between coming into being and passing away, sparkling with reflected light. They gently make fun of the sculptural tradition of a static finished work, under the absolute expressive control of the artist, by opening the creative process to other forces. Medalla's *Sand Machine* introduces an element of human participation by allowing the spectator to interfere and remodel the furrows in sand being ploughed by a mechanised 'snake'.

Around 1967 Medalla's work underwent a change. Sensitive to cultural trends in the world at large, he moved away from the established art world and looked for another context, another field of operation for creative work.

I felt at that time a deep dissatisfaction towards all art that derives solely from a single person, and is determined by one person's ideas and wishes … I wanted to share my thoughts and feelings with the spectator, who has been kept at an unreachable distance by the established art of our time. I wanted to break down the invisible barrier between 'creator' and 'spectator' in order that these static conditions cease to exist gradually, and art be a living process in which one, two, or several people formulate suggestions that others take up and develop in different directions ... London in the beginning of 1967 was full of fermenting creativity, of signs of renewal ... I thought: why not create a situation where dance, poetry, singing, and painting and sculpture could cooperate and inter-penetrate one another as they did in the great historical cultures? And with that intention I went round London, among strangers and friends, and invited all interested to join me in the creation of such a dynamic climate. I called my original suggestion 'The Exploding Galaxy' as I thought this name sufficiently flexible to contain and inspire all sorts of activities.[10]

What is particularly interesting here is the way in which Medalla's kineti-cism metamorphosed into the participatory, performative model of the Exploding Galaxy. Movement, change, interaction, freedom from 'art deriving solely from one single person', were expressed in Medalla's kinetic machines through the metaphor of physical forces, of nature. And it was essentially the same interactive model that he now translated to other people and the social world (it is interesting to note that Auguste Comte, who coined the word 'sociology' in 1830, originally described it as 'social physics').[11]

The Exploding Galaxy was an experience that strongly marked those who took part in it, most of whom were very young at the time. It was a live-together, work-together grouping of fluctuating membership which shared a house in Balls Pond Road, North London, from where they issued forth to perform collectively-devised dance-dramas in the 'streets, buses, tubes, market places, post offices, social security offices, railways stations, museums, cafés, cinemas, lavatories, squares and parks in London'. There was a mood to reinvent everything, to discover the poetry in any object or action from making a pot of tea to designing a costume from waste found in the street, for, ideally at any rate, 'the Galaxy makes it possible for anyone at any moment to try an infinite number of roles and functions'. Medalla continued:

A private idea, a personal vision, an individual hope can all result in a common work ... By not having choreographers, stars, conductors, directors, costume designers, lighting engineers, sales managers, etc., [we] completely avoid every hierarchy in art and life: the Galaxy has no leaders is our only proverb – the Galaxy allots to each individual the dignity of creator.[12]

Later, after the Galaxy had disbanded and individuals gone their separate ways, Medalla returned to an 'exhibition' context, and began to devise partici-patory projects for a passing public. I return to these later.

Lygia Clark and Hélio Oiticica arrived at the idea of spectator participa-tion by a route that was different from Medalla's. Both Brazilian artists evolved from a basis in geometric or concrete abstraction (Mondrian, Malevich, Albers), whose transformation in the Brazilian context is associated with the Neoconcrete movement (initiated in 1959). 'I started with geometry but I was looking for an organic space where one could enter the painting', Lygia Clark later reminisced.[13] The stages by which Clark and Oiticica accomplished that goal, between the late 1950s and early 1960s, are broadly similar and one of the most inspiring perceptual/conceptual processes in twentieth-century art. Having explored its own surface spaces, edges, thickness and limits, the painting came off the wall, descended to the floor as sculpture (after a period of free hanging reliefs in Oiticica's case) and entered into haptic, sensorial dialogue with the spectator's body. This process takes us from Clark's black/white reliefs, through her *Bichos* and *Obras Moles*, to her first 'Relational Objects'; and from Oiticica's *Metaesquemas* to his *Bolides* and *Parangolé Capes* to be worn, explored and opened to bodily movement and expression.[14]

It is fascinating that both Clark's and Oiticica's early objects are expressions of transition. The *Bichos* (see figure 3.1) still have the geometric schema but are animated by an organic and kinetic rhythmic structure which becomes apparent only in the give and take of the spectator's physical engagement with this nexus of hinged planes. Oiticica's early *Nucleuses* and *Penetrables* are paintings that you enter and which surround you. 'The world is round me, not in front of me' – the philosopher and phenomenologist Maurice Merleau-Ponty's declaration, roughly contemporary with Oiticica's and Clark's work, chimes perfectly with their aims, especially as it suggests that the perception of the world as 'in front' of one corresponds to the way one faces, and is faced by, a painting.

Both Oiticica and Clark felt that their work implied a reorientation in space of cosmic proportions. This was of sufficient seriousness to challenge the entire human sense of self, and with it the roles of 'artist' and 'spectator'. In Clark's case the geometric plane disappeared from her work after the *Bichos* and she announced its 'death':

> The plane is a concept created by humanity to serve practical ends: that of satisfying its need for balance. The square, an abstract creation, is a product of the plane. The plane arbitrarily marks off the limits of a space, giving humanity an entirely false and rational idea of its own reality.
>
> … The square took on a magical meaning when the artist understood it as carrying a total vision of the universe. But the plane is dead. The philosophical conception that humanity projected onto it no longer satisfies – no more than does the idea of an external God.
>
> … In becoming aware that it is a matter of an internal poetry of the self that is projected into the exterior, it is understood at the same time that this poetry must be reintegrated – as an indivisible part of the individual.

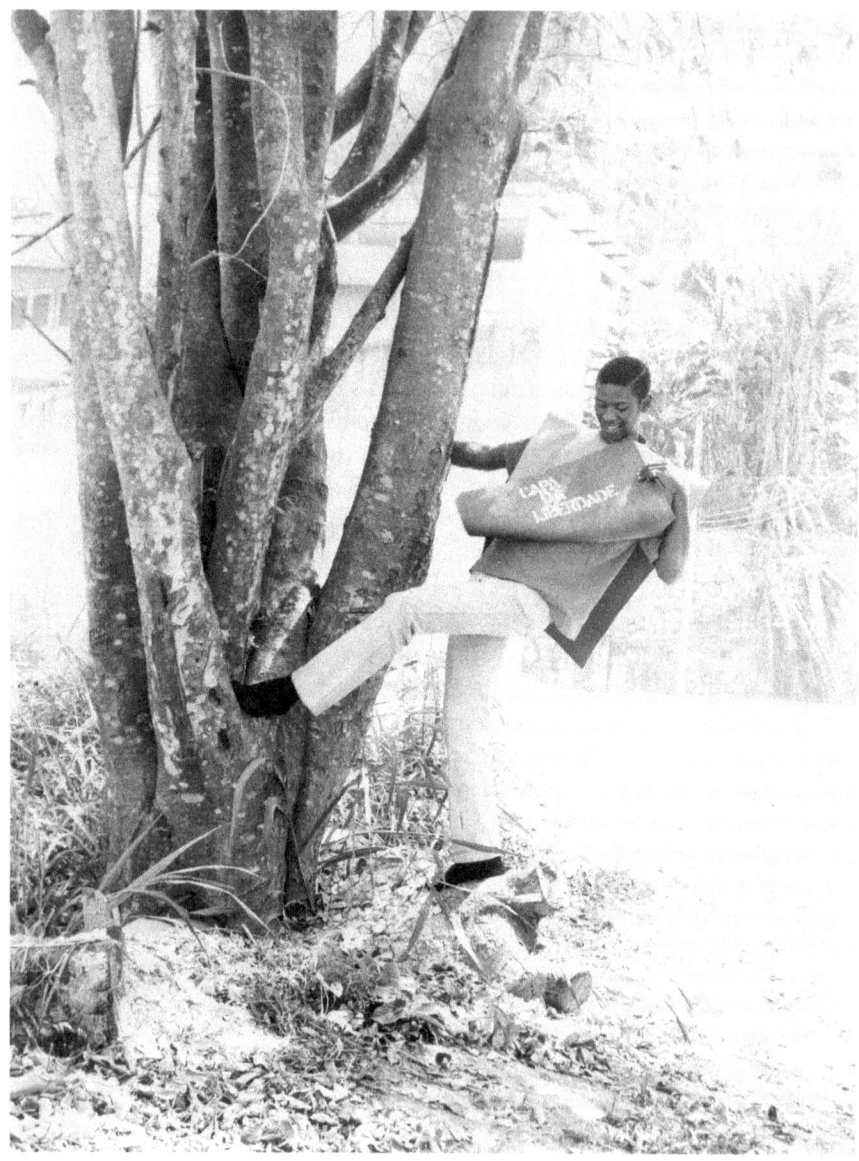

2.2   China of Mangueira wearing *Parangolé Cape 8, Capa da Liberdade* ('*Liberty Cape*'), by Hélio Oiticica and Rubens Gerchman, 1966. Cloth and lettering.

> … We plunge into the totality of the cosmos; we are part of this cosmos, vulnerable on all sides – but one that has even ceased having sides – high and low, left and right, front and back, and ultimately, good and bad – so radically have concepts been transformed.[15]

Later Lygia Clark would write of 'learning to live on the basis of what is precarious'.[16] A typical expression of Clark's cosmology as it related to her art was to equalise and incorporate the most extreme opposites: 'The experience is lived at that instant. Everything happens as if man today could capture a fragment of suspended time, as if a whole eternity dwelt in the act of participation'.[17]

Oiticica's early work is characterised by a highly individual experimentation with colour. In the process of liberating colour from its traditional support of the painting (he described his *Bolide* boxes and containers as manifesting 'the pigment mass extra-painting')[18] he also sought colour's inner energies, a meticulously material quest for which he wrote explanatory and speculative notes as he went along. A corollary, or necessary outcome, of this process was to diminish the role of the artist's own aesthetic choices and open the work increasingly to reality, to life. It is this quality, this feeling, that Oiticica and Clark, and Medalla too, doubtless imply by 'cosmic' – a word with reverberations as mystical as they are material. Oiticica wrote of a work giving a *vivência* (life-experience) of colour, 'neither totally contemplative, nor totally organic, but cosmic'[19] or a work 'so full of cosmic plenitude that the author is irrelevant'.[20] The social implications of this cosmology can be found in Lygia Clark's desire to plunge into the popular mass, to 'throw my work in large numbers at the man in the street';[21] they can be found too in Hélio Oiticica's description of the populated streets of Rio as the 'cosmic', 'that is, the non-naturalistic, the multi-transformable',[22] and in David Medalla's particular vision of inclusive structures that could include anyone who wishes to get involved.

Lygia Clark described the relationship between her work and Oiticica's in a now-celebrated simile: 'Hélio and I are like a glove. Hélio is the outside of the glove, very much linked to the exterior world. I am the inside, and the two of us exist from the moment there is a hand which puts on the glove'.[23] Clark moved towards the inner world of psychology and the self, Oiticica towards the social world of human community. Of course, these two worlds are not separated: there is an exterior/interior overlay in both artists' work, which is one of their most poignant connections. Both artists concurred in regarding the objects they made as empty shells unless animated by a human presence or expressivity. Both artists from their different vantage-points explored the relation between individual and collective. And both artists took the body as the primary vehicle for these experiments (Oiticica wrote of taking the body as 'life's first probe')[24], experiments which ranged from the most delicate tactility to the space of architecture and dwelling: '*The House is the Body*' as Lygia Clark affirmed in the title of her penetrable labyrinth for the Venice Biennale of 1968.

The interplay between individual and social being, between self and other, realised through participatory structures in the work of Medalla, Clark and

Oiticica is a fascinating subject to study. There is only space here to sketch out some general outlines. These were processes that engendered feelings ranging from the blissful or playful to the uncomfortable and even frightening. Lygia Clark, for example, would concentrate on an intense feeling of the interiority of one's individual body by proposing the *Abyss Mask* (1968), a sort of harness worn on the body, incorporating a blindfold and large airbags weighted down by stones attached to rubber bands, bags which, when touched or embraced, stimulated the sensation of a huge space inside oneself (figure 2.1). Using similar materials she would then construct webs to link groups of people together in what she called Collective Bodies, elastic structures in which each individual's movements would immediately affect everyone else's.[25] An encounter between individual interiority and the intimate proximity of others was brought to a testing intensity in the extraordinary scenario of *Baba Antropofágica* (1973), a work which evolved out of her classes with her students in Paris. The experience of taking part in the work, as the person lying on the floor is covered in multi-coloured cotton threads fallen from the mouths of the others surrounding her body, has been vividly described by Suely Rolnik.[26] Clark commented:

> 'Collective body' ... in the last analysis is the exchange between people of their intimate psychology, brought about by the group's experience of communal propositions. This exchange is not a pleasant thing. The idea is that a person 'vomits' life experience (*vivência*) when taking part in a proposition. This vomit is going to be swallowed by the others, who will immediately vomit their inner 'contents' too. It is therefore an exchange of psychic qualities and the word communication is too weak to express what happens in the group.[27]

In 1969 Hélio Oiticica constructed his *Eden* at the Whitechapel Art Gallery in London. It was to be an 'experimental campus, a kind of *taba* [Brazilian Indian settlement], where all human experiments will be allowed – human ones, concerning human species possibilities. It is a kind of mythical place for feelings, for acting, for making things and constructing one's own interior cosmos'.[28] Later, while living in New York, he made many plans for penetrable structures of considerable complexity, which he committed to notebooks in the absence of spaces and funds to realise them. In all of these projects the relationship of solitary to communal spaces was explored with great precision and imaginative insight. Space was concrete but not literal because each cabin, enclosure or circulation area, while an abstract distillation from the real, sensory world, created a nexus of interlocking poetic fields: spaces for making, rapping, performing, or solitary reverie. In *Eden*, having left your shoes and socks at the entrance you might step into water in a covered-in place, lie down in a dark cabin full of a strange scent, stand alone in a booth where there are large flat leaves on the floor, or make a habitation out of any

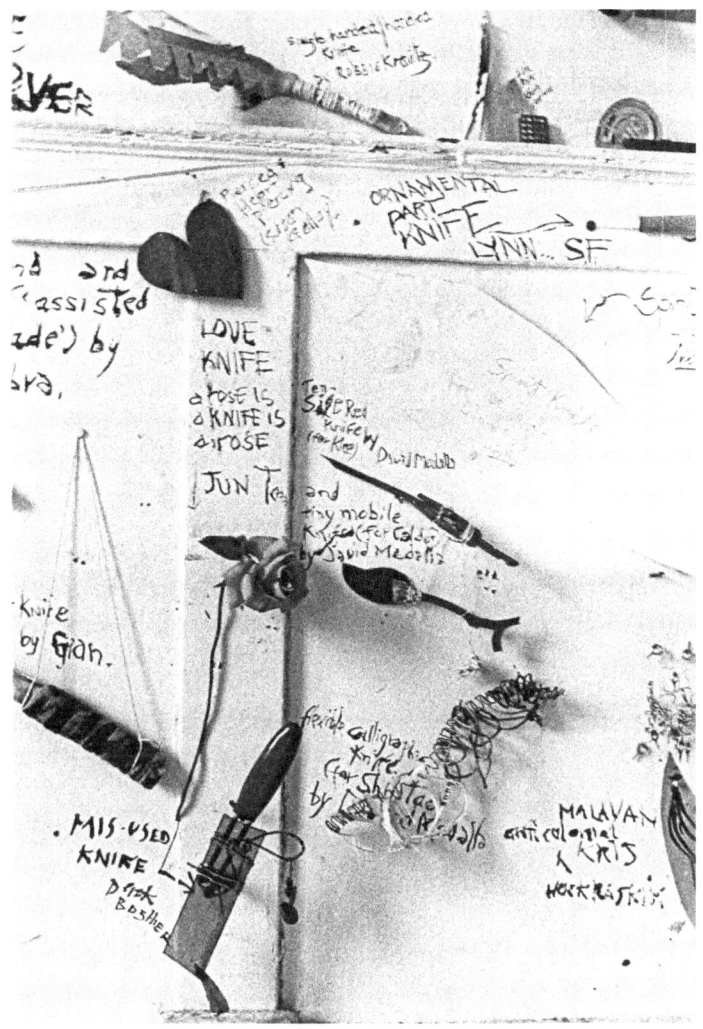

David Medalla, *Eskimo Carver, a participation-production-propulsion*, Artists for   **2.3**
Democracy, London, 1977.

materials you liked in one of the six nest-cells grouped together and separated by thin muslin screens.[29]

If Clark concentrated on psychological phenomena, and Oiticica on constructed social space, David Medalla was more concerned with human beings as producers. He called some of the interactive works he produced in the 1970s *Participation-Production-Propulsions*. This was a subdivision of his more general category of *Cosmic Propulsions*. Radically politicised by his travels in the developing world during 1968–70, and reading Marxism voraciously, he started to invent structures which would engage the public in a form of making – stitching, modelling, assembling – which would grow potentially without limit. Medalla stressed that his propositions were easy to enter, requiring no necessary skill or knowledge of art. 'People can walk in and out of my situations … they are dependent on each person falling back on his/her own resources … [their aim] is to infuse people with a certain kind of enthusiasm, to trust their own capacities to be creators'.[30] 'If you put such a proposition in a public space, literally it is an endless proposition, there is no end to people coming in and making [something]. I could easily inundate, say, the Tate Gallery'.[31] We will briefly consider one of these works – *Eskimo Carver* – which took place at Artists for Democracy in London in 1977 (figures 2.3 and 2.4). As I described it at the time, Medalla had been considering a performance in which the periods of human history, from the caves to the twentieth century, would each be represented by a knife singing its own song (for example, the Palaeolithic flint knife, Leonardo da Vinci's scalpel for cutting the cadaver, etc.). At the same time, he came across Tom Lowenstein's re-translations of the Danish-Inuit anthropologist Knud Rasmussen's transcriptions of Eskimo oral poems made originally in the 1930s. These were thrown into sharp relief by current stories in the English newspapers about the building of an oil pipeline in Inuit territory in Alaska – a huge project undertaken by transnational companies.

Medalla's event consisted of several elements. There was an exhibition of his drawings and transcriptions of Eskimo poetry, and a performance, *Alaska*

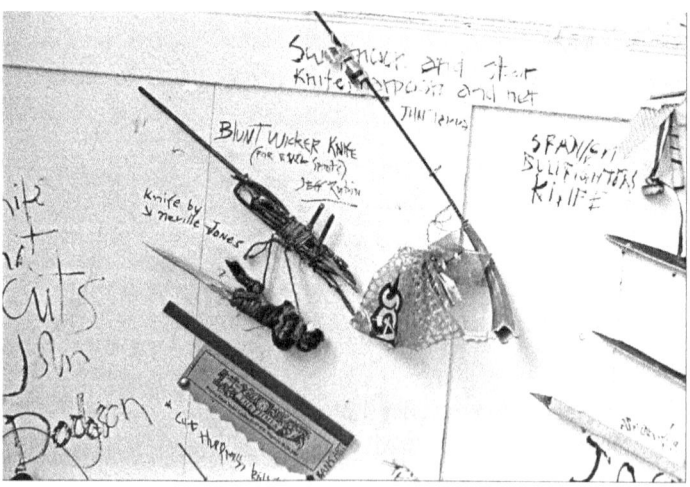

2.4   David Medalla, *Eskimo Carver, a participation-production-propulsion*, Artists for Democracy, London, 1977. Detail: some of the 'knives' made and titled by visitors from scrap collected locally.

Pipeline, in which the British tabloid newspapers' glorification of pioneering pipe-layers, combined with a racist denigration of Eskimos, effectively condemned itself. The third part was an invitation to visitors to make knives out of non-perishable garbage that had been collected in the neighbourhood and piled in a corner. The ambience opened people's minds in a certain way. The Inuit people have given some of the most succinct and eloquent descriptions that exist of the mixture of desire, anxiety and pleasure which is present in the human urge to compose poems and songs. They traditionally have a democratic, non-professional practice of creating them. Everyone knew the feeling of being poetically inspired. As Orpingalik, a Nestilik Inuit put it: 'Songs are thoughts which are sung out with the breath when people let themselves be moved by a great force, and ordinary speech no longer suffices.'[32]

As the collection of knives grew, everyone, including the artist, was astonished by the variety of people's contributions. The process revealed certain things about the psychology of people, Medalla reflected, because their contributions ranged from 'very functional-looking knives to an amazing kind of fantasy'.[33] The artist was intrigued by what he had set in motion because, while made up of hundreds of highly personal and individual assemblages, the whole aggregate exceeded the bounds of any individual personality, including the artist's. At the same time, the communal nature of the undertaking instilled a kind of desire to excel, whether by hard work, by the economy of wit, by metaphoric imagination or by a baring of the psyche.[34]

I believe one can grasp the cultural vitality of the participatory models described by comparing them with some related art manifestations of the time. At one level, for example, Medalla's *Eskimo Carver* anticipated a wave of British sculpture of the early 1980s consisting of installations and objects made from the scavenging and re-presentation of waste, such as dumped plastic bottles (Tony Cragg), obsolete washing-machines (Bill Woodrow), and so on. The process of recycling was seen by the more radical critics of the time as implying a critique of capitalist society. For Medalla, however, the problems of commodity production, in art as in society, and consumerism, could not be illuminated by the mere creation by the artist of a new object, since it was bound up in the relationship between artist and spectator (producer and consumer).

The originality of *Eskimo Carver* was to link one part of the system – the context of contemporary art – with another part, the context of ethnographic art, and the image made by ethnographic museums of 'other cultures'. These museums embody a disturbing paradox. They present objects as evidence of cultures as communities, as seamless systems of shared beliefs and communal practices which we consume individually and privately, almost as voyeurs. It becomes hard to make any bridge between these assumed poles of individuality and collectivity. At one level *Eskimo Carver* was a kinetic experiment in overcoming this estrangement. The device of mass participation, the element of giving something of oneself in return rather than merely taking or consuming, was the key to the experiment. Since it was not pedagogical but unrestrained in its subjectivity and affectivity, this collaboration was potentially a way of receiving information about another culture, and of another people's historical predicament, without objectifying it in order to alienate and control it. This, in turn, rebounds upon the nature of the contemporary artist–public relationship.

Close comparisons with some other artists' work are highly revealing in Lygia Clark's case too. A superficial similarity between Lygia Clark's *Goggles* (1968) and Julio Le Parc's optical devices worn as spectacles, *Lunettes pour une Vision Autre* (1965), allows one to compare their respective models of participation. Le Parc's *Lunettes* were made about three years before Clark's *Goggles* (and she may have known of the Argentinean's work), but this does not substantially affect the point of a comparison between them. Le Parc was a member of the Groupe de Recherche d'Art Visuel (GRAV), a collective of artists based in Paris in the 1960s, which made a radical critique of received, 'bourgeois', notions of the autonomous art object, the artist as the unique author, and the passivity of the audience. The group issued manifestos and staged public events in the streets, inviting the public to engage physically with various sorts of object and installation, which challenged the stability of perceptual systems.[35] Their devices were often witty and entertaining but on the whole remained limited to a simple behavioural model of stimulus and response. Le Parc's *Lunettes*, just one of many devices he invented, destabilised the visual field of the wearer, multiplying and fragmenting it, not unlike a prismatic kaleidoscope.

Lygia Clark's *Goggles*, on the other hand, while also breaking up the visual field, did so in a way that raised searching questions about the structure of the inner self, and the relation of oneself to another. The goggles, adapted from rubber masks made for underwater swimmers, were extended by a system of hinged mirrors. The wearer could manipulate these to give a patchwork of partial views. By turning them flat, one looked past them to the 'real' world; by twisting them, one could produce reflected views up, down, or behind, or look back into one's own eyes. A double set of goggles allowed the heads of two people to be brought into intimate proximity producing complex modulations of the experience of looking away or into the other's eyes. According to the way the mirrors were positioned there could be a disturbing ambivalence between the experience of one's left and right eye: one eye looking into the other person's and the other reflecting one's own eye.

Hélio Oiticica was preoccupied with these questions too. In a letter to me of October 1967 he made a distinction between a simple and a complex/deep understanding of participation:

I would consider as simple sensorial problems those related to 'stimulus-reaction' feelings, 'a priori' conditioned, as occurs in Op Art and those arts related to it ... When a proposition is made of a 'feeling-participation' or a 'making participation', I want to relate it to a supra-sensorial sense, in which the participator will elaborate within himself his own feelings that have been 'woken up' by these propositions. This 'wake-up' process is a supra-sensorial one: the participator is shifted off his habitual field to a strange one that *wakes up his internal fields of feeling* and gives him a consciousness of some area of his Ego, where true values affirm themselves.[36]

Oiticica's phrase, which I have italicised, bears a striking resemblance to one of Clark's quoted earlier: the desirability of moving towards 'an internal poetry of the self'. The phrase comes from her text 'Death of the Plane', written when she was still working within the conceptual limits of the visual arts, and is extraordinarily prophetic of the underlying motivation of her *Therapy with Relational Objects*, the last, most audacious, phase of her work (see below). Oiticica's affirmation of the internal took him to the concept of 'Creleisure' (*Crelazer*). This was a creative state which he saw as pushing beyond the work/leisure dichotomy typical of modern capitalist societies, resulting in the promotion of activities which 'only divert and sublimate, and always end in unhappiness and frustration'.[37] Oiticica's Creleisure anticipates a 'world which creates itself through our leisure, around it, not as an escape, but as the apex of human desires'.[38]

It is worth bearing Oiticica's words in mind when considering a further comparison between two phenomena of the early history of participatory art. This concerns two notable exhibitions, or experiments, that took place in London at the turn of the 1960s–1970s: Oiticica's at the Whitechapel Gallery (1969) where the previously-mentioned *Eden* was installed, and Robert Morris's at the Tate Gallery (1971) (see figures 6.1–3). Both Oiticica's and Morris's exhibitions represented audacious departures for British public galleries at the time. Oiticica's was the first one-person environmental show the Whitechapel had ever held. At the Tate, a fairly conventional survey of Morris's existing work had been planned, but a few months before the opening, the artist came up with a project for a sequence of structures which (in the words of the catalogue) 'although they resemble in their uncompromised simplicity Morris's earlier sculpture, invite the physical participation of the public'.[39] Yet, after only two or three days of boisterous, sometimes violent use, the structures were considered dangerous and the show was closed to the public – a closure which created a sensation in London at the time.

I respect Morris's work and I do not wish to describe the Oiticica exhibition only by way of contrast. Yet clearly it had a different ethos and origin. It was the proposal of what, as we saw, he termed Creleisure (a neologism combining 'creation', 'growth', 'leisure', 'pleasure', and perhaps 'creole'). You took off your shoes and socks before stepping onto the sand of *Eden*, as the central environment was called, otherwise you could not enter. Rather than a simple and mechanical form of behaviourism, Oiticica's *Eden* was an invitation to play and reverie whose ends were open and unconditioned. There were *Bolides* to be explored by hand, and sometimes by smell, cabins for solitary occupation and other, more communal, spaces (see figure 1.4). There were *Parangolé Capes* to be worn and danced in, and there were the *Nest-Cells*, a cluster of boxes each about 2 m × 1 m, divided by veils, which the visitor was invited to make habitable with found materials of their own choosing and entirely in their own way.

All in all, Oiticica took a different inspiration from the geometric forms of twentieth-century constructive art, which had inspired his formative years. Instead of the confrontational, irreducible 'objecthood' of the Minimalists, he proposed open voids to be entered and inhabited. His environment, though minimal, had a sinuous rhythm, again in contrast to Minimalism's serial standardisations. It allowed a subtle exploration of the relationship between the subjective and the social, the poetic and the material.

One thing that struck me at the time about the two exhibitions was that, although Morris invited people's participation, he did so in a way that emphasised individualism. He brought people together but kept them apart, and this was one of the reasons for the explosion of misdirected energy. We were in proximity physically but psychologically, each in our isolation was directed single-mindedly at the artist's work in order to master it – hence the friction, the bumping, the jostling. This led to the spending of energy frantically between yourself and the artwork without the possibility of renewal. The set-up was uni-directional whereas Oiticica's was poly-directional.

Rather than on mastering, the emphasis in the Oiticica was on sensuous receptivity to the world, reverie, communality ('the internal sun of non-repressive leisure', he called it).[40] Integral to his receptivity, in fact underlying all Oiticica's work, was to see creativity in terms of a life cycle. When, for example, he felt that his work-concept of the *Bolide* was over time becoming acculturated and rigidified as an 'art object',[41] he invented a ceremony, the *Counter-Bolide: To Return Earth to the Earth* (1978), to reverse the original process. Rich, black earth was brought to a wasteland site in Rio de Janeiro and deposited inside a rectangular frame. When this was lifted away the earth remained on the earth. It was the burial of the *Bolide* as an object and its rebirth as what he would call a 'life-act'.

It was around a set of renewable and reciprocal relations that Oiticica's participatory method flowered in the concept of Creleisure. And this was an immense paradox, because for Oiticica, the origin of Creleisure was closely associated, not with comfortable bourgeois holidays, but with the precarious, dangerous and rebellious life of Rio de Janeiro *favela*-dwellers: the 'desperate search for happiness', which he had identified in the life and death of Cara de Cavalho ('horse face'), a *favela* outlaw he had met and who was ambushed and shot by police.[42]

Although this chapter has dealt with events in the 1960s and early 1970s, explicitly to investigate how certain processes began, it would be wrong to confine these three artists to that period. Their experiment continued and evolved, and since the art world has not changed greatly in its basic assumptions, their challenge has lost none of its power. One of the key problems that their work raises is the nature of the relationship between 'audience/public' and 'participant'. This undergoes complex and qualitative changes as time passes. It is a question that has been tackled differently by each of the three artists. In Lygia Clark's case, the evolution of the forms and devices of participation – her *Relational Objects*, falling into various conceptual clusters: *Body Longing, Collective Body, Man Living Support of a Biological and Cellular Architecture, Structuring the Self*, and so on – was accompanied by changes in the nature of the public with whom she worked. This developed from works addressed to the spectator (the gallery-goer, and so on), to passers-by in the street, then to ongoing processes with more initiated and constant groups such as her students at the Sorbonne at the turn of the 1970s, eventually to the closed, private encounter between herself and the participant in the course of a therapeutic treatment. Here, she employed her *Relational Objects*, one to one, in a form of healing based on the object's capacity to reconnect with a person's earliest pre-verbal experiences still held, she believed, in the cells and skin of the body. From this process the 'public' was excluded and could have no knowledge of it except in the mediated form of photographs and verbal testimonies of those she had treated. Photographs and films of her *Terapia* (*Therapy*), visually striking though they are, give only an external reference to an experience in which the object, in Lula Wanderlay's words, 'is lived in an imaginary inwardness of the body where it finds signification'.[43]

In keeping with Clark's metaphor of the glove, Oiticica retained a strong external component in his work, which existed in a fluid relationship with the internal. The *Parangolé Cape*, typically, combined an inner structure and tactility for the wearers to absorb themselves in while at the same time broadcasting a feeling or thought to the public around. A public/private dialectic was generated and interwoven in the body's movements. Sometimes this fluidity had a tactical purpose, for example in *Cape 16 'Guevarcália'* (made in the politically volatile late 1960s), the portrait of Che Guevara was sewn into the structure and could either be shown or hidden by turning the fabrics inside out. Similarly with the *Capa da Liberdade, Cape 8*, 1966, where the word LIBERTY was hidden under a flap and could be revealed by the wearer by pulling up the cloth with a kind of flourish (figure 2.2). *Parangolé* was for wearing and watching, as Oiticica said himself. He did not eschew the element of spectacle but questioned its one-sided creation of a passive audience. His *Quasi-Cinema* experiments of the early 1970s were attempts to loosen the hypnotic hold of the projection screen on the spectator. He devised various playful scenarios in which people would lie about in hammocks or on sandy slopes playing with some given object while listening to the collage of music/sounds and watching oblique slide projections on wall and ceiling which themselves presented the images as a continuous cosmetic make-over.

The notion of participation, for Oiticica, connected naturally with the great number of creative collaborations he undertook in his short lifetime: with Nildo of the Mangueira *favela* during the early formation of the *Parangolé*; with artists Rubens Gerchman, Antonio Dias and Antonio Manuel during the period of the 'protest capes'; with Neville d'Almeida for the *Cosmococa* series of *Quasi-Cinema*; with poet Waly Salomão for the *Head Parangolé*; with Ivan Cardoso on the highly inventive documentary about Oiticica's work, *HO*;[44] with the many texts he wrote for other artists: and those collaborations which continued posthumously like the poet Haroldo de Campos's *Hagoromo*, a theatrical event in which the poet made a correlation between the *Parangolé Cape* and the feather-mantle, which is the theme of a classical Japanese Noh play.

At first sight, Lygia Clark's exclusion of an audience in her late work might appear to be the complete opposite of the inclusiveness that has continued to animate David Medalla's work since the 1960s – his idea that his propositions were open to 'any number of people'.[45] But opposites can easily turn into one another and one could say that both practices are different ways of resisting the pressures of institutionalisation, financial speculation and heedless consumption, to which the work of artists is so susceptible. True to his nomadic lifestyle and a love of the ephemeral, we find Medalla today wandering the world giving performances, making installations and objects, woven in with an endless series of informal encounters and meetings with the aim of stimulating, totally unofficially, artistic activity, whether funds are forthcoming or not. Earlier participation proposals, such as *A Stitch in Time*,[46] are reconfigured for new contexts and seem to gear people up to sew in their contribution with the same inexhaustible diversity as others had twenty-five years previously; performances are given in which there is often a participatory element; and groups and gatherings are brought about, the latest being the London Biennale, a sort of benign *ballet des pauvres* carnivalising the art world's globalisation.[47]

By calling these three artists pioneers I do not wish to imply that they are responsible for what has followed after them, or that they would necessarily approve of what is being called participatory art or 'relational aesthetics' today. When one thinks of Lygia Clark's late work such phrases sound banal, shallow and driven by the packaging considerations essential to marketing. I believe we have to look for their influence in a qualitative rather than quantitative sense, in a way which answers some of the conditions I proposed at the beginning, above all, seeking a transformative relationship with life, a non-institutional destiny for art, an open structure to which the other brings their subjective charge. As a legacy, this is much more significant than formal or stylistic derivations. It is non-prescriptive, non-literal, non-dogmatic and open to surprises. There is actually no end to the way a participatory aesthetic and ethic can be defamiliarised and reinvented, as Oiticica hints in the quote that begins this chapter.

Notes

1 Rose English, quoted by Guy Brett, *Carnival of Perception* (London: Institute of International Visual Arts, 2004), p. 4.
2 For another discussion of Hélio Oiticica's and Lygia Clark's work, see also Chapters 3 and 11.
3 Jean-Christophe Royoux, 'Introduction', *Omnibus*, special issue on *Documenta X* (October 1997), 2.
4 Harry Laus, quoted by Anna Dezeuze, 'Tactile dematerialisation, sensory politics: Hélio Oiticica's *Parangolés*', *Art Journal*, 63:3 (Summer 2004), 65.
5 Pierre Restany in conversation with the author, 1980s.
6 Lygia Clark, diary entry, 22 August 1971, in Guy Brett et al., *Lygia Clark* (Barcelona: Fundació Antoni Tàpies, 1997), p. 281. Clark may have made the analogy to medieval burning of witches and heretics to refer both to the 'healing' practice she later developed (in the Middle Ages some of those persecuted as witches were 'wisewomen' healers), and to her heresy in relation to artistic convention.
7 Hélio Oiticica, 'The possibilities of Creleisure' (1970), in Guy Brett et al., *Hélio Oiticica* (Rotterdam: Witte de With Centre for Contemporary Art, 1992), p. 137.
8 Hélio Oiticica, unpublished introductory text for a planned book of photographs by Desdémone Bardin, Rio de Janeiro, 1966.
9 László Moholy-Nagy, *Vision in Motion* (Chicago: Paul Theobald, 1947), p. 238.
10 David Medalla, 'The exploding galaxy', *Paletten*, 1 (1968), n. p.
11 David Medalla was not alone in making such a transition. Hans Haacke at the beginning of the 1970s also moved from nature-kinetics to 'society'. He kept the model of interdependent systems and applied it to reveal and clarify social and political processes, in forms which were open to the intervention of the public. In 1970 he converted his space in the *Information* exhibition at the Museum of Modern Art, New York, into a poll-booth where people could express an opinion on the implication of Nelson Rockefeller (then Governor of New York State, with strong family connections with the running of the MOMA) in a policy of support for the war in Vietnam.
12 Medalla, 'The exploding galaxy', n. p.

13 Lygia Clark, quoted in *Véja* magazine (December 1986).

14 For a discussion of Lygia Clark's and Hélio Oiticica's early work, see my 'Lygia Clark: in search of the body', *Art in America* (July 1994), 56–63 and 108, and 'The experimental exercise of freedom', in Brett et al., *Hélio Oiticica*, pp. 222–39.

15 Lygia Clark, 'Death of the plane' (1960), reprinted in *October*, 69 (Summer 1994), 96.

16 Lygia Clark, 'To capture a fragment of suspended time' (1973) in Brett et al., *Lygia Clark*, p. 187.

17 Ibid. At this time, a related work to hers, which Lygia Clark particularly appreciated, was the American artist John Dugger's *Perennial* (1970). A slender polythene tube was wound around the hand and covered by a thin plastic mesh, which was rolled back from the tube's end. Then placed on the table, the *Perennial* gradually unwound in a sensuous way and freed itself from the mesh.

18 Hélio Oiticica, 'To return earth to earth' (1979) in Brett et al., *Hélio Oiticica*, p. 202.

19 Hélio Oiticica, 'Colour, time and structure' (1960), in ibid., p. 37.

20 Hélio Oiticica, diary entry, 25 November 1960, in *Aspiro ao grande labirinto* (Rio de Janeiro: Rocco, 1986), p. 24.

21 Lygia Clark, letter to Guy Brett, c.1967.

22 Hélio Oiticica, 'World-shelter', unpublished text, 1973.

23 Lygia Clark, quoted in *Véja* magazine (December 1986).

24 Hélio Oiticica, letter to Edward Pope, 17 August 1974.

25 Parallel experiments with the notion of a 'collective body' were made in Brazil by Lygia Pape, although she did not use the term. Her *Divisor* of 1968 consists of a giant sheet of cloth, nearly 100 feet square, holding together, yet apart, a crowd of people whose heads protrude through evenly spaced holes. They are free to move, to bunch together or to spread out within certain limits. *Divisor* is an ambivalent metaphor: either referring to an atomisation, the 'massing together of man, each inside his own pigeon-hole' or to community. Lygia Pape, in *Lygia Pape* (Rio de Janeiro: Funarte, 1983), p. 46.

26 Suely Rolnik, 'Um singular estado de arte', *Folha de São Paulo* (4 December 1994), Caderno 6, 6.

27 Lygia Clark, in *Lygia Clark* (Rio de Janeiro: Funarte, 1980), p. 41.

28 Hélio Oiticica, 'Eden' (1969), in Brett et al., *Hélio Oiticica*, p. 12.

29 For a detailed record of the Whitechapel Experiment and its historical context, including reminiscences by people involved, see Guy Brett and Luciano Figueiredo (eds), *Oiticica in London* (London: Tate, 2007).

30 Steve Thorn, unpublished interview with David Medalla, May 1977. Quoted with the author's kind permission.

31 Ibid.

32 Orpingalik, in *Eskimo Poems from Canada and Greenland, from Material Originally Collected by Knud Rasmussen*, ed. and trans. T. Lowenstein (London: Alison & Busby, 1973), p. xxiii.

33 Medalla, unpublished interview with Thorn.

34 Although not directly related, it is revealing to connect Medalla's *Eskimo Carver* which centres, however playfully, around some notion of the will, discipline, planning, etc., involved in human production, to Susan Hiller's participatory

exploration of the involuntary activity of dreaming, and her experiments in creating a 'collective of dreamers', particularly in *Dream Mapping* (1974). These investigations were, in Hiller's words, 'deliberately non-theatrical. They are conducted among creative equals in the spirit of a collective endeavour, for which all participants are responsible.' Susan Hiller quoted in *Susan Hiller* (Liverpool: Tate, 1996), p. 50.

35 See Chapter 5.

36 Hélio Oiticica, letter to Guy Brett, October 1967 (my italics). The letter is in English.

37 Hélio Oiticica, 'Apocalipópotesis' (1969), in Brett et al., *Hélio Oiticica*, p. 232.

38 Ibid.

39 Michael Compton (ed.), *Robert Morris* (London: Tate, 1971). See Chapter 6 in this volume for an extensive discussion of this exhibition.

40 Oiticica, 'The possibilities of Creleisure', p. 136.

41 *Bolide* – fireball or meteor in English – is the generic title of a series of boxes, basins, bottles, flasks and other containers (including even a bed), which Oiticica produced in the 1960s and later. They remove a quantity of earth, or pigment, liquid, shells, eggs, etc., from the world, the totality, to create an energy-centre which in turn reaffirms the 'all'.

42 See Oiticica's lengthier response to this vexed question in a letter of 1967, reprinted in Brett et al., *Hélio Oiticica*, p. 25.

43 Lula Wanderlay, to whom Clark taught her method and who continues to use it in his own psychotherapy, has given a vivid account of the process:

The person lies down over a huge object, a mattress made of transparent plastic filled with small Styrofoam balls. Its surface does not offer resistance. It allows for empty space inside and thus facilitates a perfect accommodation of the body. I cover the person's eyes with a small object, place sea-shells to his ears to bring about a sense of inwardness. I gently massage the person's head, press, gently and firmly, the joints' ends against each other. This brings many people to experience a sense of unity.

I touch the person's body with relational objects in a kind of massage and let the objects lie over the body, enveloping it. This, the longest step (about 40 minutes) … is when the language of the relational objects becomes strongest, without the touch of the mediator-therapist, who just stays away waiting.

A rounded pebble wrapped in a net has been placed in the person's hands. We call this pebble 'proof of reality'. Being totally different from the other objects, since it is compact, has well-defined contours, etc., the gesture of holding it makes a counterpoint to the whole process and, simultaneously, is part of it.

Slowly and gently I remove the objects. I massage the body with another huge object, a kind of blanket made of very light material and stuffed with small Styrofoam balls. After the person is seated, the eyes open, I hand an object of air for the person to touch his/her own body in a gesture of transition on the way back to an attitude of verbalization. I then converse with the client about what was experienced during the whole session.

*O Dragão Pousou no Espaço: Arte Contemporânea, Sofrimento Psiquico, e
Objeto Relacional de Lygia Clark*. Rio de Janeiro: Rocco, 2002, pp. 42–3.

44 *HO*, dir. Ivan Cardoso, Rio de Janeiro, 1979, 16 mm.

45 Writing on Medalla, Dore Ashton invoked 'Everythingism' to describe his attitude. Launched by the poet Ilya Iliazd and the painter Mikhail Ledentu in Russia around 1913, the short-lived movement allowed artists to 'use and combine all the forms of art known in the past'. 'While most avant-garde movements are pointedly exclusive', Ashton comments, 'this was pointedly inclusive, and aimed to make use of everything … in a resounding affirmation of diversity.' Dore Ashton, 'An impromptu for David Medalla and Guy Brett', in Guy Brett, *Exploding Galaxies* (London: Kala Press, 1995), p. 9.

46 *A Stitch in Time* (initiated in 1968) invites people to sew anything they like on long sheets of cotton suspended in a rope and bobbin construction. There have been many versions over the years, no two exactly the same, in venues including Gallery House, London (1972), *Documenta 5*, Kassel (1972), The Hayward Gallery, London (1991). More recently, there has been the Musée d'Art Moderne de la Ville de Paris (1996 – people were invited to sew on a pair of suspended striped pyjamas in a version Medalla said was a homage to French artist Daniel Buren), Tate Gallery St Ives (1997), MOCA in Los Angeles (1999) and the ICA in Boston (2003).

47 Inspired by the mushrooming of art biennales in cities formerly marginalised in the international art world, but also highly critical of the exclusive, strictly limited and controlled nature of artists' participation in most of these events, Medalla wanted to initiate something that would be open to any artist anywhere in the world. He sees it as a do-it-yourself biennale. There is no building or office or administrator. It is up to artists to find a venue and funding for their shows: the venues could be anywhere, from someone's front room, to a gallery, to a cemetery, to a boat on the Thames. The idea is to delve into London's complex and heterogeneous fabric as much as possible, and to facilitate a creative gathering as open as possible. To register as a participant artist in the Biennale is a poetic rather than a bureaucratic act. One simply has to make or find an 'arrow' and be photographed, or collage one's image, against the Eros statue in Piccadilly Circus (the so-called 'hub of the universe' across which Eros aims his arrow of love). These postcard-sized images constituted the registration document.

'Open work', 'do-it-yourself' artwork and *bricolage*

Anna Dezeuze

Visitors to the third Neoconcrete exhibition at the Museum in São Paulo in 1961 would have encountered various kinds of objects scattered on white plinths. Perched on one of the higher vertical pedestals, a small blue cube occupied the centre of a white rectangular base of around 40 × 50 cm. Viewers could grasp the cube and lift it, revealing a single word hidden beneath it: *lembra* (remember). Moving to a lower plinth, visitors would have bent down to look at an aluminium sculpture made out of slim, hinged geometric planes whose folds created a proliferation of angles, gleaming surfaces and hidden spaces. Spectators could fold and unfold these hinged surfaces into various configurations, shifting the sculpture's position and shape through gestures made awkward by its sharp edges and heavy bulk.

Ferreira Gullar's *Poemas-objeto* (*Object-Poems*) and Lygia Clark's *Bichos* (*Beasts* or *Animals*) (figure 3.1) are two examples of works produced by the Neoconcrete movement, founded in 1959 in Rio de Janeiro. Once the group disbanded, shortly after this show, Neoconcrete artists Lygia Clark, Hélio Oiticica and Lygia Pape would go on to develop works and theoretical reflections which marked a transition from manipulable objects in the tradition of geometrical abstraction, to participatory works made out of everyday materials of little or no intrinsic value (see figures 1.1, 2.1, 2.2, 3.3).[1] In these works the tactile and bodily dimension of the participant's experience is paramount, as he or she needs to handle or wear objects.

Leafing through the pages of the 1963 book entitled *An Anthology of Chance Operations, Concept Art, Anti-art, Improvisation, Indeterminacy, Meaning-less Work, Natural Disasters, Stories, Diagrams, Poetry, Essays, Compositions, Dance Constructions, Music, Plans of Action, Mathematics*, readers will come across a range of texts and graphic notations, arranged alphabetically by artist's name and described by categories such as poetry, music, essays, dance and mathematics.[2] Described as 'poetry' is Emmett Williams's 1958 *Cellar Song for Five Voices*, a compact arrangement of words produced by the systematic permutation of five phrases (somewhere/bluebirds are flying/high in the sky/in the cellar/even blackbirds are extinct), creating over a hundred combinations. Another page, bearing black vertical and horizontal segments of varying lengths and widths, is listed as a musical score by composer Earle Brown (*December 1952*). The unspecified performer, it seems, must decide how to interpret these signs as pitch, duration, intensity and timbre.

Elsewhere, instructions for George Brecht's 'music', such as his *Card-Piece for Voice*, are given verbally rather than through graphic notation. Phoneme cards, we are instructed, should be read according to cues given by ordinary playing cards: the selected suits indicate how to pronounce the phonemes, the numbers serve to quantify the durations of sounds in seconds. *An Anthology* was initially assembled from 1960 by composer La Monte Young for a planned issue of a periodical called *Beatitude East*, but was finally designed and published by George Maciunas, who had by then brought together an international group of artists, based in Europe and the United States, under the name of Fluxus. Instruction pieces such as Brecht's – also known as event or word scores – would serve as the basis for Fluxus performances in New York and Germany from this time onwards, and would be combined from 1964 with everyday objects in Fluxus publications packaged and distributed by Maciunas (see figure 11.2).

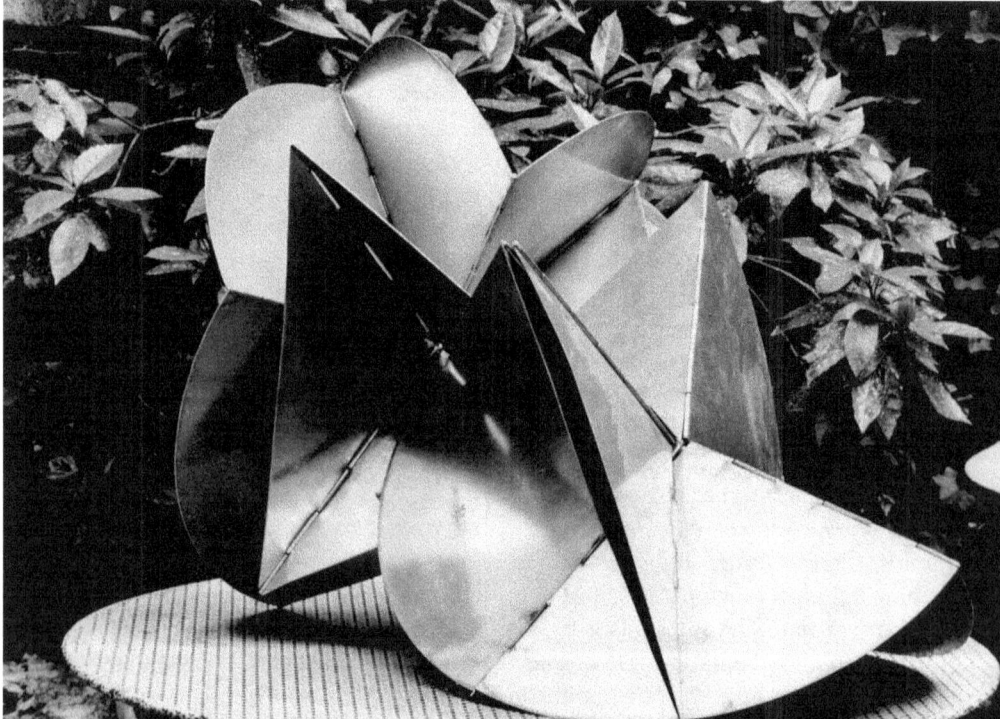

3.1   Lygia Clark, *Bicho*, 1963. Anodised aluminium.

Using Neoconcrete works and early Fluxus event scores as starting points, this chapter accounts for the emergence of spectator participation in specific practices developed independently from each other across three continents in the late 1950s and early 1960s. Situating them within a wider network of issues arising from experimental music, poetry and geometric abstraction, I bring to light little-known connections between these disparate practices, and explore some of the common preoccupations shared by these artists. In this context, I demonstrate how spectator participation emerged as one of the possible outcomes of a broader redefinition of the artwork as an 'open work', a notion theorised from 1958 by the Italian writer Umberto Eco.[3] In order to analyse the origins of spectator participation in the early 1960s, I explore the ramifications of the semantic relation between the notion of a 'do-it-yourself' artwork and the French word *bricolage*, defined by Claude Lévi-Strauss in his 1962 book *The Savage Mind*. (Although the terms *bricolage* and *bricoleur* have no precise equivalents in English, as the translator of the 1966 English edition of Lévi-Strauss's book remarked, they can be associated with a variety of 'do-it-yourself' activities ranging from functional 'odd jobs' to arts and craft hobbies.)[4] This relation, I argue, provides a new perspective on two major points in the development of spectator participation in the 1960s: first, the central role of the open work in the emergence of participation in the early 1960s, and second, the evolution from an open work, in which spectator participation is a secondary concern, to a do-it-yourself artwork which can no longer exist without the viewer's intervention. In this way, I develop new tools through which to analyse different types of spectator participation, and to address wider issues in the development of 1960s art.

A 'science of the concrete'

Drawing examples from twentieth-century poetry, painting and music, Eco attempted to map out in *The Open Work* a common desire among modern and contemporary artists to create works characterised by an ambiguity of meaning, and a plurality of interpretations. Eco theorised this new kind of 'openness' as the articulation between a static, 'closed' order embodied in forms, structures or systems, on the one hand, and, on the other, that which 'escapes' from the control of this order: chance, indeterminacy, events, matter and mobility. In 1955, the Brazilian poet Haraldo de Campos had written an article in the *Diário de São Paulo* on 'the open artwork' in which he referred to the poet Mallarmé, the writer James Joyce, the artist Alexander Calder, and the composer Pierre Boulez – all figures subsequently mentioned in Eco's *Open Work*.[5] De Campos defined 'open works' as 'short organisations embodying a realm of possibilities (*um possível*)' opposed to 'the fixity of conventional solutions' of the 'perfect', 'classical' artwork.[6] Two years later, George Brecht,

Allan Kaprow and Robert Watts explained in a collective text how the 'new advance guard' in the United States was characterised by 'a general loosening of forms which in the past were relatively *closed*, strict, and objective, to ones which are more personal, free, random, and *open*'.[7]

Thus, on different continents, in the second half of the 1950s, artists, poets and composers seemed to be similarly concerned with 'opening' up artworks which they felt to be somehow locked into fixed, static or 'closed' forms. There were, of course, differences in the general types of practice, and the specific contemporary works, to which each writer was responding at the time; the oppositions they set up can certainly each be inscribed within their own context of historical lineages and rhetorical strategies. I would argue, however, that these three definitions bring to light a crucial dynamic that emerged as a widely shared interpretative framework during this period: what Eco called 'the dialectic movement between form and openness', which 'determines the limits within which a work can accentuate its ambiguity … while keeping its existence as a work'.[8] My contention, here, is that this dynamic can be usefully described in terms of the operations of *bricolage* described by Lévi-Strauss in his discussion of 'mythical thought'. Where the *bricoleur*'s construction is typically made out of everyday objects and materials, the open work is assembled from visual, verbal and auditory elements; the analogy lies in the kind of process involved in both types of creation. The *bricoleur*, Lévi-Strauss tells us, selects his means from a stash of previously accumulated, largely used material ('odds and ends'), which he then uses to construct a unified whole. Similarly, the artist according to Eco explores through the open work a variety of options within a set field of possibilities, by mapping out a 'constellation' of elements within a single form.

This 'stash' of elements used to assemble the open work, I would argue, consisted in the remains left behind by the unprecedented explosion, in post-war experimental music, poetry and geometric abstraction, of new systems and methods bent on breaking down each aesthetic field into its basic formal and sensory constituents. Haraldo de Campos belonged to the Noigandres group, founded in São Paulo in 1952, who developed a form of 'concrete poetry' whose primary material, they claimed, was 'the word (sound, visual form, semantic charge)'.[9] Closely associated with Noigandres was Ruptura, one of the first groups of Brazilian artists to develop a vocabulary of geometric abstraction. The 1956 *First National Exhibition of Concrete Art*, which took place in São Paulo and travelled to Rio de Janeiro, included, along with poets such as Haraldo de Campos and Ferreira Gullar, both the Ruptura group and the Rio de Janeiro-based group Frente, which counted among its members Lygia Clark, Lygia Pape and Hélio Oiticica. This new trend of geometric abstraction in Brazil can be partly attributed to the influence of the Swiss artist Max Bill, who had won the sculpture prize at the first São Paulo Biennial five years earlier. Bill described his type of abstraction as 'concrete art', following Theo van Doesburg's use of the term in 1930. The central premise of concrete art, according to van Doesburg, was that 'nothing is more concrete, more real, than a line, a colour, a surface'.[10]

A musical equivalent of this premise can be found in the teachings of American experimental composer John Cage, whose classes were attended by George Brecht and Allan Kaprow, as well as poets such as Jackson MacLow and Dick Higgins, who were both included in *An Anthology*.[11] Cage started his course on 'Experimental Composition' at the New York School for Social Research in the summer of 1958 by listing the constitutive elements of sound: frequency, duration, amplitude, overtone-structure and morphology.[12] Out of these five determinants, Cage selected duration as the principal means to structure his compositions because it was the only characteristic common to both 'events in sound-space' as he called them, and silence. What Brecht, Higgins and MacLow took away from this definition was that any event occurring in time could be perceived as music. According to Higgins, dance, poetry and drama could be considered as so many specific types of 'musical activity', distinct only in their emphases.[13] This logic is clearly at work in the grouping of artists, composers, poets and dancers in *An Anthology*, as many works blur the boundaries between media (as a poem may involve sounds as well as words, and a music composition may ask the performer to walk and jump), while new forms of notations developed in these different fields converged in their shared use of verbal instructions such as Brecht's *Card Piece for Voice*.[14]

Implicit in most forms of concrete art and poetry was the ideal of a universal language, which fostered an increasingly international network of artists. Anthologies of concrete poetry in the 1960s include Fluxus poets such as Emmett Williams, MacLow and Higgins alongside the Noigandres group,[15] while Max Bill's 1960 exhibition *Concrete Art: Fifty Years of Development* in Zurich brought together European, North and South American artists working in the language of geometric abstraction, including members of the Brazilian groups Ruptura and Frente. When George Maciunas used the term 'concretism' in a 1962 manifesto, read out during a concert inaugurating an early series of Fluxus manifestations in Germany, he was reflecting the very international, interdisciplinary context from which this loose grouping of artists had emerged.[16] Maciunas had initially considered staging these concerts at the Cologne studio of artist Mary Bauermeister, where concrete art, concrete poetry and experimental music had previously been brought together.[17] As Wilfred Dörstel has retrospectively pointed out, Fluxus did indeed share common principles with concrete art, in particular the use of visual, verbal or musical elements which 'connote nothing other than themselves', as well as an 'overcoming of the subjective gesture'.[18] These two closely related central tropes – of 'letting' the physical features of sounds, words, lines or colours 'be themselves' as Cage would put it,[19] and of avoiding any form of individual self-expression – certainly run through most definitions of concrete art, poetry and experimental music at the time, underlying their aspirations to both universality and objective reality.

What emerged, then, in the post-war period could be called, after the title of Lévi-Strauss's chapter on mythical thought as *bricolage*, a new 'science of the concrete'. The reasons for this recurrent appeal to the concrete and the literal, the search for direct, unmediated access to materials, were undoubtedly very varied. While Mary Bauermeister, who studied at Max Bill's Hochschule für Gestaltung in Ulm, and turned to concrete art after the war had discredited in her eyes other forms or concepts,[20] Brazilian artists adopted the language of concrete art and poetry in the far more optimistic context of their country's new aspirations to progress and modernity.

At the same time, in the United States, Allan Kaprow defined the 'new concrete art' not through geometric abstraction, but rather as a turn to the everyday, away from the painterly concerns of Abstract Expressionism.[21] Maciunas's own even broader (and idiosyncratic) definition of 'concretism' posited the 'non-artificial' as an artwork's most concrete quality – whether it took the form of 'non-art, anti-art, nature', or 'reality'.[22] The category of the concrete work that I propose, then, spanned a wide variety of forms, contexts and discourses, and provided the conditions for the development of the 'open work' in the late 1950s and early 1960s. Through concrete art, a new 'field of possibilities' for art, poetry and music was being mapped out in the same way as the *bricoleur*, according to Lévi-Strauss, always starts his project by making an inventory or catalogue of the possibilities contained in his stash of objects.[23] Indeed, images of the artist as *bricoleur* abound in the rhetoric surrounding both concrete and open works. Both Emmett Williams and John Cage speak of 'raw materials' to describe the basic elements used by concrete poetry and the performer of a score by Earle Brown, respectively.[24] Similarly, concrete poetry's aim to 'present poetic material that the reader could do with as he saw fit' (according to Daniel Spoerri) is comparable to Eco's characterisation of a music piece by European composer Karlheinz Stockhausen, which is 'handed over to the performer more or less like the components of a construction kit'.[25]

Spectator participation and the 'open work'

'[T]he primary contribution of a truly concrete artist', according to Maciunas, 'consists in creating a *concept* or a *method* by which form can be created independently of him'.[26] Compositional devices ranging from systematic methods to chance processes all ensured the elimination of authorial control. While concrete poets such as de Campos or Emmett Williams subordinated the composition of their poems to rigid structures determined by permutations, repetitions and divisions of single words or phrases, concrete painters and sculptors often subjected regular geometric shapes and planes of colours to mathematical processes which involved adding, subtracting, dividing or multiplying a set number of modules. Cage pioneered the use of random chance processes in composition. For example, to determine the organisation of sound events within a time structure, he would often list in a chart all the event materials which he wanted to use, and then throw dice in order to determine their characteristics and order, sometimes using the Chinese book of changes, the *I-Ching*.

An Anthology is rife with such chance devices. In Brecht's *Card Piece for Voices*, performers are invited to use randomly picked playing cards as cues for their actions, while in Dick Higgins's *Telephone Music* the performer throws a dice to determine how he or she will respond to a ringing phone. In both systematic and chance processes, the author starts with a vocabulary of forms/words/sounds and arranges it according to a 'concept' or 'method', as Maciunas put it. If the use of systematic and indeterminate methods certainly let sounds, words and forms 'be themselves' to a greater extent than ever before, it also raised new problems. Sometimes, the authorial process remains opaque to the reader/performer/viewer, who may not know how the possibilities were chosen from the initial field, as in the cases of many works by Cage. Most crucially, it is often impossible to determine whether the composition was guided by chance or by a series of authorial choices (systematic or other). At some point in the early 1960s, experiments of concrete art, poetry and music, complete arbitrariness and inner necessity were collapsed together, as both were reduced to methods 'by which form can be created independently' of the artist. One of the most fruitful – if paradoxical – lessons of concrete art, then, would be that chance and mathematical calculation were, in fact, equivalent.[27]

The crucial rupture within the field of the concrete and open work, I would argue, should thus not be located within the debates over the merits of chance versus mathematical calculation. The origins of participatory works are to be found instead in another distinction, suggested by Maciunas, between 'indeterminate-chance' (or, I would add, 'systematic') 'compositional methods' on the one hand, and 'the form of an independent performer' on the other hand.[28] Within this new framework, the central question becomes who, exactly, takes on the role of the *bricoleur* in the open work: the artist, or the viewer (or reader/performer) who is now being directly given the 'raw materials' in order to develop the work independently from the author? Eco never addressed this distinction because for him any open work allows the reader/performer/viewer to trace back the field of possibilities from which the author was working, and hence imagine the alternative paths that could have been chosen to create a different object from the same 'raw material'. In this sense Eco's paradigm approximates Lévi-Strauss's contention that the viewer of the *bricoleur*'s assemblages can grasp 'the other possible forms of the same work; and in a confused way, he [the viewer] feels himself to be the creator'.[29] In this sense, many concrete works can be described as 'open' in Eco's (and Haraldo de Campos's) definition; what I would like to suggest here is that works concerned with participation pursued this drive towards 'openness' in substantially more radical ways.

Cage himself acknowledged the qualitative difference between the use of chance procedures at the level of *composition* and the introduction of indeterminate elements in the *performance* of musical works.[30] In a 1958 lecture, he pointed out that the latter had been explored less substantially by himself than by his colleagues in the so-called New York School, including Earle Brown and Christian Wolff, who were both represented in *An Anthology*. What emerged from Brown's and Wolff's brand of experimental music were new types of notation which allowed performers to make their own decisions regarding specific aspects of the work, be it the duration, sequence, pitch or tempo of each sound (as in Brown's *December 1952*, mentioned earlier). Brown had studied the Schillinger method which, like certain forms of concrete art and poetry, involved subjecting the raw materials of composition (sounds, in this case) to mathematical rules. As a reaction, Brown turned away from this 'overly mechanistic and mathematical basis' in favour of 'experiments in purely intuitive and spontaneous actions'.[31] Inviting performers to make their own decisions was a way of liberating musicians at the same time as 'letting the sounds be themselves'.

While George Brecht followed Cage in singling out Earle Brown's scores for the range of choices they offered the performers, the event scores written by Brecht and other Fluxus artists took this form of experimentation one step further by removing abstract musical notation altogether, and reducing the score to verbal instructions. The freedom given by Earle Brown to his musicians was extended to any possible performer: neither musical training nor a concert situation are required to perform Fluxus scores. The conception of music as an 'activity', pioneered by Brown, was taken to new lengths by Fluxus artists as they decided that music could be redefined as incidental to any activity. An activity could be performed that produced noise, imperceptible sounds, or even no sound at all. It could take place anywhere, and for durations exceeding the span of a public performance.

Earle Brown's personal trajectory from 'overly mechanistic' method to 'intuitive' experimental 'activity' strikingly parallels the debates that emerged as the two groups of Brazilian concrete artists, Ruptura and Frente, officially became rival factions around 1958, and some Frente artists led by Ferreira Gullar went on to found the Neoconcrete group. The language of Concretism, the Neoconcrete artists argued in their manifesto, was suffering from a 'dangerous rationalist exacerbation'.[32] Against the 'scientific' claims of Concretism and its emphasis on formal characteristics such as efficiency and rapidity, the Neoconcrete poets called for an 'intuitive, affective' dimension, closer to a 'living reality' (*realidade viva*) which would not exclude 'subjectivity'. More specifically, Lygia Clark complained that viewers of concrete art were invited to read 'space in a purely optical manner in which time is expressed in a merely mechanical way'.[33] Instead, Clark wanted spectators to 'participate actively' in works that were no longer addressed to the eye only – the Neoconcrete artists wanted to appeal to the viewer's 'eye-body'. Rather than serial forms to be understood mathematically, viewers of Neoconcrete art were invited to experience forms that evoked movement and life in a temporal process of apprehension.[34] Similarly, Neoconcrete poets sought to bring words to 'life' by staging a spatial, dynamic encounter with them in poem-objects such as Gullar's *Lembra*, described earlier. The appeal to tactile manipulation in Neoconcrete poetry was shortly mobilised in Clark's *Bichos* (figure 3.1) and Pape's *Livro da Criação* (*Book of Creation*), which invited readers to assemble each page. Oiticica, for his part, extended his exploration of colour from painting to hanging and environmental structures to be apprehended in space. 'The spectator', he noted in 1962, 'has now become the "discoverer of the work," revealing it part by part.'[35] For Clark, the dialogue between the spectator and the *Bicho* shifted the viewer's experience from an optical encounter to an embrace (*corpo-a-corpo*, the Brazilian term used by the artist, literally means 'body-to-body').[36]

Just as performer choice, for composers such as Earle Brown, emerged as an alternative to chance and systematic composition in the field of experimental music, the appeal to spectator participation in Neoconcretism was little more than a side effect of the desire to introduce an organic, 'subjective', 'intuitive' dimension into the language of concrete art. Through viewer and performer participation, a crucial shift occurred from chance to choice, and from the mechanical time and space suggested by some forms of concrete art and poetry to the viewer's experienced time and space in participatory works. This shift allowed artists, composers and poets to pursue their exploration of the objective and universal aspirations of the concrete idiom, while at the same time acknowledging some aspects of specificity and subjectivity. Rather than a regression to types of individual self-expression previously rejected by concrete art, these new elements of specificity and subjectivity signalled a move to another form of expression: that of the spectator/reader/performer encountering forms in his or her own here and now.

Play, contingency, economy

Lévi-Strauss pointed out that, semantically, the term *bricolage* originated in the fields of games, hunting and racing, where it described the incidental movement of a horse avoiding an obstacle in a race, or a ball accidentally bouncing off a billiard table. This obsolete usage points to three important structural characteristics of *bricolage*: movement, play and contingency. These features, it seems to me, are intrinsically linked to the 'precarious' 'balance' that Lévi-Strauss defined elsewhere as the tensions, at the heart of every artwork, between 'structure' and 'event'.[37] By displaying the ways in which closed, fixed 'structures' can be disrupted and transformed by singular 'events' – whether generated by chance, indeterminacy or viewer/performer participation – open works, like the *bricoleur*'s assemblage, reveal the very contingency of their existence. This conception of the work resonated strongly with contemporary changes in scientific worldviews, as many artists in the 1950s and early 1960s became attracted to new theories of mathematics and physics that were being popularised at the time.

Brecht, who was a professional chemist before becoming an artist, pointed in a 1957 essay to three concepts in particular that seemed to encourage a perception of the artwork as contingent and mobile. Firstly, he emphasised the centrality of the indeterminacy principle defined in 1927 by the physicist Werner Heisenberg. Heisenberg suggested that the causal model of classical physics was flawed and needed to be replaced by a probabilistic model, in which, as Brecht explains, 'the best we can do is to make statements with a high degree of probability'.[38] Eco similarly referred to 'the general breakdown in the concept of causation' of classical physics.[39] Replacing the binary model of an 'either true or false' proposition, quantum physics introduced a new probabilistic model of 'universes' or 'fields' of possibilities – new concepts that were central, as we have seen, to definitions of the open work. Brecht also concluded that nuclear physics had led to a redefinition of matter since it was no longer possible to 'consider the structure of an atom without feeling that an object is becoming an event and that every event is an object'.[40]

Clark seemed to have shared similar concerns, as she noted in 1960: 'Static things do not exist. Everything is dynamic. Even an object that appears to be static is not at a standstill.'[41] The mobile nature of matter was suggested in different ways in Clark's articulated *Bichos* and in Brecht's 1959 exhibition *Toward Events*. Works included in this exhibition included *The Case*, which presented visitors with objects displayed in a box, which they were invited to handle, and replace freely (figure 3.2). Brecht was less interested in the objects on display than the participants' actions, which, for him, constituted a musical 'event'. The third major lesson of modern physics for artists was, as Brecht put it, the 'inseparability between observer and observed': every

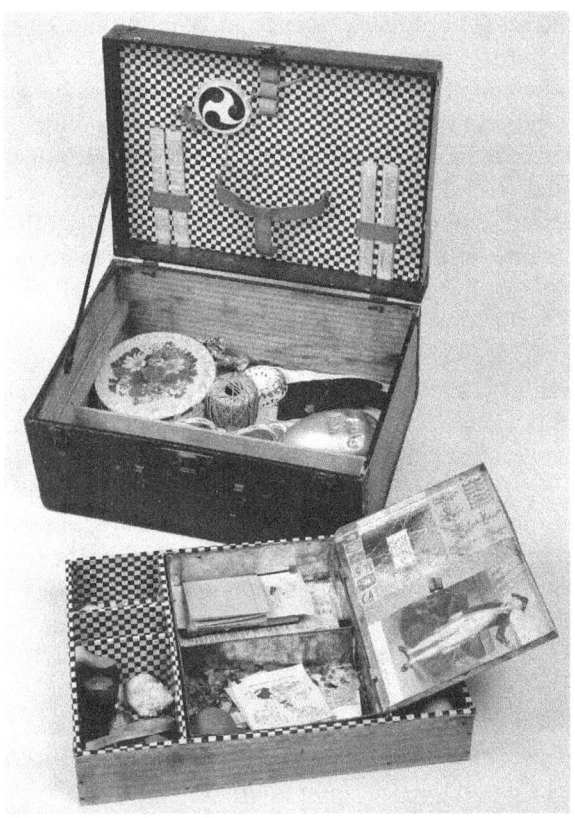

George Brecht, *Suitcase*, 1959. Mixed media, 20 x 41 x 30 cm.   **3.2**

observation is in fact an intervention within the very 'field of possibilities' that is being studied.[42] This, of course, would be a further justification for the need to introduce spectator and performer participation in artworks. As one physicist explained, the observer of scientific experiments should be called a 'participator', and the universe should be redefined as a 'participatory universe'.[43] One of the logical implications, according to Brecht, of this new 'participatory' role was that, 'There is no absolute chance or random event, for chance and randomness are aspects of the way in which we structure our universe.'[44] If every observation could be perceived as a way of structuring the universe, then spectator participation appeared as a far more effective means of introducing randomness within an artwork than complex chance operations set up by the author. What Brecht called his 'resolution of the distinction between choice and chance' can be seen both in participatory objects such as the *Case* and in his scores, as he left behind chance methods such as those used in *Card Piece for Voice*.[45]

This overall sense of mobility, change and contingency encouraged a new conception of the artwork as play. When Roland Barthes described, in a 1971 essay, the production of a text by the reader's intervention, he used the French verb *jouer*, to play, in its three different semantic meanings. The first, more technical sense of the word '*jeu*' is often applied to a machine to describe the necessary but restricted movement between its fixed parts. As Roger Caillois explained in his 1958 book on play, '*jeu*' in this context 'signifies the freedom which must remain at the heart of rigour itself for it to acquire or preserve its efficiency'.[46] This form of play bears a striking resemblance to the dialectical tensions at the heart of the open work: the 'precarious balance' between form and matter, fixed structures and events, order and disorder. The second and third meanings of *jouer* listed by Barthes are more common. The reader, according to him, is invited to play with the text 'as one *plays* a game' but, 'in order that that practice not be reduced to a passive, inner mimesis', he or she must also play the text 'in the musical sense of the term'.[47] Although Barthes was probably thinking of other composers than Cage when he evoked the 'post-serial' score in this essay, it is highly significant that he turned to experimental music as a model for his discussion of reader/author relations; music had similarly allowed Fluxus artists to introduce spectator participation in both their event scores and their manipulable objects. The final meaning of *jouer* evoked by Barthes – to play *with* something – emphasises the strong connection between the performance of a musical score and the manipulation of objects which can be conceived as toys or games. This relation lies, of course, at the centre of the definition of the 'do-it-yourself' artwork as a form of participatory practice that exceeds formal categories and comprises both text-based and object-based works.

While this text by Barthes effectively maps out the role of the reader/performer as a 'player', it is to an earlier essay that we need to turn for an explicit articulation of the relation between play and *bricolage*. In this 1957 article, Barthes contrasts contemporary fashions in children's toys with a more creative form of play that he associates with the *génie de la bricole* – the 'spirit of do-it-yourself'.[48] Abstract, 'invented' forms made out of building blocks for example 'offer dynamic forms', unlike ready-made figurines, model houses and doctors' toys, which appeal to the child as a 'user' rather than a 'demiurge'. The spirit of do-it-yourself involves creating new forms out of a limited range of available means. Rather than possessing a specific function, the elements chosen by the *bricoleur* 'each represent a set of actual and possible relations' ('*un ensemble de relations, à la fois concrètes et virtuelles*').[49] *Bricolage* thus sets up a specific kind of economy, which lies at the heart of the do-it-yourself artwork as a form of play. This economy, I would argue, is precisely what Brecht seemed to be describing in 1957 when he defined 'the primary function' of his art as 'an expression of maximum meaning with a minimal image, that is, the achievement of an art of multiple implications, through simple, even austere, means'.[50] Brecht's 'art of multiple implications' – like the 'fields of possibility' set up by the 'open work' – hinges on structures, made with simple words or forms, that can evoke a variety of meanings or take on a number of visible arrangements.

This is nowhere more apparent than in those of Brecht's scores that bear a strong resemblance to Japanese haiku, poems characterised by a fixed, three-line structure and a reliance on the suggestive power of a limited number of words and images.[51] Both Brecht and Higgins moved away from lengthy, complex instructions such as those included in *An Anthology* in favour of shorter instructions, sometimes reduced by Brecht to a single word. For her part, Lygia Pape recalled in an interview how she and the Concretist poets were fascinated by the haiku as an 'image-based poem'.[52] The economy which characterises her *Livro da criação* could indeed be compared to the logic of the haiku, as a simple square painted green evokes the plains and forests inhabited by the first human beings, or a yellow square pierced with a square opening refers to the creation of light. The viewer's or reader's imagination is awakened precisely by the simplicity of the basic forms of the *Livro da criação*: each page is conceived as a set of components in a construction kit allowing participants to construct their own personal narratives of genesis – thus turning them, as Barthes would have it, into 'demiurges'.

In a 1960 presentation, Fluxus artist Yoko Ono compared 'the poetry of origami' to haiku in terms of their economy. Origami, she explained, 'consists of a square sheet of paper which becomes many different and exciting objects merely by folding'.[53] Clark's *Bichos*, which yield their multifarious forms through folding and unfolding, can be compared to origami; Ono's suggestion that in origami 'the process of folding … is as important as the object' could easily be applied to Clark's hinged sculptures, which focus on the 'dialogue' between the viewer and the object. The *Bichos*' poetry, like that of origami objects, lies in the 'ingenuous' 'underlying geometric arrangement' of a simple structure. As viewers fold them, shapes are superimposed, divided and multiplied: a circle becomes a semi-circle, a square is transformed into a pyramid. As Ono put it, origami enables the participant to 'achieve a maximum of beauty with a minimum of manipulation'.[54]

'Techniques du corps'

Whereas a haiku, according to Alan Watts, is an 'image of a concrete moment in life', Brecht's event score 'is a signal preparing one for the moment itself'.[55] Brecht noted this crucial shift from the descriptive mode of the haiku to the more instructive event score in 1961: performers of his scores, he argued, are invited to encounter these 'moments in life' in the present as well as the future. This shift can be seen in Brecht's score for *Drip Music*, which consists of the single word 'dripping'. The score first emerged from the context of the Cage class, where students were encouraged to explore new sound-producing activities such as water being poured in a vessel. By 1961, however, Brecht could suggest that listening to the sound of a tap dripping somewhere in one's everyday environment could in itself be a realisation of his score. No activity is required, apart from the act of noticing.

The huge body of Fluxus scores does not systematically reflect this specific shift from a musical context to the context of everyday life, since many Fluxus artists continued to write both kinds of scores throughout the 1960s. Among the other artists who along with Brecht invite us, through their scores, to consider our most everyday activities in a new light, is Alison Knowles, whose 1961 *Proposition*, for example, simply instructs us to 'make a salad'. *Proposition* easily inscribes itself within the daily context of cooking, which is no less complex a framework than music – as sociologist Luce Giard has demonstrated, cooking involves a rich network of traditions, conventions and culture. In her analysis, Giard draws in particular on Marcel Mauss's 1934 definition of '*techniques du corps*' ('techniques of the body') as 'the ways in which men, in each society, use their bodies' in socially and culturally determined ways.[56] For Giard, the practice of cooking is a *technique du corps* characterised by 'the skill involved in adapting the gesture to the conditions of realisation and the quality of the obtained result'.[57]

It was to this very concept of *techniques du corps* that Brazilian critic Frederico Morais referred in relation to Clark's and Oiticica's works in a 1970 text.[58] In this essay, Morais discussed the works developed by Clark and Oiticica after the end of Neoconcretism in 1962, as both artists left behind the language of geometric abstraction and created tactile objects out of everyday objects and materials. Clark further explored the potential of spectator participation, first developed in the *Bichos*, in her 1966 series of *Sensory Objects*, also known a *Nostalgia do Corpo*. In *Air and Stone*, for example, viewers are invited to hold a transparent plastic bag, filled with air, on which is balanced a round stone (see figure 1.1); *Breathe with Me* involves participants making a loop out of a rubber tube, normally used in diving, and extending and retracting it repeatedly.

Oiticica's search for 'the body of colour' was the drive for the evolution of his Neoconcrete work from painting to hanging structures, and, after Neoconcretism, led him to experiment with box-like containers in which viewers can plunge their hands to discover pigment, cloths and poems (the *Bolides*); as well as colourful capes, flags and tents made out of jute and plastic bags, painted or printed fabrics and pockets filled with objects (the *Parangolés*) (see figures 2.2 and 3.3). In these situations, argued Morais, the spectator's body has becomes a 'motor' of the work. Just as the term *techniques du corps* redefines the body as a tool, the spectator's body in these works is conceived as the means through which objects are discovered by the participant. Indeed, the objects created by Clark and Oiticica act as bridges between the participants' bodies and the realm of tools and clothing. As they are handled and worn, they take the form of prosthetic extensions of our bodies. The rubber tube becomes my third lung in *Breathe with Me*, as my own breathing spontaneously starts to adjust to its rhythms; when I dance around in a *Parangolé* cape, my arms seem extended into wings, while the play between hidden and visible elements in the fabric evokes the porous membrane of my skin.

In Fluxus instructions and the mid-1960s works of Clark and Oiticica the *bricolage* operations of the 'open work' are extended and transposed to encompass the viewers' bodies and their everyday gestures as a whole. The artwork is no longer an autonomous object caught up between conflicting forces of order and disorder, control and indeterminacy: it becomes inseparable from the viewer's interactions with it. This shift is not, however, a rupture. Rather, it is a transposition of the problematics of the open work to a wider field of experience. The figure of the *bricoleur* remains a key reference, but he has extended his remit in significant ways. From a means to construct meaning from the raw materials of sound, light and colour, *bricolage* has become a model for understanding another type of technical formation: the *techniques du corps*, described by Mauss as 'montages' of 'a physio-psycho-sociological series of actions'.[59]

The 1959 Neoconcretist manifesto explicitly invoked Maurice Merleau-Ponty's definition of the phenomenology of perception as an embodied process in which subject and object are indissociable.[60] Merleau-Ponty, as it happens, was a friend of Lévi-Strauss, and *La Pensée sauvage* is dedicated to his memory. As Stephen Melville has pointed out, both Lévi-Strauss's chapter on 'the science of the concrete' and Merleau-Ponty's later writings exemplify a 'particular strand of materialism' emerging in France in the 1950s and 1960s.[61] This particular materialism, according to Melville, proposed a new conception of matter, not as opposed to thought, but as articulating and being articulated by thought. The polarities of order and disorder, chaos and control, articulated by the dialectics of the open work can thus be inscribed within this emerging materialism, which paved the way for wider questionings of the intrinsic relations between matter and bodies, on the one hand, and conscious and unconscious thoughts on the other hand.

The contingency, play and economy characteristic of the 'open work' can thus be recast as guiding principles for a new do-it-yourself artwork in the expanded field of the *techniques du corps*. The minimal 'neo-haiku' economy of Fluxus was highlighted by George Maciunas as its distinguishing feature, which demarcated it radically from the 'neo-baroque' aesthetic of happenings.[62] Even the most sensory experiments in Fluxus, I would argue, stand apart from

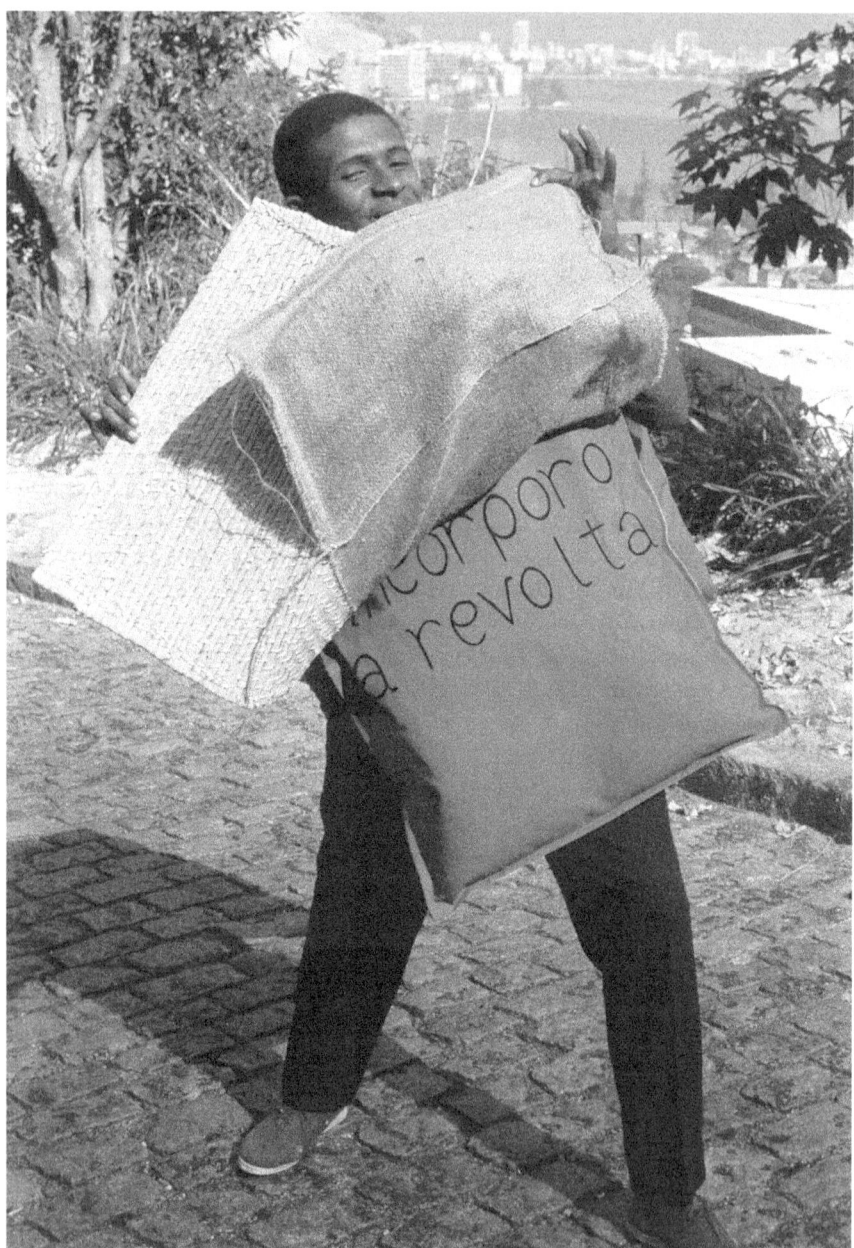

3.3 Nildo of Mangueira wearing *Parangolé P15 Cape 11 Incorporo a revolta* ('*I Embody Revolt*'), by Hélio Oiticica, 1967.

the aesthetic of multi-sensory environments or simultaneous performances that would become widespread in the 1960s. Rather than a multiplication of sensations, Fluxus primarily explored what Ono herself defined as 'a sensory experience isolated from other sensory experiences, which is something rare in daily life'.[63]

The concrete lineage of Clark's and Oiticica's sensory works may be more difficult to trace, since the rupture from Neoconcretism certainly marked a shift away from the language of geometric abstraction (as plastic bags, rubber tubes and stones replaced the hinged metal disks and squares of Clark's *Bichos*, or soft jute and cotton fabrics succeeded Oiticica's angular painted reliefs and boxes). Nevertheless, in the works that Clark and Oiticica produced in the mid- to late 1960s at least, the relation to Neoconcretism can be observed in the persistence of formal concerns within the new bodily experiences offered by the artists. Specific dynamics of forms, colours, shapes and contrasts are articulated through minimal structures involving sets of polarities. When they are worn, the *Parangolé* capes articulate the opposition between concealment and display, self-consciousness and liberation, which, as I have suggested elsewhere, may have been linked to the ambivalent relations between high art and popular culture experienced by Oiticica when he first became involved with inhabitants of the Mangueira *favela* in Rio de Janeiro.[64] Clark's exploration of contrasts between heavy and light, warm and cold, natural and artificial materials in works such as *Air and Stone* or *Breathe with Me* allowed her to further expand her Neoconcrete interest in an 'organic' space: as the distinctions between inside and outside, body and space become blurred, a new sense of the self moulded by the world around it emerges. If the *Bicho* had involved an 'embrace' between the viewer and the object, the *Sensory Objects* invited a further dissolution of the viewer-object distinction.

A new conception of the body is what would attract Oiticica to Yoko Ono's scores in the 1970s.[65] Oiticica singled out, for example, her 1963 *Pulse Piece*, which invites readers to: 'Listen to each other's pulse by putting your ear on the other's stomach.' In order to describe the new relation to the body suggested by Ono's score, Oitica coined the compound word 'body-play' (*corpo-play*) by combining the English word 'play' and the Portuguese '*corpo*' (body). This 'corpo-play', argues Oiticica, reveals 'the body as a phenomenon of sensory play' rather than as an 'element of linear integrity'.[66] While these reflections correspond to a later stage in Oiticica's work, it is tempting to read the *Parangolés* as operating a similar transformation of the body beyond 'linear integrity'. With the emergence of the do-it-yourself artwork as a *technique du corps*, play is transposed from a way of transforming the autonomous artwork into an open field of possibilities, to a remapping of the viewer's body itself. 'Letting' sounds, words, forms 'be themselves' – the catchphrase for 1950s concrete art – would logically lead to letting our bodies 'be themselves'.

The appeal to spectator/performer participation in the early 1960s, rather than a novelty gimmick, presented itself as the logical outcome of converging preoccupations, embodied in the notion of the open work, with a new kind of concrete reality, new ways of structuring this reality, and the ensuing shifts in conceptions of authorship. Although the evolution from open works to do-it-yourself artworks focusing on experiences rather than objects was not a linear process, the characteristics of contingency, economy and play that feature in a number of Fluxus practices and in works by Clark and Oiticica can be traced back to the defining features of the open work, and serve to set these do-it-yourself practices apart from other participatory works of that period. Moreover, the truly international tendencies intersecting within the notion of the open work allows us to revise accounts of 1960s art traditionally centred on North American Minimalism and Pop.

Most importantly, I would argue here that the concrete materialism of the open work – with its relation to Lévi-Strauss's 'science of the concrete' and Merleau-Ponty's phenomenology of perception – became the starting point for one of the most radical 'rethinkings of materiality' that would characterise, according to Michael Newman, conceptual art from the late 1960s onwards.[67] As the spectator's body became a motor for action and thought within the do-it-yourself artwork, a new conception of the artwork emerged in which matter and form, object and subject, became more intrinsically intertwined than ever before.[68]

Notes

1 For an extended discussion of the works of Lygia Clark and Hélio Oiticica, and references to some of Lygia Pape's work, see also Chapter 2.

2 La Monte Young (ed.), *An Anthology* … was originally published in 1963 (New York: Jackson Mac Low and La Monte Young). A second edition was published in 1970 (New York: Heiner Friedrich).

3 Umberto Eco first discussed the 'open work' in a paper presented in 1958 at the XVII International Congress of Philosophy, and first published an article on the subject in 1961. Published in Italian in 1962 (Milan: Bompiani), *Opera aperta* was translated into French in 1965 by Chantal Roux de Bézieux with the help of the French experimental composer André Boucourechliev (*L'Œuvre ouverte*, Paris: Seuil). The only existing English translation to my knowledge is not complete, as it was edited by Eco and David Robey who selected some chapters from the original and added other writings. *The Open Work*, trans. Anna Cangogni (London: Hutchinson Radius, 1989).

4 See translator's note in Claude Lévi-Strauss, *The Savage Mind*, trans. anon. (London: Weidenfeld & Nicolson, 1966), p. 17. The discussion of *bricolage* is included in Chapter 1.

5 Haraldo de Campos, 'A obra de arte aberta', *Diário de São Paulo* (3 July 1955),

in Augusto de Campos, Haraldo de Campos, Décio Pignatari, *Teoria da poesia concreta: textos críticos e manifestos 1950-1960* (São Paulo: Edições Invenção, 1965), pp. 28–31. Unless otherwise stated, all translations in this essay are mine.

6 Ibid., pp. 30, 31.

7 George Brecht, Allan Kaprow and Robert Watts, 'Project in multiple dimensions' (1957–8), in Joan Marter (ed.), *Off Limits: Rutgers University and the Avant-garde, 1957–1963* (Newark: Newark Museum, 1999), p. 155 (my italics).

8 Umberto Eco, 'Introduzione alla II edizione', in *Opera Aperta* (Milan: Bompiani, 3rd edn, 1980), p. 16.

9 Augusto de Campos, Haraldo de Campos, Decio Pignatari, 'Pilot plan for concrete poetry' (1958), in Richard Kostelanetz (ed.), *The Avant-garde Tradition in Literature* (Buffalo: Prometheus Books, 1982), p. 258.

10 Theo van Doesburg, 'Das Manifest der konkreten Kunst' (1930), reproduced in Max Bill (ed.), *Concrete Art: Fifty Years of Development* (Zurich: Helmhaus Zurich, 1960), p. 23.

11 Cage's influence on Fluxus has been the subject of a range of studies. See Michael Nyman, *Experimental Music: Cage and Beyond* (Cambridge, New York and Melbourne: Cambridge University Press, 2nd edn, 1999), chapter 4; Bruce Altshuler, 'The Cage class', in Cornelia Lauf and Susan Hapgood (eds), *FluxAttitudes* (Buffalo: Hallwalls Contemporary Arts Center, 1992), pp. 17–23; Douglas Kahn, 'The latest: Fluxus and music', in Elizabeth Armstrong and Joan Rothfuss (eds), *In the Spirit of Fluxus* (Minneapolis: Walker Art Center, 1994), pp. 103–20; Joseph Jacobs, 'Crashing New York à la John Cage', in Joan Marter (ed.), *Off Limits*, pp. 65–99; Liz Kotz, 'Post-Cagean aesthetics and the "event" score', *October*, 95 (Winter 2001), 55–89.

12 See George Brecht, *Notebook I, June–September 1958*, vol. I (Cologne: Walther König, 1991), pp. 3–4.

13 Dick Higgins, 'Postface', in *Postface and Jefferson's Birthday* (New York, Nice and Cologne: Something Else Press, 1964), p. 42.

14 For a discussion of these developments, see my 'Origins of the Fluxus score: from indeterminacy to the "do-it-yourself artwork"', in *Performance Research*, 7:3 (September 2002), 78–94.

15 See Emmett Williams (ed.), *Anthology of Concrete Poetry* (New York: Something Else Press, 1967); Stephen Bann (ed.), *Concrete Poetry; an International Anthology* (London: Magazine Editions, 1967); Mary-Ellen Solt (ed.), *Concrete Poetry: A World View* (Bloomington: Indiana University Press, 1968).

16 Maciunas's 'Neo-dada in music, theatre, poetry, art', was read out in German at the concert *Après John Cage* in Wuppertal on 9 June 1962. The English version is reproduced in Jon Hendricks (ed.), *What's Fluxus? What's not! Why* (Brasília: Centro Cultural Banco do Brasil, 2002), pp. 89–90.

17 See Wilfred Dörstel, Rainer Steinberg, Robert von Zahn, 'The Bauermeister studio: proto-Fluxus in Cologne, 1960–62', in Ken Friedman (ed.), *Fluxus Virus, 1962–1992* (Cologne: Galerie Schüppenhauer and Kölnischer Kunstverein, 1992), pp. 56–62. This is an abridged translation of a longer essay by Wilfred Dörstel, '"Knollenwächs" und "Rongierstelle": Europäische konkrete Kunst und

amerikanischer Konkretismus im Atelier Mary Bauermeister', in Dörstel (ed.), *Intermedial, Kontrovers, Experimentell: Das Atelier Mary Bauermeister in Köln 1960–62* (Köln: Emons, 1993), pp. 136–49.

18 Dörstel et al., 'The Bauermeister studio', p. 61.

19 John Cage, 'Indeterminacy' (1957), in *Silence: Lectures and Writings* (London: Marion Boyars, 1978), p. 10.

20 See Mary Bauermeister, interview with Wilfred Dörstel in Dörstel (ed.), *Intermedial, Kontrovers, Experimentell*, p. 15.

21 See Allan Kaprow, 'The legacy of Jackson Pollock' (1958), in *Essays on the Blurring on Art and Life* (Berkeley and London: University of California Press, 1993), pp. 1–9.

22 Maciunas, 'Neo-dada', p. 89.

23 See Lévi-Strauss, *The Savage Mind*, pp. 18–19.

24 Emmett Williams, 'Foreword', in *Anthology of Concrete Poetry*, p. vi. Cage, 'Composition as process II: indeterminacy' (1958), in *Silence*, p. 38.

25 Umberto Eco, *The Open Work*, pp. 1, 4. The original Italian reads '*pezzi di un meccano*', which refers in fact to the construction game, Meccano, which has existed in Europe and North America since the beginnings of the twentieth century. *Opera Aperta*, p. 35.

26 Maciunas, 'Neo-dada', p. 90.

27 Wilfred Dörstel mentions this characteristic of concrete art in Dörstel et al., 'The Bauermeister Studio', p. 61; Yve-Alain Bois develops this issue in his 'Ellsworth Kelly in France: anti-composition in its many guises', in Yve-Alain Bois et al., *Ellsworth Kelly: The Years in France, 1948–1954* (Washington: National Gallery of Art, 1993), pp. 9–36.

28 Maciunas, 'Neo-dada', p. 216.

29 Lévi-Strauss, *The Savage Mind*, p. 24. Lévi-Strauss is in fact speaking here of miniatures, but is comparing them to *bricolage*.

30 Cage, 'Composition as process II', pp. 35–40.

31 Earle Brown, 'Some notes on composing' (1963), in George Chase (ed.), *The American Composer Speaks: A Historical Anthology 1770–1965* (Baton Rouge: Louisiana State University Press, 1966), p. 301.

32 Ferreira Gullar et al., 'Manifesto neoconcreto' (1959), in Aracy Amaral (ed.), *Arte construtiva no Brasil: coleção Adolpho Leirner* (São Paulo: Dorea Books and Art, 1998), p. 270.

33 Lygia Clark, 'Ligia (sic) Clark busca na pintura a expressão do proprio espaço', *Folha da manhã*, 27 September 1958. Lygia Clark Archives, Rio de Janeiro, Museu de Arte Moderna, MFN 1125.

34 For an overview of Neoconcretism, see Ronaldo Brito, *Neoconcretismo: Vertice e Ruptura do Projeto Construtivo Brasileiro* (1975) (São Paulo: Cosac & Naify Edições, 2nd edn, 1999).

35 Hélio Oiticica, 'A Transição da cor do quadro para o espaço e o sentido de construtividade' (1962), in Luciano Figueiredo, Lygia Pape and Waly Salomão (eds.), *Aspiro ao grande labirinto: textos de Hélio Oiticica (1954–1969)* (Rio de Janeiro: Rocco, 1986), p. 53.

36 Lygia Clark, '*Bichos*' (1960), in Guy Brett et al., *Lygia Clark* (Marseilles: MAC, galeries contemporaines des Musées de Marseille, 1998), p. 121.
37 Lévi-Strauss, *The Savage Mind*, pp. 40, 25.
38 George Brecht, *Chance Imagery* (New York: Something Else Press, 1966), p. 9.
39 Eco, *The Open Work*, p. 15.
40 Michael Nyman, 'George Brecht: Interview', *Studio International*, 192: 984 (November–December 1976), 258.
41 Lygia Clark, 'O Vazio-pleno' (1960), in Brett et al., *Lygia Clark*, p. 112 (my translation).
42 George Brecht, 'Statement', in Brecht, Kaprow and Watts, 'Project in multiple dimensions', p. 158.
43 John Wheeler, *The Physicist's Conception of Nature* (Boston: Reidel, 1973), quoted in Michael Crichton, *Jasper Johns* (London: Thames & Hudson, 1977), p. 77.
44 Brecht, *Chance Imagery*, p. 15.
45 Ibid.
46 Roger Caillois, *Les Jeux et les hommes: le masque et le vertige* (Paris: Gallimard, 2nd edn, 1967), p. 15.
47 Roland Barthes, 'De L'Œuvre au texte' (1971), in *Œuvres Complètes, vol. II, 1966–1973* (Paris: Seuil, 1993), p. 1216.
48 'Jouets' (1957), in *Œuvres Complètes, vol. I, 1942–1965* (Paris: Gallimard, 1993), p. 597. Translated as 'Toys', in *Mythologies*, trans. A. Lavers (London: Vintage, 1993), p. 53.
49 Lévi-Strauss, *The Savage Mind*, 18. *La Pensée sauvage* (Paris: Plon, 1962), p. 27.
50 Brecht, 'Statement', p. 158.
51 Brecht mentioned haiku in 1961 in 'Events. (assembled notes)', extract from an unpublished letter to George Maciunas, written around May or June 1961 n.p. New York, Gilbert and Lila Silverman Fluxus Collection. My thanks to Jon Hendricks for access to documents in the Silverman archive.
52 Lygia Pape, *Entrevista a Lúcia Caineiro e Ileana Pradilla* (Rio de Janeiro: Lacerda Edições and Centro de Arte Hélio Oiticica, 1998), p. 40. Pape compared the 'forest' page of her *Livro da criação* with a haiku in a conversation with the author, Rio de Janeiro, 27 April 2001.
53 Yoko Ono, 'The poetry of origami', unpublished text, *c.*1960, n.p. New York, Gilbert and Lila Silverman Fluxus Collection.
54 Programme for an untitled event at the Department of Graphic Arts & Illustration, Pratt Institute, New York, 23 March 1960, n.p. New York, Gilbert and Lila Silverman Fluxus Collection.
55 Brecht, 'Events. (assembled notes)', n. p.
56 Marcel Mauss, 'Les Techniques du corps' (1936), in *Sociologie et anthropologie* (Paris: Presses Universitaires de France, 3rd edn, 1968), p. 365. Luce Giard, 'Faire-la-cuisine', in Michel de Certeau, Luce Giard, Pierre Mayol, *L'Invention du quotidien, vol. 2: Habiter, Cuisiner* (1980) (Paris: Gallimard, 1990), p. 285. All translations from these texts are mine.
57 Giard, 'Faire-la-cuisine', p. 285.
58 Frederico Morais, 'O corpo é o motor da obra' (1970), in *Artes plásticas: a crise da hora atual* (Rio de Janeiro: Paz e Terra, 1976), p. 32.

59 Mauss, 'Les Techniques du corps', p. 384.
60 Gullar et al., 'Manifesto neoconcreto', p. 272.
61 Stephen Melville, 'Counting/As/Painting', in Philip Armstrong, Laura Lisbon and Stephen Melville (eds), *As Painting: Division and Displacement* (Columbus: Wexner Center for the Arts, 2001), p. 6.
62 This opposition figures, among other instances, in Maciunas's 1966 diagramme detailing 'relationships of various post-1959 avant-garde movements', reproduced in Hendricks (ed.), *What's Fluxus?*, p. 174.
63 Yoko Ono, 'To the Wesleyan people who attended the meeting, a footnote to my lecture of January 13, 1966', in *Grapefruit: A Book of Instructions by Yoko Ono* (New York: Simon & Schuster, 2nd edn, 2000), n. p.
64 See my 'Tactile dematerialization, sensory politics: Hélio Oiticica's *Parangolés*', *Art Journal*, 63:3 (Summer 2004), 58–71.
65 Hélio Oiticica, unpublished *Notebook, 22 Junho 1973*, p. 47. Hélio Oiticica Archives, Rio de Janeiro, Projeto Hélio Oiticica, Notebook 2/13.
66 Ibid.
67 Michael Newman, 'The material turn in the art of Western Europe and North America in the 1960s', in Milena Kalinovska (ed.), *Beyond Preconceptions: The Sixties Experiment* (New York, Independent Curators International, 2000), p. 73.
68 See Chapter 11 for a further discussion of the politics of these do-it-yourself artworks' materiality.

'Creative acts of consumption' or, death in Venice   4

Judith Rodenbeck

Death in Venice

The city is the physical and tropological fact of modernity. Formulated by Nietzsche and put into play by Baudelaire, a sense of the city in which personal experience rather than rationality or morality became the arbiter of meaningfulness, as Carl Schorske has argued, characterises modernism. 'The modern city,' Schorske observes, 'offered an eternal *hic et nunc*, whose content was transience, but whose transience was permanent. The city presented a succession of variegated, fleeting moments, each to be savoured in its passage from nonexistence to oblivion.'[1] Over the course of the twentieth century this flow would be entered again and again by cultural workers pressing against what Henri Lefebvre would call its 'abstract space', from the rainy trip to St. Julien-le-Pauvre organised by Dada artists in 1921, to the 1958 Situationist psychogeography of Venice, to the 1968 discovery (under the paving stones of Paris) of the beach.[2]

If, in such projects of drift and *dérive*, the city operated as a giant readymade, in the regulatory idealism of modern architecture and planning, its flow was in need of organisation and control. As Dorothy Rowe puts it, 'The collision between aesthetic modernity and bourgeois modernity is made manifest through modernist architecture, dependent as it is on networks of capitalism to sustain its development.'[3] Le Corbusier, for instance, visiting New York in 1935, confronted a chaotic 'fairy catastrophe' of cluttered streets and congestion, a 'Great Waste' of disorderly movement, exchange: grand, nearly-functional elements in a messy and dysfunctional pile.[4] The role of the modern planner – the obverse of the psychogeographer – was to bring some sense of hygiene and rationality to the flow of the city; one solution involved Le Corbusier's 'Law of Ripolin', a vast, imaginative whitewashing on which, one could argue, the 'white cube' of the modern gallery is modelled. And forty years after Le Corbusier's visit, when the architect Peter Blake blithely predicted that projects of architectural renewal would turn New York into 'the new Venice', Manfredo Tafuri again invoked liquidity, citing Nietzsche with knowing ambivalence: 'One hundred profound solitudes form the whole of the city of Venice – this is its spell. An image for the man of the future.'[5] For Tafuri, rather than conjuring an image of urban rehabilitation, of revitalised communal values, or of organised and cooperative flow, La Serenissima evoked 'the city as a *system of solitudes*', of drift and blockage and alienation. Against the backdrop of a post-Second World War urban boom of conservative megaplanning and of the counter-discourse of resistance, of micropolitics, and of urban grain to which it gave rise, this image of Venice as a liquid and distracted city, atomised, labyrinthine, imperial, emblematises a profound critique of modernism's regulatory, hygienic vision.

One of the most immediately influential post-war theorisations of the city in the arts is the elegy to Jackson Pollock written by New York artist Allan Kaprow in 1958.[6] Giving voice to explorations in materials, form and process that were taking place throughout the developed world, Kaprow's formal argument proposed the expansion of painting – as both material and as practice – into temporal, architectural, and even urban space (see figure 4.1). Environments and happenings, for Kaprow, were passive and active versions of a radically extended visual practice, an expansion most properly understood in terms of the turn to process and participation in the arts. And he concluded: 'Not only will these bold creators show us, as if for the first time, the world we have always had about us but ignored, but they will disclose entirely unheard-of happenings and events, found in garbage cans, police files, hotel lobbies; seen in store windows and on the streets; and sensed in dreams and horrible accidents.'[7]

Inasmuch as Kaprow's text hinged on the violent automotive death of one of the previous generation's leading lights, its call for attention to the details of the everyday was not simply anodyne, but suggested a kind of forensic realism as well. In what is perhaps the most often quoted of his statements, he urged forward-looking artists to: 'become preoccupied with and even dazzled by the space and objects of our everyday life, either our bodies, clothes, rooms, or, if need be, the vastness of Forty-second Street'.[8] It was a call for an engagement with the processes of the everyday environment (and with its potential violence) that was echoed and nuanced by a number of other artists. For example, Claes Oldenburg wrote in 1961: 'I am for an art that is political-erotical-mystical, that does something other than sit on its ass in a museum … I am for an artist who vanishes, turning up in a white cap painting signs or hallways.'[9] Or Wolf Vostell, in 1963: 'Decollage is your understanding / Decollage is your accident / Decollage is your death …'[10] These artists actively engaged with the world around them, often beginning experiments with figuration and then expanding those experiments into action in space.

The happenings presented an aleatoric performance paradigm structured by a score, with varied options for roles, site, props; importantly, action was task-driven and discrete rather than narrative, and scores resembled charts and musical notation more than they did traditional theatrical scripts. Kaprow developed a typology that ranged from the highly-orchestrated and scored 'something to take place' of his *18 Happenings in 6 Parts* (1959) to a radically dispersed self-reported execution of various structured (scored) activities. Happenings had no plot and were indeterminate, though not unrehearsed; they were alogical assemblages of concrete but compartmented events. The happenings thus put into play the tension between the variability of abstraction and concrete actuality. Participation in happenings extended from the simplistic interiority put into relief by John Cage's *4′ 33″*, in which audience members experienced themselves and their surrounds as co-extensive with, and therefore part of, a visually cued timeframe, to physical engagement in a delimited spatio-temporal field (as with the sound cues of *18 Happenings*, which indicated when audience members were to move from one space to the next), to the imaginative co-creation of a score's enactment. A radically spatialised and temporalised open form of collage, the happening as a form was open enough – and intentionally so – that the term could encompass the precise event-style of Dick Higgins, the quasi-narrative of a Jim Dine, the lyricism of a Kaprow or a Carolee Schneeman and the improvisation of a

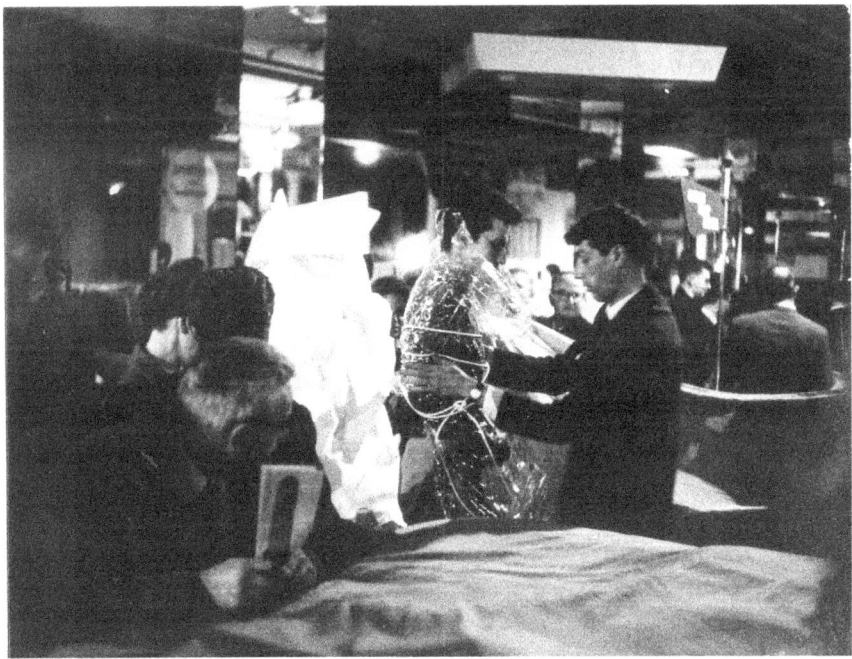

Allan Kaprow, *Bon Marché*, Bon Marché department store, Paris, 1963. Photo: Shunk-Kender. In the dark department store, spectators watch as one performer wraps another in plastic film.   **4.1**

Jean-Jacques Lebel or an Al Hansen. For drama critic Richard Schechner, they contained the 'message-complexity' of the street, but explicitly played with perceptions – the signal-processing – of that complexity.[11]

Happenings (both the term and the form) proliferated internationally. But where statements by American artists seem generally focused on form (and then secondarily on the scene of artistic production and consumption), those of Europeans seem much more critically engaged with the dialectics of production, consumption and obsolescence that had been foregrounded, indeed magnified, by post-war political tensions. For instance, in London, Gustav Metzger's 'Auto-destructive art manifesto' (1960) decried: 'The immense productive capacity, the chaos of capitalism and of Soviet communism, the co-existence of surplus and starvation; the increasing stockpiling of nuclear weapons – more than enough to destroy technological societies; the disintegrative effects of machinery and of life in vast built-up areas on the person …'[12] (This was in great contradistinction to his colleagues at the Institute of Contemporary Art, working in and around the Independent Group and developing British Pop.) Similarly, the German Wolf Vostell, writing in 1966, rephrased Kaprow's still rather romantic language pointedly:

> the accident is already in the automobile as it drives, the obsolescence is already prefabricated and built in. events in the street and airports and in supermarkets are more interesting and more significant for our time than those in a theater or museum. torn posters erasures distorted television pictures happenings and action music contain many layers of information. Happenings and events are frames of reference for experience of the present – a do-it-yourself reality.[13]

In the heady days of 1968, Jean-Jacques Lebel updated this framing yet again, casting happenings as a kind of radically unmediated direct cinema: 'The "going-beyond" postulated by the authors of Happenings has only just begun … The Happening … carries out transmissions and introduces the witness directly into the event …'[14] And in the late 1990s Vostell remembered: 'I saw my first happening when I was nine years old. It was during an air raid, and we had to evacuate the school and run out into the countryside. Each child was told to hide under a different tree. From my tree I watched an aerial battle and saw the bombs fall from the sky to the ground, like great flocks of birds.'[15]

And yet, though the American works appeared to eschew political engagement, this very avoidance may have been (explicitly for at least some practitioners, implicitly in the structure of the works themselves) strategically related to an analysis of liberalism, and of what Herbert Marcuse would call 'repressive tolerance', in which a defined and positive commitment would have been ripe for cooptation.[16] Indeed, for at least one critic this apparent refusal provided the most significant political implication of the happenings: a kind of vaccine against the consumption of 'messages'. As Schechner observed, in their 'rejection of packaging', the happenings effectively '[forced] on the receiver the job of doing the work usually done by the artist/educator/propagandist'. If the notion of an audience member as a 'receiver' evoked mediated passivity, inasmuch as that receiver had a 'job', he or she was transformed by (Cageian) self-consciousness into a participant. And if the open structure of the happening presented, in the potential range, scope, and generality of its 'messages', a kind of saturation 'that propagandists have long recognized' as 'the mark of mass persuasion', nevertheless, Schechner suggested, 'just as Pop Art has made us somewhat immune to certain kinds of advertising, so, perhaps, we become somewhat immune to other forms of mass persuasion after participating in a Happening'.[17]

The initial theorisation of environments and happenings by Kaprow proposed them as emerging from an expansion of painting into architectural and then temporal space. But the very concepts 'environment', 'process' and 'participation' that are mobilised by this work must also be read in the broader context of the radical post-war alteration of neighbourhoods and urban fabrics under central planning, and the concomitant and increasingly activist recognition of the vitality of street life. In the following discussion, I want to reframe the late 1950s development of environments and happenings in relation to the discourses of contemporary architecture and urbanism, and by implication, to issues of street life. Out of necessity I discuss architecture, urbanism and happenings at a certain level of abstraction. But what I hope emerges is a sense of the relation between those projects and the discourse of space around them.

As these artistic experiments began to take shape, they touched on architectural, urbanist and critical themes. Kaprow's early constructions, which he would expand into the temporised form of the happening, were explicitly architectural in ambition.[18] They emerged from the careful parsing of a number of compositional problems, from the artist's encounter with the work of Robert Rauschenberg (first the *White Paintings* and then combine/stage props such as the 1954 *Minutiae*) to his theorising of the participatory. With *Penny Arcade* (1956), for instance, Kaprow intentionally mimicked the contingent architecture of urban street fairs, initiating a chain of metaphors – and a morphological shift – that altered the white cube of the gallery into the raucous huckster environment of Coney Island, and the contemplative beholder into boardwalk *flâneur*. And Kaprow's *Rearrangeable Panels* (1957–59), which had an alternate life as *Kiosk*, restaged the billboard hoarding as newsstand or pavilion, the different conformations serving alternately as surround and as shelter. In this sense, Kaprow's free-standing proto-environmental projects are part of a broader set that includes the *désaffichages* of artists associated with Nouveau Réalisme – for instance, Raymond Hains's first billboard project, *Palissade des Emplacements Réservés* (1959) (a removed hoarding covered with torn posters), and projects like Wolf Vostell's 1958 *Tour de Vanves* (an 'interpretive tour' of billboards) – and the gritty early projects of British Pop, particularly the Brutalist 'Patio and Pavilion' at the 1956 ICA exhibition *This is Tomorrow*; and it predicts by four decades similar work by artists like Thomas Hirschhorn and Rirkrit Tiravanija.[19] Kaprow's project was a formal expansion of 'architecture' into temporal space and environmental scale – and eventually, as this expansion became something a viewer walked into rather than around, like *Apple Shrine* (1960) or *Yard* (1961), into junk space.[20]

Other projects, such as Claes Oldenburg's *The Street* (1960) and *Snapshots from the City* (1960), which took place in *The Street*, and Wolf Vostell's 'dé-coll/age' street works in Paris (*Tour de Vanves, Theater is in the Street*, 1958) and in Cologne (*Cityrama*, 1961), explicitly dealt with an anti-idealised street life: Oldenburg's works addressed homelessness, indigence and immigration in a gritty, emphatic material recoding of source material, from the bebop argot of French novelist Céline to the hard-boiled gutter realism of Jules Dassin's 1948 film *The Naked City*, while Vostell's tours recovered the bombed-out, trash-strewn, repressed sites of post-war, post-Holocaust Europe.[21] As artists explored possible uses of and interventions into urban space, the critique of consumption and of planned obsolescence pressed urgently. One expression of that critique can be seen in the exploration of non-art sites and aleatory trajectories through urban space, or in Kaprow's later analyses of 'throw-away architecture'; another was grounded in consumption.

Claes Oldenburg's month-long performed work *The Store* (1961) (figure 4.2), in which the artist's store-front studio became a mimicked mom-and-pop store, selling everything from chewing gum to stockings and wedding dresses – all handmade out of chicken wire and plaster – drew attention to the process of gentrification and urban renewal even then reshaping the neighbourhood (the East Village), its demographics, and its rhythms of social exchange. At the same time, Oldenburg's project, which came equipped with business cards, letterhead and invoices, as well as the plethora of quirky material 'goods', mined a curious nostalgia for *things*: not just the bought and sold, from perishable edibles to evanescent fashion items, but the tokens and mechanics of that social exchange, from display vitrines to cash registers to hand-written receipts. The studio space was an artisanal one – the evidence of production visible in the back room – and labour was compensated in view of the site of its deployment – a vertically integrated business. The intensity of *The Store*'s peculiar fetishism – a leitmotif in Oldenburg's work of the period – was echoed later in his environmental *Bedroom Set* (1964), in which the space of intimacy has been transformed into a lurid motel room straight out of Vladimir Nabokov's *Lolita*; it presents for purchase on credit an entire packaged fantasy. The city, here, penetrates into the interior through its very rejection: the jungle-motif décor, the oblique distortion of the angles, the

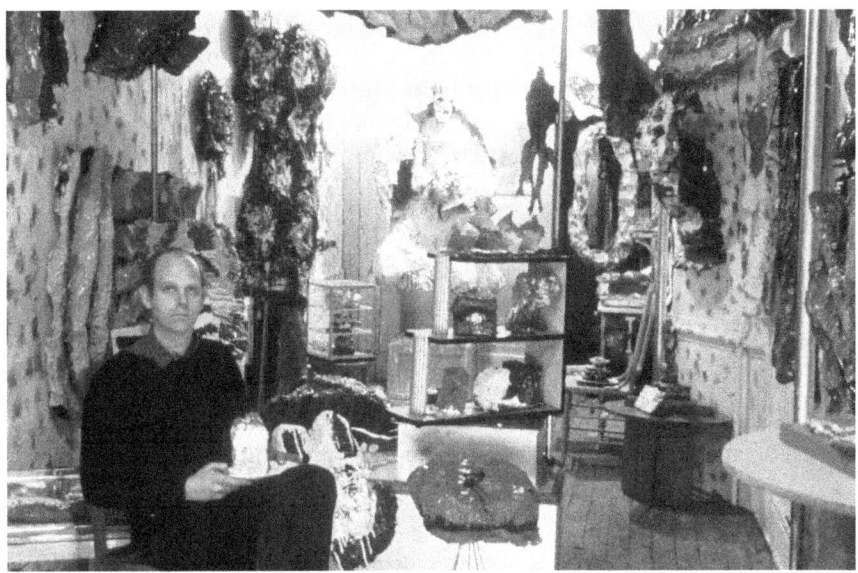

Claes Oldenburg in *The Store*, 1961.   **4.2**

drawers inhabited by tightly folded (plaster and kapok) shirts in a fetching array of colours.

To read happenings in relation to the city is to understand them not just in their emergence from the formalist endgame of Abstract Expressionism but also in the context of several specific formations: first, the development, detailing and theorisation of a dynamic urbanism in the late 1950s; second, the related development (and psychologising) of social categories for the inhabitants of those urban spaces; and third, the 'conspicuous consumption' that came to characterise the economic boom of the late 1950s and early 1960s. The environmental and temporal experiments engaged in by artists in a variety of urban centres in the late 1950s and early 1960s problematise the gallery space and demonstrate not only a sensitivity to the shape of the physical environment but also an awareness of the performativity of that environment and its inflection of post-war subjectivity. Though this had local permutations, as critical projects addressed to the conditions of production and consumption – in 'art' as well as in 'life' – these activities were dispersed internationally in scope, effect and consequence. The discussion that follows examines a two-part story: that of the movement of modernist architectural discourse from its emphasis on a Corbusian functionalism before the Second World War, to the emphasis on a more anthropologically-inflected notion of 'habitat' that characterised the mid-1950s, and that of the related development of a particular discourse of urban subjectivity that concurrently came to the fore.

The happenings addressed these formations thematically, formally and materially by using urban sites, ordinary participants, and randomised compositional structures, by confronting and inhabiting both the 'fairy catastrophe' and the Ripolin. Inasmuch as they did so, their insistent urbanism may have been in some ways as symptomatic of these formations as it was critical. I want to approach this question, but I do so by way of a detour. It is a route that takes us through one of the discourses of high modernism (architecture) and some of its effects.

Urbanisation

In the twentieth-century discourse on urbanism one important node is marked out by the Congrès Internationaux d'Architecture Moderne (CIAM), which between 1928 and 1959 gathered together many of the most outstanding figures of modern architectural practice, counting among its active members Le Corbusier, José Lluís Sert, Siegfried Giedion and, later, Aldo van Eyck, Georges Candilis, and Peter and Alison Smithson.[22] Initially founded as a sort of disciplinary think tank, the CIAM concerned themselves in the late 1920s and early 1930s with questions of functionalism, notably the notion of *existenz-minimum* (minimum liveable – and therefore mass-produceable – housing). During the fourth meeting in 1933, devoted to the 'Functional City', members had drafted a controversial document now known as the Athens Charter. (It was actually drafted on a boat headed to Athens.) The Athens Charter asserted that 'On both the spiritual and the material planes, the city must ensure individual liberty and the advantages of collective action.'[23] In this, 'the official codification of functionalist urbanism', as Joan Ockman has put it, CIAM called for a new model of urbanism based on a green-belt zoning plan that would abut high rises with open space and central arteries.[24]

The early emphasis by CIAM on planning, standardisation and urban reconfiguration was grounded in its identification of four primary functions – dwelling, work, transportation, recreation – and by the time the Athens Charter was actually published in 1943 many of its arguments had become widely accepted though its functionalism was roundly criticised. As Ockman points out, during the hiatus between drafting and publication the issue of 'converting the vast war machine to the needs of peace' had become paramount, supplanting, in its predictive way, more straightforward functionalist concerns. The war had demonstrated the effectiveness of functionalist models; yet, as would become horrifyingly clear by the close of the conflict, it also demonstrated their inherent anti-humanism.

Meeting again in 1947, and responding awkwardly to world-historical events, the group retained its functionalist commitment but shifted emphasis slightly to address what now, in the face not only of shattered cities but also of internal anxieties about the extremely problematic role of industrial order before and during the war, seemed urgent questions of aesthetics, or poetics, and of everyday experience. CIAM was very involved in immediate post-war plans for the reconstruction of Berlin, in conjunction with the Marshall Plan for European Recovery. As Walter Gropius put it, the 'job of the reconstruction planners' was to ensure the irreversibility of the interment of the 'political corpse buried in Germany's rubble'.[25] One way this would be accomplished was by breaking cities into smaller units; indeed, the post-war valorisation of the 'neighbourhood' (which had different overtones in different contexts) was an international consensus vis-à-vis urban restructuring. The goal was 'smaller, cellular urban units.'[26] And overall, the perception on the part of European planners was that the war had actually had a fortuitous effect in terms of city planning.[27]

The eighth congress, held in July 1951 in a country house in Hoddesdon, 20 miles north of London, was devoted to the theme of the 'Heart of the City'. Attempting to strike a balance between the individual and the collective, the conversations emphasised walking in the city and the praise of spontaneity – though what precisely was meant by the latter seemed more often than not to consist of throw-back romantic eruptions of imagination and reverie. The 'core' of the city was understood as its 'heart', and much was made of the physiological and emotional metaphor. The antinomies of this functionalist poetry generated some odd propositions. For example, José Lluís Sert opened his talk with a quote from Ortega, who believed in a 'natural elite' and had argued that European fascism was the result of the rise of the masses and the decline of a natural elite. In his talk, Sert argued for conceiving the urban core as a kind of media centre, with television and radio. In the published version this alarmingly centralised concept is modified along lines proposed by Giedion in favour of community centres and personal discussion. And again and again, conversations turned to Piazza San Marco in Venice as a great example of heart or urban core – with only the occasional renegade pointing out that without tourists Venice would be dead. Years later, Peter Smithson dryly recalled, 'At CIAM 8 they thought community equaled a piazza. Community doesn't equal piazza.'[28] Indeed, the Venetian malaise emblematised by the piazza is neatly summarised in 'the new forms of public space, including shopping malls, renewed downtowns, and theme parks, that came to characterize urbanism in the rapidly decentralizing cities of the 1950s and later'.[29]

In 'The disappearing city', urban critic Lewis Mumford decried the absorption of the city into two forms of anti-city, 'formless urbanization' driven by consumption alone: 'urbanoid' identical high-rises set along arteries (rationalised flow) and the 'grey building' of the suburbs.[30] He identified two hopeful divergences from the deadening technicity of modernism (and, implicitly, of CIAM's old guard). One was exemplified by those CIAM rebels who insisted on architecture as 'more than the art of building' and rather saw it as 'the art of transforming man's entire habitat'; the other was signalled by the demands of younger architecture students for historical instruction in both architecture and planning 'not for forms to imitate, but for experience and feeling to assimilate'.[31] In the immediate aftermath of the war, as younger architects had become involved in CIAM, and increasingly critical of its old guard, this was reflected in the urgency of a new focus on 'habitat', a term which called for nuanced sociological, environmental, even poetic approaches to urban planning (supplanting the dry, teutonic *existenz-minimum*'). The change in focus was marked out by the shift from 'The Functional City' through the suburban discussions of its 'Heart' to 'The Charter of Habitat' – the latter a major topic from 1952 forward and the title of a never-written 1953 report. And by the time of the meeting in the summer of 1953, full-scale hostilities had broken out as open challenges to the notion of the functional city issued on the part of younger architects, particularly the architects who would form Team 10, including Peter and Alison Smithson.[32]

For the Smithsons (and for others involved in Team 10) these concerns – for an affective, anthropological and historical sensitivity – reshaped their entire approach to planning. 'Whole levels of association are missed in our mechanically democratic society', they lamented.[33] Definable city elements had shifted from CIAM's set of functions (dwelling, work, transportation, recreation) to a set of contact zones (house, street [physical contact], district [social contact]); the city itself was understood as an intellectual contact zone.

> The street in the late nineteenth, early twentieth century was where the children were, and where people talked and all that, despite the climate being against it. The street was the arena of life. To perceive that the invention of another sort of house was the invention of another kind of street, of another arena, or maybe not an arena, wasn't a question of saying the street must be revived. It is a matter of thinking what the street did, and what is the equivalent of it if it is no longer necessary, if the street is dead.[34]

The shift was thus both positive – towards complexity – and negative – away from nostalgic idealism.

Tropologically, topologically, Venice must make one more appearance here. 'In 1949 at Peggy Guggenheim's palazzo in Venice', write the Smithsons, 'we saw the first manifestation of the new ordering, in the painting of Jackson Pollock.'[35] This new ordering would be 'complex, timeless, n-dimensional and multi-vocative'. Articulating the shift, the Smithsons observed:

> In the twenties a work of art or a piece of architecture was a finite composition of simple elements, elements which have no separate identity but exist only in relation to the whole; the problem of the fifties is to retain the clarity of

intention of the whole but to give the parts their own internal disciplines and complexities. This kind of ordering, as opposed to geometric ordering, must be the basis of all creative endeavour from the city to the object.

The new compositional strategy involved the fluid articulation of relatively autonomous parts rather than their subordination to an idealised geometric schema – a kind of discrete all-over strategy; importantly, this was predicated on the careful observation and detailing of the vernacular and of everyday life as well as respect for its materiality. Describing their project, the Smithsons write: 'the "as found" was a new seeing of the ordinary, an openness as to how prosaic "things" could re-energise our inventive activity. A confronting recognition of what the postwar world actually was like. In a society that had nothing. You reached for what there was, previously unthought of things …'.[36] In 1958, the new key words were: '*cluster, growth, change* and *mobility*. Around which stones you can roll your own snowballs'.[37] These principles, including the 'roll-your-own' principle, precisely echo those at work in many of the happenings. The snowball was mobile, fluid, changeable, impermanent; it was action-oriented, vernacular, thing-based. 'For after all,' the architects observed, 'when the basic kitchen has been achieved what can possibly follow? Only Dada followed another road which we have taken twenty years to redis-cover.'[38] As for Kaprow in New York, for the Smithsons in London Pollock pointed to a kind of complexity, a different type of structuring principle, one rooted in Dada and vested in process – though, importantly, one that was not triumphant but rather more ordinary.

The lonely crowd

The radical post-war alteration of neighbourhoods and urban fabrics led to a concomitant and increasingly activist recognition of the vitality of street life. Clearly, everyday life itself had changed. It became a topic of research, from the development of sociologically inflected urban studies to increasing activist intervention in urban fabric to the material planning activities that took into account what in other contexts would be called 'psychogeographic' consid-erations. In the visual arts, commodity production and advertising provided new cultural reference points. Techniques of mass production suggested elimination of hand, seriality, while the recuperation of ready-made strate-gies provided another model for the appropriation of the familiar and mass-produced, which in the 1950s was extended to the incorporation of signage, image/text and, arguably, of urban space. And certainly 'cluster, growth, change and mobility' stand as watchwords for late 1950s compositional strategies.

The very concepts 'environment', 'process' and 'participation' put into play in the late 1950s by artists in places as far from each other as New York,

Paris and Düsseldorf (as well as Osaka, Buenos Aires and Rio de Janeiro) should also be read in a broader context. For one decade after the end of the Second World War, American economic hegemony had begun to reshape the cultural and physical landscape of Europe.[39] Although anxieties about food and housing were the norm throughout Europe in the late 1940s, and even as late as 1950, large swathes of Berlin remained rubble-strewn, post-war European governments spent massively on modernising infrastructure. While consumer spending initially was constrained (partly out of cultural habit, partly out of necessity), the rapid replacement of infrastructure combined with increased international trade and an increasingly efficient, urbanised and organised labour force – and, importantly, a major baby boom – contributed to the general economic recovery emblematised later in the founding of the European Economic Community. Whereas in pre-war Europe, as historian Tony Judt points out, 'most people did not shop or "consume" in the modern sense; they subsisted', by the mid-1950s, demographic changes and increasing household disposable income complemented increasing productivity. Judt notes that 'America in 1950 had three fifths of the capital stock of the West and about the same share of output, but very little of the proceeds flowed across the Atlantic.'[40] What was shared was the consumer revolution. 'Europeans were now gaining access to the unprecedented range of products with which American consumers were familiar: phones, white goods, televisions, cameras, cleaning products, packaged foods, cheap colourful clothing, cars and their accessories, etc. This was prosperity and consumption as a way of life – the "American way of life".'[41]

Fantasmatic America was libertarian, pragmatic, empiricist and business-oriented, and typically emphasised status rather than class. And in the transatlantic narrative modernity European (cultural) dominance was over: the story was overtaken by a New World avatar. In this newly integrated model of consumer capitalism (it had actually been an object of fascination for European businesses and governments since the turn of the century) production was organised on Fordist lines: streamlined and morally efficient, grounded in Weberian aspiration. Importantly, leisure itself was produced as a commodity. As recently as 1947, Europe as a whole had suffered a near-famine; but by the early 1950s consumption became not only a possibility but an ideological construct, morally imperative. Judt notes that, 'For young people the appeal of "America" was its aggressive contemporaneity. As an abstraction, it stood for the opposite of the past; it was large, open, prosperous – and youthful.'[42] And for anti-Americans, 'America was a land of hysterical puritans, given over to technology, standardisation and conformism, bereft of originality of thought.'[43] Post-war affluence relied upon a cycle of consumption focused on the commodity sphere, domestic luxury and hygiene, and the by-products of mass culture. These became, in fact, socially defining, both in terms of distinction from the crowd and of elision into the norm, a process reinforced by market research, mass communications and the culture industry, and the growth of an affluent 'middlebrow' consumer culture.[44]

One significant discursive aspect of this cultural transition involved the development of specific sociological categories defining very particular subsets of consumers. In its early stages this had gone hand in hand, in the inter-war years, with development of market research, the proliferation of mass media, and the growth of the advertising industry. In the 1950s, the focus shifted dramatically under the pressure of a growing recognition of 'youth culture', on the one hand, and of a critically inflected extension of the psychological studies on both the culture of consumption and of traumatic socialisation that had begun under the aegis of the advertising industry in the inter-war years and continued under military sponsorship during the Second World War. In a large-scale and critical study of the American culture of consumption, *The Lonely Crowd*, sociologist David Riesman traced out the effects of advanced capital on the psyche in sociological terms. The typical post-war American, he argued, was increasingly 'other-directed': cosmopolitan yet with indistinct personal boundaries, at home everywhere and nowhere, bombarded by and constantly absorbing data, including psychosocial cues, from the mass media, profoundly if complacently alienated from a sense of tradition rooted in place and family yet alienated, too, from any unmediated sense of personal agency or responsibility. The 'autonomous' personality put forward by Riesman as a possible counter-force to complacent alienation was to achieve that autonomy by, as Richard Wolin wryly put it, '[embracing] creative acts of consumption in the very mass culture which gave rise to other-directedness in the first place'.[45] The potential heroes at the conclusion of Riesman's book were, interestingly enough, city planners, who had to some extent become, '[with] their imagination and bounteous approach … the guardians of our liberal and progressive political tradition'.[46] Creative consumption could be exercised, then, in the form of consuming 'not only packages of groceries or books but the larger package of a neighborhood, a society, and a way of life'.[47]

Riesman's argument operated at the level of relatively abstract sociological analysis, but it laid the ground for one of the most profoundly important revisionings of post-war urban life, Jane Jacobs's 1961 critique of modernist city planning, *The Death and Life of Great American Cities*.[48] Jacobs's book was directed as much against the local effects of large-scale urban redevelopment projects as it was to more general examples of urban mismanagement. The vast, Corbusian, automobile-driven vision of the metropolis, a vision of a functionally consolidated and streamlined city, was, in its fundamentally modernist outlines, perversely and profoundly atomising – as Jacobs stunningly demonstrated with her description of vital, 'organic', mixed-use, communitarian and, most importantly, actually existing counter-models inhabited by citizen-activists.

If modernism at its 'purest' had eschewed the external, in its very Olympian overstatement, the rhetoric of purity, sublimity, self-consciousness and mastery had required the sentimental foils of kitsch and popular culture; the two were co-implicated, 'torn halves' of a whole.[49] For Riesman, Jacobs and other progressive social critics, the evident failures of instrumental reason necessitated a strategic shift. Jacobs was a pragmatist and an empiricist, and she urged three tactics: an emphasis on the dynamics of process; the use of inductive reasoning based on the examination of existing particulars; and an attention to the small-scale and exceptional, which would, she suggested, reveal the complex operations of the large-scale and general. And Jacobs's urban inhabitant-activist – the autonomous subject invoked by Riesman – would adopt a strategy whose relation to modernism operated at the material *and* the operational levels by probing the wastage of planned obsolescence – the haphazard, the crummy, the habitual, even the formless aspects of the urban everyday – and its organisation, the packaging *and* the package.

Jacobs's counter-Corbusian urban model was one of self-organising, proto-rhizomatic social complexities based on mixed use rather than on functional discretion per se. Yet, as theorist Henri Lefebvre has observed, though Jacobs 'did very forcefully demonstrate how destructive this space can be, and specifically how urban space, using the very means apparently intended to create or re-create it, effects its own self-destruction', she 'did not go so far as flatly to incriminate neocapitalism, or as to isolate the contradictions immanent to the space produced by capitalism (abstract space)'.[50] Thus, if one result of Jacobs's intervention was a new type of city planning based on representative advocacy, this type of planning, as Lefebvre points out, produced a type of 'expert' little different from the originally problematic overseers of urban redevelopment. The failure to 'incriminate neocapitalism' (his term for a post-war techno-cratic capitalism organised around the distribution of information) represents a failure to *theoretically* bind the description of urban spaces to the analysis of their production. Lefebvre advocated an examination of the micrological, the uneventful, the ordinary – those historically contingent and otherwise elided facts of daily life in which the most profound ideological effects of modernity are embedded. Lefebvre's 'everyday life' is, writes Kristin Ross, 'what remains when all specialised activities have been eliminated'.[51] If the everyday, a concept which for Lefebvre encompassed the somatic and the habitual, was posed alongside and against modernity, the loving description of it, he claimed, provided the possibility of resistance to the very (modern) alienation that had produced it as a concept.

If the notion of 'creative acts of consumption' now seems a curious artefact, taken in this revised sense as the careful detailing (though not necessarily the recuperation) of the everyday in all its material contingency, it may nevertheless serve as an introduction to certain forms of cultural production that emerged in the 1950s. For if numerous artistic projects in the late 1950s and early 1960s borrowed themes and materials from the street, the store, the house, the supermarket, the office, the factory, the motel, the automobile, the newspaper, the snapshot, those borrowings represented a fundamentally canny critique of the logic of planned obsolescence on which aesthetic modernism's alleged 'autonomy' – in both its art and anti-art manifestations – had rested.

Leben mit Pop

Earlier, I suggested that certain works initiated a tropological shift in which the space of the gallery was rendered isomorphic with the space of the most absurdist commerce, the street fair. And I suggested that one set to which those projects belonged included quasi-architectural projects that explored the 1950s involution of domestic and public space, the dialectic of obsolescence and objecthood. In concluding, I want to explore one specific project, a happening that mobilised the material and the operational aspects of 'consumption', deploying Ripolin as a version of 'fairy catastrophe'.

[It] was resolved to hold a demonstration as follows:

a) The whole furniture store, exhibited without modification.
b) In the room set aside for the exhibition, a distilled essence of the demonstration. An average living room as a working exhibit, i.e., occupied, decorated with suitable utensils, foods, drinks, books, odds and ends, and both painters. The individual pieces of furniture stand on plinths, like sculptures, and the natural distances between them are increased, to emphasize their status as exhibits ...[52]

The year was 1963, the setting a furniture store in Düsseldorf, the occasion not a 'sale' but a peculiar two-man exhibition of paintings (figure 4.3). The artists Gerhard Richter and Konrad Lueg, students at the Düsseldorf Academy, included themselves as objects in the exhibition on the third floor. Visitors were herded through the building in groups of six to ten, their numbers called out by loudspeaker. Though 'disciplined behavior' is requested, 'most of the visitors fail to observe the prescribed itinerary and scatter or stray into the various departments'.[53] The exhibition room soon fills up and within a half hour visitors have consumed the food and drink on display and even looted some of the cupboards. Richter reports that

By approximately 9 pm, all the visitors have reached the kitchen department. They seat themselves in the 41 display kitchens and drink the beer provided. One visitor (an art student) protests against the Demonstration by removing all his clothing except a pair of swimming trunks. He is escorted from the

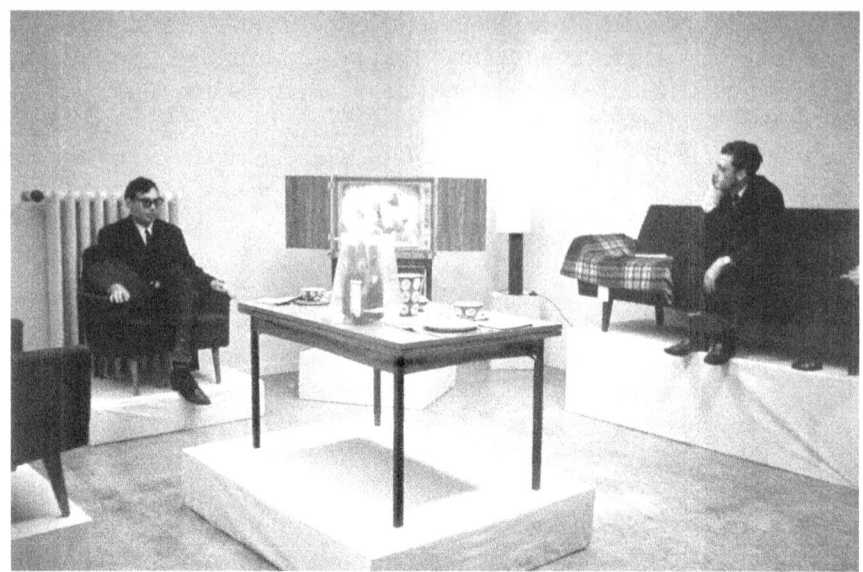

4.3   Gerhard Richter and Konrad Lueg, *Leben mit Pop*, furniture store, Düsseldorf, 1963.

building with his clothes under his arm.[54]

Though little known among scholars of performance, *Leben mit Pop* was one of a series of similar 'demonstrations' that took place in the early 1960s in West Germany. In 1961 and 1962, Georg Baselitz and Eugen Schonebeck had staged mysterious exhibitions in a dodgy Berlin tenement, while earlier in 1963 Richter and Lueg, with two other colleagues, had held an 'exhibition' of 'Capitalist Realism' in a run-down commercial space. Richter had also proposed, though not executed, several performed interventions that importantly located themselves in the spaces of visual consumption. In an interview with Hans-Ulrich Obrist, he recalls a plan to show a picture of the Alps in Paris on the roof of the Galeries Lafayette with a Paris skyline cut-out. 'And', he adds, 'there are some lovely views in the Neanderthal area; we wanted to take people out there in buses and announce: "Here is our art."'[55]

While Richter's early work is often, given its salient graphic features, aligned with Pop painting, Richter himself disavowed links to American Pop, noting instead the significant influence of Fluxus (which he had encountered in 1962 and 1963 and the cynicism of which he valued) and, interestingly, of Viennese Aktionism.[56] Certainly, artists in Düsseldorf would have read with alacrity the magazine Wolf Vostell began publishing there in 1962, *Dé-coll/age*, which featured gory images of vehicular accidents alongside happenings scores and documentation.[57] For Vostell, Richter and Lueg, but for Richter in particular, the affinities with American practice were felt with respect to a deadening of subjectivity rather than an enlivening of experience. Richter had travelled to Paris with Lueg, visiting the Galerie Iris Clert and introducing themselves to Ileana Sonnabend as 'German Pop'. On his trip to Paris, Richter, who was then interested in Yves Klein, could have seen the latter's work at Iris Clert's gallery. And, though it is highly doubtful that this connection was made, Richter and Lueg could, in 1963, have witnessed another work-inside-a-department-store: Allan Kaprow's *Bon Marché* (which took place in the eponymous Parisian emporium that July as part of the Festival du Théâtre des Nations) (see figure 4.1).

Leben mit Pop was a discomfiting exercise in second-order representation. Richter showed four paintings: *Neuschwanstein Castle* (1963), *Stag, Pope, Mouth* (the latter two are destroyed), while he and Lueg served as 'living sculptures'. Richter's images in particular were images that, in a techno-rationalist 1960s, would evoke a set of repressed identities – Catholic, mythopoetic, romantic – and orders of eschatological desire and fantasy destined always for disappointment. As Margit Brehm has pointedly put it: '"Neuschwanstein Castle" in this context illustrates the multiple meanings with which visitors to the demonstration were confronted – in a picture featuring Ludwig the Second's fairy-tale castle painted literally "along the lines" of a *Stern* magazine cover (the "highly colored" weekly of the 'sixties), skirting the subject itself by tracing only its outlines, yet presented as a wall decoration in the middle-class living room.'[58] Seen through this lens, the decision to locate the exhibition in one of the palaces of consumption (and to entomb it in the furniture department) yields an unmistakable contrast between idealism and banality, between what Alex Potts has called 'heroic' and 'casual' autonomy, repeated by the contrast between 'art' and 'commerce' and emphasised by the confrontation of 'shoppers' with 'artists'.[59] This point was, of course, blatantly restated in the elevation of the furniture, the atomisation of the inhabited interior plan, and the coarse adherence to the auditory codes of the bourgeois department store.[60] *Leben mit Pop* rearticulates the paradigm of consumption in art space by rethinking spatial negotiation itself through the ordered passage of shopping.

Leben mit Pop inhabits the department store, calling attention to the 'mass' production of paintings and the commercialisation of artists and to the latent paternalism of models of consumption. The 'architecture' of the store – its spatial extension, routes of ingress and egress, clustering and organisation – provides a massive, engulfing ready-made. The 'bourgeois interior' represented in the living room is evacuated, rendered impossible, imploded from within its consumptive core. The department store is neither Venice nor Neuschwanstein Castle; neither interior nor exterior it, nevertheless, points accusingly at both dismal imperium and proto-Disneyland; no longer a functionalist way-station or shop of fantasies, it has become a contact zone.

Notes

1 Carl Schorske, 'The idea of the city in European thought: Voltaire to Spengler', in Oscar Handlin and John Burchard (eds), *The Historian and the City* (Cambridge: MIT Press and Harvard University Press, 1963), pp. 109–10.

2 See Henri Lefebvre, *The Production of Space*, trans. D. Nicholson-Smith (Oxford: Blackwell, 1991). In April 1921, the Parisian Dadas made an excursion to 'a deserted, almost unknown church in totally uninteresting, positively doleful surroundings'. The trip 'was a complete failure. It rained, and no one came.' See Hans Richter, *Dada Art and Anti-Art* (London: Thames & Hudson, 1997), pp. 183–4. 'Psycho-geography', a key Situationist iteration of this Dada gesture, was defined as 'the study of the precise effects of geographic environment, consciously planned or not, acting directly on the affective behavior of individuals'. The psychogeographic, then, was 'that which manifests the direct action of the geographic environment on affect'. *Internationale Situationniste*, 1 (June 1958), 13 (my translations). On Ralph Rumney's psychogeography of and 'disappearance' in Venice, see *Internationale Situationniste*, 1 (June 1958), 28. Both are reprinted in *Internationale Situationniste 1958–1969* (Paris: Fayard, 1997). See also Guy Debord, 'Introduction to a critique of urban geography', *Les Lèvres nues*, 6 (September 1955), reprinted in *Situationist International Anthology*, ed. and trans. K. Knabb (Berkeley: Bureau of Public Secrets, 1989, no copyright), pp. 5–8. These activities, he wrote, 'can contribute to clarifying certain wanderings that express not subordination to randomness but complete *insubordination* to habitual influences ...' 'Under the paving stones, the beach' was a Situationist slogan used by students in May 1968 Paris. And watery Venice plays a bit-part in the image stream of Guy Debord's Heraclitean 1973 film, *Society of the Spectacle*.

3 Dorothy C. Rowe, 'Introduction to part III', in Abigail Harrison-Moore and Dorothy C. Rowe (eds), *Architecture and Design in Europe and America, 1750–2000* (Malden and Oxford: Blackwell, 2006), p. 327.

4 On Le Corbusier and 'flow', see David Pinder, *Visions of the City: Utopianism, Power and Politics in Twentieth-Century Urbanism* (New York: Routledge, 2005), esp. pp. 68–110. The terms 'fairy catastrophe' and 'Grand Waste', quoted on p. 95, are from Le Corbusier's *When the Cathedrals Were White: A Journey to the Country of Timid People* (New York: Reynal & Hitchcock, 1947), p. 34. On Le Corbusier's purifying solution to modern urbanism, the 'Law of Ripolin', see Pinder, *Visions of the City*, pp. 97ff.

5 Manfredo Tafuri, *The Sphere and the Labyrinth: Avant-Gardes and Architecture from Piranesi to the 1970s*, trans. P. d'Acierno and R. Connolly (Cambridge: MIT Press, 1990), p. 291; Tafuri is citing Nietzsche's *Aurora*. In the back of his mind, certainly, was the International Charter for the Conservation and Restoration of Historic Sites, otherwise known as the Venice Charter of 1964, which codified principles for the preservation of cultural (and architectural intervention in) heritage sites.

6 Allan Kaprow, 'The legacy of Jackson Pollock', *Art News* (October 1958), 24–60, reprinted in Allan Kaprow, *Essays on the Blurring of Art and Life* (Berkeley: University of California Press, 1993), pp. 1–9.

7 Ibid., p. 9.

8 Ibid.

9 Claes Oldenburg, 'I am for an art' (1961), in Kristine Stiles and Peter Selz (eds), *Theories and Documents of Contemporary Art: A Sourcebook of Artists' Writings* (Berkeley: University of California Press, 1996), p. 335. In an interesting twist on Le Corbusier's 'Law of Ripolin' Oldenburg paints everything white during the events recorded in Robert Breer's *Pat's Birthday* (1962) – repeating the gesture of house-painterly white-out Jim Dine had made building the set for his 1960 happening *Car Crash*.

10 'Manifesto', in Stiles and Selz (eds), *Theories and Documents*, p. 723.

11 Richard Schechner, 'Happenings', in Mariellen Sandford (ed.), *Happenings and Other Acts* (New York: Routledge, 1995), pp. 216–19.

12 Gustav Metzger, 'Manifesto [of] Auto-Destructive Art', in Stiles and Selz (eds), *Theories and Documents*, p. 402.

13 Wolf Vostell, 'de-coll/age' (1966) in Stiles and Selz (eds), *Theories and Documents*, p. 725.

14 'On the necessity of violation', in Stiles and Selz (eds), *Theories and Documents*, p. 720.

15 Vostell, 'To remind men that they must not behave savagely', in Valerio Dehò et al., *Vostell: I disastri della pace* (Milano: Edizioni Charta, 1999), p. 51.

16 See Herbert Marcuse, 'Repressive tolerance', in Robert Paul Wolff, Barrington Moore, and Herbert Marcuse, *A Critique of Pure Tolerance* (Boston: Beacon Press, 1969), pp. 95–137.

17 Schechner, 'Happenings', p. 218. In contrast to the heroic moment of high modernism, this was, as Alex Potts succinctly put it, 'a moment when the emphasis in assertions of artistic autonomy shifted from opposition to bourgeois values and norms to opposition to the mechanisms of the market and its capacity to transform even the most radical-seeming artistic gestures into commodities and spectacle.' Alex Potts, 'Autonomy in post-war art, quasi-heroic and casual', *Oxford Art Journal*, 27:1 (2004), 47.

18 William Kaizen, 'Framed space: Allan Kaprow and the spread of painting', *Grey Room*, 13 (Autumn 2003), 80–107.

19 Tiravanija's work is the focus of Chapter 9, and both artists' works are discussed in Chapter 14.

20 On this 'throwaway' aspect of Kaprow's projects and analysis, see my entry on Allan Kaprow in Helen Molesworth (ed.), *Work Ethic* (Baltimore: Baltimore Museum, 2003), pp. 171–3; see also Kaizen, 'Framed space', 99ff.

21 Jules Dassin's 1948 film noir, *The Naked City*, was shot entirely on location on the Lower East Side of Manhattan, not far from Oldenburg's future studio (a spin-off television series, also shot on location in New York, was aired from 1958 to 1963). Visually indebted to the photographs of Weegee, the film famously closes with the lines: 'There are eight million stories in the naked city. This has been one of them.'

In 1959 Guy Debord borrowed the title for a psychogeographic mapping project. On Oldenburg's relation to urban renewal, see Joshua A. Shannon, 'Claes Oldenburg's *The Street* and urban renewal in Greenwich Village, 1960', *Art Bulletin*, 86:1 (March 2004), 136–62; on Vostell, see Claudia Mesch, 'Vostell's ruins: De-Coll/age and the mnemotechnic space of the postwar city', *Art History*, 23:1 (March 2000), 88–115.

22 Much of the following discussion relies on Eric Mumford, *The CIAM Discourse on Architecture and Modernity, 1928–1960* (Cambridge: MIT Press, 2002). See also Claire Zimmerman's review of this book in *Journal of the Society of Architectural Historians*, 60:1 (March 2001), 98–100. On CIAM IX in particular, see also: www.team10online.org/team10/meetings/1953–Aix.htm (accessed 13 April 2009).

23 Cited in Nathaniel Coleman, *Utopias and Architecture* (London and New York: Routledge, 2005), p. 2.

24 Joan Ockman, 'Introduction', in Joan Ockman (ed.), *Architecture Culture 1943–1968: A Documentary Anthology* (New York: Columbia University and Rizzoli International, 1993), p. 14.

25 Walter Gropius, 'Reconstruction: Germany', *Task*, 7/8 (1948), cited in Eric Mumford, *The CIAM Discourse*, p. 162.

26 Dirk Schubert, 'The neighbourhood paradigm: from garden cities to gated communities', in Robert Freestone (ed.), *Urban Planning in a Changing World: The Twentieth Century Experience* (New York: Routledge, 2000), p. 132. Schubert points out that this valorisation was not only a post-war phenomenon: Nazi urbanists had also valued this scalar division.

27 David Hamer, 'Planning and heritage: towards integration', in Freestone (ed.), *Urban Planning*, pp. 200–1. The Blitz was also good for urban archaeology.

28 Beatriz Colomina, 'Friends of the future: a conversation with Peter Smithson', *October*, 94 (Autumn 2000), 9.

29 Mumford, *The CIAM Discourse*, p. 215. 'Malaise' is my term.

30 See Lewis Mumford, 'The disappearing city' (1962), in Donald L. Miller (ed.), *Lewis Mumford Reader* (Athens: University of Georgia Press, 1995), p. 110.

31 Lewis Mumford, 'The case against "modern architecture"' (1962), in Miller (ed.), *Lewis Mumford Reader*, p. 83.

32 I am indebted to Patricio del Real for discussions on this rupture and its ramifications.

33 Alison and Peter Smithson, *Ordinariness and Light: Urban Theories 1952–1960 and their Application in a Building Project 1963–1970* (Cambridge: MIT Press, 1970), p. 81.

34 Colomina, 'Friends of the future', 9. See also Ben Highmore, 'Between modernity and the everyday: Team 10', paper delivered at the conference *Team 10: Between Modernity and the Everyday*, Faculty of Architecture, University of Delft, 5–6 June 2003. Available online www.team10online.org/research/papers/delft2/ (accessed 13 April 2009), pp. 35–45.

35 Alison and Peter Smithson, *Ordinariness and Light*, p. 86. The following two quotations are from the same page.

36 Alison and Peter Smithson, 'The "as found" and the "found"', in Claude Lichten-

stein and Thomas Schregenberger (eds), *As Found: The Discovery of the Ordinary: British Architecture and Art of the 1950s, New Brutalism, Independent Group, Free Cinema, Angry Young Men* (Baden: Lars Muller, 2001), p. 40.

37 Alison and Peter Smithson, *Ordinariness and Light*, p. 137.

38 Ibid., p. 84.

39 I rely here on Tony Judt's masterful *Postwar: A History of Europe Since 1945* (New York: Penguin, 2005).

40 Ibid., p. 351.

41 Ibid., p. 353.

42 Ibid., p. 351.

43 Ibid., p. 353.

44 See David Riesman, with Reuel Denney and Nathan Glazer, *The Lonely Crowd: A Study of the Changing American Character* (New Haven: Yale University Press, 1950; abridged reprint 1961). See also Jean Baudrillard, *The System of Objects*, trans. J. Benedict (London: Verso, 1996). And for an interesting contemporary revision, see Adam Arvidsson, 'On the pre-history of the "panoptic sort": mobility in market research', *Surveillance and Society*, 1:4 (2004), 459–74.

45 Richard Wolin, 'Freudianism', in Richard Wightman Fox and James T. Kloppenberg (eds), *A Companion to American Thought* (Oxford: Blackwell, 1995), p. 251.

46 Riesman, *The Lonely Crowd*, p. 306.

47 Ibid., p. 307.

48 Jane Jacobs, *The Death and Life of Great American Cities* (New York: Random House, 1961).

49 Both 'bear the stigmata of capitalism, both contain elements of change (but never, of course, the middle term between Schoenberg and the American film). Both are torn halves of an integral freedom, to which however they do not add up.' Theodor Adorno, letter to Walter Benjamin, 3 March 1936, in Ernst Bloch et al., *Aesthetics and Politics* (London: Verso, 1977), p. 123.

50 Henri Lefebvre, *The Production of Social Space*, p. 364. See also James Donald, *Imagining the Modern City* (Minneapolis: University of Minnesota Press, 1999).

51 Kristin Ross, *The Emergence of Social Space: Rimbaud and the Paris Commune* (Minneapolis: University of Minnesota Press, 1988), p. 9. See Henri Lefebvre, *Critique of Everyday Life*, vol. 1, trans. J. Moore (London: Verso, 1991).

52 Gerhard Richter, 'Programme and report: the exhibition *Leben mit Pop – eine Demonstration für den Kapitalistischen Realismus,* Düsseldorf, 11 October 1963', in *The Daily Practice of Painting: Writings 1962–1993* (Cambridge: MIT Press, 1995), p. 19.

53 Ibid., p. 21.

54 Ibid.

55 'Interview with Hans-Ulrich Obrist, 1993', in Richter, *The Daily Practice of Painting*, p. 254. See also Jürgen Harten, 'The romantic intent for abstraction', in Jürgen Harten, *Gerhard Richter: Bilder/Paintings 1962–1986* (Cologne: DuMont Verlag, 1986), pp. 9–63. The 'bus tour' was explored also by Wolf Vostell in Wuppertal in 1963.

56 That *Leben mit Pop* was a happening was confirmed in the interview with Hans-

Ulrich Obrist.

57 Richter also disavowed Vostell's dé-coll/age project. But assiduous art students would have read Vostell's neo-Dada magazine. The fourth issue of *Dé-coll/age*, published in 1964, contained documents relating to Oldenburg's work as well as Kaprow's *Push and Pull: A Furniture Comedy for Hans Hofmann* and *Bon Marché*.

58 Margrit Brehm, 'The constitution of visual truth during painting', in Jochen Poetter (ed.), *Gerhard Richter, Sigmar Polke, Arnulf Rainer: Sammlung Frieder Burda* (Baden-Baden: Staatliche Kunsthalle Baden-Baden, 1996), p. 45.

59 See Potts, 'Autonomy in post-war art'. See also Allan Kaprow, 'The artist as a man of the world' (1964), in *Essays on the Blurring of Art and Life*, pp. 46–65.

60 On the happenings' use of people as materials, particularly their manipulation through behaviourist cues, see my 'Madness and method: before theatricality', *Grey Room*, 13 (Autumn 2003), 54–79.

5

Instability: the visual/bodily perception of space in kinetic environments

Arnauld Pierre

The flagrant dearth of critical and historical reception from which optical-kinetic art has suffered is not a recent phenomenon. Already in 1965, the exhibition *The Responsive Eye* received mixed reviews. This show, curated by William Seitz, can retrospectively be considered as the site of a confrontation between two opposing conceptions of modernism, and their attendant definitions of opticality. Many American reviewers perceived the hypnotic fascination exerted by optical art's patterns as an impediment to the full engagement of the viewer's critical and intellectual faculties, therefore directly hindering his or her independent ability to look at art. Like television or the most ambivalent spectacles of popular culture, Op Art (as it was named in order to emphasise this denigrating comparison) was suspected of nothing less than a subliminal manipulation of perception. Moreover, the way optical art appeared, at times, to visually assault the viewer seemed to imply a specific physiological response much too radically at odds with the largely disembodied modernist visuality defined by Clement Greenberg.[1]

This was not the first time that the artificial separation produced by the classical western *episteme* between the senses and the mind, and the corollary perception of the mind's domination over the senses, had led to the devaluation of a kind of art that was founded on the pure and simple exploration of visuality. Works such as those of seventeenth-century Dutch painters, which belonged to a culture that valued the gaze as the cognitive foundation of our knowledge of the self and the visible world, have often been deemed meaningless and even inferior in their very nature.[2] Also included within this recurrent criticism is Impressionist and Neo-Impressionist opticalism, to which Seitz explicitly referred as a precursor for Op Art in his introduction to *The Responsive Eye*. The accusations of intellectual insufficiency that have inevitably greeted this tendency culminated at the beginning of the twentieth century with Marcel Duchamp's radical denigration of the 'retinal', which logically ended up being directed at optical-kinetic art: 'The Ops do return to pure retinal painting, retinal art, and I deplore it, because I'm against retinal, as you know [;] we began that way, and we have to get [back] into it with the retinal Ops.'[3]

Thus, the protagonists of the Groupe de Recherche d'Art Visuel (GRAV)[4] had their work cut out for them when they declared, in one of their first collective tracts: 'The HUMAN EYE is our starting point',[5] and they proposed to substitute the word 'art' with the expression 'visual experience situated in physiological perception'.[6] It did not help matters that, for these artists, this change of focus was always closely related to a deliberate, conscious refusal of any reference to anything but visuality. For Joël Stein, a painting was a 'purely visual phenomenon whose components have no other aim than to create an optic, rather than a literary or psychological, situation'.[7] Yvaral went even further: 'Our project is to restore vision to its preeminence by eliminating from our works any reference to external signifieds.' It was a matter of producing 'works that essentially revolve around the exercise of visual perception and of the artist's and spectator's awareness of vision', and even of 'freeing "the eye from the mind" by eliminating all extra-plastic criteria'.[8]

For seventeenth-century Dutch artists, suspending narration in order to emphasise the act of seeing was a way of redirecting an attempt to better explore the universe, since any knowledge of the world must necessarily begin with the visual. Now, in the context of optico-kinetic art, this situation came to be reversed: rather than a privileged means of access to knowledge, the eye itself became an object of study, both for its physiology (the GRAV's first labyrinth in 1963 displayed at its entrance an anatomical plate showing a cross-section of the human eye), and for the way in which perception operates. 'Our essential preoccupation is to establish … the codification of signs, networks and specific physical or optic constants. Our aim is the knowledge of the "visual phenomenon"', claimed yet another collective GRAV tract.[9] From being the reflection of a certain state of visual knowledge about the world, painting thus became the instrument for measuring and gauging the reactions of the eye confronted with the visual situations to which it is exposed by the picture. Painting, in this case, submits the eye to extreme perceptual situations, placing it in unusual states of stimulation, by means of which certain permanent features in its way of functioning, and in human optic-perceptual organisation, could come to light through experimentation.

As the precise vocabulary that they used already shows, most of these artists did not set out on this enquiry unarmed: depending on the case, they drew on empiricism and pragmatism, along with systematic approaches in a quasi-scientific spirit. While Victor Vasarely's generation drew on Bauhaus Gestalt pedagogy (as taught by Josef Albers, in particular), the following generation learned about visual phenomena from still more direct sources. This is the case for two Argentinean members of the GRAV, Julio Le Parc and Horacio Garcia-Rossi, and for Hugo Demarco, who as students at the Art College of Buenos Aires in the 1950s learned much from the course on 'The Psychology of Shape and Vision' taught by Hector Cartier, the disciple and translator of

Kurt Koffka, one of the principal theoreticians of Gestalt, along with Wolfgang Köhler and Max Wertheimer. François Molnar, who was one of the GRAV's founding members in 1960, would have preferred the group to focus on pure theoretic and experimental laboratory research, which would not necessarily have resulted in the production of objects aimed at traditional art circuits – an ambition that he would fulfil by abandoning, for his part, all artistic creation for a research career in the psychology of vision at the Centre National de la Recherche Scientifique. Although he remained outside the GRAV's everyday activities, Molnar was able to continue to play the part of an unofficial yet powerful authority on theory for some of its members. François Morellet for example co-wrote a long text with him in 1963 revolving around the idea that 'the materialist theory of knowledge must above all be based on the physiology and psychology of the sensory organs' and that 'any theory of knowledge must necessarily begin with perception.'[10]

This position was not specific to French artists: it was a feature of the optico-kinetic trend as a whole. (Optico-kinetic artists across Europe met several times during the 1960s under the label 'Nouvelle Tendance' or 'New Tendency'.)[11] In particular, the Italian section of Nouvelle Tendance, which included the Groups N (Padua) and T (Milan), was well-informed about such questions thanks to the lively tradition of psychological studies in that country, around Gaetano Kanisza, Paolo Bonaiuto or Fabio Metelli, and the popularisation of Gestalt theory through the 1954 Italian translation of Rudolf Arnheim's book, *Arte e percezione visiva*.[12] References to the problems of perception abound in the writings of Gianni Colombo (Group T) and his colleagues. One of them, Manfredo Massironi (Group N), like an alter ego to François Molnar, would also leave his artistic practice behind at the end of the 1960s in order to devote himself to his work in experimental psychology.

Is this to say that these trends in optico-kinetics were completely dominated by visuality and that they only related to the optical materialism with which their work is, most of the time, identified in such a caricatured way? In fact, optical and kinetic art's approach to the sensory reflects much more complex questions, which often brought with them contradictions that would be resolved with uneven success. For example, the single question of spectator participation, which was absolutely fundamental for these artists as a group, raised from the beginning a series of problems relating to the psycho-sensory definition of this spectator: How long would it be possible to reduce the viewer to a single functioning eye that was artificially hypostatised and cut off from the rest of sensory experience, when one's stated aim was the spectator's total stimulation, ultimately implying a more complete sensory involvement?

For the more consistent thinkers, the study of vision would only be a starting point. Julio Le Parc, who, as a member of the GRAV, was among those who most significantly exceeded visuality, wrote, in a note dated 22 July 1960, that it was necessary to 'learn about the physiological mechanisms of ocular movement and how it was interconnected with the mind, *in order to move on consciously, and step by step, to conquering the rest of the sensory and mental mechanisms* and to successfully configure visual elements in accordance with the knowledge attained about the *nature of the relationship between the human eye and the human being*'.[13]

From the eye to the body

Indeed, the very specific way in which the spatialisation of visual situations was justified in the GRAV's collective proposals should not go unnoticed – it accounts, in fact, for much of what is original about the group's positions. During the first three years, the GRAV conceived most of its actions around the theme of 'instability': this notion appeared in the GRAV's first texts[14] and was subsequently used as a name for several exhibitions from 1962 on,[15] as well as for their first labyrinth, exhibited at the Paris Biennale the following year. 'Instability' referred to borderline states of perception where the laws of Gestalt no longer apply, and where the constructive drive that spontaneously manifests itself in normal visual activity fails in its simplest mechanisms, such as the recognition of 'good forms' or the distinction between form and background. In 'natural' vision, form is always apprehended through a central (foveal) vision. That is, form is situated in the part of the perceptual field to which the eyes naturally turn, and where perception is at its fullest and its most detailed. In contrast, the background is always apprehended through peripheral vision.

It is this very traditional hierarchy that was undermined in the works of Morellet, Stein, Yvaral, Le Parc, Garcia-Rossi, Francisco Sobrino, or in those of Horacio Garcia Miranda, who was briefly part of the GRAV. Miranda used repetitive, non-compositional, non-focused, all-encompassing structures that eliminated any centre of attention by homogeneously covering the whole surface with visual stimuli. These programmed structures give rise to exploratory eye movements as the eye vainly attempts to focus on and to adjust to a centre which has disappeared, which has been abolished, or evacuated from the work. The viewer's gaze also ends up being excluded from the work, as it is dragged along the all-over grid's lateral expansion. The feeling of disorientation or instability stems from the gaze's inability to rely on the usual discrimination, within the perceptual field, between foveal vision and peripheral vision. This was the GRAV artists' first achievement in their ambition to 'displace the eye's habitual function (its way of gaining knowledge about the world through forms and their relations to each other) towards a visual situation based on the peripheral vision field and *instability*'.[16]

The next stage was directly concerned with the kinetic environment: it consisted in increasing the stimulation of peripheral vision yet more, by surrounding the spectator in a sensory and dynamic environment, which would make demands on his or her responses from all sides at once, often in a particularly aggressive way. For example, in his *40,000 Squares*, Morellet covered all the walls in the first cell of the 1963 *Labyrinth* with a grid, while Le Parc's 1967 *Surprise Movements* blinded visitors to the Musée d'Art Moderne de la Ville de Paris with pulsating lights. Many examples could also be listed among the Italian artists, who were in close contact with the GRAV: there, similar concerns led to the creation of light environments such as the *Strutturazione cine-visuale abitabile* (*Kinetic-visual Inhabitable Structure*) presented by Gianni Colombo in the context of the Nouvelle Tendance in Paris in 1964, or the projects of Giovanni Anceschi (the 1963 *Ambiente a chocs luminosi* [*Flashing Light Environment*]), Davide Boriani (his 1963–64 *Spazio + linee di luce + spettatore* [*Space + Lines of Light + Spectator*]) or Gabriele De Vecchi (*Strutturazione triangolare × 4* [*Triangular Structuration × 4*] of 1963–64).

The range of devices mobilised in these works acknowledge the retinal persistence phenomena which occur when lights are flashed according to a random and unsynchronised rhythm (*After Structures* was the title of an environment created by Colombo in 1966, whose principle was very close to several neon installations by his friend Morellet). The more these effects are heightened, the more they force the viewer to maintain a frantic attention in all sectors of his vision, by triggering a series of motor reflexes which are the result of his attempts to adjust to situations that eventually push his disorientation to the point of instability. 'The visitors came out of the labyrinth distraught but delighted and in their disorientation, they tried to regain their grip on a stable universe beyond *moiré* and transparent surfaces.'[17]

The disorientation in question here was literal. While foveal vision gives priority to the recognition and identification of objects, peripheral vision in normal perceptual conditions is used to perceive the environment, giving information about close surroundings and allowing spatial orientation.[18] To call upon peripheral vision in the extreme conditions of perceptual instability created by these artists is thus to attack the viewer's sense of his situation in space, which eventually risks being more than slightly unsettled. Julio Le Parc, especially, worked to generate conflicting spatial situations in different ways. First, he acted exclusively on the spectator's vision by constraining it in the 1965 series of *Lunettes pour une vision autre* (*Glasses for another kind of vision*), which were given out to spectators of the GRAV's trails.[19] With these glasses on, the viewer's visual field underwent different kinds of alterations: kaleidoscopic fragmentations due to the effect of prisms or fluted glass, vertical or horizontal inversions by means of small stationary or swivelling mirrors, lateral dilations or frontal omissions triggered by the use of lenses.

Thus profoundly transformed, vision was no longer a sufficiently reliable guide, even in the simplest kinds of behaviour; on the contrary, it became a source of errors and clumsiness, which could result in knocks and falls. Le Parc's glasses thus forced subjects to focus on a heightened bodily consciousness in order to allow them to relearn the most basic kinaesthetics.

The *Glasses* fall into a group of experiments that were staged around this time with similar anti-visual aims in mind, notably by Stelarc with his *Helmets* (1968–1972), which disoriented vision, or by Lygia Clark with her own set of mirror-*Goggles* (1968), and her *Sensory Masks* (1967), whose ocular orifices were obstructed by different devices hindering the exercise of normal vision. Le Parc's *Glasses* were, however, related above all to the distorting spectacles used in experimental psychology to create conflicting situations between visual and proprioceptive kinds of information in order to understand how they interact in the perception of surrounding space.[20] (The term 'proprioceptive' describes the set of tactile, muscular, vestibular and kinaesthetic perceptions experienced in everyday perception.)[21] Experiments using inclined mirrors that throw the visual frame of a whole room out of kilter were also conducted with analogous aims,[22] and came to be repeated more or less consciously in the context of optico-kinetic art, by the GRAV, by Manfredo Massironi, who used mobile mirrors in his *Struttura dinamica* (*Dynamic Structure*) (1961), and still more by Christian Megert, whose environments were modified by walls of mirrors disposed at irregular angles, and thus immersed the viewer in a space full of conflicting landmarks (in his 1962 *6 Spiegeln* [*6 Mirrors*]).

The destabilising experience triggered by these environments does not stem, as in the case of the conflicting glasses, from the alteration of visual perception, but rather from the multiplication of mutually exclusive pieces of visual information: each point of view on the mirrors reorganises the site of the optic experience according to different configurations, in which a vertical axis in the visual space can become slanted to the right or to the left according to the chosen angle of vision. Joël Stein also gave an interpretation of these polyc-entric spaces with his kaleidoscopic tunnels into which spectators were asked to look or even put their heads when the tunnels were big enough. At least the number of reflections was controlled (as in the exactly contemporary environ-ments by Yayoi Kusama)[23] by a symmetrical system allowing the restoration of a logical spatial organisation, which was not the case in the multi-directed mirrors of an artist such as Megert.

In the multiplicity of viewing points presented by this type of environ-ment, from which perceptive centre can the viewer organise his behaviour? At the beginning, Wertheimer and Koffka had been able to assert that keeping one's balance when confronted with these specific conditions of experience could only be attributed to a process of visual adaptation, of which the observ-able posture reflexes were only a secondary expression. Soon after the Second

World War, H.A. Witkin, who had perfected Wertheimer's inclined mirror devices and systematised his experiments, thought he was in a good position to confirm all these conclusions.[24] Ten years earlier, however, James J. Gibson had already qualified these results when he declared that 'both the visual and the postural vertical are determined by visual factors and gravitational factors acting jointly, *with orientation to gravity, however, as the more decisive factor in cases of real conflict between the two types of sensory data*'.[25] Later, the same author prolonged the controversy, identified in terms of the classic opposition between Gestaltists and behaviourists, by emphasising that keeping a good balance presupposed the use of both visual *and* proprioceptive information and by referring back, ultimately, to the bodily perception of gravitational forces that determine the orientation of space according to a vertical called 'gravitational vertical' or 'true', 'physical' or 'postural vertical', considered to be more reliable in certain circumstances than the apparent visual vertical.[26] In any case, this background of psycho-cognitive enquiries can enrich theories of kinetic art and belie its early emphasis on opticality. It allows us to understand how the theme of instability shifted from the analysis of peripheral vision, as it was being excessively stimulated, to broader issues concerning the body and its balance.

Corporeal space, proprioceptive space

In this context, it is not surprising that 'questioning behaviour' became one of the GRAV's watchwords,[27] and was particularly applicable to Julio Le Parc's contributions, which made the most effective use of body-constraining devices. The first devices appeared in the labyrinth installed in 1964 at the Musée des Arts Décoratifs during the exhibition *Propositions visuelles du mouvement international Nouvelle Tendance* (*Visual Proposals from the International Movement of the New Tendency*), where they took the form of steps to be climbed, a passageway with a soft and uneven floor, and a corridor obstructed by staggered walls. The following year at the Paris Biennale, the GRAV's *Proposition pour une salle de jeu* (*Proposal for a Play Room*) included an invitation to play with a ball hanging over a floor covered with moving, tilting slabs – those would later be reused, with the addition of seats mounted on springs, in the course of the well-known *Journée dans la rue* (*A Day in the Street*) organised in different public locations in Paris on 19 April 1966. These methods of kinaesthetic stimulation reached their peak with the *Parcours à volume variable* (*Variable Volume Trail*), which was integrated within the visitors' journey around the exhibition *Lumière et mouvement* (*Light and Movement*) at the Musée d'Art Moderne de la Ville de Paris in 1967 (figure 5.1). On this occasion, the GRAV built three parallel trails, which disrupted each of the three fundamental coordinates of architectural space in turn. The

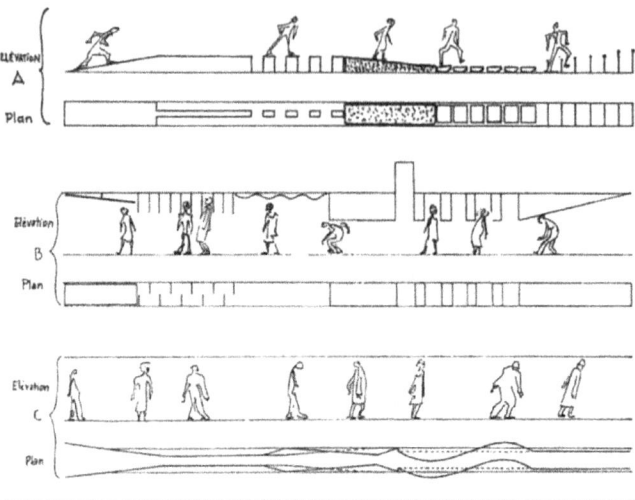

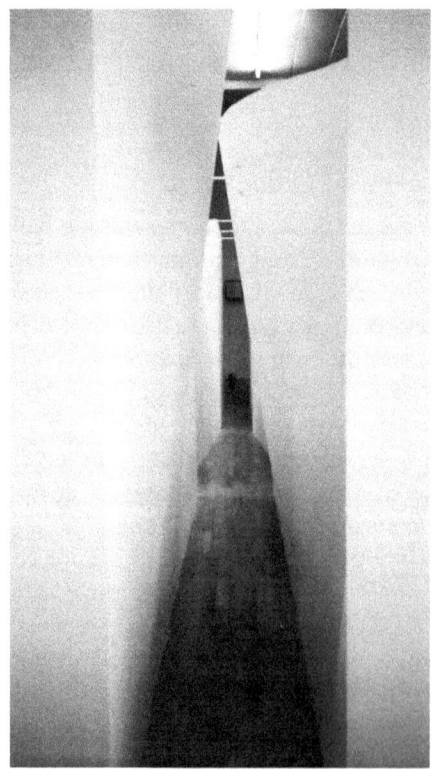

5.1   GRAV (Groupe de Recherche d'Art Visuel), *Parcours à volume variable* (*Variable Volume Trail*), 1967. Top to bottom: cross-section, and reconstruction at Le Magasin – Centre national d'art contemporain de Grenoble, 1998.

first trail tackled the floor, which was split into different heights, and covered with soft materials, unstable slabs, narrow beams, footbridges and obstacles of increasing size; the second was a transformed corridor in which the ceiling was lowered throughout, and offered visitors various kinds of slants, mobile elements, battlements, funnels and undulations; the third was a narrow tunnel with walls that were successively curved, slanted, bent and funnel-like. As a whole, the spaces were meant to trigger a 'chain of situations and environments that brings about different kinds of behaviour'.[28] These kinds of behaviour (bending, standing up, moving to one side, brushing and leaning against the wall) are all connected to a series of postural adjustments, composed of reflex or anticipated movements that are, generally speaking, ultimately aimed at adapting one's moves to the constraints of an unpredictable, uneven, fragmented, partitioned and confined setting. In this sense, this installation alone was a behaviourist manifesto in itself: it turned behaviour into a perceptual activity in its own right, to be carried out in relation to the characteristics of space – bearing in mind that the space that viewers in the *Parcours à volume variable* were allowed to discover was a physical and perceptual frame, along which they could pace up and down, and which they could measure with their own bodies through the very act of walking.

Installations by the GRAV have seldom appealed less to the viewer's gaze: movement, and the elaboration of the best behavioural strategies to determine such movement, were the only things that mattered. The spatial configuration presented by the *Parcours à volume variable* was basically only an exacerbation of the most everyday situations, since the smallest movement of any part of the body is always the result of a change in balance, compensated for by postural readjustments without which a fall would be inevitable. Through the exaggerated use of constraints, the GRAV turned a mechanism, which is unconscious most of the time, into a consciously motivated perceptual act: the spectator caught up in these environmental disruptions was faced with the simple, obvious fact of the interdependence between his locomotion and his postural balance. When it was possible to see anything, vision remained entirely subjected to this rule; most of the time, however, it was prevented, by obstacles and various constraints, from playing its traditional scouting role during locomotion. Thus, vision, which was often ineffective, was less important here than another kind of broader perceptual system founded on the many modes of proprioceptive sensibility that are constituted by the kinds of information, coming from the external ear, the muscles and the joints, that are necessary for body motion and balance.

That all these experiments about space were ultimately about disturbances in physical balance is confirmed by the features of a fourth trail, which remained unrealised, most probably due to technical difficulties that are obvious from the initial description: 'The fourth trail rotates the volume (floor, wall, and ceiling) through a helical torsion, so that to cross it the spectator (*in a state of normal gravity*) is forced to walk in turn on the floor, on the left wall, on the ceiling and then on the right wall before finding himself on the floor again.'[29] The reference to gravity figures only in brackets, like a detail added at the last moment, almost by chance, but it is crucial. It conveys an accurate intuition: when the visual crutches that make up the most elementary frame of reference (such as are provided by the verticals and the horizontals of architecture) are no longer operative, the destabilised spectator has no other option than to rely on other bearings. His bodily, proprioceptive perceptions will then indicate the coordinates of another spatial framework entirely directed by the gravitational pull which the skeleton and muscles continually resist, and which unmistakably provide a sense of the 'true vertical'. Therefore, in the last analysis and in certain exceptional conditions, the most relevant frame of reference for the body is not visual but gravitational: 'Through my weight, I know where I am.'[30]

Within the optico-kinetic tendency as a whole, no one demonstrated the accuracy of this intuition better than the Milanese artist Gianni Colombo, who pursued this logic to its ultimate consequences. Indeed, Colombo's entire work from the mid-1960s on seems driven by a desire to highlight this gravitational frame of reference and a specific proprioceptive space. As a founding member of Gruppo T and an active participant of Nouvelle Tendance, where he was close to the GRAV (and to Morellet in particular), he won the Grand Prize for painting at the Venice Biennale in 1968 for his most famous work *Spazio elastico* (*Elastic Space*) (1967), which, ironically, set out to subvert traditional pictorial space. *Spazio elastico* can indeed be understood as a spatialised version of the perpendicular frame on which the perspectival grid hangs (as it happens, a later version of this work would be installed in a church in Cesare Maderno in 1975, so that it related to the perspectival grid of an altarpiece). In its first version, *Spazio elastico* took the form of an almost cubic space cut through by a network of extendable white threads that crossed at right angles and at regular intervals; this network was connected to several motors hidden outside the room that acted on it by deforming and dilating it in all directions. Plunged into near obscurity, the observer would initially try to find his bearings by looking at the only available spatial points of reference: those provided by the white threads lit by a Wood's (ultraviolet) lamp. But these reference points are all moving and perpetually subjected to modifications, generating a feeling of spatial ambiguity, and even a sort of physical vertigo in which lies the whole point of the experiment.

Colombo created several such environments under the preferred title of '*ambiente*' (a term borrowed from Lucio Fontana, a spiritual father for this generation),[31] questioning the most commonplace coordinates and spatial limits, acting on the floor (*Campo practicabile* [*Practicable Area*], 1970), the walls and the ceiling. To do this, many environments relied on light effects. *Five Squares* (1969) was a translucent cube on whose walls were projected five luminous square cut-outs. These intensely coloured square areas dilated and contracted in turn, and at different rhythms, with a zoom effect that could be seen as an attempt to propose a spatial, and above all temporal, equivalent of the way in which perspective operates – acting as a spatio-dynamisation of perspective, so to speak. In its effective destabilisation of the viewer, this apparatus calls to mind certain psychology experiments that consist in placing the observer in a small room where the walls may be moved, through translation, while the floor remains still. It was found that the subject of this kind of experiment tended to attribute changes in his visual field to changes of position in his own body rather than to the real cause, which lay in shifts in the limits of the room in which he found himself. By a phenomenon of reflex adaptation, which is for the body what accommodation is for vision, the subject instinctively modified his posture according to this sensation of movement: since this reaction was not, in fact, adapted to reality, it led to a loss of balance, to stumbling and even to falling.[32]

In Colombo's work, the illusion of an expanding or shrinking visual field was created by the dilation and contraction of the squares that zoomed in and absorbed the spectator as if he were travelling back and forth in a space seemingly hollowed out by light – here the multiple changes in intensity and direction called upon the viewer from all sides at once, thus making perception more complicated. What this environment induced was a sensation of vection, that is, the illusory sensation of the viewer's own body going towards the focal point of the expanding visual field.[33] This sensation originates in the information that Gibson called visuo-proprioceptive, in which visual modality (the ability to see) dominates that of the body itself – even when the latter would have proved itself to be more relevant for the understanding of a given situation. Under the circumstances that they recreated experimentally, Gibson or Colombo demonstrated that visuo-proprioception can in short lead to a misuse of visuality, where vision encroaches on corporeal sensations to the point of inducing anomalous behaviour.

Gianni Colombo's *ambiente* effectively acted as breaking machines for the correlation between visual and proprioceptive crutches, which usually work together in constructing a feeling of space, in orientation and balance. His most effective work in this regard was certainly *Tre zone contigue a inclinazioni diverse* (*Three Diversely Inclined Contiguous Zones*) (figure 5.2), presented for the first time in an exhibition of the Nouvelle Tendance in 1965 and numerous times thereafter – notably at *Documenta 4* in 1968. This environment consisted of a strongly tilted cubic room that the visitor could reach and leave by two narrow corridors, which were themselves slanted in different directions. In a variation, the slant of the corridors was accentuated still more by networks of reflecting lines, lit by a Wood's lamp, which completely twisted the space.

Using an architecture of inclined planes was obviously the most expedient means of accomplishing a very immediate physical loss of balance, without the visuo-proprioceptive subtleties of the preceding *ambiente*. Yet the destabilising effect of this work should not be attributed only to the changes in the visitor's basis of support: the visitor also had to overcome the surprise effect caused by the unusual position of his most ordinary visual reference points, that is, the expected horizontality-verticality of the walls, floor and ceiling. When the visitor entered this space, his conditioning as to the ordinary organisation of the surrounding world made him instinctively identify an apparent visual vertical that contradicted the true postural vertical that he had to adopt to prevent himself from falling. Even the light fitting in the space was artificially stiffened so as to slant in the same direction as the architectural lines, and so became one of the slyly contradictory cues tricking the visitor: logically, the fitting should have hung straight down like a plumb line, indicating the true vertical direction. Under these conditions it is the spectator's body that was called upon to play the role of the plumb line in order to rediscover the direction of gravity which alone was capable of reorienting a viable space.[34]

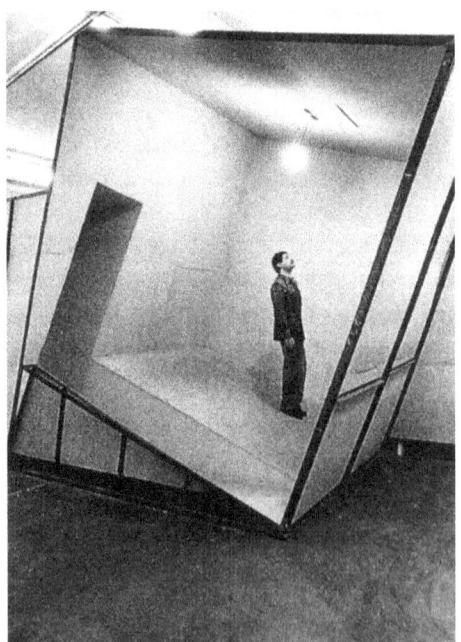

5.2   Gianni Colombo, *Tre zone contigue a inclinazioni diverse* (*Three Diversely Inclined Contiguous Zones*), 1965–68. Reconstruction at the Studio Marconi, Milan, 1977.

Here Colombo put the spectator in the same situation as in numerous experiments carried out in order to answer the question that Gibson formulated in the following way: 'Of the two kinds of available cues, the lines on the retinas on the one hand and the vestibular-kinaesthetic stimuli for bodily equilibrium on the other, which are decisive in the event of conflict between them?'[35] The experiment of the tilted room and the movable armchair, in which the seated observer is asked to align his position with the direction which seems to him to follow the true vertical, counts among the most frequently staged in this context (figure 5.3).[36] Either the observer trusted the visual data, followed the reference points provided by the architecture of the tilted room, but became aware of a loss of bodily balance; or he relied on his proprioception and proposed a vertical that no longer coincided with the apparent visual vertical, but around which he could, however, maintain his physical balance.

Contradicting the conclusion of the Gestaltists (Wertheimer, Koffka), who believed that the space of the tilted room would eventually seem upright if the subject maintained his observation long enough, Gibson suggested 'that a sense of the physical vertical persisted and the artificial environment continued to look tilted by reference to it'.[37] What Colombo, agreeing with Gibson, made clear in an installation like *Tre zone contigue* was the insufficiency of the purely visual frame of reference of Gestalt theory – and above all, its totally abstract character, cut off from the real forces that operate in concrete space. Gestalt, said Gibson, imposes on the phenomenal world the coordinates of abstract geometric space, like a transparent grid by which the relative position of bodies could be understood.[38] Now, it was this very model that revealed its flaws at each attempt to formulate a theory of perception taking the observer's bodily, sensory-motor reality into account.

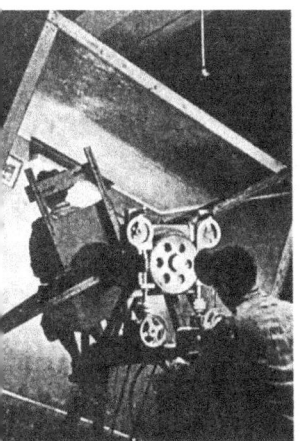 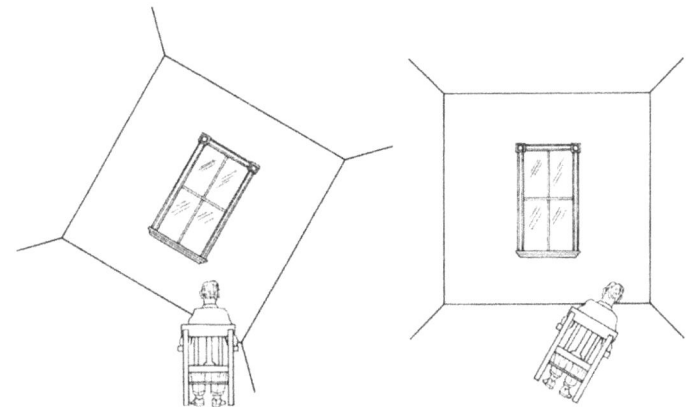

'Tilting-Room-Tilting-Chair Test'.   **5.3**

The oblique function

The concept of new 'inhabitability' that Colombo put forward concerning his experiments suggests a connection with the similar intuitions underlying certain contemporary architectural utopias.[39] The most obvious example is Claude Parent and Paul Virilio's theory of the oblique function, which presents the additional advantage of highlighting the debate about the senses underlying all research on instability. Parent is the architect of the Villa Drusch in Versailles (1963–65), one end of which is in the shape of a cube tilted at a 45° angle and apparently precariously balanced on one of its edges. For Parent, 'the visual element is no longer the preferred source of information' in this architecture of strain and constraint, which, instead, privileges the body through which sensations of weight are experienced:

> The body is mobilised through a more intense sensitivity to gravity. The individual's weight is experienced and expressed on a slope even in a stationary position, for in this case one must mechanically make a muscular effort to keep one's balance. Becoming aware of one's body, even in immobility, has the effect of making one much more acutely perceptive when walking along the ramps.[40]

In this way, life on the oblique would create no less than the establishment of a new sensory regime abolishing the 'adulterated and alienating world of visualisation':

> The second specific physiological occurrence is that of TACTILITY. As it is encountered, the slope can be sensed directly through one's feet via the phenomenon of adhesion. Feet, which are essential factors in the equilibrium polygon, transmit direct, un-coded data regarding the steepness of the slope, the difficulties in the path, losses in adhesion, etc. … We are liberated as human beings from the pernicious, and noxious, hierarchy of information which, through the predominance of the visual, used to obscure our judgment and to encode it to such an extent that our thinking was always dominated by different ideologies about the perception of experienced space.[41]

For Paul Virilio, who was at that time associated with Parent within the Architecture Principe group, life on the oblique challenged the most usual 'body techniques' and required an awareness of gravity, no longer as a constraint, but as the driving force of movement:

> At the origin of the group's theory, there is … the idea of loss of balance and of motor instability. The idea that gravity, the pull of the earth, is a motor to be used like the wind in a ship's sails. … But what became hotly contested and challenged *was the classical postural schema*, the reference to the essentially static and fixed proprioception of a stationary body. The purpose was to finally bring the human habitat into the dynamic era of bodies in movement. … It was

a question of transforming the inhabitant's posture by using his weightiness dynamically according to the reality of a living being, *to bring back to life the 'locomotor' body* [Virilio also used the term 'automotor' later in the text] *as a totality open to the world.*[42]

The most significant architectural counterpart of the manifesto for the oblique function was Virilio and Parent's installation of the French Pavilion for the 1970 Venice Biennale (figure 5.4). Created in collaboration with a group of artists including François Morellet, an ex-member of the GRAV,[43] the installation constituted a prelude to many other ephemeral walk-through installations, built in different French cities until 1973, which often became the sites of spontaneous gatherings during the flurry of post-May 1968 cultural and political events.[44] In Venice, long slanting walkways at contradictory, more or less, steep inclines covered with reflecting materials (contributing, along with Morellet's flashing neon lights, to the environment's Op Art feel), defined a space whose 'principal characteristic was to refuse any contemplation directed by individual artists' signatures, and to be simply offered to the visitor's experience'.[45] The visitor 'is so absorbed in his progress through the environment, in the sensation of his own body, in the brand new idea of voluntary balance, and in the physical effort, that he is freed from the trap of the visual. He is no longer sensitive to its aggression. He is neither dominated nor coerced by it', for 'to walk on the oblique is to rediscover one's body and change one's ideas of balance'.[46]

The theory of proprioceptive perception developed by Parent and Virilio can be connected to some of August Schmarsow's suggestions at the beginning of the twentieth century in his *Fundamental Principles of the Science of Art* (1905) and, above all, in Heinrich Wölfflin's *Prolegomena to a Psychology of Architecture* where one can already read that 'the architectural impression, far from being a kind of "reckoning by the eye", is essentially based on a direct bodily feeling', through empathy with the material properties of the world.'[47] 'As human beings with a body that teaches us the nature of gravity, contraction, strength, and so on, we gather the experience that enables us to identify with the condition of other forms.'[48] Thus, 'we interpret the physical world through the categories ... that we share with it', and for example, 'the basic elements of architecture – material and form, gravity and force – are defined by our experiences of ourselves'.[49] Wölfflin's text calls for the development of a kind of bodily sense of the perception of place, site, of physical space in general; it is an invitation to cultivate what one could call, using a neologism borrowed from Colombo, a true 'topoesthesia'. Indeed, *topoestesia* was the generic term that the artist used, after *Tre zone contigue*, for a large number of installations based on the repertory of architectonic forms (post and architrave, arch, pilaster, column) voluntarily misused (arrhythmia, conflicting inclinations, overhangs) in a continually renewed attempt to disorient the observer by altering his visual frame of reference. He would go as far as creating an incoherent cacophony of angles, a 'cacogoniometry' (in *Architettura cacogoniometrica*, Lyon, Espace Lyonnais d'Art contemporain, in 1983–4).

Moreover, another of Colombo's neologisms underscores how accurately he understood our bodily perception of space as a set of phenomena. From 1975 on, *bariestesia* designated works in the form of irregular and asymmetrically inclined steps, which considerably increased the difficulty of such a simple an action as climbing stairs, exactly like the modules *Variations sur l'escalade* (*Variations on Climbing*) presented by the GRAV in Buffalo in the 1968 exhibition *Plus by Minus*. The term 'baryesthesia', in other words, the perception of weight, comes from the Greek '*barus*' meaning heavy, weighty, 'grave' in the archaic sense.[50] Once again we are led back to taking into account the gravitational framework that is implicit in any theory of perception that seeks to include data other than those deriving from visual modality alone. Such a theory opens on to a comprehension of a true 'somesthesia', a total bodily sensitivity.

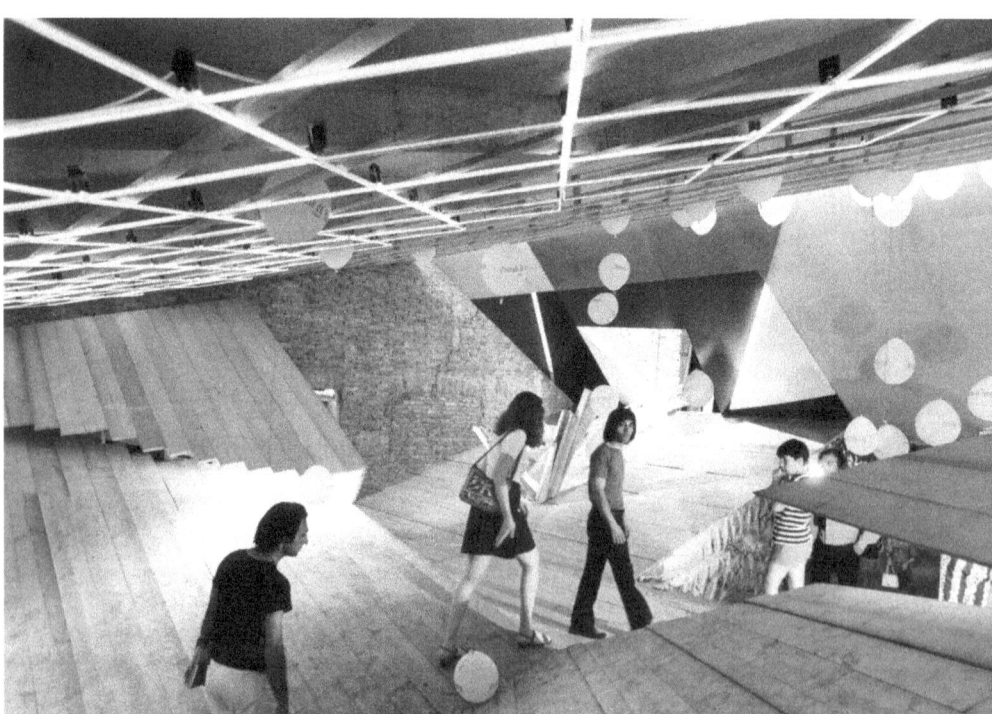

5.4   Claude Parent, French Pavilion, Venice Biennale, 1970.

The gravitational vertical

A theory of perception based exclusively on the valorisation of the optic components of space alone would indeed be missing one of its essential dimensions. When kinetic environments play with bodily constraints, strains and physical instability, they allow viewers to become aware of the existence of another spatial coordinate: that which the pull of gravity creates spontaneously: the force of gravity. Space is, in effect, entirely oriented by gravity: just as the compass needle unfailingly spins towards the magnetic north, all weighty bodies fall vertically, in the direction of the Earth, its centre, a common centre for all bodies subjected to the pull of gravity (*les 'graves'*). This is why this spatial dimension can be identified more precisely as a *gravitational vertical*.

The *gravitational vertical* indicates the direction of a movement without return, with no possibility of going back up. In contrast with the optical vertical, it can only go in one direction and its definitive groundward orientation does not allow for any back-and-forth movement along its directional axis. That the gravitational vertical can be confused under habitual circumstances with the optic vertical that structures visual space should not for all that make us forget that, in order to understand the perception of physical space in all its complexity, this perception must be acknowledged to be based on the integration of different kinds of sensory data. For the gravitational vertical structures a space that is not the one in which the royal illusion of the gaze makes us believe, but rather a space filled with real forces, tensions and reactions, a fabric in which our bodies are caught. The gravitational vertical differs in its very nature from the optical vertical in that it is experienced, and manifests itself, through sensations that are bodily rather than exclusively visual: it allows the subject to substitute, for a point of view, a 'point of being' or a 'point of body' which, in comparison, may turn out to be more reliable under certain circumstances. This 'body point', which coincides, at the sensory level, with our proprioception, is precisely the one through which the gravitational vertical passes.[51]

What I have identified as the gravitational vertical is thus the coordinate that structures a space that is not exclusively optic, but also and above all tactile, muscular and kinaesthetic, a space which was, in my opinion, the site of the most interesting and seminal revitalised forms of sculpture and of three-dimensional art around 1970, from Anti-form to Process Art, from certain forms of performance to choreography (twentieth-century dancers in particular had become more acutely aware than ever that the 'kinesphere' defined by Rudolf Laban is entirely determined by the pull of gravity).[52] In fact, some of these issues are mentioned by Dan Graham in 'Subject matter', a 1969 text which refers, in particular, to a quote by James J. Gibson about 'the earth's gravity' as 'a continuous downward force pulling bodies of material downward', to discuss works by Carl Andre, Bruce Nauman and Richard Serra in terms of proprioceptive perception and the kinaesthetic mobilisation of the spectator.[53] From the GRAV to Robert Morris's playful, participatory installation at the Tate Gallery in 1971, from Gianni Colombo's *ambiente* to Bruce Nauman's corridors: it would be easy to go beyond traditional geographical and historical distinctions in order to examine, from the same angle as in this chapter, the many different forms that the act of falling took in the art of this period.[54] In this context, phenomenological accounts of this period could be explored further by looking more precisely at the very bases from which phenomenology itself developed.

Notes

This chapter is a translation from the French, by Anna and Karen Dezeuze, of an abridged and revised version of 'De l'instabilité. Perception visuelle/corporelle de l'espace dans l'environnement cinétique', *Les Cahiers du Musée national d'art moderne*, 78 (Winter 2001–2002), 41–69.

1 On this polarisation between American and European conceptions of modernism, see Frances Follin, *Embodied Visions: Bridget Riley, Op Art and the Sixties* (London: Thames & Hudson, 2004), in particular chapters 1.2 and 4.
2 This is the argument addressed by Svetlana Alpers, *The Art of Describing: Dutch Art in the Seventeenth Century* (London: Penguin, 1989).
3 Marcel Duchamp, 'Interview with the BBC' (1968), quoted in Francis M. Naumann, *Marcel Duchamp: the Art of Making Art in the Age of Mechanical Reproduction* (New York: Harry A. Abrams, 1999), p. 306.
4 The GRAV existed between 1960 and 1968 and included Paris-based artists François Morellet, Julio Le Parc, Joël Stein, Horacio Garcia-Rossi, Jean-Pierre Yvaral and Francisco Sobrino. While each of them pursued his personal career, they organised collective exhibitions and wrote theoretical and polemical texts that were distributed to visitors. For an inventory and chronology of their activities, see Yves Aupetitallot and Marion Hohlfeldt (eds), *Stratégies de participation. GRAV – Groupe de Recherche d'Art Visuel* (Grenoble: Le Magasin – Centre national d'Art contemporain, 1998).
5 GRAV, 'Assez de mystifications' (September 1961), in Aupetitallot and Hohlfeldt (eds), *Stratégies de participation*, p. 71. Unless otherwise specified, all translations are by the translators.
6 Quoted in Otto Hahn, *Yvaral* (Paris: Galerie Denise René, 1969), n. p.
7 Joël Stein, '[untitled text]', in *Nove Tendencije* (Zagreb: Galerija Suvremene Umjetnosti, 1969), in Aupetitallot and Hohlfeldt (eds), *Stratégies de participation*, p. 70.
8 Jean-Pierre Yvaral, '[untitled text]' (April 1965), in Aupetitallot and Hohlfeldt (eds), *Stratégies de participation*, p. 158.
9 GRAV, 'Recherche d'art visuel', *Melpomène*, 16 (December 1964), 11.
10 François Molnar and François Morellet, 'Pour un art abstrait progressif', in *Nove Tendencije 2* (Zagreb: Galerija Suvremene Umjetnosti, 1963), n. p.

11 The most thorough account to date of the activities of the Nouvelle Tendance is to be found in Lea Vergine (ed.), *Arte programmata e cinetica 1953–1963: l'ultima avanguardia* (Milan: Palazzo and Mazzotta, 1983).

12 Cf. Vittorio Fagone's interview with Gillo Dorfles: 'Joe & Gianni Colombo a Milano fra arte e design', in Vittorio Fagone (ed.), *I Colombo* (Bergamo and Milan: Galleria d'Arte moderna e contemporanea, and Mazzotta, 1995), p. 23. In 1968, Dorfles significantly called this group of artists 'peceptivists'. Quoted by V. Fagone, 'Gianni Colombo, l'artista e il suo mondo', in *Gianni Colombo* (Tokyo: Sogetsu Art Museum, 1999), n. p.

13 Julio Le Parc, 'Pour un manifeste' (1960), in Jean-Louis Pradel, *Julio Le Parc* (Cernusco Sul Naviglio: Severgnini, 1995), p. 262 (my emphasis).

14 'Propositions sur le mouvement' (1961), in Aupetitallot and Hohlfeldt (eds), *Stratégies de participation*, pp. 96–7.

15 *L'Instabilité* opened at the Maison des Beaux-Arts in Paris in April 1962. The Gruppo N invited the GRAV to present the same exhibition in Padua a month later.

16 GRAV, 'Transformer l'actuelle situation de l'art plastique' (25 October 1961), in Aupetitallot and Hohlfeldt (eds), *Stratégies de participation*, p. 74.

17 Joël Stein, 'Homo ludens', *Robho*, 2 (November–December 1967), n. p.

18 Claude Perrin, *L'Homme et ses espaces: Plasticité et limites de l'équilibration* (Nancy: Presses Universitaires de Nancy, 1991), p. 56.

19 *Translators' note*: the French word used by the GRAV to describe their participatory works was '*parcours*' which evokes a discovery trail as well as an adventure or obstacle course.

20 A brief history of these experiments, starting from G.M. Stratton's in 1896 and 1897 can be found in James J. Gibson, *The Senses Considered as Perceptual Systems* (London: G. Allen & Unwin Ltd., 1966), pp. 300–2. During his classes in the 1950s, Maurice Merleau-Ponty made his students wear spectacles that inverted their visual fields in order to note the persistence of phenomena after prolonged use. (My thanks to Jean-Pierre Criqui for bringing to my notice this fact, which was witnessed by Hubert Damisch. This confirms the strong phenomenological orientation displayed by optico-kinetic art in its methods for stimulating specific kinds of behaviour.)

21 The term 'proprioception' was coined by Charles S. Sherrington in *The Integrative Action of the Nervous System* (New Haven: Yale University Press, 1906).

22 The first experiments were conducted, it seems, by Max Wertheimer, who described them in 'Experimentelle Studien über das Sehen von Bewegung', *Zeitschrift für Psychologie*, 61 (1912), 257ff.

23 Kusama was in contact with the GRAV from 1962, at the moment of the group's exhibition at the Contemporaries Gallery in New York in December. For more on Kusama's relation with the Nouvelle Tendance, see Laura Hoptman, 'Down to zero: Yayoi Kusama and the European New Tendency', in Lynn Zelevansky (ed.), *Love Forever: Yayoi Kusama, 1958–1968* (Los Angeles: Los Angeles County Museum of Art, 1998), pp. 42–59.

24 S.E. Asch and H.A. Witkin, 'Studies in space orientation: I. Perception of the upright with displaced visual fields', *Journal of Experimental Psychology*, 38:3 (June

1948), 325–37. This article is unfortunately not illustrated, but it includes a wealth of details regarding mirror devices used in the experiments it describes.

25 J.J. Gibson and O.H. Mowrer, 'Determinants of the perceived vertical and horizontal', *Psychological Review*, 45 (1938), 300–23.

26 James J. Gibson, 'The relation between visual and postural determinants of the phenomenal vertical', *Psychological Review*, 59:5 (September 1952), 370–5. The idea of the 'true' vertical also appears in Perrin, *L'Homme et ses espaces*, pp. 65–78.

27 GRAV, 'Parcours à volume variable', in Frank Popper (ed.), *Lumière et mouvement* (Paris: Musée d'Art moderne de la Ville de Paris, 1967), n. p.

28 Ibid.

29 GRAV, 'Parcours à volume variable', n. p. (my emphasis).

30 These are Bonnie B. Cohen's words, quoted by Laurence Louppe, *Poétique de la danse contemporaine* (Brussels: Contredanse, 2000), p. 67.

31 Colombo himself emphasised the importance of Fontana's legacies in a long interview with Jole De Sanna: 'Storia come filtro della qualità', in Fagone (ed.), *I Colombo*, pp. 289–92.

32 Perrin, *L'Homme et ses espaces*, pp. 141–2.

33 See Gibson, *The Senses Considered as Perceptual Systems*, pp. 34, 37–8.

34 An Italian precursor for this work by Colombo can be found in the spectacular *Suspended House* built by Vicino Orsini, with inclined walls and ground, at the sacred wood of Bomarzo between 1552 and 1580. See Antonio Pinelli *Belle Manière: Anticlassicisme et maniérisme dans l'art du XVIe siècle*, trans. B. Arnal (Paris: Le Livre de Poche, 1996), pp. 252–4.

35 Gibson, 'The relation between visual and postural determinants of the phenomenal vertical', 370.

36 Such devices were described and illustrated by H.A. Witkin, *Psychological Differentiation: Studies of Development* (New York and London: John Wiley & Sons, 1962), pp. 36–9. See also S.E. Asch and H.A. Witkin, 'Studies in space orientation: II. Perception of the upright with displaced visual fields and with body tilted', *Journal of Experimental Psychology*, 38:4 (August 1948), 455–77; and G.E. Passey, 'The perception of the vertical: IV. Adjustment to the vertical with normal and tilted visual frames of references', *Journal of Experimental Psychology*, 40:6 (December 1950), 738–45.

37 Gibson, 'The relation between visual and postural determinants of the phenomenal vertical', 370.

38 Ibid.

39 'The *ambiente* created here tends to highlight the habitability potential of a space conditioned by kinetic actions.' Gianni Colombo, 'Environnement variable', *Robho*, 3 (Spring 1968), n. p.

40 Claude Parent, *Vivre à l'oblique* (Paris: L'Aventure urbaine, 1970), p. 31.

41 Claude Parent, *Vivre à l'oblique*, p. 35. The architect's own sister, Nicole Parent, would develop in turn the '*Incliplan*' method, which is a kind of gymnastics on inclined planes for therapeutic purposes. 'On an oblique plane', she explained, 'the smallest movement up- or downwards is an acceleration or a brake. As in yoga practice, one thus rediscovers the sensation of one's body's weight.' Quoted by

Michel Ragon, *Claude Parent: monographie critique d'un architecte* (Paris: Dunod, 1982), p. 85. See also Nicole Parent, *L'Incliplan* (Paris, Robert Laffont: 1972).

42 Paul Virilio, 'La désorientation', in Paul Virilio and Claude Parent, *Architecture Principe 1966-1996* (Besançon: Editions de l'imprimeur, 1996), pp. 8–10. (In this book are reprinted nine issues of the magazine *Architecture Principe*, published in 1966. Of particular interest is issue 1 (February 1966) on 'La Fonction oblique'.) Virilio owes his own discovery of instability and the oblique partly, at least, to a kind of tragic, contemporary Bomarzo: the bunkers on the Atlantic coast which have been become unstable and slanted through the movement of the dunes. 'The children's favourite game at the time was to slip into these colossal toppled frames and to run along their inclined floors, looking for strange sensations of vertigo and unbalance. I started to imitate these practices and realised how the use of inclined planes within a closed volume transformed my sense of size, directions, movement, and the quality of my sensations and movements itself.' Virilio, 'Architecture Principe. Pour mémoire', in Ragon, *Claude Parent*, p. 193.

43 When he declared, for example, that, 'The function of the oblique forces a conscious participation', Parent seemed very close to the GRAV's ideas. 'Structures', *Architecture Principe*, 3 (February 1966), translated by Pamela Johnston in Pamela Johnston (ed.), *The Function of the Oblique: the Architecture of Claude Parent and Paul Virilio, 1963–1969* (London: AA Publications, 1996), p. 70.

44 On some of the political implications of Parent's ideas, as well as the GRAV's, during this period, see Anna Dezeuze, '"Cinétisme du corps" et participation du spectateur', in Arnauld Pierre (ed.), *L'Œil moteur: art optique et cinétique, 1950-1975* (Strasbourg: musée d'art moderne et contemporain de Strasbourg, 2005), pp. 90–3.

45 Parent, quoted by Ragon, *Claude Parent*, p. 173.

46 Claude Parent, *Entrelacs de l'oblique* (Paris: Le Moniteur, 1981), pp. 84, 107. In the context of the debate about the senses, which underlies his comments, it is unsurprising that Parent introduced a reference to blindness: 'Elsewhere, a blind people's association visited the "*praticable*" for an hour, without a guide, walking up and down along 25% and then 50% slopes by clinging to the balustrade, thus confirming that feet are more useful than eyes when it comes down to the oblique function.' Ibid., p. 94.

47 Heinrich Wölfflin, 'Prolegomena to a psychology of architecture' (1886), in Harry Francis Mallgrave and Eleftherios Ikonomou (eds), *Empathy, Form, and Space: Problems in German Aesthetics, 1873–1893* (Santa Monica: The Getty Center for the History of Art and the Humanities, 1994), p. 155.

48 Ibid., p. 151.

49 Ibid., pp. 152, 158.

50 *Translators' note*: although this archaic meaning exists in English, it is better known in French in the expression 'chute des graves', used by thinkers such as Descartes in order to describe specifically the fall of heavy bodies when discussing gravity.

51 'The point of being is the proprioceptive point, it is the point from which one knows that one is somewhere.' Derrick de Kerckhove, 'Propriodéception et autonomation', in Mario Borillo et Anne Sauvageot (eds), *Les Cinq sens de la création* (Seyssel: Champ Vallon, 1996), p. 140.

52 That the space of dance is the 'gravitational space' *par excellence* is suggested by the title of an interview with Paul Virilio by Laurence Louppe and Daniel Dobbels in Laurence Louppe (ed.), *Danses tracées* (Paris: Dis Voir, 1991), pp. 47–71.

53 See Dan Graham, 'Subject matter' (1969), in *Rock My Religion: Writings and Projects, 1965–90* (Cambridge: MIT Press, 1993), pp. 38–51.

54 This is what I am working on in my current research project entitled *Chute des corps et formes de l'art dans l'espace gravitaire 1960–1970*, which deals with the themes of the perception of weight and of falling bodies in 1960s and 1970s art. For a discussion of Morris's 1971 retrospective and Bruce Nauman's corridors, see Chapters 6 and 8 respectively in this volume.

Part II

Performing participation

6

The rules of engagement: displaced figuration in Robert Morris's mise-en-scène

Catherine Wood

See-saw

Robert Morris's writings and interviews in the late 1960s and early 1970s frequently emphasised the importance of sculpture's 'essentially tactile' nature, distinct from the 'optical sensibilities involved in painting,'[1] as well as the viewer's 'physical participation' in contemporary sculpture's 'extended situation'[2] comprising the relations of shape, light and space. With this emphasis in mind, it becomes intriguing to consider the extent to which his particular conception of 'participation' in this period was, in fact, mediated via a complex relationship with pictures. Specifically, these were pictures associated with the cultural context in which both his dance and sculpture work were made and disseminated in the mid to late 1960s: namely the theatre tableau and the photographic publicity image. Morris's 1971 Tate Gallery 'retrospective', for which he made the controversial decision to install, rather than existing works, a newly-made series of interactive plywood, stone and rope objects (see figures 6.1 and 6.2) – while past artworks were to be represented by slides and films installed alongside them – might be seen as the clearest manifestation of the complex, antagonistic relationship between the utopian capacity the image and physical actuality that his participatory work negotiated. In this chapter, I consider how Morris's 'blank form' sculpture was, in fact, underwritten by a particular, image-informed cultural consciousness that prefigured its immediate relationship with the spectator's body.

The fact that Morris began his artistic career as a painter is perhaps less important in this discussion than the early influence of his personal and artistic involvements with the dancer and choreographer Simone Forti, and – later – with choreographer and film-maker Yvonne Rainer.[3] Throughout the early to mid-1960s, in parallel with initial presentations of his own sculpture, Morris made and appeared in dance works alongside these and other dancer-choreographers at the Judson Dance Theater in New York's Greenwich Village. His grey painted plywood sculptures made in the same period, were, notoriously, negatively interpreted alongside work by Minimalist peers Donald Judd, Carl Andre and Tony Smith by the critic and art historian Michael Fried, in his

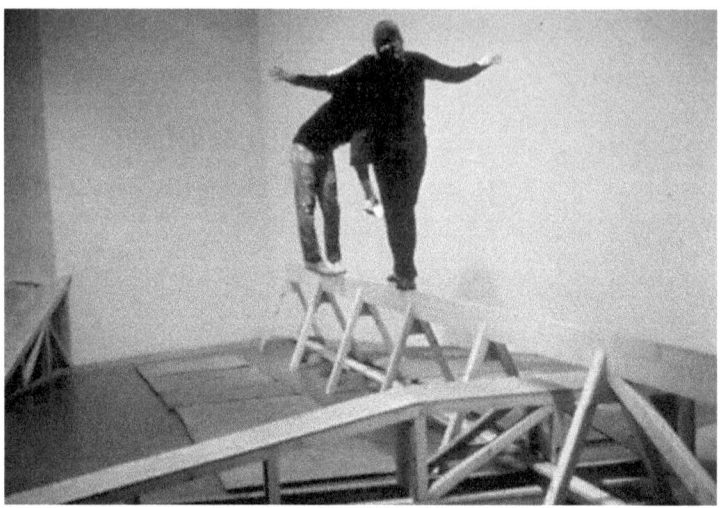

6.1   Exhibition view of *Robert Morris* (beam), Tate Gallery, London, 1971.

1967 essay on 'Art and objecthood', as being problematically 'theatrical'. Such was the open and discursive nature of the cross-disciplinary environment in New York during this period that Judd and Andre had, in fact, contributed sculptural props to occasional performances.[4] Morris's sculpture had, however, much stronger ties to performance as his work had, quite literally, been born from a context of theatrical presentation.

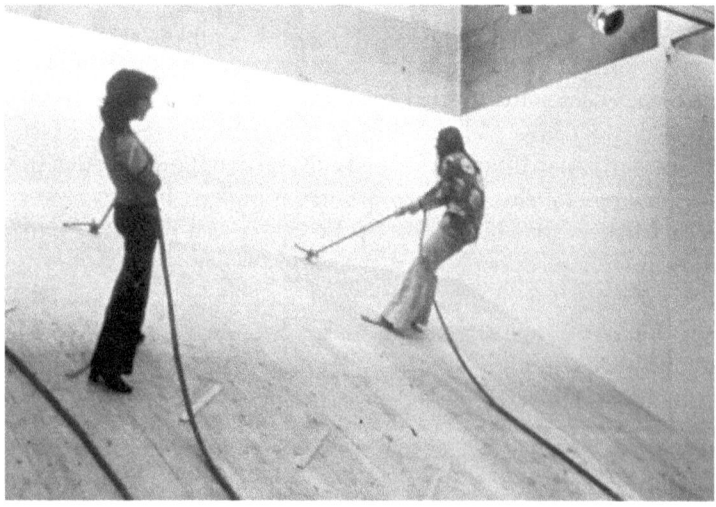

6.2   Exhibition view of *Robert Morris* (slope with ropes), Tate Gallery, London, 1971.

Morris's experiments with rudimentary 'geometric carpentry'[5] began around the time of his participation in Simone Forti's experimental choreography, *See Saw*, which was presented in December 1960 as part of one of the then frequent concerts that took place in Yoko Ono's loft space. The performance involved Morris and Rainer – who was at that time sharing a studio with Morris and Forti – balanced on either end of a pivoted plank of wood that he had constructed for the purpose, he at one end reading, she at the other, occasionally screaming; both walking back and forth along its length and attempting to balance.[6] Forti's subsequent piece, *Slant Board* (1961), likewise utilised a wooden structure designed by Morris, in an attempt to test the ordinary movement of bodies against gravity and alter their passage through space. Morris also presented an early corridor piece at Ono's loft in the same period, *Passageway* – a piece constructed 'out of plywood that curved for some fifty feet, narrowing to a closed point at the end; the progressively squeezed spectator had no choice, on discovering the dead end, but to return to the entry, where he or she appeared on emergence as an inadvertent performer'.[7]

Rainer recalls in her biography that Morris's own first work for the theatre stage, *Column* (1961), recycled a sculptural prop that she had had made for use in her own dance piece, *The Bells*, which had been presented in the same space, the Living Theater, the previous year. Morris had simply 'found it in the wings, and painted it grey'.[8] *Column* was the first of Morris's own complete works to stage a direct relationship of cause and effect between the body and object – or, at least, an attempt to. In a telling prefiguration of the physical accidents which caused his Tate Gallery retrospective to be closed after only five days a decade later, Morris was injured in the rehearsal of the piece.[9] Though he had planned to stand inside the box, which was to appear onstage when the curtains opened, standing vertically upright for three and a half minutes, before falling and lying prone on the floor for the same time again, on the night of its actual presentation the fall was initiated by use of invisible wire instead. The object's dimensions clearly signified its relationship to an upright and then horizontal body and to the performance capacities of both.

Through his involvement with the community of choreographers and dancers associated with the Judson Dance Theater, Morris created and performed in a number of dance pieces that were presented – for the most part – by, and for, a dedicated dance and art world who closely followed the scene. Reviews and photographs of the work regularly appeared in *Dance Magazine* and *The Village Voice*. The Judson context was heavily influenced by John Cage's compositional strategies using chance procedures, and the legacy of the interdisciplinary experiments of Cage, Merce Cunningham and Robert Rauschenberg born at Black Mountain College in the 1950s. The Judson dancers prioritised aesthetic approaches that were spoken of, at the time, in universal terms, but were clearly, in retrospect, ideologically and culturally specific: an aesthetic of everyday, pedestrian movement and found props was explored with a vocabulary that invoked 'democracy' and the 'ordinary'. The latter terms were employed in written form by Yvonne Rainer in particular,[10] but characterise an ethos shared by many of the dancers.

Steve Paxton's *Proxy* (1961), for example, involved within its composition a sequence in which a number of ordinary people simply walked back and forth across the stage. In parallel, Simone Forti was choreographing influential pieces such as *Rollers* and *Huddle* that used the 'neutral' structures of tasks and games as the basis for movement improvisation, incorporating into these games forms that Morris had made as props, which 'imposed some restriction or distortion on the performer's normal repertoire of movement'.[11] Judith Dunn, another key member of Judson, choreographed a duet for herself and Morris titled *Speedlimit*, for *Concert #5* in Washington on 9 May 1963. This piece involved Morris rolling Dunn in a cart, both artists performing on a gym mat and balancing each other, as well as Morris '[vaulting] up against a wall by means of a pole'.[12]

According to a description by the *Village Voice* dance critic Jill Johnston, Dunn was dealing with dance in a way that seemed to operate according to the general laws of physics, with 'basic physical problems [such] as balancing, bracing, pulling'. 'The dance was a horizontal level of tension', she wrote, 'the speedlimit is slow, there seemed no reason to hurry beyond one or two accelerations that erupted naturally from the action. … [The dance] includes props – car, pole, flag, ropes – which are secondary to the movement but which bring further dimension to the "environment" and to the field of physically motivated impulses.'[13] Sculptor Charles Ross designed a setting that resembled a 'jungle gym' made of steel pipe, plywood and rubber tyres, for the performance of Yvonne Rainer's *Room Service* at Judson in 1963.

Overall, then, the dance context within which Morris began his exploration of physical interaction with sculptural objects and environments was one in which the rigour of ballet training was indeed no longer necessary for participants. It could not be said, however, to have been entirely democratic or ordinary. With its basis in Cagean aesthetics and the phenomenological philosophy of Maurice Merleau-Ponty, it is important to remember that this participatory dance context comprised a particular community of interest that championed a specific conception of the 'everyday' as an aesthetic language with unique status within the hybrid real, yet utopian, space of the stage. Personal photographs of Rainer with Morris from the time show her in clothes that are more 'marked' by fashion (flower patterned fabrics, and so on) than the studiedly neutral T-shirts and sneakers of the Judson's staging of ordinariness.[14] Likewise, the Judson movement repertoire was observed and drawn from certain kinds of activities such as sports games and from physical tasks which conjured images of 'work' and 'labour' that did not in fact correspond with the everyday experiences of 'ordinary' workers in the post-industrial economy of 1960s New York.

In the same period, between 1963 and 1966, Morris choreographed five dance pieces that incorporated his own approaches to movement, speech and sculpture within the frame of this shared aesthetic: *Arizona*, *21.3*, *Site*, *Waterman Switch* and the less well-known work, *Check* that was performed in the auditorium of the Stockholm Museum in Sweden in 1966. These works varied a great deal but all, more or less, created forms of demonstrative tableaux that staged particular kinds of relations between the gestures of the body and sculpture, with an explicit awareness of art history. *21.3* was performed in February 1963 at the Surplus Theater in New York as an art history lecture, in fact a reading from the introduction to Erwin Panofsky's *Studies in Iconology*. Morris began his lecture with the sentence, 'Let us then try to define the distinctions between subject matter or meaning on the one hand and form on the other', while making his own movements and gestures the subject of his lecture's analysis: pointing to his action of the greeting of 'lifting one's hand' as a 'western residue of medieval chivalry', and so on. The lecture was performed as pure gesture – typical actions performed by a lecturer including the shuffling of papers or the sipping of water from a cup were framed as 'dance' – as he lip-synched to a recording of his own voice that occasionally, deliberately, fell out of synchronisation to indicate its fakery. In this way, the capacity of recording technology was incorporated into the live situation, deliberately undermining its authenticity, and the emphasis on live theatre's 'presence' that was a key to much performance of this period.

Site, performed in March 1964, created a live tableau image of Manet's *Olympia* (played by Carolee Schneeman) as Morris 'de-constructed' a box around her to reveal her naked, deathly-white-painted body, before reconstructing and encasing her again. *Waterman Switch*, presented at both the Judson Church and the Festival of the Arts Today in Buffalo, March 1965, involved the manipulation of large rubber objects and a grey plank by dancers, performed in a characteristically 'matter-of-fact' manner, as well as a sequence in which a 'totally nude' Morris and Rainer 'clasped one another face-to-face and made a slow round trip of the floor, chaperoned by Lucinda Childs (totally dressed)'.[15] A voice-over states at one point, 'I eventually hope to have slides done of this dance so I can show them at the same time … I could of course show slides of this section while this section is playing; but that has been done.'[16] *Check* (1966) involved Morris changing all the seating for the audience during the performance's interval and positioning the performers around the edge of the seating, performing repetitive gestures using their bodies as well as props, such as flags. Whether through his attention to the iconographic significance of gestural conventions, the history of figurative painting or the capacity of photographic or other media to interrupt one's experience of 'live-ness', Morris's performances exhibited a consistent concern with testing relations between visual perception, technological mediation and the expanded physical encounter.

It is intriguing to return to the more familiar territory of Morris's sculptural practice with awareness of these experiments in choreography in mind. In parallel with his investigation of dynamic relations between body and object in these theatrical tableaux, Morris had begun making gallery installations of sculptures that closely resembled the dance props. He began to have a number of major shows at the same time: of his 'grey sculptures' (Green Gallery, 1964; Dwan Gallery, April 1966), his 'Permutation Pieces' (at the Castelli Gallery in March 1967), moving on to the open-ended 'anti-form' and process work in 1968–69. During the latter part of this period Morris began to publish his four-part 'Notes on sculpture' in *Artforum* (1966–71). It was not only the direct physical encounter with these works that was evidently important for Morris, as his writings attest, but also the implication of their own performative capacities. Morris 'staged' many works as movable elements, and his sculpture as a whole would have been understood with reference to *Column* or *Site* – boxes that literally contained and concealed live bodies. Moreover, some pieces carried implicit references to the history of their own construction, echoing the performative history contained in Morris's early work, as in *Box with the Sound of its own Making* (1961), which played a recording of the sawing, drilling and nailing that had brought it into being. The performative capacity underlying Morris's conception of his sculptures as modular units that could be placed in different configurations was highlighted by the photographs of them that were circulated at the time. As Alex Potts notes, the approximately human-scaled *L-Beams*, which were 'propped in different positions to show the situation-dependent nature of their character as objects', were 'so brilliantly posed in the photograph by Rudolph Buckhardt that later actual reconstructions seem by contrast rather lacking in substance and presence'.[17]

Clearly, a relationship between the pictorial space of the theatre tableaux – the 'fourth wall' – and the spatial experience to be had by a visitor between the four walls of the gallery situation was already being tested. As the work progressed, it became clear that the apparent 'open-ness' of his permutation, process and anti-form work, especially in the major project *Continuous Project Altered Daily*, was – as with his use of recording technologies in the live work – in fact laced through with the insertion of retrospective analyses that marked each shift via the 'progressive incorporation into a work of progressive photographs of its preceding states' and worked against its apparent spontaneity.[18] In *Continuous Project*, '[the] relationship of record to event was dramatized' to the extent that 'on the last day almost nothing was left in the empty room but the traces on the floor (a sort of reference to action painting) and the photographs of the series of stages stuck on the wall'.[19] Morris also experimented with image-recording technology as a means to mediate chains of actions. For example, his 1969 *Finch College Project* involved

> a cine camera erected in a revolving stand and set going while Morris and an assistant first set up, and then took down, in sequence, mirrors on one wall and photographic portraits on the facing wall, starting at opposite corners and going on until they overlapped … At the end the film was developed and run through a projector revolving at the same speed.[20]

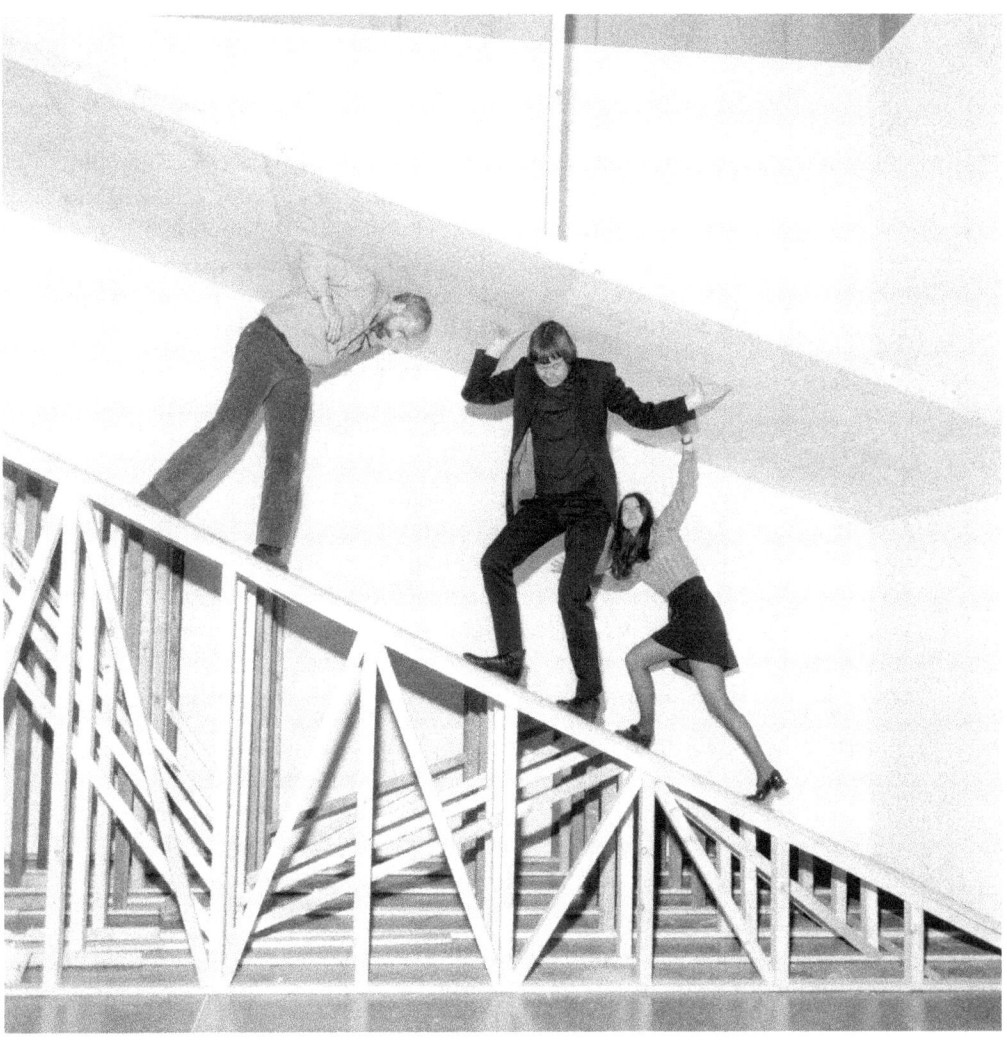

Demonstration photograph displayed at the exhibition *Robert Morris*, Tate Gallery,   **6.3**
London, 1971.

The object in Morris's work, then, was always a point of mediation that had become not 'less important, but less self-important',[21] as he put it. The key aspect of this mediation, for Morris, was in the direct encounter between object and embodied viewer who, radically, existed 'in the same space as the work'.[22] But despite the artist's apparent prioritisation of that primary encounter, the object's secondary mediations through image technologies and through theatre performance were, it seems, highly significant as regards the actual reception and understanding of his work, determining the actual nature of the encounter. His manipulation of images of the sculptural objects made via the pictorial media of theatre and photography was telling, also, in terms of his pre-emptive inherent understanding of the post-modern 'mediatization' of culture, as Philip Auslander has described it,[23] that developed from this period via absurdist investigations of 'feedback loops' in Bruce Nauman's antagonistic participation works such as *Live-Taped Video Corridor*[24] and into the technologised practices of artists such as Joan Jonas or Cindy Sherman in the late 1970s and 1980s, which put the mediation and fragmentation of action via image to poetic and critical ends. Both in terms of his concern with the creation of 'situations', and of his use of recorded media, Morris's 1971 show is, thus, positioned at the very 'crux' of Minimalism's general transition from formal modernism into post-modern site-specificity described by Hal Foster.[25]

Pictures

Morris's 1971 Tate Gallery retrospective staged perhaps his most ambitious investigation of spectator participation with his sculptural work. The major part of the exhibition comprised a three-part sequence of structures for increasingly complex interaction and manipulation. These structures included configurations of bars, beams (see figure 6.1), weights, platforms, rollers, tunnels and ramps (see figure 6.2) built from materials such as plywood, stone, steel plate and rope, and intended to effect what he described as:

> alterations of the architectural elements of passages and surfaces to the body relating to its own conditions … [T]he progression is from the manipulation of objects, to constructions which adjust to the body's presence, to situations where the body itself is manipulated. I want to provide a situation where people can become more aware of themselves and their own experience, rather than more aware of some version of my experience.[26]

Morris's emphasis was, thus, resolutely placed on creating new work that was radical within a museum context in its requirement for physical inter-action. In a letter to Michael Compton at the planning stages for his Tate Gallery exhibition, he proclaimed: 'I'd rather break my arm falling off a platform than spend an hour in detached contemplation of a Matisse.'[27] 'Time to press up against things', he insisted, to 'squeeze around, crawl over … to acknowledge that the world begins to exist at the limits of our skin and what goes on at that interface between the physical self and external conditions doesn't detach us like the detached glance.'[28]

Despite these dismissals of opticality and vision, Morris's very approach to the invitation to stage a 'retrospective' and his reversal of its conventional terms was negotiated via a strong reliance on supplementary images. Though the visitor-participant's close physical contact with his work may have appeared to collapse the act of seeing into acts of pure bodily immediacy, the presence of the set of photographs that Morris commissioned to be presented alongside the work and – equally importantly – the images of participation created within his sculptural installation, as people activated them in real time, demonstrate the importance of the externalised image plane in creating a displaced element of figuration in the work. Alongside the apparently open forms that invited interaction, Morris strictly specified that a certain amount of didactic visual information should be on display, including 'illustrative photos which demonstrate the possibilities of each set of objects or device' (see figure 6.3).[29] Carefully staged with the collaboration of members of Tate staff, these photographs showed men and women elegantly balancing on wooden beams and platforms, walking the tightrope, hauling themselves up a slanted board with the aid of ropes or manipulating a huge rolling drum by standing inside it. With their ordinary work clothes and pedestrian bearing, the staged photographs clearly – and not coincidentally, it would seem – resembled publicity and archive images such as those taken by photographer Peter Moore and others of performances at the Judson Dance Theater in the 1960s. Just as the circulated publicity shots of his sculptures communicated their modular choreographic potential, the 'demonstration photographs' and the live tableaux created in the installation combined, for viewers, to play a significant role in creating an understanding of what the work was about.

Morris's conception of the way in which these pictures would operate in relation to the work at Tate had much in common with how he had thought of his works made for the stage in the same period. In an article in the *Tulane Drama Review* in 1965, he had written explicitly of the way in which his theatrical staging of the encounter between body and object may be seen as evidence of his own ideal for the later sculptural work, as a kind of demonstration of its potential rather than a process of experimentation with the object's design:

> The objects I used [in performances] had no interest for me but were means for dealing with specific problems … by the use of objects which could be manipulated I found a situation which did not dominate my actions nor subvert my performance. … My efforts were bound up with the didactic and

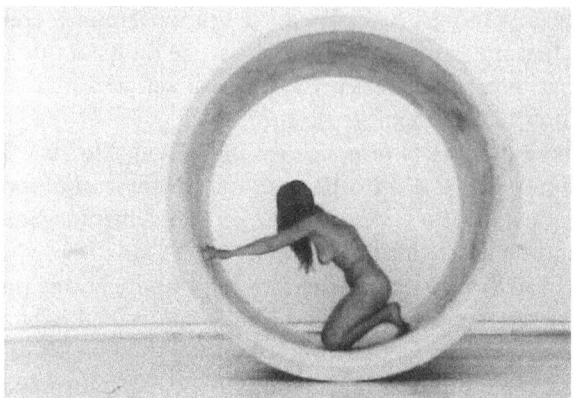

6.4   Robert Morris, *Neo-Classic*, 1971. 16 mm film displayed at the exhibition *Robert Morris*, Tate Gallery, London, 1971.

the demonstrative and were not concerned with the establishment of a set of tools by which works could be generated.[30]

The demonstration photographs at Tate seemed to be an attempt at a kind of fast-track 'mediatization' for the viewer-participant into that apparently 'ordinary' community of participation with which Morris had been involved in New York, aiming to prompt a certain kind of experience by creating a form of what one might describe as a pre-determined 'memory' for their instruction. Morris believed that by the end of the sculptural sequence in the Tate's lengthy Duveen galleries the images (and audio tapes that he had originally planned) would no longer be needed: 'This information will diminish as one approaches the back of the museum.'[31] In parallel with these prescriptive pictures, the Tate catalogue was conceived to include the major 'retrospective' element of the exhibition as a sequence of installation photographs of previous works set out in chronological order, with accompanying descriptions. Furthermore, a curious black and white film titled *Neo-Classic* that depicted a naked female model (named Jill Purse) 'interacting' with various of the sculptures was made just two days before the exhibition opened and was introduced into the installation adjacent to the actual objects (see figure 6.4).

Despite the care that was taken to underwrite the participatory work with a retrospective understanding of the nature of Morris's concerns and his prescriptive prefiguration suggesting how the physical aspects might be tackled, the exhibition was, notoriously, closed down after only five days. The decision to close it was due to what the director, Norman Reid, described in a press statement as 'the exuberant and excited behaviour of some of the visitors' which had caused minor injuries and may, it was felt, also cause 'more serious accidents.'[32] Though the exhibition's curator, Michael Compton, wrote in his explanatory letter to Morris detailing all the problems that had been encountered with the various works that, 'in spite of all this I do not regard the show as having been a failure,'[33] the show has been critically assessed in terms of a failure of the experience to meet expectations on the part of the artist and institution alike.

Jon Bird, Alex Potts and others have since analysed what may have been at stake here. Potts infers a certain solipsistic naivety as regards the 'dichotomy between private and public domains of experience'[34] – between the artist's studio environment and the open museum – at play in the artist's conception of how people might interact with his sculptural environment, pointing out that in his 1967 interview with David Sylvester, 'Morris consistently refuses to take up Sylvester's leads to reflect on how a viewer coming to his work as a relative outsider might respond to it.'[35] Bird frames the divergence between ideal and real as a part of the artist's complex investigation, in gendered terms, of 'the body as a site of turbulence and parody'; 'a metonym for the embodied subject in a tactile and libidinal relationship to the world'.[36] Potts, as did many contemporary critics writing at the time, considers the relationship between *Neo-Classic* and the sculptural objects which are featured within it as a clue to this divergence between 'real' and 'ideal'. Potts writes that '*Neo-Classic* exemplifies how the interactive works are ideally to be handled'.[37]

David Sylvester, likewise, believed that *Neo-Classic* indicated that 'Morris idealised his concept into something where the interactions between the objects and the visitors would happen in a state of contemplative calm.'[38] Reyner Banham believed that the film proposed 'a refined, gentlemanly and contemplative aestheticism'.[39] The exhibition's curator, Michael Compton, also thought its serene calm was indicative of Morris's expectation that 'people would barely be able to touch things because of the exhibited or tacit rule against touching sculpture in museums. Perhaps he even thought that we British are especially inhibited so would behave in a contemplative manner.' Though he added: 'Everything he said suggested that, but he didn't, as far as I recollect, say so outright.'[40]

If naivety came into the equation, it could perhaps have been evident in the apparently universalised phenomenological terms used by the artist and curator to discuss how participation with the sculptures might take place, while the exhibition was in preparation. Hal Foster identifies the problematic sense of the universalism underlying discussions of Minimalism at the time when the work was being made, observing that 'Minimalism's critique of the subject is initiated in abstract terms'. Foster problematises the way in which perception was considered in phenomenological terms 'as somehow before or outside history, language, sexuality and power', without regarding 'the subject as a sexed body positioned in the symbolic order of the gallery/museum as ideological apparatus'.[41] In the catalogue, Morris's 1970 *Artforum* article is quoted thus:

the entire enterprise of art making provides the ground for finding the limits and possibilities of certain kinds of behaviour … This extended profile is composed of a complex of interactions involving factors of bodily possibility, the nature of materials and physical laws, the temporal dimensions of process and perception as well as resultant static images.[42]

Clearly, also, these apparently ahistorical universals had been disseminated to the press. Reviewing the show in *The Guardian*, Caroline Tisdall wrote knowledgeably of Morris's concern to banish 'allusion' from his work; 'in the case of the Tate show this demands that you put aside any fleeting associations with playgrounds, gymnasiums or army assault courses and concentrate on the physical experience each object gives you'. Viewers were expected to concentrate on 'the sensation and awareness of gravity … and of time'.[43]

Philip Auslander and others have analysed the extent to which television has become an 'organic' 'facet of our 'mediatized environment',[44] informing our behaviour subconsciously. In Morris's show, people behaved in ways that demonstrated the extent to which their own frames of reference – games, competition, sporting activities – were inspired, not so much by the demonstration photos they had just encountered on the museum walls but, according to Michael Compton and the *Guardian* critic alike – by what they had seen on the then concurrent television footage of the (Winter) Olympic Games. Once the contemplative atmosphere of the museum had been broken, other 'rules of engagement' came into play that drew on a whole different set of cultural references.

So rather than being the pure phenomenological experiment that Morris may (or may not) have originally intended, the retrospective represented a crux – I believe – that was a contradictory, pivotal point for modernist sculpture: between Minimalism and the technologically mediated image. The relations within the exhibition between objects and images represent an axis point between an investigation of 'pure presence' as an authentic capacity for the participating spectator (certainly a concern in Morris's work of the early 1960s) and the interference of technologies in shaping experience (which artists in the 1970s and 1980s were to explore in depth). The failure, I believe, was rooted in the fact that though the image plane was clearly of importance to Morris in his own understanding of his work, the participants could not picture themselves in relation to the sculptures acting out this participation. As Caroline Tisdall noted, 'These same forms were used in Morris's performance in a balletic way. Now there is no specific performance and the same materials are there for people to manipulate themselves. The effect may still look balletic … But each individual will be too concentrated on his own physical effort and coordination to see himself in that context.'[45]

As Andrew Murphie has observed, 'through various processes of video, photography, scanning and imaging, we are increasingly coming to know our bodies as "foreign objects" viewed from outside'.[46] What complicated the potential capacity for image technology to work as both document and assist self-knowledge was the fact that the photographs Morris used in this work – unlike his process-based use of photographs to document and subsequently determine the changes in a work as it evolved through time in *Continuous Project* – were strictly predetermined and pre-staged.

Auslander distinguishes two 'types' of performance photography: the documentary and the theatrical. In the first category he places the photographers who captured the live work of Morris's peers such as Babette Mangolte and Peter Moore, whose recordings of performance are generally read as forms of 'message without a code'.[47] In the second are the performative manipulations of Yves Klein's *Leap into the Void*, of Cindy Sherman or Matthew Barney's staged tableaux, where 'the space of the document becomes the space in which the performance occurs'.[48] The problem with Morris's demonstration photos is that they tried to substitute the latter category with the former, and at the same time excluded the *actual performers* themselves from participation in their creation. Rather than acting as mirrors – the facility that a dance studio would have in order that the dancers could check their posture and form – the photographs were propositions about behaviour that lacked reciprocity with the actions of the viewer. Had the photographs somehow shifted and openly reflected the actual images that were being created of people engaged in actual activities, including the dangerous ones, would the outcome have been different? Whilst in *Continuous Project* and other works photographs were used as a form of mediation in the ongoing process of changes in the sculptural work, the Tate situation petrified the use of the photograph as mediation by presenting it as a framed fait accompli to which participants had no access.

Perhaps the failure of 'successful' participation lies here in the fact that unlike Morris and his Judson peers, who frequently reviewed documentation and critical appraisal of what they were doing, the Tate participants had no way to see themselves. Without the self-consciousness that is literally provided as feedback by the image, the ideal of the body–object relationship becomes threateningly unsteady. How different the project might have been today, visited by people with cameras on their mobile phones.[49] Michael Fried's criticism of Morris recognised theatre's need for an audience in his anxiety that 'it exists for one – in a way the other arts do not', observing that 'literalist work depends on the beholder, is incomplete without him, it has been waiting for him. And once he is in the room the work refuses, obstinately, to let him alone'.[50] In his conception of how his work would work for its participants, Morris seemingly failed to recognise the doubling of the 'beholder's role' that its framing within the museum would generate. The active 'beholder' who completed the literalist structures by participating with them would in fact provide an ideal image of the work to another beholder looking on from a position outside the participatory act.

The complexly interwoven histories of theatre, photographic image, film, sculpture, and mirrors in Morris's preceding work serves to cast doubts on assumptions of a naive relationship between an image signifying 'intention' and the participatory actuality.[51] The apparent divergence between Morris's 'ideal conception' and the events that occurred is muddied, I believe, by the conflation of his didactic photographs (theatre posed as documentary) (see figure 6.3) and his film, *Neo-Classic* (see figure 6.4). Whilst the photographs were clearly intended, from the beginning of the exhibition's conception, as demonstration pieces with the intention of directing or prompting a certain kind of visitor experience, I propose that rather than serving as evidence of naive idealism on the part of the artist, *Neo-Classic* critically pre-empted the inevitable clash of interests that was played out as people interacted with the work within the heavily loaded environment of the European museum. While Morris's conception of the body as universalised, unmarked and 'ordinary' did indeed prioritise what Edward Lucie-Smith identified as the 'physical aristocracy of the young fit male',[52] the chosen image of a nude female serenely encountering his works cannot have been without awareness of its exaggerat-edly idealised (Neo-classical) implications. If his demonstration photographs of idealised interaction with his sculptural props were, as I believe, heavily inflected by his involvement within the particular community of the Judson dance performances, which created a kind of 'blueprint' for relations between body and object, his critique of the institutional setting for this work evident in *Neo-Classic* was undoubtedly, in part, a product of his engagement with the politics of Judson participants Carolee Schneeman or Yvonne Rainer's proto-feminist attitudes. *Site*, in any case, had made explicit his own awareness of the politics of gender representation in art history.

The space of the museum, as he no doubt encountered it afresh on arriving to make and install the show, far from offering an 'ordinary' or 'neutral' situation for a purely phenomenological encounter that paid attention to light, space and shape, was heavily loaded with the elitist traditions of classical painting, neo-classical architecture and a certain atmosphere of 'museum behaviour'. It was a long way from the warehouse, church hall or loft spaces of the Downtown New York scene. As the author of *Site*, *21.3* or *Waterman Switch*, Morris had already shown himself to be an artist acutely aware of iconography and art historical convention as regards gesture, gender, physical signification. *Neo-Classic* was, I believe, part-pastiche, part-lament, created in tandem with Morris's *own* actual encounter with the site in which his work was to be on show; a piece that operated in a manner deliberately at odds with the original aims for which the demonstration photographs were conceived, as evidence of the particular antagonisms at stake in creating this kind of contemporary exhibition situation within a conventional museum. In other words, the film seems to have been intended not, as the photographs were, as a useable demonstration but as a performative work of representation, inserted as an asymmetrical equivalent to the paintings and sculptures that would have been on show in the museum at that time. While the plywood sculptures and participatory planks, ropes, pipes and beams were dismantled and recycled, according to the artist's wishes, back into the material economy, *Neo-Classic* survives as an indigestible remnant of the exhibition that has been misread as a document or statement of intent. It seems, rather, to be a curious, hallucinatory vision, barbed with latent critique.

Notes

1 Robert Morris, 'Notes on sculpture, part 1' (1966), in Gregory Battcock (ed.), *Minimal Art: A Critical Anthology* (New York: Dutton, 1968), p. 224.
2 Ibid., p. 231.
3 Forti and Rainer were involved in Anna Halprin's Dancers Workshop Co., founded in 1955, as well as with dancer Trisha Brown and composer La Monte Young. See Thomas Crow, *The Rise of the Sixties: American and European Art in the Era of Dissent 1955–69* (London: Weidenfeld & Nicolson, 1996), p. 123. Morris and Forti later began their own workshop in San Francisco, which evolved from Forti's experience of, and dissatisfaction with, Halprin's teaching.
4 Carl Andre's *Styrofoam Beam* is listed among the props used in Yvonne Rainer's 1967 performance titled *Carriage Discreteness*, which was presented as a part of *9 Evenings of Theatre and Engineering*, a series of theatre, dance, music and performances at the New York 69th Regiment Armory in 1966. See Rainer's annotated plan for the event, held in Yvonne Rainer archive at the Getty Research Institute Library. The other nine artists included in the series were: Robert Rauschenberg, John Cage, David Tudor, Deborah Hay, Robert Whitman, Steve Paxton, Alex Hay, Lucinda Childs and Öyvind Fahlström.
5 Crow, *The Rise of the Sixties*, p. 125.
6 These details are recalled by Yvonne Rainer in her autobiography, *Feelings are Facts* (Cambridge: MIT Press, 2006), p. 196.
7 Crow, *The Rise of the Sixties*, p. 125.
8 Rainer details this episode in *Feelings are Facts*, p. 235.
9 Rainer notes that he 'cut his lip in rehearsal'. Ibid.
10 See 'A quasi survey of some "minimalist" tendencies in the quantitative, minimal dance activity, midst the plethora, or an analysis of Trio A', in Battcock (ed.), *Minimal Art*, pp. 263–73, and *Work 1961–1973* (Halifax: Nova Scotia School of Art and Design Press, 1974).
11 Crow, *The Rise of the Sixties*, p. 125.
12 Sally Banes, *Democracy's Body: Judson Dance Theater 1962–64* (Durham and London: Duke University Press), 1993, p. 125.

13 Ibid.

14 Personal photographs of Rainer and Morris are kept in the Yvonne Rainer archive at the Getty Research Institute Library.

15 Review of *Waterman Switch* at the Judson Church, March 1965, in *Dance Magazine* (May 1965), 64.

16 The video documentation of the performances is held in the Jerome Robbins Dance Division of the New York Public Library, Lincoln Center, New York.

17 Alex Potts, *The Sculptural Imagination: Figurative, Modernist, Minimalist* (New Haven and London: Yale University Press, 2000), p. 240.

18 Michael Compton, 'Box with the sound of its own making', in Michael Compton and David Sylvester (eds), *Robert Morris* (London: Tate, 1971), p. 11.

19 Robert Morris cited in Compton and Sylvester (eds), *Robert Morris*, p. 115.

20 Ibid.

21 Robert Morris, 'Notes on sculpture, part 1', p. 222.

22 Ibid., p. 231.

23 Philip Auslander, 'Postmodern culture as mediatized culture', in *Presence and Resistance* (Ann Arbor: University of Michigan Press, 1992).

24 For a discussion of this work, see Chapter 8.

25 See Hal Foster, 'The crux of Minimalism', *The Return of the Real* (Cambridge and London: MIT Press), pp. 35–69.

26 Robert Morris, letter to Michael Compton, 5 March 1971. Tate Gallery archive.

27 Robert Morris, letter to Michael Compton, 19 January 1971. Tate Gallery archive.

28 Ibid.

29 Morris, letter to Michael Compton, 5 March 1971.

30 Robert Morris, 'Notes on dance', *Tulane Drama Review* (Winter 1965), 180.

31 Robert Morris, letter to Michael Compton, 5 March 1971.

32 Press Announcement for the Robert Morris exhibition by Sir Norman Reid, 7 May 1971. Tate Gallery archive.

33 Michael Compton, letter to Robert Morris, 13 May 1971, p. 4. Tate Gallery archive.

34 Potts, *The Sculptural Imagination*, p. 255.

35 Ibid., p. 242.

36 Jon Bird, 'Minding the body: Robert Morris's 1971 Tate Gallery retrospective', in Jon Bird and Michael Newman (eds), *Rewriting Conceptual Art* (London: Reaktion, 1999), p. 106.

37 Potts, *The Sculptural Imagination*, p. 249.

38 Cited by Bird, 'Minding the body', p. 88.

39 Reyner Banham, 'It was SRO – and a disaster', *New York Times* (23 May 1971). Tate Gallery archive.

40 Interview with David Sylvester for 'Tate Extra', published as part of *Tate: The Art Magazine*, supplement to 12 (Summer 1997), n. p.

41 Foster, 'The crux of Minimalism', p. 43.

42 Robert Morris, 'Some notes on the phenomenology of making', *Artforum* (April 1970), quoted in Compton and Sylvester (eds), *Robert Morris*, p. 115.

43 Caroline Tisdall, 'Robert Morris', *The Guardian* (28 April 1971). Tate Gallery archive.

44 Philip Auslander, *Liveness: Performance in a Mediatized Culture* (London and New York: Routledge, 1999), p. 2.

45 Tisdall, 'Robert Morris'.

46 Andrew Murphie, 'Negotiating presence: performance and new technologies', reproduced in Philip Auslander (ed.), *Performance: Critical Concepts in Literary and Cultural Studies* (London and New York: Routledge, 2003), p. 351.

47 Philip Auslander, 'On the performativity of performance documentation', in Barbara Clausen (ed.), *After the Act* (Vienna: MUMOK, 2007), p. 22.

48 Ibid., pp. 23–4.

49 The example of creative spectator participation at Tate reached its peak with Olafur Eliasson's 2003 Turbine Hall installation, largely due to the fact that it had a mirrored ceiling in which people could watch themselves forming groups, shapes, choreographies, even words.

50 Michael Fried, *Art and Objecthood: Collected Writings* (Chicago: University of Chicago Press, 1998), p. 163.

51 Morris had, after all, long been fascinated by the mirror in works such as his *Mirrored Cubes*, of which Annette Michelson said 'the physical space of a perception was perceived as the mental space of paradox'. Annette Michelson, 'Robert Morris: an aesthetics of transgression', in *Robert Morris* (Washington: Corcoran Gallery of Art, 1969), p. 35.

52 Edward Lucie-Smith, 'Robert Morris', *The Times* (28 April 1971). Tate Gallery archive. The reviewer shows his own rather than Morris's prejudices here as most of Morris's collaborators were of course young, fit women.

7

Marina Abramović: approaching zero

Frazer Ward

> The experience I drew from this piece was that in your own performances you can go very far, but if you leave decisions to the public, you can be killed.[1]

Marina Abramović, a Yugoslav artist born in Belgrade in 1946 and now based in Amsterdam and New York, began making performances in the late 1960s. Abramović concentrated on individual performances (along with video and film) from 1973 to 1976, and then in 1976 she began a partnership with Uwe Laysiepen (Ulay/Abramović), which lasted until 1988. Since then she has worked on her own again, in various media: relatively rarely among those artists who achieved some prominence for it in the 1970s, she continues to do performance work.

The work on which this chapter focuses, *Rhythm 0*, was the last in a series of individual performances made in 1973 and 1974 that was concerned with capacities and limits. Characteristically, a particular strand of performance work at that time tended to be concerned with the capacities and limits of the body, as in the instance of Vito Acconci's brute, empirical tests of physical parameters. Tactics used by artists involved in these investigations included the setting up of risk situations, endurance tests, and various forms of training exercises. For American artists, at least, for whom phenomenology had been introduced into aesthetic discourse with Minimalism, the interest in the body broadened, to take in questions of the relations between body and subjectivity, and of the limits and contingency of subjectivity.

In relation to this, Abramović's *Rhythm* series looks to have been particularly concerned with the status of agency; in different ways, the five performances in the series put pressure on any presumed identity between agency and subjectivity, or agency and activity. They did so without reference to depth psychology, and I would suggest that they tend to be anti-psychological, in so far as they are concerned with the continuity between conscious and unconscious states, and are not concerned with motivations for, or explanations of, individual behaviour. When Abramović's agency exceeds her conscious control, at least during the performances, this is not to be attributed to the actions of the unconscious in any psychoanalytical sense: if Abramović speaks of her work in terms of preparing the mind to reach some higher consciousness, her position is anti-rationalist and closer to a Zen view that emphasises being 'in the moment', rather than any causal or therapeutic model.[2] Of course, there is an intentional framework: Abramović herself set up these situations, in which her agency was to be surrendered or transformed; and the works may rely on or manipulate patterns of behaviour, but, even so, the outcomes were not predictable.

The first work in the series was *Rhythm 10* (1973). In the initial performance at the Edinburgh Festival, Abramović recorded herself stabbing between the fingers of her left hand, as fast as she could, with each of ten knives in turn, changing knives each time she cut herself. She then rewound the tape and played it back, while reperforming the action to the rhythm of the first part. Abramović claims to have cut herself in the same places, and has written that in this performance, 'the mistakes of time past and time present are synchronised'.[3] Presumably, if you practised at this, you might improve, both at missing your fingers, and in your ability to reproduce the initial rhythm. Except, however, that if you got really good at missing, you might actually disable the work (there would be nothing to repeat): which is to say that in Abramović's farcical repetition, history is bound to error. (But then, as we shall see, perhaps performance more generally puts in play effects which are to do with error and memory.) Whether or not Abramović actually cut herself in the same places is less important than the fact that – however wilfully – she subjected her activity to an anterior scheme (or rhythm), over which she had limited control.

If we view the series as a developing sequence (risking the benefits of hindsight), perhaps she still had too much control. *Rhythm 5*, the second work in the series, was performed in Belgrade in 1974. Abramović constructed a five-pointed star of wood shavings within a wooden frame, the shavings soaked in gasoline. Ritualistically, Abramović lit the star, walked around it, cut her hair, fingernails and toenails and threw them into the points of the star, then entered the space in the centre and lay down. Her intention was simply to lie there until the star burned out, which might have been to enact a relatively straightforward, passively sacrificial gesture. However, a five-pointed red star was the dominant symbol of Tito's Yugoslavia, and a native has impressed upon me its everyday importance and ubiquity. Given that, *Rhythm 5* might be seen as a political provocation, an aestheticised flag-burning; or else, Abramović might have been pointing to, or participating in, and/or enacting her victimisation by – to borrow the words of my informant – 'the fanaticism of the red star'.[4] Or, given her sacrificial gesture, when the fire had burned out, Abramović might have emerged, as it were, ritually purified.

Whether a critical provocation or an attempt at transcendence, *Rhythm 5*, in its original formulation, appears as a risky encounter with history, in which Abramović's behaviour was to some degree given over to the local historical conditions unavoidably symbolised by that star. In the event, however, the outcome was not predictable: the burning gasoline apparently consumed the oxygen in the space, and Abramović passed out. When flames touched her leg and she still did not move, two members of the audience went and lifted her out. In shifting beyond Abramović's intention, *Rhythm 5* became more complicated: her survival became less an arguably tendentious aestheticised provocation or ritualised transcendence, and more a matter of urgency, which required audience members to choose whether to intervene. Metaphorically as well as actually, the performance was no longer constrained by the framework of the star: to press the work a little, here one might speculate about the formation of a public, founded in Abramović's failure to anticipate what would happen, which refused to respect the star as a barrier.

In terms of the internal development of the *Rhythm* series, *Rhythm 5* was important because it prompted Abramović to ask 'how to use my body in and out of consciousness without interrupting the performance'.[5] Her first attempt at this was *Rhythm 2* (Zagreb, 1974), in which she first took a drug usually given to catatonic patients to make them move, then, after the effects of that had worn off, a drug given to schizophrenic patients to calm them down. In Abramović's account of Part I, her muscles contracted wildly until she lost control of them: 'Consciously I am very aware of what is going on but I can't control my body.' In Part II, she first felt cold and then completely lost consciousness, 'forgetting who and where I am'. The performance finished when the medication lost its effect, and Abramović gives the time period as six hours.[6]

That you might watch someone forget herself seems potentially not uninteresting, but it is not clear how you would know what you were watching. So *Rhythm 2* seems rather too formulaic (at worst, stunt-like). The idea of performance and agency exceeding consciousness is more precisely communicated – after the fact, at least – in relation to *Rhythm 4* (Milan, 1974). In one room, Abramović approached a high-pressure air blower; in another room the audience saw a video monitor, focused on her face without the blower. As she bent over the blower, Abramović passed out (again), but, she writes: 'this does not interrupt the performance. After falling over sideways the blower continues to change and move my face … [T]he performance lasts 3 more minutes, during which the public are unaware of my state.' She concludes: 'In the performance I succeeded in using my body in and out of consciousness without any interruption.'[7] Here, I think, there is a link between Abramović's preservation of intention and the manipulation of the viewers, who are disallowed from seeing exactly what is happening (unusually, in Abramović's work), and presumed not to know what they are looking at, while watching its representation. In *Rhythm 4*, almost as if correcting the interruption of *Rhythm 5*, Abramović prevented any intervention by viewers, but at the cost of a live audience.

According to the cumulative logic to the series, *Rhythm 0*, which Abramović describes as having concluded her 'research on the body when conscious and unconscious,'[8] established, or at least represented, the continuity between consciousness and unconsciousness by a different method, an extraordinary and paradoxical effort of will (roughly, the willed abandonment of will). And it more or less demanded the intervention of the audience. *Rhythm 0* was performed in a gallery in Naples in 1974. In the gallery, viewers, or visitors, found a table covered with a white cloth, on which were arrayed a series of objects (figure 7.1). Abramović has described the work as follows:

> Instructions.
> There are 72 objects on the table that one can use on me as desired.
> Performance.
> I am the object.
> During this period I take full responsibility.
> *Duration*: 6 hours (8 pm – 2 am).[9]

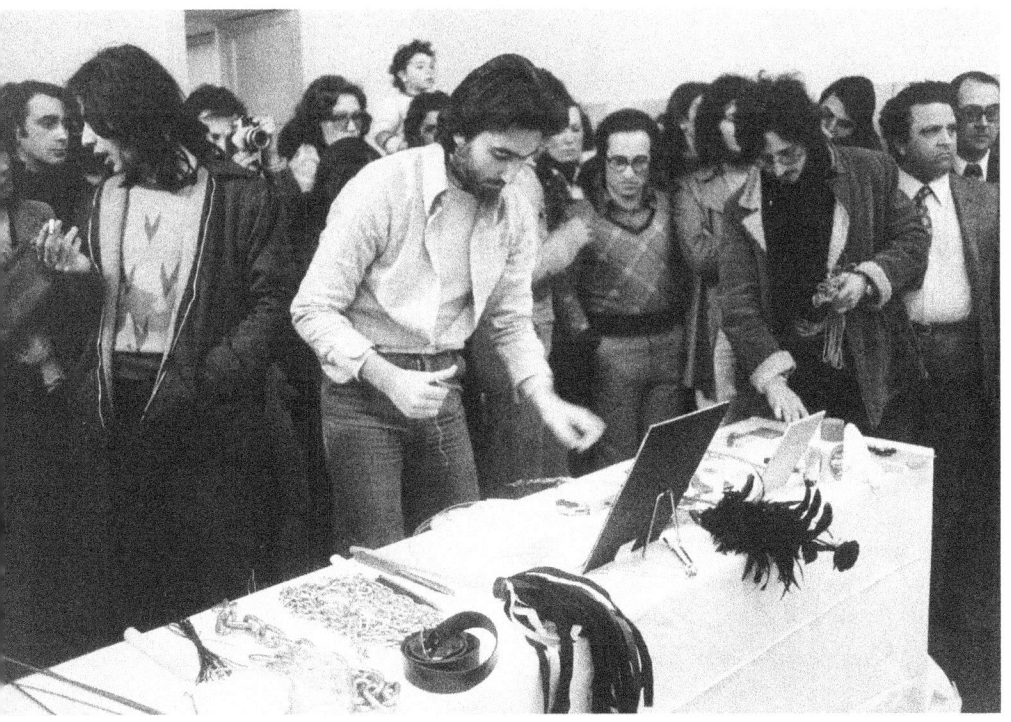

Marina Abramović, *Rhythm 0*, Studio Morra, Naples, 1974.   **7.1**

What happened in broad terms seems clear, but it is necessary to mention discrepancies among descriptions of the work: subsequently, Abramović herself has provided another account that adds 'There are objects for pain, objects for pleasure' to the instructions, and specifically mentions the 'gun with one bullet'.[10] Perhaps this is not a crucial change, because in any case it seems that it must have been clear that the objects suggested a range of uses. In two different texts, Thomas McEvilley writes that the gallery director announced to the audience that Abramović would remain completely passive, for six hours. Paul Schimmel has borrowed this description, describing the predetermined length as a Cagean strategy giving a nonlinear event a beginning and an end. In the compendium *The Artist's Body*, edited by Tracey Warr, no mention is made of duration, and we are told that the instructions took the form of a text on the wall;[11] and, in relation to the work's duration, RoseLee Goldberg, Warr and McEvilley have written that the work ended, not because the preset time ran out but because part of the audience 'put a stop to it', 'halted it', or declared it over.[12]

The question of announcement or text does not seem especially important, although a spoken announcement interpellating the people there as participants might have focused or shaped the group more than having them find and read a text, individually. Abramović herself is clear as to duration: 'After six hours, at 2 in the morning, I stopped, because this was exactly my decision: six hours.'[13] It may remain a significant question whether or not critics understood that there was a predetermined duration. (McEvilley has two contradictory versions, in one of which, 'perilously, Marina completed the six hours'.)[14] It is not clear whether any of these critics were present at *Rhythm 0*. Most, clearly, were not. But such discrepancies, especially either on the part of the artist or in the face of the artist's own recollections, point to a methodological issue in dealing with performance art. Broadly, I would describe this as the after-the-factness of performance. There is one tendency in the history of performance art that says, in effect, that you had to be there. Hence, for instance, the title of RoseLee Goldberg's essay, 'Here and now'. But of course, hardly anyone ever was, there and then, so that a complex set of relations is put into play, between an event that happened in a particular place and time, and its subsequent mediation, not only in photography, film or video (the status of the 'document' has been extensively discussed),[15] but also in description and memory. So, to the extent that performances, like other relatively ephemeral practices, generate a community of memory (whether or not that is even the memory of people who were present), they may also generate a community of error. Clearly, performances themselves become screens onto which people project, just as much as the body of the artist in performance.

Bearing this qualification regarding memory and error in mind, the most detailed description of what happened comes from McEvilley (and I suspect that his description tends to be recycled by other commentators):

> It began tamely. Someone turned her around. Someone thrust her arm into the air. Someone touched her somewhat intimately. The Neapolitan night began to heat up. In the third hour all her clothes were cut from her with razor blades. In the fourth hour the same blades began to explore her skin. Her throat was slashed so someone could suck her blood. Various minor sexual assaults were carried out on her body. She was so committed to the piece that she would not have resisted rape or murder. Faced with her abdication of will, with its implied collapse of human psychology, a protective group began to define itself in the audience. When a loaded gun was thrust to Marina's head and her own finger was being worked around the trigger, a fight broke out between the audience factions.[16]

McEvilley made an important and problematic addition to this in a subsequent essay, noting that the audience was comprised of 'a random crowd brought in off the street, along with some art world aficionados', and that the event was declared over, 'when the art world constituency rebelled against the aggressive outsiders'.[17] Perhaps this is true, but it is not a division to be accepted without better evidence: there are enough instances in the history of performance in which specialist audiences have taken aggressive roles or not intervened in other ways, or in which non-art viewers have rescued artists, that this certainly should not be taken for granted.

A brief sketch of the critical response to *Rhythm 0* shows what is available for consideration. McEvilley describes it as 'a classic of passive provocation', and Goldberg sees it as an exercise in 'passive aggression'. Chrissie Iles relates it to Duchamp – the body as ready-made – and, like Schimmel, to Cage, via its passivity. More substantively, Kathy O'Dell, while not addressing this work in particular, discusses similar works in terms of an idea of masochism derived from Gilles Deleuze's *Coldness and Cruelty*, with its emphasis on the 'masochistic contract'. Writing about Chris Burden's *Shoot* (1971), for instance, she says:

> Each of the individuals involved, therefore, agreed to tacit or specified terms of a 'contract' with the artist … [T]he crucial implication of such masochistic performances concerns the everyday agreements – or contracts – that we all make with others but that may not be in our own best interests.[18]

The effect of this, for O'Dell, is to reveal the alienation bound up with such everyday agreements. Generally, the 'masochistic' artists of the 1970s, 'wanted to reactivate a meeting of the minds, specifically in the form of a negotiation of differences between individuals or negotiation among the various identities inherent in one's own being'.[19] In a similar vein, Kristine Stiles has written, regarding so-called 'masochistic' performances: 'While certainly expressing the inversion of external suffering back on the self, they were accomplished neither for the sake of personalised erotic pleasure or desire, but as vital culturally shared communications between the artists and tiny groups of individuals partaking in the context and experiences metaphorically enacted and metonymically shared.'[20] More generally still, Amelia Jones has written that the 'artist's body has functioned as a kind of "resistance to a power" in relation to the body itself through its performance as socially determined and determining.'[21]

It is clear that *Rhythm 0* depends on a form of passivity, and in the perform-ance art of the period passivity often appears provocative or aggressive, as it stymies and frustrates audience expectations. Abramović has avowed an interest in Cage. But the body cannot be a ready-made, to the extent that it cannot be separated from a subject and cannot quite be an object. (As Chris Burden once observed of the demands he placed on a gallery director with one of his own passive pieces, 'I wanted to force him to deal with me by presenting myself as an object. But I'm not an object, so there'd be this moral dilemma.')[22] Rather, the body, as the quote from Jones suggests, is better regarded as a process.

I remain unconvinced by masochism and the masochistic contract as explanatory devices: first, because a work like *Rhythm 0* seems to me to rely on a disavowal of psychology; second, because the outcome was not predeter-mined to involve pain; third, because the idea of a contract does not account for the manipulation of the audience, and fourth, because if its end result is a 'meeting of the minds' or 'vital culturally shared communication', then it seems to me to misunderstand the nature and perhaps the radicality of avant-garde modelling of experience. On the contrary, Abramović's passivity might represent a pointed resistance to the very idea of shared communication.

To move toward a different interpretation: *Rhythm 0* might seem at first to have owed something to the passivity and risk involved in works like Yoko Ono's *Cut Piece* (1964) (see figure 12.1), in which Ono allowed audience members, one by one, to cut off her clothes with a pair of scissors, and Burden's *Shoot*, in which he was shot in the arm by a friend, in front of a small audience.[23] What differentiates it from the earlier works is that it was struc-tured by Abramović's extraordinary willed inertia, her refusal or reservation of private subjective interiority, and by time, whether predetermined or open-ended (see figure 7.2). Whatever was to happen during those six hours was evidently far less precisely imagined or organised than the possibilities posed by Ono's scissors, or by Burden's very specific activity. I think it is very impor-tant that the objects on the table were not *only* dangerous or threatening. As Abramović's own (mis?)remembrance makes clear, they were 'objects for pleasure as well as pain' – including flowers, soap, cake and olive oil, as well as a gun, whip, axe and chains.[24] So the aggression toward Abramović and the violence that developed would seem not to have been the only possible

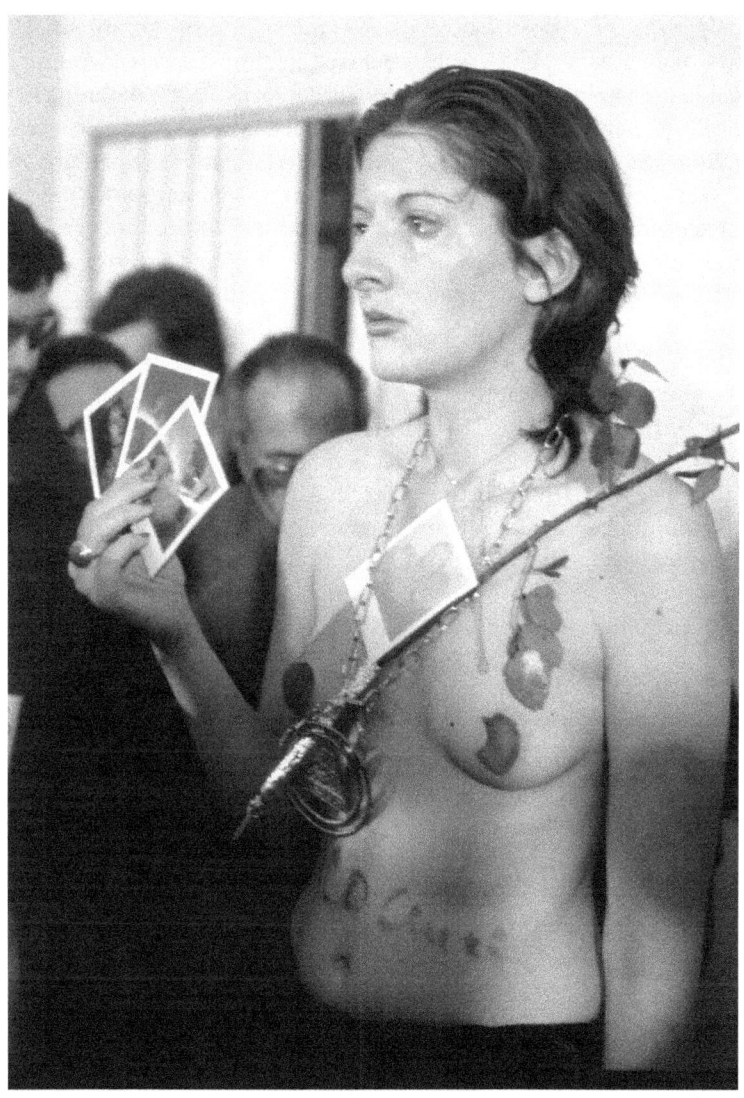

Marina Abramović, *Rhythm 0*, Studio Morra, Naples, 1974.   **7.2**

outcome (although it should be noted that photographs of other works in
the series on the walls of the space might have affected what happened).[25] It
seems to me that it is possible to imagine another version in which Abramović
is tickled or massaged or fed cake for six hours, or one in which audience
members enact their own dramas in front of her (even if the work did not
court such a response). In that regard, *Rhythm 0* might have its public as a
participatory construction. But what actually happened was that it generated

an amalgam of the exposure of gendered fantasy, and the adumbration in the negative of an ethical public realm. It did so in almost as aversive a form as it is possible to imagine, generating a crudely contestatory public arena in which violence was met with violence, as the audience factionalised.[26]

Rhythm 0 suggests a question, one that is particularly pertinent for women, in the face of sexual violence: what, if anything, guarantees whatever sense you have of the integrity of your body as private? Is it the state, and its laws? The body is a kind of mobile border between public and private: we assume a kind of 'ownership' of our bodies and their capacities, even though we must recognise that this is not entirely true, or not always the case. In *Rhythm 0*, Abramović effectively declared her body to be, if not public, then not private. That is, she gave up the normative indicators of ownership of her body, so that the normal or normative distinction between public and private did not apply. She undid the binding between property *and* subjectivity, and the public/private split. This is what is terrifying about the performance. If my body is not mine, if it is not my property, whose is it? And where am 'I', then? The effect of a woman, particularly, giving up this – in any case, fictional – relationship to her body was to expose the gendered and pathological effects – or, the pathologically gendered effects – of abandoning the public/private distinction. In the face of the pathological effects of Abramović's abandoning that split, what evidently happened was that some people literally fought to reassert that distinction, as if to say that those six hours of art could not take place beyond that other fiction.

It is possible to take this a little further. The general claim I would make about works by artists like Abramović, Ono and Burden is that they established situations in which viewers had to decide what to do; Ono's *Cut Piece* perhaps makes it clearest that that decision might take one into a public arena (people who decided to go and use the scissors had to walk up onto the stage), but that is in place in *Rhythm 0*, too; whatever you did, you did in front of, if also within, an audience. Your actions, too, were available for judgement (if also encouragement); in fact, your actions were at least as available for judgement as Abramović's (and perhaps that was intolerable to some of the people there). And viewers of the work's documentation, after the fact, may be prompted to think about what they might have done, in that situation (another form of a community of error, perhaps). So if *Rhythm 0* did not establish a kind of ethical testing zone, the situation was at least traversed by ethical questions. And as Abramović's description suggests, these were not to be separated from questions of individual desire: 'There are 72 objects on the table that *one* can use on me as *desired*.' Any question of the ethics of desire is put in play and mediated by Abramović's willed abandonment of will.

Iles remarks that Abramović 'operated like a mirror onto which the public projected themselves. The three main roles they constructed for her were

Madonna, mother and whore.'[27] Perhaps this description should be inverted, to suggest instead that viewers *failed* to see themselves reflected: Abramović became a projective screen, not a mirror. And if Iles is right, Madonna and whore are figures bound up with overdetermined systems of representation of women and familiar discourses of desire. More to the point, however, audience members' need to 'construct roles' for Abramović, to name her or to call her something, one way or another, speaks to the connection between ethics and recognition claims. O'Dell touched on this, in her remarks about the negotiation of differences between individuals. But here we would have to revise or make a little more explicit the everyday encounter with ethics, asking something like: What should I do, in this situation, in relation to this other, among these others?

What I am referring to here is a familiar contention that, in order to behave ethically, one must recognise and respect the difference of the other. As a matter of fact, what usually 'requires recognition is a group-specific cultural identity' (such that the politics of recognition comes to mean 'identity politics').[28] In relation to this, what becomes so interesting about *Rhythm 0* is Abramović's resolute refusal of any such group-specific identity, her refusal to *be* identified. Arguably, this is what was intolerable to those members of the audience who became aggressive. In case there is a presumption that it was male audience members who became aggressive, Abramović's gloss is fascinating: 'It was a very strange situation in Naples: women did very little, were hardly active, but were telling men what to do.'[29]

One way to interpret what happened in *Rhythm 0* is to say that Abramović became subject to promiscuous identification, including, if we follow Iles, identification as Madonna and whore, which is to say that she was ascribed a position within a system of representation of women that serves to control difference (and desire – certainly women's desire); and, whether or not we think Iles is right, even the fact that she interprets fragments of the event in this way suggests the persistence and power of those fully spectacularised and commodified images. Yet, in her passivity, Abramović remained indifferent to these and any other positions; she refused to recognise them or to be recognised by them. So one conclusion that might be reached is that *Rhythm 0* is a hyperbolic demonstration of the construction of female subjectivity from without, or of female subjectivity as purely exterior, an imposition; a subjectivity without identity except in so far as it is defined, called something, by a group (what is more, a group internally divided over what it should be called).

Iles also writes: 'At one point someone put a mirror in her hands and wrote in lipstick on it "Io sono libero" (I am free).'[30] But Abramović gave no sign of seeing herself in this, either. Her evacuation of interiority, or of the signs of interiority, maintained equal indifference to Madonna, whore, Eros, or freedom, that is, she enacted indifference to all properties, to anything she might be called, to any and all categories she might be asked to stand for. Such an observation suggests that, as against the sometimes pious discourse of interactivity or participation, one way to think about this work is in terms derived from the philosophical critique of community in the work of Jean-Luc Nancy and Giorgio Agamben.[31] Despite their differences, what can be taken from Agamben and Nancy is the sense of community as a horizon of experience that is anything but empirical, and defined as much in the breach as in any positive way. (This underlies my earlier remarks about a community of error.) In this context, if for various audience members Abramović could be made to *stand for* this or that category, she herself refused to answer to them. She performed the refusal even to acknowledge what she was called.

In this instance, though, performance and refusal verge on the same thing – the autonomy and/or alienation of the generic or common underpinning of existence, that is, language. This is why notions of a meeting of the minds or of vital, shared communication (with their implications of communities of interest) miss the point. This is not to suggest that Abramović directs us to some idealist notion of the beyond of language to which we all belong. On the contrary, her refusal to be what she is called, the assumption of singularity in her 'indifference with respect to [any] common property',[32] which has the effect of generating the promiscuous identification that I have referred to, suggests that the one thing to which Abramović was not indifferent was the *fact* of being-called, and her alienation from that. In this regard, perhaps the effect of *Rhythm 0* was to model a subject without representable identity, a being, 'whose community', as Agamben puts it, 'is mediated not by any condition of belonging'.[33]

Notes

1 Marina Abramović, 'Body art', in *Marina* Abramović (Milan: Charta, 2002), p. 30.

2 For instance, Abramović has spoken of the extremity of her performances in terms of letting 'the danger focus you; this is the whole idea – to put you in the focus of now', in an interview with Hans-Ulrich Obrist. 'Talking with Marina Abramović, riding on the bullet train to Kitakyushu, somewhere in Japan', in Marina Abramović, *Artist Body: Performances 1969–1998* (Milan: Charta, 1998), p. 44. In the same interview, she said that 'your body and mind have to be prepared. And then the idea comes totally as a surprise, like a click, like a blip in consciousness … It is very Zen' (49), and that 'going to the non-personal space where the ego is depersonalised, is really important' (50). She spoke of her refusal of the 'frustrating rationalism of Western society' in an interview with her brother, Velimir Abramović, also in *Artist Body*, p. 403. Such remarks may lend support to the interpretation of the works as emptying out typical, affective markers of subjective interiority.

3 Abramović, *Artist Body*, p. 56.

4 My thanks to Indira Mesihovic.

5 Abramović, *Artist Body*, p. 69.

6 Ibid., p. 70.

7 Ibid., p. 76.

8 Ibid., p. 80.

9 Ibid.

10 'Instructions were: "There are seventy-two objects on the table that one can use on me as desired. I'm taking the whole responsibility for six hours. There are objects for pain, objects for pleasure." Duration was from 8 p.m. to 2 a.m. There was also the gun with one bullet so there was the possibility of being killed.' Abramović, 'Body art', p. 30. The slightly less formal syntax in this statement perhaps suggests that it represents a mix of description and remembrance.

11 See, respectively, Thomas McEvilley, 'Marina Abramović/Ulay, Ulay/Marina Abramović', *Artforum*, 22:1 (September 1983), 52 and 'The serpent in the stone', in Chrissie Iles (ed.), *Marina Abramović: Objects Performance Video Sound* (Oxford: Museum of Modern Art Oxford, 1995), p. 46; Paul Schimmel, 'Leap into the void: performance and the object', in Schimmel (ed.), *Out of Actions: Between Performance and the Object 1949–1979* (Los Angeles and London: Museum of Contemporary Art and Thames & Hudson, 1998), p. 101; Tracey Warr, 'Works', in Warr (ed.), *The Artist's Body* (London: Phaidon, 2000), p. 124.

12 RoseLee Goldberg, 'Here and now', in Iles (ed.), *Marina Abramović*, p. 11; Warr, 'Works', p. 124; McEvilley, 'The serpent in the stone', p. 46.

13 Abramović, 'Body art', p. 30.

14 McEvilley, 'Marina Abramović/Ulay', 52.

15 See, for instance, Philip Auslander, *Liveness: Performance in a Mediatized Culture* (London and New York: Routledge, 1999); Amelia Jones, '"Presence" in absentia: experiencing performance as documentation', *Art Journal*, 56:4 (Winter 1997), 11–18; Peggy Phelan, *Unmasked: The Politics of Performance* (London and New York: Routledge, 1993).

16 McEvilley, 'Marina Abramović/Ulay', 52. This is confirmed to a degree by Abramović's recollection: 'I was really violated: they cut my clothes, they put the thorns of the roses in my stomach, one person put the gun in my head and then another one took it away. It was a very tense and aggressive situation.' 'Body art', p. 30.

17 McEvilley, 'The serpent in the stone', p. 46.

18 Kathy O'Dell, *Contract with the Skin* (Minneapolis: University of Minnesota Press, 1998), p. 2.

19 Ibid., p. 63.

20 Kristine Stiles, 'Uncorrupted joy: international art actions', in Schimmel (ed.), *Out of Actions*, p. 306.

21 Amelia Jones, 'Survey', in Warr (ed.), *The Artist's Body*, p. 22.

22 Jim Moisan, 'Border crossing: interview with Chris Burden', *High Performance*, 2:1 (March 1979), 6.

23 For a detailed account of *Cut Piece*, see Julia Bryan-Wilson, 'Remembering Yoko Ono's *Cut Piece*', *Oxford Art Journal*, 26.1 (2003), 99–123; on *Shoot*, see my 'Gray zone: watching *Shoot*', *October*, 95 (Winter 2001), 115–30.

24 Abramović, *Artist Body*, p. 81.

25 Thanks to Sharon Corwin for this point. Images of *Rhythm 0* in *Artist Body* show what look like large-scale photographs of *Rhythm 10* (see pp. 85, 87) and *Rhythm 2* (pp. 88, 93) on the gallery walls.

26 In McEvilley's account of random and art-world factions, this effect is seen to be engineered, by presuming the hostility of the non-specialised audience.

27 Iles, 'Cleaning the mirror', in Iles (ed.), *Marina Abramović*, p. 21. This 1995 remark seems to pre-empt Abramović's own 2002 comment that the public 'projected three basic images on me: Madonna, image of the mother and image of the whore'. 'Body art', p. 30.

28 Nancy Fraser, 'Recognition without ethics?' in Marjorie Garber et al. (eds), *The Turn to Ethics* (New York: Routledge, 2000), p. 99.

29 Abramović, 'Body art', p. 30.

30 Iles, 'Cleaning the mirror', p. 22.

31 See Giorgio Agamben, *The Coming Community*, trans. M. Hardt (Minneapolis: University of Minnesota Press, 1993), and Jean-Luc Nancy, *The Inoperative Community*, trans. P. Connor et al. (Minneapolis: University of Minnesota Press, 1991).

32 Agamben, *The Coming Community*, p. 1.

33 Ibid., p. 86.

Space, body and the self in the work of Bruce Nauman   8

Amelia Jones

In the 1974 piece *Body Pressure*, a pink sheet of paper is printed in plain font with the following exhortation:

Body Pressure
Press as much of the front surface of your body (palms in or out, left or right cheek) against the wall as possible.

Press very hard and concentrate.

Form an image of yourself (suppose you had just stepped forward) on the opposite side of the wall pressing back against the wall very hard.

Press very hard and concentrate on the image pressing very hard.

(the image of pressing very hard)

Press your front surface and back surface toward each other and begin to ignore or block the thickness of the wall. (remove the wall)

Think how various parts of your body press against the wall; which parts touch and which do not.

Consider the parts of your back which press against the wall; press hard and feel how the front and back of your body press together.

Concentrate on tension in the muscles, pain where bones meet, fleshy deformations that occur under pressure; consider body hair, perspiration, odors (smells).

This may become a very erotic exercise.

The artist plays the role of directing the visitor to press her or his body into the gallery wall: the three elements involved in what we call 'art' are co-articulated in an almost violent intertwining.

Body Pressure parallels the actions in his two 1973 video pieces *Tony Sinking Into the Floor* (figure 8.1) and *Elke Allowing the Floor to Rise Up over Her, Face Up* – in the latter, you see a woman's body sprawled in a grey featureless room that seems to swallow up her body (and, in discussing the pieces, Nauman described how psychologically fraught was the experience of attempting to merge with the floor when he tried it himself).[1]

Nauman's words – like the voices, materials, bodies and architectural spaces evoked, performed and addressed in his works – function as *hinges* between two or more elements. As hinges, they bend and connect rather than dividing. They facilitate openings and intertwinings (of doors, concepts, subjects, experiences, materials) rather than discriminating one side or one thing from another. Activating these pivots across elements, then, Nauman's works produce us in relation to a range of other things and subjects (including what we perceive to be attributes of the artist himself) – elements that inhabit, surround, penetrate, envelop and otherwise saturate our experience for the moments in which we engage them.

This effect is linked to a complex and mostly subterranean tendency in French avant-garde art and philosophy of activating the body/mind complex through the production of objects that propose a relation of *hinging* that precludes the polarisation of qualities or things. Marcel Duchamp's 1927 *Door, 11 rue Larrey*, a door with two-way hinges (figure 8.2), exemplifies this tendency, as does his concept of *infra mince* (generally translated as *infra thin*). Simultaneously welcoming and sending visitors away, sweeping a full 180 degrees so that it potentially slaps against its own door frame or against the wall, the *rue Larrey* piece, which was originally installed in Duchamp's studio at this address, functions itself as a giant hinge between the 'outside' world and the 'inside' domain of artistic creativity (a domain marked with irony across Duchamp's oeuvre as essentially analogous to a site of industrialised production) – a hinge between the viewer's body and the spaces of creative

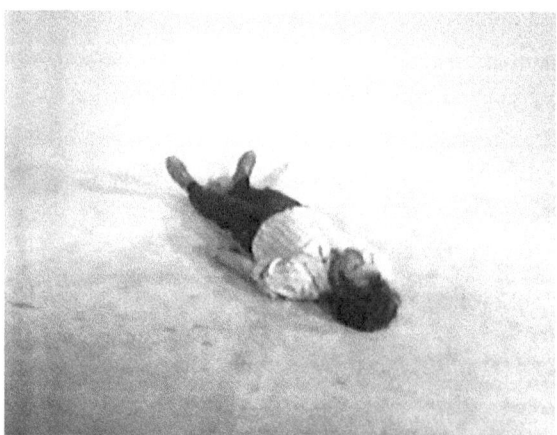

8.1   Bruce Nauman, *Tony Sinking Into the Floor, Face Up and Face Down*, 1973. Video (colour, sound), 60 minutes, to be repeated continuously.

production and display. In a sense, *Door, 11 rue Larrey* could be said to be a three-dimensional actualisation of Duchamp's concept of *infra thin*, which he developed in his notes written in the teens and collected in *A l'infinitif*, also known as the *White Box*.[2]

    Infra thin is a concept that can only be exemplified or described and not defined. Duchamp portrays it in the notes as a bodily as well as psychic

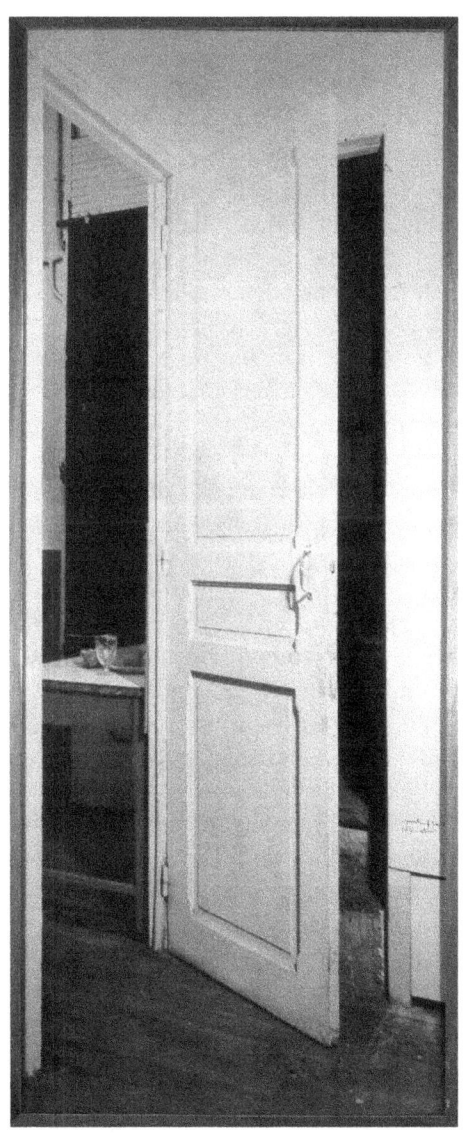

Marcel Duchamp, *Door, 11 rue Larrey, Paris*, 1927/1964. Type C print, 250 × 100.   **8.2**

phenomenon in the following way: 'the possibility is an infra thin ... The possibility implying a becoming – the passage from one to the other';[3] 'the bearers of shadow represented by all the sources of light (sun, moon, stars, candles, fire) ... work in the infra thin';[4] 'the heat of a seat (that was just vacated) is infra thin';[5] 'when the tobacco smoke also smells of the mouth which exhales it the two odors are married by infra thin';[6] 'a painting on glass viewed from the non-painted side gives an infra thin [effect]';[7] 'the (dimensional) difference between 2 objects made in a series [come from the same mould] is an infra thin when the maximum of precision is obtained.'[8]

Duchamp's infra thin is thus a *process* that implicates the passage of one possibility to another, linking the live body to the things around it through intangible signs of the body as *hinge* between presence and absence (the 'heat of a seat [that was just vacated]'), the air with the bodies that breathe it ('smoke ... [that] smells of the mouth which inhales it'), and the act of seeing and making with the space that engulfs the seeing/making body. Infra thin is the 'difference' (so infinitesimal that it is not difference at all) between two objects 'from the same mould'.

Functioning across the senses, the infra thin, like *Door, 11 rue Larrey* and like all of the spoken, visible and enacted elements of Nauman's works, operates as a hinge connecting and co-articulating rather than opposing or differentiating two (or more) bodies, spaces, concepts, or forms. As such, the infra thin offers a radical alternative to dominant oppositional modes of making sense of the world in post-Renaissance Euro-American thought. The myth of coherence promised by the most instrumentalising forms of perspectivalism (the system of logic and representation developed in the Renaissance whereby the seeing subject, situated in an optimal, centred position vis-à-vis the scene, can apprehend everything fully) and of Cartesianism (the mode of understanding the mind as transcendent and so distinct from the immanent body, developed by René Descartes in the seventeenth century) – this myth of coherence, which relies on the sustaining of oppositions, can no longer be sustained in global late capitalism.

This logic of oppositions in Cartesianism, as it became reified in modern Euro-American conceptions of the self, is also foundational to western aesthetics itself, particularly in reductive versions of Kantian aesthetics in modernist formalism. As has been extensively argued, in the art theory of British critic Roger Fry in the early twentieth century or American critic Clement Greenberg mid-century, and their followers, the complex arguments attempting to bridge the gap between human-made objects and subjects in the world articulated in Immanuel Kant's 1790 *Third Critique* are simplified such that the work of art is positioned in diametric opposition to the viewer /interpreter, who must remain 'disinterested' (not invested in a bodily way) in order for the work of art to retain its supposed universal, objective

value.[9] It is the *body* in particular, then, with its 'interested' sensual investment in the work of art, which must be suppressed for the 'objectivity' and
'transcendence' claimed by modernist formalism at its most reductive to be
sustained. For, if the viewing/interpreting subject were invested in a bodily
way in the work of art, his judgement could certainly not be claimed to be
universal, neither could he be said to be transcending his body through pure
thought – rather the relation between the subject and the work of art would
be obviously invested and so 'interested'. It is both the anxiety about the body
and the dualistic logic of this matrix of beliefs that Nauman's work compli-
cates and challenges by activating a relation of hinging. Like Duchamp's *infra
thin*, Nauman's hinging explores a way of thinking interrelations among
things, bodies, subjects and spaces without lapsing back into Cartesian and/
or perspectival logic to resecure a sense of the self as knowable and as centred
in knowledge.

Nauman's centring/decentring 'infra thin' project

Nauman's project can be viewed, then, as an extended process of exposing
and reworking the perspectivalism and Cartesian dualities built into western
aesthetics and crystallised in Euro-American modernism. In works such as
the 1972 *Floating Room: Lit from Inside,* Nauman explicitly points to the way in
which our impulse to centre ourselves, which motivates the oppositional logic
of self and other, underlies much of our defensive behaviour in the world. In
Floating Room Nauman literalises the search for coherence by encouraging the
visitor to make a congruence between the centre of his body and the centre
of the room – this congruence would be an infra thin hinge connecting the
body with architectural space. In the text advertising *Floating Room* Nauman
thus notes:

> We are trying to get to the center of some place: that is, exactly halfway between
> each pair of parts.
>
> We want to move our center (some measurable center) to coincide with such
> a point.
>
> We want to superimpose our center of gravity on this point.
>
> Save enough energy and concentration to reverse.[10]

Ultimately, as the text suggests, centring ourselves is a reversible action: in
a sense we produce spaces around us to secure our feeling of being centred.
They then produce or reinforce this feeling of wholeness. To point to the hinge
between body and space is to expose the feeling of being centred as contingent
on a production (say, of perspectivally rendered architectural space), not
inherent. *Floating Room*, which explicitly evokes our desire ('we want') to

centre ourselves in spaces and relative to others, exemplifies the way in which Nauman's continual evocation of hinges between things links up with the philosophical concepts underlying Euro-American beliefs about subjectivity: the hinge between body and space in relation to the act of centring indicates the *constructedness* of the concept of the centre.

Nauman is quite explicit about the underlying anxiety that motivates our desire to centre ourselves (an anxiety he explicitly exacerbates in installations such as *Acoustic Pressure Piece*, where the visitor experiences pressure on the body through sound waves, disorienting her or his physical body through sensory input). In discussing *Floating Room*, he further notes that visitors to the show tend to 'block out' the disorienting experience of finding themselves aggressively positioned in an architectural structure within the gallery, musing that they were blocking out this experience 'because it was, in a way, a pretty frightening thing, too. I think it has to do with fear, but it also has to do with the way we normally control space, or fill up space.'[11]

In the trapezoidal, harshly-lit yellow room of *Left or Standing*, a text describes the sense of unease produced physiologically in the visitor's body by the disconcertingly skewed space of the room. As Nauman said of *Left or Standing*, '[I am] seeking an art that puts you on an edge: it forces you into a heightened awareness of yourself and the situation. Often without you knowing what it is that you're confronting and/or experiencing. All you know is that you're being pushed into a place that you're not used to and that there's an anxiety involved in that.'[12] And, in the 1973 *Flayed Earth/Flayed Self (Skin/Sink)*, which consisted of a spiral of words spewing out from a central point on the floor, the text ends with the exhortation:

> Squirm into my mind so I can get into
> your mind your body our body …
> … Has to do with your
> ability to give up your control over space.[13]

With words, spaces, bodies and other elements Nauman disorients us – but not by splitting us in half (returning us to the oppositional logic of seeing and being seen). He disorients us as if to encourage us to relinquish ourselves to space, to embrace the hinge between our bodies and other bodies, spaces, and things – to 'give up our control over space'.

This exploration exposes to view and challenges the tendency in western patriarchy to propel oneself into the social world aggressively, to cohere oneself by sealing oneself off and projecting an illusion of wholeness, in many cases, an illusion that takes shape through the debasement of others. Drawing on the early nineteenth-century model of the 'master/slave' dialectic developed by Hegel, wherein the master needs (even produces) the slave in order to remain master and the slave needs the master to retain his known and felt identification as 'slave', twentieth-century theorists from Frantz Fanon to Simone de Beauvoir have thus pointed out how such oppositional 'othering' devices work discursively, institutionally, materially and psychologically to secure the oppression of blacks and women. As de Beauvoir puts it: 'The terms *masculine* and *feminine* are used symmetrically … as a matter of form, as on legal papers. … [T]he relation of the two sexes is … [asymmetrical but also oppositional], for man represents both the positive and the neutral … whereas woman represents only the negative …: she is the Other …'.[14] Or, in Fanon's terms, 'what is often called the black soul is a white man's artifact' and, through this othering, the black man suffers a 'corporeal malediction'.[15]

The white and/or male master projects the depraved immanence of his other, the slave, in order to prove his empowerment and his supposedly transcendent incorporeality. *This* is the fundamental opposition Nauman's works implicitly either refuse, expose, pervert or parody – an opposition that, as de Beauvoir pointed out, was never symmetrical in the first place and is now replaced by a relation of hinging that connects each side irrevocably (and in bodily and enfleshed ways) to the other. It is surely not incidental that Nauman was finding ways to create hinged interrelationships just as the women's and civil rights movements were exploding onto the scene in the United States, challenging the oppression of women and blacks and often through an equally oppositional strategy of reversal. While I am not claiming that Nauman is literally or even consciously providing a different way of imagining difference, his work effectively poses an alternative to the polarised politics of the United States around 1970.

Nauman and the self/other as hinge

In Nauman's work, relations between self and other are constructed as oppositional – they are not inherently so. A parodically exaggerated opposition between the sexes is, for example, enacted in the video installation *Violent Incident* via the heterosexual white male/female couple, who violently propel each other into antagonistic opposition. The 'violence' between two lovers (played by actors who are obviously enacting scripted roles, overtly exacerbating the apparent constructedness of the situation) develops as part of the 'threat' that each poses to the other's fantasised transcendence or wholeness. The fact that Nauman has the man and woman exchange roles in different parts of the video narratives indicates the fundamental reversibility of power: there is no *inherent* reason why women are so often disempowered in relation to men. Nauman notes that in his installations,

> My intention was to deal with the relationship of public space to private space. When you are alone, you accept the space by filling it with your presence; as

soon as someone else comes into view, you withdraw and protect yourself. *The other poses a threat, you don't want to deal with it.* The best example of this is when someone steps out of a crowded street and into a phone booth. On the one hand you go in there to get acoustic privacy and on the other hand you make yourself a public figure. It is a conflicting kind of situation. What I want to do is use the investigative polarity that exists in the tension between the public and private space and use it to create an *edge*.[16]

The other *poses a threat, you don't want to deal with it.* To open this out, Nauman explicitly notes his interest in 'creat[ing] an edge' – exposing the anxiety that motivates the construction of oppositions between self and other, public and private, body and space. The 'edge' is not a divider of one thing from its opposite but a kind of *hinge* that makes their connectedness and inter-relation evident. This is another infra thin relation.

One of Duchamp's examples of infra thin, which indicates sexual identity both as difference and as sameness, reads: 'better / than screen, because it indicates / interval (taken in one sense) and / screen (taken in another sense) – separation / has the 2 senses male and female.'[17] Male and female must be *made* separate in order for heterosexual patriarchy to sustain itself – they are not inherently oppositional.

What the construction of infra thin hinges or connectors in Nauman's work does is effectively expose the tenuousness of the subject as discrete and coherent (a construction, as noted, that can only function in an illusory way and that only by suppressing the role of the body in connecting the self to the world). Psychoanalytic theorist Parveen Adams, writing about Nauman's work, evokes Jacques Lacan's model of the gaze: 'Lacan, writing about perspective, has shown how the visual structure of the world is organised, not around an object but around a hole … When the whole of the visible world is projected (that is, the space in front of and behind the subject) there is the gap that you cannot see, between the anterior and posterior horizons.'[18]

In fact what we are really afraid of, as Nauman's comments about our fear of giving up our control over space and his ongoing efforts at positioning us in radically disorienting ways indicate, is acknowledging that we are this *hole*. We – embodied subjects located materially and psychically in space – are the gap that ruins the possibility of imagining that the world can be fully known through perspectival vision. We are the hole that ruins the fantasy that all subjects can be neatly divided into self (full, present, knowing) and other (seen, known). Adams notes: 'In kicking us out of the picture, Nauman has unraveled perspectival space. We are speaking of the creation of distance, of a noncontinuous space between the viewer and the scene. This is a distance that cannot be reduced; we cannot fill in the gap that intervenes between us and [the disorienting object].'[19] Adams's wording – this 'kicking out of the picture' – evokes aesthetics, a way of defining and describing visual art that is invested in making the positioning device of perspective invisible so that it seems 'natural' or 'true'. As Adams suggests, if we are 'kicked out' of the perspectival structure, we are profoundly disoriented, forced on some level to acknowledge our decentredness, our occupation of the world as a hole or gap.

Returning to *Body Pressure* – it proposes to the gallery visitors that they mesh themselves with the space of viewing that western aesthetics insists is a neutral or invisible frame for the art it displays (an extension of the disinterested subject attitude called for within the same model). We are told to press ourselves insistently and with vigour against the wall of the gallery. In this way, far from sustaining the invisibility required of the institutions of art within the logic of aesthetics (where artworks are seen and judged as if they have no context and are entirely 'neutral' in their presentation), the wall becomes more and more present as brute material architectural form, and a form we cannot transgress, erase, or (in fact) mesh with.

In fact, through works such as *Body Pressure* Nauman marks out the wall, potentially imagined to be (but never successfully, in fact) coextensive with the visitor's body, *as not only* not *neutral but as integral part of the work itself.* If the wall is the work of art, my body pressing into it (in an exchange he explicitly notes to have an *erotic charge*), then there is no separation between the aesthetic object and the viewer, the aesthetic object and the spatial or institutional frame that defines it as such. (And yet, of course, the pressing of the body fails to mesh with the wall – there is a lingering, stubborn, but infinitesimal difference – an infra thin separation – that defines them as distinguishable entities but not opposed.)

In western aesthetics, art is defined as both connected to the artist as maker (this is what makes it 'art', after all) and as radically *other*, as a thing that is brutely objective – an object-ness defined and secured by its placement within the architectural and institutional frame of the art gallery. As frame, the institution of the art gallery (and its activating myths and architectural supports) operates to show us what is properly art by sustaining this opposition that is simultaneously a connection. But as frame, French philosopher Jacques Derrida has noted, it also produces an irreducible split – an insurmountable *difference* – between the work of art and those who apprehend and interpret it (and thus between the maker of the work of art, who is implicated in our understanding of the work, and this work as well as between the maker and us, its interpreters).[20]

In Derrida's analysis, which focuses on the model proposed by Kant in the *Third Critique*, the institutional and discursive frames through which 'art' is defined and displayed function paradoxically both to produce this radical difference between art and those who apprehend it and to construct a *bridge* between the artist, the artwork, and the future viewers: aesthetics pivots around a simultaneous production of radical difference and attempt to bridge it.[21] And yet, as Derrida notes, this bridge itself can never fully breach the gap between self and other (the artwork and its makers and interpreters).[22] Aesthetics is a bridge or hinge and this bridge is infra thin, both marking and disavowing difference. Correlatively, the artwork both 'is' and 'isn't' the artist; it both 'is' and 'isn't' me as I engage with it. And all of these hinged (rather than fully or clearly oppositional) concepts are enacted via the *body*, the hidden or repressed factor implicit in the most basic concept of 'art'. After all, it is the body that *makes* the work; it is the body through whose senses it is experienced and interpreted or given meaning – as much as Fry, Greenberg, and their followers would rather disavow this dependence of our relationship to the object on our bodily senses, as linked through apprehension and cogitation to interpretation and value-making judgement.

Nauman's directive in *Body Pressure* is precisely posed, with great irony, as a demand that the visitor attempt to erase the gap between herself and the work (which is also the institutional wall that displays it), only to make her more acutely aware that she cannot in fact erase it. At the same time, the piece is not (in the context of Nauman's work as a whole) about this impossibility as a confirmation of radical difference – as the glance towards eroticism suggests (remember the manufactured antagonism in *Violent Incident*). It is, I am arguing, an attempt to make us see that the idea of self and other as irrevocably oppositional, an idea that we have seen is foundational to western concepts of subjectivity, is itself an impossible fiction. That is, if we assiduously follow the directives of the absent artist 'Nauman', attempting to merge with the wall of the gallery, we express the dual wish to *be* Nauman (to mesh with the wall through the words that are his work of art) and to *have* him – we act like lovers yearning to merge with the one we desire. (As Nauman states in *Body Pressure*, 'This may become a very erotic exercise.')

This points to something profound about art but also about subjectivity in general. The self and other are *not* radically different. Nor are they the same. They relate to each other via a condition, it could be said, of *infra thin* – a condition that is always already about the body as the means through which we are subjects. They smell of one another like the smoke issuing from a smoker's mouth smells of this mouth; through touch they warm each other, changing the temperature of each other's bodies; they may gaze at each other through a projective perspectival looking that, in the first instance, would function to produce the other as radically opposed, but this gazing is reversible and intertwining (as Duchamp would have it, as if through a painted glass, seen from the wrong side).[23]

In aesthetics, as I suggest above, the spectator must have nothing at stake (must be 'disinterested' in the image or object being viewed) for the aesthetic (bridging subject and object) to function.[24] And yet Nauman's *Body Pressure* is forcing us to activate ourselves physically – to perform the stake that we have in the gallery as an invisible frame defining the work of art *qua* art. And to perform the stake that we have in the artist.

Bruce Nauman's work, at its best, exaggeratedly enacts and so exposes the limits of this bridging function of the aesthetic (turning it into a flexible *hinge* rather than a fixed and inflexible *bridge*). As overtly articulated or clearly visible hinges between things, people, or concepts, Nauman's works deinstrumentalise the artist/artwork/viewer system.

As hinges, Nauman's words, spaces, bodies and other connecting elements produce links between maker, artwork, viewer that illustrate the extent to which all 'art' (by which I mean the network of human-made objects/images/concepts and the subjects, both making and viewing, they propose and imply) is about an eroticised exchange that is *never* disinterested, but highly charged and invested – an exchange that activates the infra thin connections among the artist, artwork and viewer.

Infra thin hinges

Nauman's work joins subjects and things and spaces in often ambiguous and conflicted relationships through elements that function as hinges (or infra thin membranes). In works such as *Eat Death* (1972) language becomes a hinge (rather than a divider) interconnecting the interior and exterior of the subject, the self and other. In the 1984 video *Poke in the Eye Nose Ear*, skin is activated (as in *Body Pressure*) as the hinge between the body and the world – not divider, but infra thin connector of the inside and outside of the body (think of the skin of the vaginal wall or hymen: it does not divide inside from outside as much as it indicates a passage in an infra thin way).[25] As Nauman states in a 1966 piece entitled *Codification*, which consists of a list of infra thin qualities:

1 Personal appearance and skin
2 Gestures
3 Ordinary actions such as those concerned with eating and drinking
4 Traces of activity such as footprints and material objects
5 Simple sounds – spoken and written words …[26]

Architectural space is manipulated such that it functions as a hinge between our body and the other, our body and the world. And, often in Nauman's practice architecture is extended and manipulated conceptually and spatially through videotapes of body/space actions that produce the video screen as another hinge between the artist's body/space relation and ours, as in *Slow Angle Walk*. The screen becomes another hinge, then, interrelating elements (in particular, the body of the artist and viewer/participant and space).

The body is articulated in Nauman's work as a hinge between inner feelings and outer expression, between experience and representation (between, of course, the self and other). In Nauman's world (versus the Cartesian world-view) the body *instantiates* thought and feeling, it is not in any way 'opposed' to or outside of the mind. To this extent Nauman produces an art that, overall, functions as a hinge between public and private, the interior self (of the artist, of the viewer/participant) and the exterior world. The art is not an 'external' expression of something interior – it is one way in which that interior knows and produces itself. In Maurice Merleau-Ponty's terms, it is a kind of chiasmus that joins the flesh of the artist with the flesh of the world, marking the fact that 'the body contributes more than it receives' in 'coupling with the flesh of the world' and that the reversibility that defines the flesh is 'capable of weaving relations between bodies that … will not only enlarge, but will pass definitively beyond the circle of the visible'.[27]

In the 1974 *Double Steel Cage Piece*, Nauman constructed a room with in a room (within, it must be said, the room of the gallery). Visiting the Tate Liverpool Nauman retrospective with my six-year-old daughter, I approached the cage with some trepidation – would I fit into this small space? Would my daughter be frightened? The piece, in fact, was constructed so that an adult of average size, like me, is forced to walk sideways between the walls of the inner cage and those of the outer cage. My daughter, however, could fit easily into the space and saw the experience as a game. For her the hinge worked in a playful way – her body being still more porous to its surround-ings, more adaptable. For me, the hinge creaked and laboured, making me acutely aware of the join between myself, the architectural space of the gallery, and the spatial manipulations of the piece. Shoving myself sideways around the inner cage I felt claustrophobic and anxious – what if I were to get stuck? The walls pressed in on me, making me aware both of the limits of my body's capacity to shape the spaces around myself and of the potentially aggressive and dangerous nature of these spaces.

And yet, rather than feeling set apart or vulnerable as a separate body, the piece evoked in me a sense of my own capacity for violence: I wanted to burst out of the confinement, strike at something, make myself as rigid and ungiving as this sculptural/architectural form. For an adult the tendency is to be provoked into aggression as a way of re-establishing the separateness that Nauman denies us. A child, it seems, can adapt to the threat of impending objects and walls. My daughter, her body lighter, smaller, more mobile, and less armoured, seemed to feel only the connectedness of her body with the spaces Nauman imagined and made material. *Double Steel Cage Piece* evokes an awareness of the reversibility of power – the hinge between master and slave (never, as Hegel pointed out, diametrically opposed – one is dependent on and coextensive with the other).

Other pieces, such as the 1968 video piece *Walk with Contrapposto* and the spatial installation resulting from it, the 1970 *Corridor Installation (Nick Wilder Installation)* also produce relations between the body and architectural space that may at first seem menacing but can (if we let go of our defensive desire to maintain the divisions that keep the self coherent by opposing it to a definable outside or other) become liberatory. In *Walk with Contrapposto*, Nauman's own body gyrates between the tight confines of the corridor. In an infra thin play, his body seems to define the limits of the space even as the space defines the limits of his body movements: we are encouraged to wonder which came first. There is a hinge between his body and the space rather than an opposition – a hinge that can link us, rather than opposing us, to the spaces we shape around us, and which inform our bodily comportment.

In the *Corridor Installation* something much more complex is happening – here, several corridors, only a few passable by the human body, divide the gallery space. In one of the corridors we are encouraged to walk down it towards two video monitors only to see ourselves on one of the monitors *receding* from our own view, and seen from behind. As Parveen Adams has eloquently described this uncanny experience, something intrudes into the public/private division when you are in this particular corridor of the *Corridor Installation*: 'It is yourself but you are somewhat unfamiliar … [T]he viewer in the installation sees him- or herself in unfamiliar ways – through the eyes of another viewer.'[28] The viewer, in fact, sees him- or herself precisely as Duchamp described the infra thin experience of looking through the non-painted side of a painted glass.

Adams argues that this seeing of yourself from behind, as another would see you, points to 'the viewer's disappearance as subject … the body becomes the stain in the picture, which disrupts the completeness of the visual field. For a moment, there is no subject of vision.'[29] (Or, in the words she used in the quotation above: the experience produces the viewer as *hole*.) While she argues this is the case *tout court*, I would insist that this disappearance of the viewer as subject is really a disappearance of the viewer as a subject *in the western or Cartesian sense*. The erasure of the 'subject of vision' is the erasure of a very particular subject as constructed within a particular ideological matrix. This is no longer a subject of vision as understood in western aesthetics – the viewer in a sense *disappears* in favour of the subject who appears to be viewing her (which is also, uncannily, herself, but herself as an other – perhaps the artist?).[30]

Interestingly, the play with space, which thus positions the gallery visitor in particular ways, becomes a play with vision that produces the visitor as reversible in relation to a non-present seeing subject. The non-present seeing subject (the person who we feel is seeing us retreating from ourselves on the screen we approach) can only be Nauman himself (I mean 'Nauman himself' as a subject whom we imagine to be behind the piece as a whole, and literally 'behind' us, seeing and filming us). The fact that, as with *Body Pressure*, he is directing us (here spatially and visually rather than verbally) and yet is not 'there', present in the room with us, points to the slippery nature of the author as an origin of the work and its meaning. Nauman's absence, furthermore, points to the larger impossibility of the subject (including ourselves) as ever being fully 'present'.

While for philosophers from the Renaissance to the early twentieth century such as Edmund Husserl, self-presence is relied upon as the guarantor of being, for poststructuralist Derrida, presence is a fantasy always already disrupted by 'irreducible nonpresence'.[31] Nauman's *Corridor Installation* paradoxically illustrates the irreducible nonpresence of the subject even to herself, confirming Derrida's insight that: 'Visibility and spatiality as such could only destroy the self-presence of will and spiritual animation which opens up discourse. *They are literally the death of that self-presence.*'[32] This is to say that the *visible* body enacted in three-dimensional space puts the lie to the idea of the 'self-presence of will and spiritual animation': if the body is there, it has not been transcended and Descartes' fantasised full spiritual self-presence (which required the transcendence of the corporeal) is shown to be impossible. Put another way, Derrida argues:

> What in effect happens in communication? Sensible phenomena (audible or visible, etc.) are animated through the sense-giving acts of a subject, whose intention is to be simultaneously understood by another subject. But the 'animation' cannot be pure and complete, for it must traverse, and to some degree lose itself in, the opaqueness of a body.[33]

Works such as *Corridor Installation*, then, narrate the impossibility of the system of oppositions on which western concepts of the subject (and, correlatively, of aesthetic meaning and value) rely. The sense of unease we feel as we see ourselves as if seen from behind, retreating, indicates a profound dislocation of the very bases on which we have come to identify our own 'coherence' as thinking and viewing subjects.

Room with my soul left out: Nauman's hinge as radical unhinging

The text for Nauman's *Double Doors: Projection and Displacement* (1973) directs the visitor as follows:

> Stand in the wedge that will allow you to see through the doors and into the further room.
>
> Become aware of the volume displaced by your body. Imagine it filled with water or some gas (helium).
>
> …
>
> Make your body fit your image.[34]

The last line – 'make your body fit your image' (an image of the body as liquid [water] or dissolved in air [gas]) – crystallises the paradox of our belief in our own coherence. It is so obviously constructed (we *imagine* ourselves to be who we are, inviolable in relation to the assaults and seductions of others, and then project our bodies into this coherence), and yet we must pretend it is not in order for this belief to carry any weight.

Nauman's engagement of the terms of contemporary visual art in the service of interrogating profound metaphysical questions about how we navigate the world, and how this everyday navigation relates to what we want and expect from art itself, takes a slightly different form in works such as his 1984 *Room with My Soul Left Out, Room that Does Not Care* – a multi-level installation that positions the visitor in relation to three intersecting black tunnels, meeting at a central grating through which he or she can look through to see a vertical shaft leading to the basement of the gallery. The visitor identifies with the building as a 'body' in its own right, but a body with orifices and passageways acting as infra thin links between inside and outside.

By his own admission, *Room with My Soul Left Out* was meant to function in parallel to aspects of Gestalt therapy:

> What interested me was the idea [from Gestalt therapy] that you go to your resistances, to whatever physical or social situation in your life or your work causes you problems. In other words, you don't try to avoid the resistance. You go straight to it, try to analyse the parts that make you uncomfortable … and then certain physical blocks will be released – or at least you will react physically to certain disruptions in the mental pattern.[35]

Nauman 'disrupts the mental pattern', as he noted, by opening an architectural space normally closed off as a 'container' for art. Rather than being a container, the building becomes the art itself and the body of the visitor, its analogue, becomes porous and incoherent. I am suggesting that the 'resistance' to which Nauman refers, and which he attempts to open up with this installation, is the resistance to accepting our incoherence and contingency on the spaces and bodies around us. Nauman thus productively chips away at our resistances, putting us in infra thin relationships with spaces, bodies and imagined (non-present) subjects, as if to turn us inside out.

This chipping away or dislocation can be as simple as in the 1969 *Lip Sync* (where a video of Nauman's mouth shown upside down and saying the words 'lip sync' gradually goes out of synchronisation) or *Work* (1994), where two video monitors show Nauman's head bouncing up and down (the top one right-side up, the bottom one upside down) saying the word 'work' over and over again. We see the hinge between body and language and yet it is out of 'sync'. In the 2005 *Three Heads Fountain (Juliet, Andrew, Rinde)*, where heads, cast in epoxy resin and hung upside down, are rent with holes through which spew fountains of water, the heads hinges between mind/body, self/other, body/space (the cascading water illustrating their permeability and interconnectedness with other heads, bodies, and spaces).

The hinge between life and death

All of these examples point to a final paradox of hinging that Nauman's work plays out in ways that activate complex levels of the human experience of the object world so central to aesthetics. Much of Nauman's work, finally, is thus (I want to argue) about the hinge between the live and the not-live – performances of bodies that are either implied (as in the architectural and corridor works) or represented through video or photography (as in *Failing to Levitate in the Studio*). The performance in *Failing to Levitate in the Studio* (figure 8.3) belies the title of the work: it appears to be a successful (if perhaps momentary) levitation that is documented. Here, the intertwining of words, bodies, actions, spaces, as well as *photographic documentation*, provokes a productive confusion between failure and success, action and stasis, the live (defined as present *now* in time, before me) is connected via the photographic *hinge* to the impossible-to-be-achieved, the fake, the not-live, the *dead*.

Aesthetics could be said to be a model of claiming the immortality of the human. It situates us in relation to the world of things, producing them as incorruptible extensions of our bodily presence in the world (often conflated with the bodily presence of the artist, thought in many cases to be secured via the artwork as 'trace' of his actions through time, frozen in perpetuity). Ultimately, I want to say that Nauman's work can be experienced not as a reified trace of the artist but as a hinge between life and death, between the actions that constitute being in the world and the ultimate end of action that constitutes death. If Nauman's works fail to secure presence and, in fact, cast doubt on our very assumption that we are 'here', in control, coherent, able to view and know the world, then they also suggest that there is no way of knowing that death is a definitive end. If there is no full presence, there is no definitive absence – there is a hinge between them that we might call human life, made experientially manifest through the production of art.

In Nauman's hands art, then, becomes a different kind of bridge from that imagined by traditional aesthetics. Rather than simultaneously marking out and disavowing the radical difference between the artwork and its maker and viewers, art becomes the hinge that co-articulates the three within a complex matrix of meaning-making – all are contingent on and coextensive with one another. Nauman will continue to haunt us whether he is 'in' the space or not. Subjects linger beyond their literal material habitation in an infra thin way. There is a hinge between being and not being, a hinge between live art and representational art, a hinge between life and death. I end appropriately enough re-speaking the words of Nauman, who seems to be present (and yet, of course, never present at all) through our experiencing of his works. These words, from the 1985 piece *Good Boy Bad Boy*, evoke the ultimate fear underlying our desire for coherence and so, perhaps, open the door for our acknowledging it and diffusing the power it has over us:

> I don't want to die.
> You don't want to die.
> We don't want to die,
> This is fear of Death.[36]

Notes

1 See Nauman's description of trying to perform these actions himself in Jan Butter-

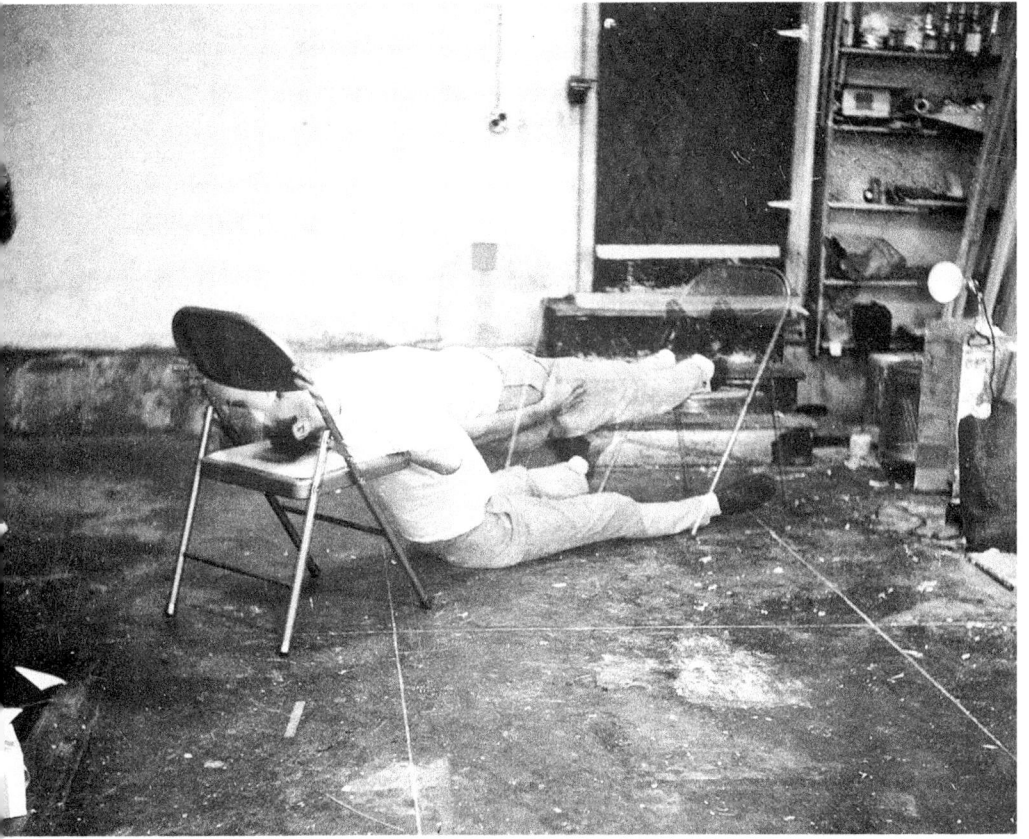

3   Bruce Nauman, *Failing to Levitate in the Studio*, 1966. Black and white photograph, 20 × 24 inches (50.8 × 61 cm).

field, 'Bruce Nauman: The center of yourself', *Arts Magazine*, 49 (February 1975), 53–4.

2 The *White Box*, also entitled *Á l'infinitif*, consists of facsimile reproductions of manuscript notes of Marcel Duchamp originally written during 1912–20.

3 In the original French: '*Le possible est un infra mince ... Le possible impliquant le devenir – le passage de l'un à l'autre*'. Marcel Duchamp, *À l'infinitif* (New York: Cordier & Ekstrom, 1966), n. p.

4 '*Les porteurs d'ombre représentés par toutes les sources de lumière (soleil, lune, étoiles, bougies, feu –) ... travaillent dans l'infra mince*'. Ibid.

5 '*La chaleur d'un siège (qui vient d'être quitté) est infra-mince*'. Ibid.

6 The text is translated in *The Writings of Marcel Duchamp* (New York: Da Capo Press, 1989), p. 194; it was originally published in the special issue of *View* (5, n. 1, March 1945) on Duchamp.

7 '*Peinture sur verre vue du côté non peint donne un infra mince*'. Duchamp, *À l'infinitif*, n. p.

8 '*La différence (dimensionnelle) entre 2 objets faits en série [sortis du même moule] est un infra mince quand le maximum de précision est obtenu*'. In *Marcel Duchamp, Notes*, ed. Paul Matisse, trans. P. Matisse (Boston: G.K. Hall, 1983), n. p.

9 On the history of modernist formalism see Caroline Jones, 'Form/Formless', in Amelia Jones (ed.), *A Companion to Contemporary Art Since 1945* (Oxford: Blackwell, 2006), pp. 127–44. See also her extensive historical and theoretical analysis of the closures of Greenbergian formalism, *Eyesight Alone: Clement Greenberg's Modernism and the Bureaucratization of the Senses* (Chicago: University of Chicago Press, 2005).

10 The final line of the text is: '(The Center of most places is above eyelevel [sic])'. 'Floating room' (1972), in Janet Kraynak (ed.), *Please Pay Attention Please: Bruce Nauman's Words: Writings and Interviews* (Cambridge: MIT Press, 2005), p. 65. Nauman described *Floating Room*, which was displayed at Leo Castelli Gallery in New York City, in the following way: 'It is in a room with a high ceiling. You are to go into the room and locate its center, which is somewhere above eye level. Then you attempt to locate the center of yourself, and then try to move your own center until it coincides with the center of the room. There is a set of instructions for people to follow (for how you might find your own center) which is intended to be a *physical* center ...' Cited in Jan Butterfield, 'Bruce Nauman: The Center of Yourself' (1975), in Kraynak (ed.), *Please Pay Attention Please*, p. 179.

11 Ibid.

12 Nauman to Coosje van Bruggen, in Emma Dexter, 'Raw materials', in Emma Dexter (ed.), *Bruce Nauman: Raw Materials* (London: Tate Modern, 2004), p. 20.

13 Text reprinted in Kraynak (ed.), *Please Pay Attention Please*, p. 67. The text was also mounted on the wall as typewritten collage and handed out in a brochure.

14 Simone de Beauvoir. *The Second Sex* (1949), trans. H.M. Parshley (New York: Knopf, 1952), pp. xv, xix.

15 Frantz Fanon, *Black Skin White Masks* (1952), trans. C. Lam Markmann (New York:

Grove Press, 1967), pp. 14, 111.

16 He is actually speaking specifically about a group of maquettes intended to function as models for (never realised) massive-scale outdoor public sculptures. See Ian Wallace and Russel Keziere, 'Bruce Nauman Interviewed' (1979), in Kraynak (ed.), *Please Pay Attention Please,* p. 187 (my italics).

17 Duchamp, *Marcel Duchamp, Notes,* n. p. (translation modified). I discuss the implications of this note at greater length in *Postmodernism and the (En)Gendering of Marcel Duchamp* (Cambridge: Cambridge University Press, 1994), 142ff.

18 Parveen Adams, 'Bruce Nauman and the object of anxiety', *October,* 83 (Winter 1998), 107–8.

19 Ibid., 105.

20 See Jacques Derrida, *Truth in Painting* (1978), trans. G. Bennington and I. McLeod (Chicago: University of Chicago Press, 1987).

21 Nauman explains: 'I have tried to break down this division [between works 'directly related to your body', per Sharp, and works that aren't] in some way, by using spectator response. These pieces act as a sort of bridge.' Willoughby Sharp, 'Nauman Interview' (1970) in Kraynak (ed.), *Please Pay Attention Please*, p. 125.

22 As D.N. Rodowick summarises this dilemma explored by Derrida: 'While enclosing and protecting an interior, the frame also produces an outside with which it must communicate. If the third *Critique* [of Kant] is to complete its teleological movement, this externality must also be enframed – a process creating a new outside, a new necessity for enframement, and so on ad infinitum.' D.N. Rodowick, 'Impure mimesis, or the ends of the aesthetic', in Peter Brunette and David Wills (eds), *Deconstruction and the Visual Arts: Art, Media, Architecture* (Cambridge: Cambridge University Press, 1994), pp. 98–9.

23 This aspect of Nauman's work resonates strongly with Maurice Merleau-Ponty's theorisation of the reversibility of vision and the world in his essay 'The Intertwining – the chiasm', in *The Visible and the Invisible* (1964), ed. Claude Lefort, trans. A. Lingis (Evanston: Northwestern University Press, 1968), where, for example, he states: 'vision is question and response ... The openness through flesh: the two leaves of my body and the leaves of the visible world ... It is between these intercalated leaves that there is visibility ... My body model of the things and the things model of my body: the body bound up to the world through all its parts, up against it → all this means: the world, the flesh not as fact or sum of facts, but as the locus of an inscription of truth: the false crossed out, not nullified' (p. 131).

24 As Rodowick sums up this aspect of western aesthetics, in such judgements the 'spectator must have nothing at stake. If the critic invests in the object, as it were, his or her judgment cannot transcend its subjective origins and pretend to universal communicability.' Rodowick, 'Impure mimesis, or the ends of the aesthetic', p. 101.

25 The hymen is a trope in Derridean philosophy, where it enacts the lack of opposition between inside and outside; see, for example, Jacques Derrida and Paule Thévenin, 'To unsense the subjectile', in *The Secret Art of Antonin Artaud*, trans. M. A. Caws (Cambridge: MIT Press, 1998), p. 75. See also Elizabeth Wilson's exploration of the hinge as a deconstructive strategy in Derridean theory, where she notes that

hinge terms such as supplement, *différance*, dissemination and hymen function as hinge terms 'to expose and internally displace [the] … operations of the binary'. In *Neural Geographies: Feminism and the Microstructure of Cognition* (New York and London: Routledge, 1998), p. 26.

26 'Codification' (1966), in Kraynak (ed.), *Please Pay Attention Please*, p. 49.

27 Merleau-Ponty, 'The intertwining', p. 144.

28 Adams, 'Bruce Nauman and the object of anxiety', pp. 107, 108.

29 Ibid., p. 109.

30 This is an enactment of the Derridean concept of *différance*: 'Intersubjectivity is inseparable from temporalization taken as the openness of the present upon an outside of itself, upon *another* absolute present. This being outside itself proper to time is its *spacing*: it is a *protostage* [*archi-scène*]. This stage, as the relation of one present to another present *as such*, that is as a nonderived re-presentation …, produces the structure of signs in general as 'reference', as being-for-something … and radically precludes their reduction. There is no constituting subjectivity. The very concept of constitution itself must be deconstructed.' Jacques Derrida, *Speech and Phenomena and Other Essays on Husserl's Theory of Signs*, trans. D. Allison (Evanston: Northwestern University Press, 1973), pp. 84–5, note 9.

31 Ibid., p. 6.

32 Ibid., p. 35.

33 Ibid., p. 38.

34 'Double doors: projection and displacement' (1973), in Kraynak (ed.), *Please Pay Attention Please*, p. 66.

35 Nauman, cited by Michael Auping, 'Metacommunicator', in *Bruce Nauman: Raw Materials*, p. 12.

36 This text is cited in Dexter, 'Raw materials', p. 21. It was one of the texts spoken over the loudspeaker as part of Nauman's *Raw Materials* installation in the Turbine Hall at Tate Modern in 2004.

9

Rirkrit Tiravanija's liability

Janet Kraynak

This chapter was first written between 1997 and 1998 and published in the Autumn 1998 issue of *Documents*, a small circulation journal founded and edited by a group of my, then, graduate school colleagues and friends: Chris Hoover, Miwon Kwon, James Marcovitz, Helen Molesworth and Margaret Sundell. At the time of its writing, participatory practices were just appearing on the contemporary art world's radar screen; *Documents*, a journal that aimed to provide a forum for serious criticism in a non-academic, interdisciplinary context, provided a perfect venue in which to explore what I perceived to be a largely uncritical reception of these new practices. The seeds of the original essay were planted as early as Rirkrit Tiravanija's, now famous, 1992 exhibition, *Untitled (Free)*, at 303 Gallery in New York. To my eye, Tiravanija's work was being addressed in exclusively celebratory and non-historical terms: neither with regards to its relationship to past socially engaged works, nor in terms of the transformed conditions of capitalism in the 1990s that inevitably impacted the critical claims that were being made in the work's reception

Documents has long been out of print and, in the years since, the issues I attempted to address in my essay have been productively expanded and retheorised by others (see for example, Miwon Kwon's 'Exchange rate: on obligation and reciprocity in some art of the 1960s and after' and Claire Bishop's 'Antagonism and relational aesthetics', both reprinted in this volume), attesting to the ongoing currency of these concerns, and to the need for more investigation into these important issues. My own research has continued to explore some of the themes formulated here, and I thank Anna Dezeuze for the opportunity to share these ideas with a new audience of readers and interpreters.

*   *   *

The contemporary art world is currently experiencing a much-noted romance with artistic strategies first developed during the 1960s and 1970s, reserving a particularly privileged status for institutional critique and the related area of site specificity. Artists, critics and art historians are clamouring to situate recent practices within this genealogy, and, in the process, to recover a historical project that is seen to have been prematurely interrupted by the 1980s, where more traditional forms of art making were reconstituted, and the politics of *representation* displaced the politics of *institutions* as a pressing concern. When appropriately self-reflexive and conscious of the dynamics of historical returns, this renewed dialogue with the past can be productive. But there has been a problematic tendency to posit a seamless continuum with this past, in which a model of criticality – born of a specific set of socio-political circumstances – and its claims for radicality, are simply transposed, unchanged, to the present. In the case of the art of Rirkrit Tiravanija, this transhistorical mapping is doubly paradoxical. Critically embraced as the artistic progeny of institutional critique – a set of practices that insisted upon the semantic determinacy of art's physical, ideological and discursive 'frames' – Tiravanija's work is frequently examined in the absence of any considera-tion of the material conditions of its context. The very attempt to consider the present in historical terms is, thus, ironically performed outside the purview of historical thinking.

In 1992, at 303 Gallery in New York, Tiravanija mounted his exhibition, *Untitled (Free)*, moving the offices, the packing and shipping department, and the mundane materials associated with the gallery's daily operations from the back private domain into the public viewing areas. The central space was now occupied by the formerly hidden contents of the gallery, including the director working at her desk, while Tiravanija set himself up in the back room with a stove and a variety of cooking ingredients and proceeded to make a pot of Thai curry vegetables, which was served with steamed jasmine rice to the gallery visitors.[1] Coming on the heels of an earlier 1990 installation at Paula Allen Gallery,[2] which similarly entailed the cooking and serving of food, the exhibi-tion secured Tiravanija's position within the legacy of institutional critique – specifically, its interrogation of the effects of commodification, both on the level of the production and the reception of art.

By physically intervening in the gallery space, *Untitled (Free)* recalls Michael Asher's 'situational aesthetics', in which the activity of making was transformed into a series of spatial displacements. For instance, in Asher's 1974 installation at Claire Copley Gallery in Los Angeles, the artist removed the wall separating the gallery offices from the exhibition space, leaving a sparse white room occupied by a desk in the corner where the employees worked. Tiravanija's reversal of the private and public realms of the gallery similarly attempts to intervene into the supposedly neutral spaces and activi-ties of the institution.[3] Yet, in the critical literature, what are persistently identified as the primary interest and meaning of Tiravanija's art are not the environments themselves, but the production of social interaction that takes place within them through various forms of consumption (of food, drink and entertainment).

Consider, for example, the following statement, taken from the essay accompanying the artist's 1997 exhibition *Untitled* (*Playtime*) at the Museum of Modern Art: 'Rirkrit Tiravanija's art is one of empathy, compassion, and hospitality. It has as its goal the transformation of public spaces into social places that celebrate convivial interaction between people.'[4] The many things extended from artist to viewer – a free screening of a Warhol film, a puppet theatre performance, a hot cup of noodles – become the means to produce the final 'object': the fostering of community.

This idealising of sociality as a resistant mechanism unconsciously mimics a classical Marxist critique of political economy, specifically Marx's notion of 'commodity fetishism', which maintains that, in capitalism, relations between people are masked as relations between things.[5] In creating social environments, we are told, Tiravanija's work actively undermines the alienating effects of capitalism and, in the process, transforms the spaces of art's exhibition and marketing into sites of harmonious human exchange, essentially exceeding the institution of art altogether. In one essay, the author characterises *Untitled* (*Free*) in such terms, going so far as to contrast the artist's position and motivations with those of his dealer: 'Ironically, while she [the gallery director] was selling art, Tiravanija was giving away the fruits of his labor.'[6] In other words, Tiravanija's art does not simply *reveal* or *critique*, but effectively *escapes* the effects of commodification, both on the level of its production and, most significantly, on the psychic and experiential level for the participant beholders.

If the above passages anchor the interpretation of Tiravanija's work to its reception, as if the work and its reception represent two conjunctive parts of the same proverbial coin, this is not unintentional. One contention of this essay is that Tiravanija's art is so overly determined by the discourse of its reception that it is an almost unavoidable sieve through which the work is encountered and experienced. While Tiravanija's art compels or provokes a host of concerns relevant to the larger domain of contemporary artistic practices, its unique status in the public imagination derives in part from a certain naturalising of the critical readings that have accompanied and, to an extent, constructed it. Unlike previous pairings of avant-garde utopianism, in which art merges happily with life, and anti-institution criticality, in which art objects are constituted in, and as, social spaces,[7] what putatively guarantees the production of uncontaminated social praxis in Tiravanija's work is the unique imprint of the artist, whose *generosity* both animates the installations and unifies them stylistically.

A host of articles have focused on the familial atmosphere of the gallery where he is represented, and other biographical details of his life, rendering a covert equivalence between Tiravanija's work and self.[8] This idealised projection seems to derive from the work itself, as the artist has thematised details of his ethnic background in his installations through references to Thai culture. Furthermore, such a subjectivising approach reflects a more recent paradigm of political critique realised as biography.[9] The artist, repositioned as both the source and arbiter of meaning, is embraced as the pure embodiment of his or her sexual, cultural or ethnic identity, guaranteeing both the authenticity and political efficacy of his or her work. In the case of Tiravanija's art, this turn to biography is reinforced by the presumption that when the artist serves something, he is offering a part of himself. The food and other objects of consumption contain his *anima*, so to speak, they are uniquely *of* him. In other words, they occupy the cultural territory of the gift and, as such, represent the perfect *anti-commodity*, fulfilling a dual imperative – implying both an economic critique of commodification and a cultural or anthropological critique of identity. But what is absent from this reading is the question of the gift itself.

In semiological terms, the gift is defined within a relational system, deriving its meaning not through any intrinsic qualities, but through its purported structural dissimilarity to the commodity. The latter is defined as an object that is impersonal, motivated by profit and bound to exchange. The gift entails a different character – personal, selfless – and a different temporality – spontaneous and unidirectional, or not contingent upon any return. Yet I want to suggest that it is the very temporal and spatial model of *economy* – that is, circulation, distribution, exchange and return – that structures both the conception and meaning of Tiravanija's art. As such, the immanent distinction drawn between the gift and the commodity cannot be presumed. But it is not simply the 'purity' of the status of these objects that is questioned. It is the more generalised dissociation of the social from the economic sphere in the dichotomous coupling of gift/commodity that is at issue. This separation, underpinning the critical readings of Tiravanija's art, is what the anthropologist Marcel Mauss challenged in his theory of the gift exchange system.

The stated subject of Mauss's seminal essay, *The Gift: Forms and Functions of Exchange in Archaic Societies* (1925), is the elaborate and highly organised systems of gift exchange in what he called 'archaic' societies: from Polynesia and Melanesia to the indigenous tribes of Northwest America.[10] Mauss's essay, however, constituted an explicit challenge to the evolutionary approach of cultural anthropology, specifically the notion that gift economies represented a more 'primitive' precedent to market economies (a type of thinking that, for one, served to justify colonialism).[11] From his extensive analysis of gift exchange within different socio-cultural systems, Mauss maintained that the development of the 'market' was not contingent upon the invention of money, but pre-existed its appearance, and moreover, that it is fundamentally a *social* system. Gift practices can be found across cultures and temporal periods, persisting even within contemporary societies based on a market economy.

Mauss defined the process of gift-giving as a 'total social phenomena'[12] in that far from being an isolated ritual, it involved every aspect of a society: its legal, political, social and religious institutions. The gift, however, enjoys a unique and almost magical status, securing its fundamental deception: 'the so to speak voluntary character of these total services, apparently free and disinterested', Mauss wrote, 'but nevertheless constrained and self-interested'.[13] It is the 'obligation to reciprocate', directly contradicting the notion of the gift as free and voluntary, which forms the crux of Mauss's investigation.

Mauss observed that during central cultural events (birth, marriage, circumcision etc.) in Polynesian society, a series of gifts were transacted, each one possessing specific attributes and functions. The exchange of actual property was formal and to an extent incidental, in that the true 'objects' in circulation were power and prestige. The receiver, upon accepting the gift, essentially incurred a debt, thus reinforcing the authority of the giver's position. Although the goods in circulation might be precious, what was more important was that they established a link between people, elevating the character of the original donor. As Mauss observed, 'What imposes obligation in the present received and exchanged, is the fact that the thing received is not inactive. Even when it has been abandoned by the giver, it still possesses something *of* him.'[14]

Mauss insisted that the gift, similar to the commodity, operates within a *cyclical* process, or what he termed a 'general theory of obligation': the demand to give, to receive and to reciprocate.[15] This triad ostensibly forms a legal tie outside of, and above, simple individual relations, economics or familial bonds. The practice of gift circulation, far from deriving from individual will, is a product of a series of rigidly structured conventions, which are sanctioned by the social body.[16] In this way, the gift anticipates the modern notion of money (itself a social contract, not a purely 'economic' one); but unlike money, the gift does not necessarily procure the return of *material* goods, but may be reciprocated with *immaterial* or symbolic property.[17]

In its most extreme form, the potlatch of Northwest native American tribes, gift-giving reached the status of rivalry and outright warfare. Potlatch ceremonies constituted a gift with no return, as they involved the complete destruction of property in order to assure that the other party *will not be able to reciprocate*.[18] Potlatch strikingly reveals the danger of the gift as something both favourable and treacherous. This duplicity, Mauss tells us, is conveyed in the German word *Gabe*, a single term that signifies both 'gift' and 'poison'.[19]

*   *   *

> Great indebtedness does not make men grateful, but vengeful; and if a little
> charity is not forgotten, it turns into a gnawing worm.[20]

For the exhibition *Economies: Hans Accola and Rirkrit Tiravanija*, the Walker
Art Center arranged for Tiravanija to travel to Minneapolis and produce
an on-site work rather than securing loans of prefabricated art objects.[21]
Tiravanija made several trips to the city in order to investigate the culture
and geography of the area and to negotiate his project with the museum prior
to his final journey to complete the actual installation. During his research,
the artist discovered a postcard from the 1970s picturing one of the museum's
galleries, with its relaxing lounge area for museum visitors, and a window
that offered an open vista onto the city. In response to his find, Tiravanija
created a multi-part work that aimed to recapture the casual comfort of the
older space, while providing a portrait of the city's socio-economic history
with a specific focus on the Hmong, Laotian immigrants with a significant
presence in Minnesota.[22] A tent was erected in the gallery, an audiotape of a
Hmong radio programme was played, two videos were put on display, one of
a local mill that makes wool blankets, and the other of the handmade embroi-
dery work of the Hmong; and artworks from the museum's own collection,
including a Dan Flavin sculpture, were reinstalled.

The 'service' provided by Tiravanija took the form of collaboration, as
museum employees, including the curators, agreed to supply different kinds
of labour during all stages of planning and executing the final exhibition. This
rearticulated relationship of artist-to-production-to-institution participates in
the larger trend in contemporary art toward post-studio forms of production.
But as demonstrated by curator Richard Flood's recounting of the procedures
that ensued, this is accompanied by a fundamental reorientation of both the
institution's goals and expectations.

> After his departure, certain areas of concentration emerged through faxes and
> phone calls … Very gently, but consistently, tasks were assigned to those of us
> who remained behind, and decisions were made concerning the configuration
> of the gallery in which he would be working. Blankets, it became clear, would
> play a part in the installation. Temporary walls, built for a previous exhibition,
> were to remain in place. Asian grocery stores would need to be accessed.[23]

Explicitly avoiding any legalistic language that would figure these arrangements in a formalised, objective manner, Flood employs benevolent and
personalised terms to characterise the organisation of Tiravanija's exhibition,
determining the artist's contribution largely through his communication and
interaction with the museum staff and the exhibition's audience. This form
of personal input is perceived to be more valuable than the production of
standardised artistic objects, deriving from a spirit of sociality and generosity,
where the artist's contribution is understood to be the inaugural gift, or the

origin point. Yet the products and services extended by Tiravanija were *already bound up within a cycle of exchange* – in effect, fulfilling the remuneration of a debt derived from a contract with the museum. In turn, his 'gifts' produced a series counter-exchanges, among which was the contribution of a local artist, Hans Accola, who was introduced to Tiravanija by the host institution that proposed the 'joint' exhibition.[24]

In other words, in its conception, execution and reception, Tiravanija's exhibition seems to embody the terms, character and symbolic geometry of gift exchange: the commodity's objective relations, consisting of the exchange of equally valued objects, are displaced by the transaction of surrogate objects, valued for the relations between the participating subjects they engender. As such, critics, curators and audience members alike enthusiastically champion the exhibitions and installations themselves as *emancipatory* sites, or ideal public spaces, free of constraint and obligation.

Indeed, in Tiravanija's interactive tableaux, where the activity of consumption is displayed and enacted, nothing is *produced*, there is no profit. But if the calculated logic of capitalist accumulation is eschewed, it is displaced by an economic relation of a different order. Take, for example, visitors flocking to the MoMA courtyard. Grasping a pencil and paper, they retreat into the seclusion of the intimately scaled-down, 'Philip Johnson' glasshouse in order to make a drawing, purportedly partaking in a completely voluntary pursuit where nothing is asked in return (or, to use the Maussian terminology, there is no 'obligation to reciprocate'). We read curator Laura Hoptman's description, and note her insistence that these acts of drawing arise spontaneously, granting the viewer absolute autonomy and control:

> Tiravanija neither forces audience participation nor attempts to manipulate it if it does occur. With a reticence approaching self-abnegation, he leaves the nature of the encounter between the audience and the artist-made situation – in effect, the artwork – up to chance. As welcoming environments conducive to any number of quotidian activities, his installations never dictate the specific experience one must have.[25]

The actual material realisation of Tiravanija's artworks is utterly contingent, however, upon a system of reciprocal obligations, in which the individual acts of consumption – drinking beer, engaging in conversation – collectively participate. But beyond these visible acts, the simple acknowledgment of the gift *returns* the gift. What I am emphasising is that the formation of any simplistic divisions between freedom and obligation, gift and remuneration, interest and disinterest, is necessarily artificial, as these series of pairs constitute not simple antitheses, but dialectical counterparts. A fundamental question arises – what Jacques Derrida has called the 'aporia of the gift': can there even be a gift without a return?[26]

It is this impossibility of the gift that is elusive; its absence from the reception of Tiravanija's art is symptomatic of its absence from the social arena, where conscious acts of giving are bound to an illusory faith in the gift. The ability of the commodity to control human actions and desires is overt and wholly legible, working itself into our behaviour and our psyches: we purchase the commodity, aware on some level that we are buying its deception as well. The gift's power, however, is far more ambiguous, because in the gift economy, not just 'objects' but intangible items – the sentiment of gratitude, the recognition of the giver's act, the social value of civic virtue – circulate.[27] Operating with such immaterial returns, this sphere of praxis is collectively determined to be *disinterested* and *anti-economic*. But acts of giving, Pierre Bourdieu insists, are prescribed within a particular logic, one which is neither determined by, nor initiated through, the generous intentions of the giver, but by the *habitus*: the internalisation of collective practices underlying all social organisation.[28] For Bourdieu, in an extension of Mauss's analysis, gift exchange represents an entire domain of economic activity of a society that, due to the 'disposition of the *habitus*', is relegated to the 'social'. What is acquired, accumulated and preserved, he maintains, is *symbolic capital*.

More ambiguous than material wealth, or 'economic' capital, it is precisely this 'market' – a symbolic economy – that has proliferated under late capitalism, arguably constituting its very expansion and transformation. If symbolic capital is intangible, ambiguous and decentring, then it is coincident spatially and temporally to western post-industrialism, in which the production of material goods has been dispersed geographically, and the expenditure of work–energy is concentrated in the areas of management, marketing and distribution. If symbolic capital, following the logic of the gift, produces relationships of dependence and domination, then privatisation, the engine of capitalist growth, must represent one of its purest forms: colonising and appropriating, it euphemistically sports a charitable face as multinational 'partnerships', philanthropy, corporate giving, and so on.[29] The tributaries of capitalism, no longer local, have extended under globalisation (itself a privatisation, or as Henry Louis Gates recently observed, an 'Americanisation', on a world scale), so that entire nations are conceived not as autonomous entities with specific histories and needs to be respected, but potential markets to be conditioned and developed.

Politicians, corporations and other beneficiaries advocate for this economic realignment in terms remarkably similar to those who idealise the cultural expansion of the art world and its institutions (such as the recent proliferation of international biennials)[30] – in the name of a harmonious global community; empowering those formerly disenfranchised; nurturing the commingling of diverse cultures. Yet without the possibility of equal contribution from nations that possess radically uneven levels of economic and political influence, what occurs is a reinscription of asymmetrical relations of power. In other words, late capitalism productively exploits what is thought to be a pre-capitalist object: it toils in the liability of the gift.

In light of the realities of the current socio-economic order, the desire to envision the spaces comprising Tiravanija's artistic universe as a sanctuary from the material conditions of contemporary life acquires an air of urgency and desperation, as one last breath in face of an historical inevitability, in which the formerly non-commodifiable is thoroughly expropriated. But I want to suggest that under the guise of putatively pleasant activities, Tiravanija's art stages this alternative economy of symbolic capital.

In Tiravanija's work, every moment in the life of the art object – from production to exhibition to distribution and acquisition – is redefined according to the laws and logic of the gift economy, which unlike 'economy' in its restricted sense (based upon accumulation and wealth, and profitable production) is characterised by use, circulation, and consumption.[31] This aesthetic of expenditure is exploited towards potentially subversive ends, in that, for example, the precondition of the purchase and continued existence of Tiravanija's art is that it must be *used*. As discussed previously, audience participation is realised as a depletion or ingestion of the artwork's offerings. Additionally, a collector (either an individual or an institution) is denied the spoils of traditional art patronage, as they acquire not a 'work' but, under the artist's directive, the mandate 'to work', redefining the very conception of collecting from a singular event, which procures a lasting object of status and taste, to an ongoing process. As the artist once commented, 'Basically I started to make things so that people would have to use them, which means if you want to buy something then you have to use it … It's not meant to be put out with other sculpture or like another relic and looked at, but you have to use it.'[32]

The act of acquisition binds the collector to the artist in a symbolic contract, in which the former is obliged to perform an operation in order for the work to become meaningful – much in the way that a collector of a Felix Gonzalez-Torres 'stack piece' is encouraged to constantly replenish the posters or candy as they are taken and eaten by passers-by. In deploying this logic, Tiravanija's work aims to frustrate the function and role of the museum itself, which historically has been bound to the accumulation and preservation of art objects *cum* products. The recuperative will of the institution, however, makes for a formidable enemy. In the following statement, the artist describes one of his artworks, a backpack, which had been purchased by the Walker museum and then quickly placed in storage. 'But it really should be used', Tiravanija inveighs,

Richard Flood and Kathy Halbreich should just put it on their backs and walk out into the garden and make a meal with it. I think even the person I made the edition with, who I spend a lot of time with, still can't come to terms with the idea that for me it's the dirt, and it's the fingerprints, and it's the drip, and it's the thing falling apart that makes it much more valuable than it being kept and preserved – it has to have a life, or it has to have a history for it to become something. It's because all of these people have touched it and used it that it becomes animated. Essentially all the marks are the recording of its life ... which is something museums try to fight. It's like Fluxus being completely contained and completely preserved. It undermines everything they were undermining. You have to think about how to undermine the situation before it undermines you.[33]

This figuring the art object as entropic was immanent to critiques of commodification during the 1960s and early 1970s. In addition to institutional critique, such aesthetic strategies as anti-form (production through destruction), dematerialisation (perceptual and material withdrawal) and performance (temporalisation versus spatialisation) challenged the traditional, metaphysical economy of the art object as a permanent, spatially definable thing.[34] Paradoxically, while this production of immaterial 'objects', and the structural collusion of an artwork with its mechanisms of distribution (a seminal example being Dan Graham's magazine project, *Homes For America*) once stood as a critique of capitalist commodification, these strategies may now formally reproduce its current, mutated form. In the rhetoric of the information society (the post-industrial era, the global economy), material and physical boundaries are dissipating into decentred networks and ephemeral flows of communication. The means to access and distribute information have become primary political and economic battlegrounds, yielding less identifiable mechanisms of control and power, which feed the fantasies (or paranoias) of popular culture.[35] Consider the wellspring of Hollywood action and thriller films in which central protagonists fight not visible, embodied enemies, but invisible media networks that due to their very *unrepresentability* assume a threat of unimaginable proportions.

The dilemma for criticism is whether Tiravanija's work self-reflexively critiques this phenomenon, or unwittingly reproduces its logic. If we follow the theoretical principles forged in the history of critical artistic practices (institutional critique included) the cultural sphere enjoys a 'relative autonomy', which affords its ability to operate as a space of contestation, outside the reach of capital's maleficent effects.[36] Yet it is this distance and division of spheres that is rapidly obliterated under the expanding symbolic economy. After all, although Tiravanija's art is located physically and conceptually in the spaces of 'art', those boundaries that have traditionally circumscribed 'art' from 'non-art' spaces and institutions are no longer so distinct.

The 'museum' (as both an actual and imaginative place) can no longer be thought of as a purely 'cultural' site, owing to its recent mutation into a surrogate branch of corporate advertising. Corporate culture and its ravenous marketing apparatus have not simply invaded the art museum (the woe of the 1960s) but, owing to the forces of privatisation, the two have become mutually dependent. Recent history has witnessed a particularly virulent displacement of public funding for the arts by what is innocently termed 'charitable giving'. Yet such acts of 'generosity' cynically benefit from the deception that marks the gift. Embraced as a panacea to a reduced political and public commitment to cultural production, they in fact proactively delegitimate the very necessity of any unrestricted public funds for artistic institutions and individual artists. Despite rhetoric to the contrary (most shamelessly evidenced in the recent corporate realignment of the Guggenheim Museum, with its 'global partners'), the, by now, institutionalised structure of private contribution and sponsorship fundamentally is neither 'free' nor disinterested, but is tied to a host of reciprocal demands (i.e. the display of company logos prominently in exhibition literature, the mounting of the names of the sponsors on exhibition walls next to wall texts, and 'free' membership extended to company employees). These forms of advertising liberally commingle with the editorial content of exhibitions, while the benefits accrued are not publicly acknowledged. Whether interpreted as a recognition on the part of cultural institutions of the economic realities of the time, or as their acquiescence to the political whims of the time, such 'giving' has resulted in an enormous sea-change in the structure of the art world and its institutions, not only in the way exhibitions are selected and mounted, but also increasing the pace of transformation of the artist into an institution, by necessity, now forced into the global marketplace of goods and services.[37] The possibility for an artistic position of 'relative autonomy' is increasingly unavailable at the behest of a system in which such distance is being compressed into obsolescence.

The object of Tiravanija's critique, however, is not simply the institutions of art (even in their state of non-differentiation from political and economic institutions) along the lines of the work of Hans Haacke or Daniel Buren, for example, who explicitly thematised these issues within the structure of their art objects. Instead of envisioning the artwork as a vehicle to perform sociological analysis (and in the process, explicitly rejecting its status as a carrier of metaphorical allusion),[38] Tiravanija (like many of his contemporaries) populates his artworks with a range of found and created stories, and other narrative tropes. These have included, among others: Thai food and cooking, which the artist has referenced to memories of his grandmother's restaurant in Thailand; the role of homemade crafts in the economic and social development of the Hmong refugees; a Viennese coffee house; and the Swedish welfare state, in the form of a scaled-down day-care centre. This deployment of storytelling on the part of Tiravanija and his artist peers (which has been reductively ascribed to an explicit rejection of the more 'cerebral' tendencies of conceptual art and the theoretical pretences of post-modernism) should be contextualised in terms of a generalised shift in historical explanation and philosophical thinking, which maintains that knowledge is understood and transmitted as a form of narrative.[39] Specifically, much recent art has responded to current discourses of cultural politics, in which the social and discursive formation of identity is investigated, and notions of community are explored.

For Hal Foster, this development represents a generalised anthropological turn in contemporary art, which, although continuing a position of critical resistance vis-à-vis artistic and social institutions, has overturned or displaced the socio-economic orientation of previous critical practices.[40] Now the artist *cum* ethnographer, defined through cultural identity, manufactures artwork by engaging in fieldwork. Under the pretence of creating art objects relevant to the communities in which they were made, Foster argues that there is, ironically, a lack of self-reflexivity regarding the implicit authority of the ethnographer's position (as 'participant observer') that the discipline of anthropology itself has laboured to undermine.[41] In Foster's analysis, this situation introduces the danger of a realist assumption, in which the 'truth' of the artist's experiences and his or her privileged position to them (and by association to his or her own subjectivity) is problematically assumed.

Foster's schema, however, unwittingly reproduces one of the central deficits plaguing the dominant discourses of identity politics, in that economic and cultural relations are held in suspended isolation, whereas it is their *convergence* – or their 'unmediated relationship' in the words of Frederic Jameson – that forms the crux of my reading of Tiravanija's art. This interpretive shift, moreover, is historically mandated, as one can no longer presume that 'identity', 'community', and 'culture' conjure forms of political resistance, in the face of their mutation into economically mediated concepts.[42] Identity – and 'difference' in general – in other words, have transmogrified from interventionist *forces* that disrupt the dominant order, to fixed, *spatialised* objects that are recuperated by the market as symbolic commodities.[43] In terms of contemporary art, one possible outcome is that a structural *de*-commodification of the art object is antinomically hinged to a *re*-commodification of cultural identity (to wit, all of the discussions about identity as a 'site').

As Foster rightly observed, this version of cultural politics is contingent upon the fantasy of the pure, outside *other*, a 'beyond' that, although an *illusion* given the interstitial spaces of globalism, confirms critical distance. In the logic of the gift, however, it is precisely this alterity, or the conceptualisation of an absolute, externalised other, that is undone: as the anthropological object to the economic object of the commodity; as the pre-capitalist, 'primitive' economy to the 'advanced', market one. The philosopher Randolphe Gasché has observed that Mauss himself retreated in fear of the logical conclusions of his own theory, which entail not simply an abolishing of the hierarchical divisions between gift-exchange and market economies, but the undermining of the very project of ethnography itself, which is contingent upon the fundamental premise of alterity, or otherness.[44] It is this essential alterity, a difference that is spatially grounded and bounded, that must exist for ethnography – and by extension, a dogmatic politics of difference – to function.

The gift, thus, indicates another critical possibility, in its refusal to produce that *beyond* that Foster rightly admonished and Jameson recognised as an impossibility given the logic of late capitalism. So to read Tiravanija's art as gift is to suggest that it potentially undermines the premise of alterity, rather than markets its promise. In *Pad Thai*, Tiravanija's installation at Paula Allen, and *Untitled* (*Free*), his exhibition at 303 Gallery, identity is produced within a principle of exchangeability. Beyond the satisfying of individual desires, the exchange and consumption of food that structures the installations has a collective significance: to realise how one's introduction to Thailand, or any culture, as a place and a set of social customs and mores, often comes about through the cooking and exchange of food. A culture is defined historically and epistemically through a continual, dynamic process of such economic *cum* symbolic encounters.

The danger is to idealise this communicative dimension, for communication, the relaying of knowledge, is rife with symbolic power relations.[45] In Tiravanija's artworks, these tensions are registered through intercultural interactions and migrations, which are predicated upon the very displacement of identity and culture, rather than their totalising representation. For example, in his project *Untitled 1993* (*1271*) at the Venice Biennale, the artist fabricated a gondola that held large cooking pots and pre-packaged Asian cup-of-noodles, ready to be distributed to exhibition visitors. The seemingly minor tale of the noodle, transported from the villages of China onto the Italian table, is merely a foil to enact the disputes over history: who determines it, who has the right to own it, and how knowledge of it is transmitted. But the cup-of-noodles, an Asian product made available for western consumption, is altered in taste, and thus threatens to melt into non-differentiation and to eradicate its specificity.

This, of course, represents the peril of globalisation itself: a place becomes a non-place, sapped of its history and specificity (the Disney effect, where all that is natural becomes artifice and simulation). The exporting of American democracy (or rather capital) necessitates such levelling, which results in an increasing sense of cultural, social and political homogenisation. When Tiravanija fabricates a mock day-care centre in a Swedish museum, it is understood as a monument to the largesse of the state. But does it simply celebrate these values, or subtly excoriate the exporting of an American-style, fully capitalised, privatised, 'democracy' which scorns precisely such values? Tiravanija's art of giving is conceptually and materially linked to governmental giving, but in light of the hysterical scapegoating of welfare, now synonymous with sloth and a lack of moral fibre, it is hard to encounter a house that embodies such giving as ideologically neutral. Indeed welfare in the American political imagination represents the *pure gift*: uni-directional, bestowed upon the undeserving and unable to reap a return.

In the day-care centre – as in the entertainment box in the museum, and the friendly bar in the gallery – the potential effectiveness, and possible ineffectiveness, of Tiravanija's art unfolds from the same source, as both are contingent upon the liability of the gift. If the gift represents the possibility to rethink the terms of criticality by destroying the oppositions and distances which it presumes, it is also so inextricably bound to the fantasy that publicly determines it (and that critically repeats it), that it allows us to sit in the glass-house that Johnson built that Tiravanija rebuilt, and simply, unreflexively, pick up a pencil and draw.

Notes

This chapter was originally published as an essay in *Documents*, 13 (Autumn 1998), 26–40.

1 Subsequent projects similarly transformed the activity of viewing into one of consumption: of drink and conversation, as in *Meet Tim and Burkhard* (1994) at neugerriemschneider Gallery in Berlin; and of entertainment, as in Tiravanija's contribution to the 1995 Whitney Biennial, which consisted of a live band playing inside an architectural interior constructed specifically for the exhibition.

2 For the project entitled *Pad Thai*, the artist cooked and served food during the opening, and then maintained the residue of the preparation and eating on tables and in Plexiglas cases throughout the course of the exhibition.

3 As both James Meyer and Miwon Kwon have written, artists from the 1960s associated with institutional critique (such as Asher, Haacke, Graham and Buren, among others) radically transformed 'site specificity' from an exclusively *spatial* understanding of site – as physical location – to a more expansive definition. The notion of 'site' thus included the economic system within which art objects circulated, and how the institutions of galleries, museums, collecting and criticism participate in assigning value to these objects. See Miwon Kwon, 'One place after another: notes on site specificity', *October*, 80 (Spring 1997), 85–110; and James Meyer, 'The functional site: an essay on contemporary site-oriented art', *Documents*, 7 (Autumn 1996), 20–9.

4 Laura Hoptman, 'Rirkrit Tiravanija', *Projects*, no. 58 (3 April–1 June 1997), exhibition brochure (New York: Museum of Modern Art), n. p. For the exhibition, Tiravanija produced a model of Philip Johnson's famous 'glasshouse' in the centre of MoMA's courtyard. Reduced to child's scale, the house was transformed into a functional place for children to visit and draw, directly countering the modernist ethos of Johnson's (the architect of MoMA) and MoMA's aesthetic.

5 See Karl Marx, 'The fetishism of commodities and the secret thereof' (1867), in Robert C. Tucker (ed.), *The Marx-Engels Reader* (New York: W.W. Norton, 1978), pp. 319–29. See also William Pietz, 'The problem of the fetish, I', *Res*, 9 (Spring 1985), 5–17; and 'The problem of the fetish, II: the origin of the fetish', *Res*, 13 (Spring 1987), 23–45.

6 Rochelle Steiner, 'Rirkrit Tiravanija', in Joan Rothfuss and Rochelle Steiner (eds), *Economies: Hans Accola and Rirkrit Tiravanija* (Minneapolis: Walker Art Center, 1995), n. p.

7 Relevant examples from the 1960s include Gordon Matta-Clark and Tina Girouard's alternative space *Food* restaurant and Tom Marioni's *Café Society*. *Food*, which opened in (then undeveloped) SoHo in 1971, operated as a restaurant, performance space and gathering site for the relatively intimate art community. *Café Society*, a series of gatherings organised by Tom Marioni (the founder of San Francisco's Museum of Conceptual Art) took place at Breen's Bar, and was an extension Marioni's earlier project, *The Act of Drinking Beer with Friends is the Highest Form of Art* (1970), in which the artist invited friends to the Oakland Art Museum after it closed to the public in order to drink beer. The remnants from the activities were subsequently exhibited during the following month. For a discussion of Marioni's activities, see Ann Goldstein and Anne Rorimer (eds), *Reconsidering the Object of Art* (Los Angeles: Museum of Contemporary Art, 1995), pp. 172–3.

8 See, for example, Roberta Smith, 'The Gallery is the Message', *The New York Times* (4 October 1992), p. C35; Judith H. Dobrzynski, 'A Popular Couple Charge into the Future of Art, but in Opposite Directions', *The New York Times* (2 September 1997), pp. C1, 13.

9 Although the discourse of identity politics derived from a critique of the subject, and the contention that sexuality, gender, race and ethnicity are external social institutions and/or linguistically constituted notions, in the past several years 'identity' problematically has been equated with autobiography. In the art world, the turning point was the 1993 Whitney Biennial. While excoriated in the press for its supposed instrumentalisation of art for political concerns, the actual problem was the exhibition's promotion of self-indulgence as politics and its reductive approach to the political. The exhibition's format (artworks framed with diaristic statements) and its celebration of a simplistic idea of 'difference' severely undermined both the complexity of the issues it sought to address and the artworks on view.

10 Marcel Mauss, *The Gift: Forms and Functions of Exchange in Archaic Societies*, trans. W. D. Halls (New York and London: Norton, 1990). Mauss's essay has been widely influential not only for anthropology and economics, but in the fields of sociology, history and feminist scholarship, the latter which has examined rites of marriage and issues of domesticity in terms of the gift economy. Among the large body of secondary and primary literature, Arjun Appadurai's *The Social Life of Things: Commodities in Cultural Perspective* (Cambridge: Cambridge University Press, 1986) provides a diverse cross-section of essays that develop issues in Mauss's theory from anthropological, historical and cultural perspectives.

11 Appadurai stresses that this bias is equally present in Marx's economic theorisation, in which 'commodities' are identified as those types of products that are attached

to money and only came into existence under modern capitalism. Appadurai, *The Social Life of Things*, pp. 6–7.

12 Mauss, *The Gift*, p. 3.

13 Ibid.

14 Ibid., p. 12 (my emphases).

15 Ibid., p. 13.

16 In Mauss's words, 'It is not individuals but collectivities that imposed obligations of exchange and contract upon each other.' Ibid., p. 5.

17 In one example, which formed the basis of a lengthier study, Mauss examined the practice of sacrifice in ancient cultures as a gift to the gods, predicated upon the understanding that the gods must reciprocate. Henri Huber and Marcel Mauss, *Sacrifice: Its Nature and Functions*, trans. W. D. Halls (Chicago: University of Chicago Press, 1981).

18 Mauss explained, 'The most valuable copper objects are broken and thrown into the water, in order to put down and to flatten one's rival. In this way, one not only promotes one's family up the social scale. It is therefore a system of law and economics in which considerable wealth is constantly being expended and transferred.' *The Gift*, p. 37.

19 Marcel Mauss, 'Gift, gift' (1929), in Alan Schrift (ed.) *The Logic of the Gift: Toward an Ethic of Generosity* (New York: Routledge, 1997), pp. 28–31.

20 Friedrich Nietzsche, *Thus Spake Zarathustra*, excerpt cited by Schrift, 'Why gift?', in ibid., p. 3.

21 Referring to Benjamin Buchloh's notion of the 'aesthetics of administration', Miwon Kwon has described the proliferation of these arrangements in contemporary art as an 'administration of aesthetics', in which artists accept commissions from institutions to travel and provide various types of services, both in addition to and, in some instances, in lieu of the actual production of material artwork. Kwon writes: 'Generally speaking, the artist used to be a maker of aesthetic objects; now, he/she is a facilitator, educator, coordinator and bureaucrat. Additionally, as artists have adopted managerial functions of art institutions (curatorial, educational, archival) as an integral part of their creative process, managers of art within institutions (curators, educators, public program directors), who often take their cues from these artists, now function as authorial figures in their own right.' Kwon, 'One place after another', 103. See also Benjamin Buchloh, 'Conceptual art: from an aesthetics of administration to a critique of institutions', *October*, 55 (Summer 1991), 105–43.

22 Many of the Hmong immigrants had served in special guerrilla units assisting the United States (specifically the CIA special forces) during the Vietnam War. After the US pullout, they were essentially abandoned, and when the Communist government was declared in Laos in 1975, they fled to Thai refugee camps before travelling to the United States, settling in concentrated groups in Minnesota, California and several other Western states.

23 Richard Flood and Rochelle Steiner, 'En route', *Parkett*, 44 (1995), 115.

24 Despite presenting the exhibition as a collaborative effort between two artists (and thus of equal contribution and importance), Flood characterises Tiravanija's

participation as a gift to the other artist, remarking: By the time his five days of seemingly improvisational installation were up, Rirkrit had made two video tapes, found two couches from the original 1970s arrangements of the gallery, erected a camp site, created a meditation chamber, and proved a nimble, generous collaborator to Hans Accola'. Flood and Steiner, 'En route', 115. For his part, Accola, during a public conversation with Tiravanija about the exhibition, emphasises the differences between their work and working process, specifically regarding the social dimension:

There's certainly not the same kind of direct invitation in my work for people to touch it or sit on it or eat from it and then leave it behind. There's a wide range of possibilities within the forms and relationships I'm putting forth, but it's a different kind of involvement. I don't know if it's a private thing that's being made or what. There's certainly a social/asocial dichotomy between our work.
I really liked how you were able to come right into the museum, embrace everybody, include people to a great extent, and still do what you do. I was much more invisible. I wanted to work at night, and I didn't want the distractions of questions all the time – "what are you going to do?" – simply because I just didn't know; that's not the way I work. I wasn't involved in the same way either. I was involved with the guards, I guess (*laughter*).

Quoted in *Economies*, n. p.

25 Hoptman, 'Rirkrit Tiravanija', n. p.
26 Jacques Derrida, *Given Time: I. Counterfeit Money*, trans. P. Kamuf (Chicago: University of Chicago Press, 1992). As Derrida emphasises, the gift paradoxically contains the very properties of its supposed 'other' (the commodity) thus rendering the opposition itself fundamentally false. The gift *qua* gift, he writes, is 'the very figure of the impossible'.
27 For a further discussion of these issues, see James G. Carrier, *Gifts and Commodities: Exchange and Western Capitalism Since 1700* (New York and London: Routledge, 1995).
28 Bourdieu writes, 'The *habitus*, a product of history, produces individual and collective practices – more history – in accordance with the schemes generated by history. It ensures the active presence of past experiences, which, deposited in each organism in the form of schemes of perception, thought and action, tend to guarantee the 'correctness' of practices and their constancy over time, more reliably than all formal rules and explicit rules.' *The Logic of Practice*, trans. R. Nice (Stanford: Stanford University Press, 1990), p. 54. What is significant in Bourdieu's model is that the *habitus* implies the internalisation of external, collective dispositions, thus maintaining the illusion of individual will and motivation. See also his 'Marginalia: some additional notes on the gift', in Schrift (ed.), *The Logic of the Gift*, p. 232.
29 An example of symbolic capital accumulated under the force of privatisation is the selling of 'naming rights' to lavish new sports stadiums. Although constructed at taxpayers' expense (sold as central features of 'community revitalisation'), these stadiums essentially become mammoth billboards of corporate advertising as well as personal corporate entertainment centres to court potential clients. Of course,

this reaps huge monetary returns (and public good will) for the corporations and their stockholders, not the communities in which these facilities exist.

30 In this spate of global Biennials, identity critiques, derived from academic discourse and cultural criticism, are hinged to the structure of the new global economy. The events, European in origin, quickly developed into propaganda for competing nations to demonstrate cultural and ideological superiority. See Laurie Monahan's 'Cultural cartography: American designs at the 1964 Venice Biennial' for an excellent discussion of the American orchestration of Robert Rauschenberg's 1964 winning of the Venice prize, in Serge Guibault (ed.), *Reconstructing Modernism* (Cambridge: MIT Press, 1990), pp. 369–416. Whether or not this institution can be exported, and operate to empower previously disempowered groups or societies, is an open question.

31 Bataille theorises this economy of expenditure as a 'sacrificial economy'. In an extension of Mauss's analysis, Bataille argues that the underlying ethos of cultures organised around a principle of sacrifice is markedly different from ours, 'Their world-view is singularly and diametrically opposed to the activity-oriented perspective that we have. Consumption loomed just as large in their thinking as production does in ours. They were just as concerned about *sacrificing* as we are about *working*.' Georges Bataille, *The Accursed Share*, vol. I, trans. R. Hurley (New York: Zone Books, 1991), p. 46.

32 Flood and Steiner, 'En route', 116.

33 Ibid., 117.

34 My use of the term 'commodification' thus needs to be understood expansively: as any process of self-containment, enclosure or atemporality.

35 One example is the merging of media empires across different communication forms (e.g. Disney Corp. and ABC/Cap Cities, in which the ability of the ABC news division to critically report on Disney's products and projects is severely hampered, if not eradicated outright). Also to be considered is Microsoft's embedding its web browser within the computer operating system, which spurned the Federal anti-trust suit; as well as the recent interest of media companies (from NBC to Walt Disney and Time Warner) in purchasing internet directory services, such as Snap and Excite, which extract large fees from the web sites to which internet users are directed. The internet itself may be the paradigmatic site of symbolic power relations – touted by techno-utopianists for its ability to create a global community unrestrained by temporal and cultural distance, and unfettered by corporate power and marketing. Every aspect of its operation is increasingly being controlled by corporate conglomerates, who are embracing the opportunity not just to charge large fees to advertisers, but to control what information is readily available to the internet public.

36 Frederic Jameson powerfully argues that under the logic of late capitalism, we must re-examine these past assumptions about the cultural sphere. '[S]ome of our most cherished and time-honored radical conceptions about the nature of cultural politics may thereby find themselves outmoded. However distinct these conceptions – which range from slogans of negativity, opposition, and subversion to critique and reflexivity – may have been, they all shared a single, fundamen-

tally spatial, presupposition, which may be resumed in the equally time-honored formula of "critical distance". No theory of cultural politics current in the Left today has been able to do without one notion or another of certain minimal aesthetic distance, of the possibility of the positioning of the cultural act outside the massive Being of capital, from which to assault this last.' *Postmodernism or, The Cultural Logic of Late Capitalism* (Durham: Duke University Press, 1991), p. 48. I thank Helen Molesworth for pointing out the relevance of Jameson's argument to my discussion.

37 One of the most interesting and, I believe, effective confrontations with this situation is seen in the work of the young collaborative artists, Eric Chan and Heather Schatz (known under the moniker ChanSchatz™). Over the past few years, they have actively sought and secured corporate and other forms of sponsorship – from the donation of expensive computer equipment, to office chairs and bolts of fabric – in order to create their projects, which utilise advanced computer imaging technologies. Without the pretence of operating outside the 'Being of capital', to appropriate Jameson's phrase, their work registers the impossibility of that position without being complicit to it. For example, on the wall of the installation, *Digital System Production*, the sponsor's names were all cited in a text panel that, owing to their sheer number, nullified the individuality and recognisability of the logo. The text panel visualises the overall effect of their work, in that the power of sponsorship, and the accumulation of symbolic capital that it engenders, is essentially subverted from within. Thus, rather than naively seeking to import the strategies of past critical practices, Chan Schatz redefine them in light of the present.

38 Extending back to Frank Stella's now infamous statement, 'What you see is what you see', made during a conversation with Donald Judd and Bruce Glaser in 1964, many artists in the 1960s strategically sought to curtail the possibilities of interpretation: from Judd once declaring that the more he withdrew allusions from his Minimalist sculpture, the more critics strained to form metaphoric readings; to Bruce Nauman's pithy remark that his performance films and installations were 'really difficult to explain'. Stella's comment is found in 'Questions to Stella and Judd', reprinted in Gregory Battcock (ed.), *Minimal Art: A Critical Anthology* (New York: E.P. Dutton, 1968), p. 158.

39 This formed the subject of my exhibition, *Pagan Stories: The Situations of Narrative in Recent Art* (New York: Apex Art, 1997), and its accompanying essay, in which I examine the inscription of narrative in contemporary art as a manifestation of this transformation, as opposed to an attempt to reinvigorate traditional modes of artistic representation.

40 Hal Foster, 'The artist as ethnographer', in *The Return of the Real* (Cambridge: MIT Press, 1997), pp. 171–204.

41 Foster refers to James Clifford's 'On ethnographic authority', a seminal text that challenged the traditional anthropological method of fieldwork, and role of the 'participant observer'. See also James Meyer's discussion of the issue of artist's subjectivity in recent site-oriented projects. Meyer, 'The functional site', 26–8.

42 An ad for IBM (1998) – in which the phrase 'Diversity works' is accompanied by a drawing of an idealised community of managers and executives of all ages, races, physical abilities and sexual orientation – demonstrates how politically progressive

thinking has been recuperated as a marketing device, whether or not accompanied by an actual ideological commitment. A useful analogy can be drawn between this commodifying of difference and Miwon Kwon's discussion of the importing of site-specific 'critical' artworks by institutions and towns as a form of tourist promotion. See Kwon, 'One thing after another', 104–7.

43 The philosopher Jean-François Lyotard refers to the spatialising of concepts as a *commodification*, in that excess energy is saved and force is contained. For example, in reducing difference to opposition within a closed system (such as in Saussurian and Structuralist linguistics) it becomes bounded as a 'concept', rather than an operation that potentially works to undo that system.

44 Gasché writes: 'The success of such a recasting of the notions and categories hitherto employed would lead, however, to an effect whose consequences would be uncontrollable: the otherness, the difference between societies, would be insurmountable and Western thought would be thrown back, for once at least, onto itself and would remain alone with its wretchedness; for henceforth the radical otherness of archaic societies could no longer be considered as the hidden essence of Western culture, its possible supplement, a remedy for difficulties, and, in a word, its *arché*. And at the same time the project as an archaeology would be reduced to a pure vanity. That apprehension, the fear of such consequences, may be precisely the reason why Mauss will abandon that approach.' Randolphe Gasché, 'Heliocentric exchange', in Schrift (ed.), *The Logic of the Gift*, p. 102–3.

45 See Bourdieu, 'Marginalia', pp. 236–8.

10

The face and the public: race, secrecy and digital art practice

Jennifer González

Today we are constantly reminded of the degree to which we are participating in public culture, in political culture, and in online digital culture. A media-saturated environment requires us to define our identities in relation to the culture we consume, while the internet invites us to take up new (and multiple) subject positions in virtual worlds or social networks sites such as Facebook. This chapter explores the way race discourse operates in contemporary digital art as a site for public encounter, and as a trope of 'participation' for artists, audiences and critics alike.

Coming face to face with racial difference has been the focus of participatory artistic practice since the 1960s. Early conceptual examples include Adrian Piper's mediated social encounters, where the formal artistic device of commonplace textual interfaces – calling cards and questionnaires – propelled sometimes unwitting participants to come to terms with their own racial bias. Other live performances in the 1980s and 1990s, like James Luna's *Take a Picture with a Real Indian*, or Guillermo Gomez-Peña and Coco Fusco's *Two Undiscovered Amerindians Visit...*, seduced audience members to enter into carefully choreographed encounters designed to draw out specific forms of racial and cultural bias in relation to the history of photography or ethnographic museum displays, respectively. The works discussed here, by Nancy Burson, Keith Piper and Mongrel, can be seen to converse with these earlier investigations, inviting viewers to attend to race politics, including the colour of their own skin, as a form of social, historical or ethical encounter. The physical actions of participants in these digital works may be fairly minimal (such as clicking a mouse or having a photograph taken) but each of these gestures, however small, proves to be effective in revealing the extent to which race is itself a radically participatory discourse.

*   *   *

The function and importance of race and race discourse in online digital spaces and in contemporary digital art revolves around an apparent paradox. On the one hand, there is a recurring desire to see online digital spaces as sites of universal subjectivity that can escape the limitations of race. This desire tends to intersect with assumptions about public space and systems of ethics that valorise the neutralisation of cultural, racial and sexual difference, as well as historical specificity. The apparently neutral space of the internet is viewed as a potentially progressive domain for overcoming barriers that may otherwise obstruct or restrict ideal forms of participation in the public sphere. On the other hand, a proliferation of racially-marked avatars and experimental hybrids (human and non-human) increasingly populate artificial worlds and online chat spaces. Race, as a set of visual cues operating in graphical interfaces, has literally become a fashion accessory to be bought, sold, traded and toyed with experimentally and experientially online.[1] This proliferation of typologies and pseudo identities provides the opportunity for the expanded display of difference, and this display seems directly and actively to undermine the prospect of the neutral, universal, online subject.

It is not a real paradox, of course, because both conditions operate in parallel to reduce cultural and racial difference to a question of appearance: the domain of visual signs. Online identity, participation and power have become tethered to images (or their elision) for social and political ends. Questions arise, however, concerning the way race discourse actually intersects with the internet, and with digital culture.[2] What are the conditions for ethical relations that entail encounters with racial difference? How do theoretical explorations of 'the face' and 'the public' bear on the subject? If vision and visibility are central to the operative dynamics of race, as has been argued not only by Franz Fanon but many others subsequently, then might it be possible to undo the power of race discourse as an oppressive regime by decoupling it from vision or the visible?[3] Or, alternately, might it be that visual culture is the very place where contemporary race discourse might be most powerfully critiqued and transformed?

These questions are central to recent theories of digital art practice that directly engage race as a dominant and pervasive visual discourse within an emerging public sphere. Technoculture is often praised for the ways it enhances democracy by realising an ideal public sphere. But this view is generally inattentive to the fact that the experience of the technocultural public sphere can also be one of aggression, exclusion and invisibility. Taking the writings of media theorist Mark Hansen as a provocative and symptomatic starting point, this essay explores how the desire for racial 'neutrality' can lead to the unintentional repression of important forms of cultural difference. Two models of ethics, grounded in the writings of Giorgio Agamben and Emmanuel Levinas, respectively, are posed as alternatives in the quest for understanding the importance of 'the face' as a device for the unfolding, or unmaking of race in the public space of the internet.

Universal address

In 2004 Mark Hansen published an essay entitled 'Digitizing the racialized body or the politics of universal address', which was later expanded and substantially revised as a chapter entitled 'Digitizing the racialized body, or the politics of common impropriety', in his 2006 book *Bodies in Code: Interfaces with Digital Media*. In both versions, Hansen argues that the internet provides an unprecedented possibility for a new ethical encounter between humans, in part, because it can render them invisible to each other. Hansen observes that digital art can produce affective states in the user that might ultimately lead to recognising incongruities or incommensurabilities between categories of identity and embodied singularity.[4] Race becomes a lens for Hansen's thinking about online identification as making possible community beyond identity, namely:

> Because race has always been plagued by a certain disembodiment (the fact that race, unlike gender, *is* so clearly a construction, since racial traits are not reducible to organic, i.e., genetic, organization), it will prove especially useful for exposing the limitations of the internet as a new machinic assemblage for producing selves. For this reason, deploying the lens of race to develop our thinking about online identification will help us to exploit the potential offered by the new media for experiencing community beyond identity.[5]

Hansen's use of contemporary art and discourses of racial (dis)embodiment to illustrate his argument are worth further analysis precisely because they signal a set of consistent, symptomatic desires within media theory regarding the potential of the internet. While I applaud Hansen's anti-racist goals, the general framework of both essays risks returning us to an overly utopian, universalising understanding of human relations that leaves little room for more subtle analyses of the concrete effects of cultural, racial and sexual difference operative online today.

Hansen's argument is engaging and nuanced, but reveals a certain racial and cultural privilege. For example, he finds that 'passing' in online environments, that is, posing as someone other than oneself, particularly in terms of race or gender, suspends 'the constraint exercised by the body as a visible signifier or as a receptive surface for the markings of raced and gendered particularity'.[6] In other words, since we are all theoretically invisible online (webcams notwithstanding), and cannot be marked or mapped visually, we can all pass. Hansen hopes that by celebrating the ubiquity of passing online (we all are equally subjected to the condition of *having* to pass) that cultural signifiers (of race, gender) will be shown to have no natural correlation to any particular body and will thus be revealed as no more than 'social codings'.[7] Hansen presents this vision of cyberspace as not merely experimental, but also pedagogical: through the transcendence of visibility, those who are engaged in passing online will, of necessity, learn the very bankruptcy of categories of identity.

Yet 'social codings' are precisely the forms of ideology that are most resistant to transformation. If race is revealed to be (or has scientifically been proven to be) a social *code*, rather than a natural or biological *condition*, this revelation has yet to transform the social function of race in the maintenance of uneven power relations. While some aspects of race, gender and sexuality are performative, as Judith Butler so convincingly argues, it must also be observed that not all forms of performance are equal, nor do they have equal effects.[8] Lisa Nakamura has effectively argued in her book *Cybertypes* that online passing frequently produces stereotypes of race that become solidified through their repeated performance through a kind of 'identity tourism'.[9] Nakamura writes, 'identity tourism is a type of non-reflective relationship that actually widens the gap between the other and the one who only performs itself *as the other*'.[10] While Hansen philosophically hopes performative repetition will render stereotypes void of meaning, Nakamura observes that it appears to merely reinforce narrow conceptions of race. Her argument is echoed in sociological studies showing that racial 'identities' may be more immutable, fixed and shallow in online interaction than offline.[11]

Passing in the real world, or online, entails more than visually choreographing one's appearance, it is a complex *psychic* activity that foregrounds precisely the ways in which subjects are generally fixed by racial typologies. Anyone who has racially passed, or who has worn black face, knows that there is nothing, truly nothing, disembodied about it.[12] Stuart Hall has argued that race is best understood as a discourse, constructed by thought and language, which responds to real, concrete conditions of cultural difference.[13] If the complexity of race discourse is grasped in the fullness of its multiple articulations, then it is not possible to discount processes of identification, fantasy and dominance that racial difference elicits simply because an online image may or may not have a 'real world' referent. Race is always an embodied discourse that acts on, and through, living human beings at the level of corporeal practices, movements, gestures,, and gazes, ultimately constructing and deconstructing the psychological states of individual subjects.[14]

In her essay 'Cyberfeminism, racism, embodiment', Maria Fernandez argues that unspoken anxieties attending the conception of race and racial difference produce a kind of physical haunting that emerges as a set of frequently unconscious and involuntary rote behavioural habits.[15] Drawing on earlier feminist analyses of embodiment, Fernandez suggests that, although much has been written about race as an ideological construct, the *performance* of racism in everyday physical and social interactions is of fundamental concern for understanding its continued reproduction.

Race as a set of embodied practices supports Michael Omi and Howard Winant's conception of race as a social formation that is constantly under revision. What they call 'racial formations' can be found both in small moments (at the micro-level) of racist encounter and in systemic (or macro-level) epistemological approaches to cultural and ontological understandings of human being.[16] Taken together, these theorists provide a framework for understanding race as a complex and nuanced discourse functioning at every level of individual and collective representation, consciousness, behaviour and organisation. Online passing is never free from the social, historical, linguistic and psychological constraints and conditions that also shape racial discourse offline. The invisibility of 'real' bodies cannot, alone, produce a racially neutral space or even racially neutral subjects.

Visual corruption, affective purity

Hansen supports his argument for the liberating aspects of the internet, not with an online art project where passing is an essential element of engagement, but rather with an offline video game called *Caught Like a Nigger in Cyberspace* (figure 10.1), which appeared on a CD-ROM that British artist Keith Piper included in the catalogue for his exhibition *Relocating the Remains* (1997). The game requires the user to encounter a series of obstacles on the way to the promising realm of 'cyberspace'. Standardised identification forms, for example, offer limited choices for the user who must select among such identities as 'tech-head' or 'Al Gore'. If the user clicks on 'Other', the application for entry into cyberspace is put on hold. At this point, the user can choose to wait indefinitely in a waiting room or click a button that says, 'Do not touch.' If one chooses to disobey and touch the button, a black male figure appears on the bottom of the screen. Seen from behind, the figure appears to be running, either toward a promising future or into the labyrinth of a hostile territory, depending on the subsequent choices of the game player. *Caught like a Nigger in Cyberspace* invites the player to identify with the running figure whose future unfolds in a dystopic landscape. Because there is no clear way to win the game, it ultimately provides a counter-discourse to utopian visions of cyberspace, and it more specifically indicates the racial divide that exists, both economically and culturally, between those with access to the internet and those without.

For Hansen, the game also offers an unusual opportunity for a new kind of feeling – frustration. He describes his own experience of struggling to succeed at playing the game, his various thwarted attempts at success and a final 'affective-overflow' that occurs when he is unable to 'correlate the sensations generated by the video game with some appropriate action'.[17] More specifically, he states:

the work compels its viewer to live through the exclusion of certain bodies from cyberspace via the frantic temporal mode of a survival exercise, thereby mobilizing the disappointment of viewer expectations concerning the payoff of video game-playing (where some kind of clear victory is an always achievable goal) in order to deliver a message about racial inequality.[18]

Hansen implies an underlying parallel between his own affective response of frustration playing the game and the materially specific situation of 'living through exclusion' from cyberspace. For Hansen, this affective response is uniquely possible in the artificial space of the digital realm, precisely because he can enter into the space of the game, experience the artificiality of racial identifications, and thereby become distanced from his own social position by recognising the 'bankruptcy' of the racialised image of the other.

Hansen argues that the 'raced image' (I presume he means images of non-white subjects) can no longer broker processes of identity formation or struggles for recognition precisely because the image is always already corrupted by the spectacle that is capitalism, as well as by the long history of racially oppressive regimes of visual representation (particularly in the human sciences) that remain in force as instruments for classification and exclusion.[19] I agree that people bring to the internet (consciously and unconsciously) the inheritance of image cultures that precede them when encountering hegemonic visual discourses online that tend to co-opt, transform, or overpower other forms of image signification. Hansen clearly grasps the ways in which

10.1   Keith Piper, *Caught Like a Nigger in Cyberspace*, 1997.

power operates unequally to create robust forms of racial oppression for different subjects. He nicely summarises Franz Fanon's discussion of the 'racial epidermal schema' in order to articulate how both black and white subjects suffer when real black bodies are reduced to racially stereotyped images.[20]

Along with Fanon, Hansen suggests that racial difference and racial oppression, can interrupt coherent forms of identification for all subjects. I agree with these observations, but not with Hansen's conclusion that the problem hinges exclusively on the *visual*. He argues that, because 'technically facilitated' forms of community suspend 'the overdetermination exercised by the (visual) image of the racial other, online identity play creates the possibility for a "zero-degree" of racial identification, a potential universality rooted in the precariousness of any identity as a fixation of embodied individuation'.[21] For Hansen, images on the internet should therefore be summarily rejected as a viable system of meaning or exchange. By pitting the concrete particularity of the visual image against the ineffable and transitory experience of *affect*, Hansen hopes to show how the 'raced image' is an always already corrupted medium 'stripped of any positive meaning for the subjects that it would mark'.[22] Affect thus emerges as a kind of pure and universal category of feeling. Hansen summarises:

> Piper seizes the empty husk of the raced image, not to rehabilitate it against capitalist fetishism, but to extract its redemptive kernel. In the various ways we have explored, he deploys this empty image as the catalyst for a reinvestment of the body beyond the image, for an exposure of the rootedness of life in a source, affectivity, that lies beyond identity and individuality and thus beyond the reach of commodification.[23]

There are two problems with this argument. First, affect is not impervious to capitalism, nor does it exist abstractly, beyond the experience of actual human subjects and their particular identities. Eliciting affect, in the form of pre-packaged desires, might be one of capitalism's most successful means of self-reproduction. Specific kinds of affect (anxiety, horror, compassion) that can be predicted and managed might even be one of capitalism's primary commodities. More to the point, affect is historical, not a-temporal, both in the life of the individual and for groups. In her essay on contemporary websites that operate through a model of collective feeling or experience (the Aryan Nations website presenting white supremacy as a form of love rather than hate, for example), Sara Ahmed writes,

> the role of feelings in mediating the relation between individual and collective bodies is complicated. How we feel about another – or a group of others – is not simply a matter of individual impressions, or impressions that are created anew in the present. Rather, feelings rehearse associations that are already in

place, in the way in which they 'read' the proximity of others, at the same time as they establish the 'truth' of the reading. The impressions we have of others, and the impressions left by others are shaped by histories that stick, at the same time as they generate the surfaces and boundaries that allow bodies to appear in the present.[24]

For Ahmed, it is structures of feeling that shape the very appearance of bodies in the domain of the visual, and provide the conditions for their legibility. Affect does not exist 'beyond' individuals and communities, nor is it separable from the circulation of signs – including visual signs – that produce it or derive from it.

Second, images cannot be 'empty' or 'full'. Images are signs deployed strategically within the context of an ongoing circulation of other signs. Whether 'raced' or not, images have different meanings for each subject who encounters them, regardless of their hegemonic or subaltern position. It is not possible therefore to argue, as Hansen does, that a given image is 'stripped of any positive meaning' a priori. If the 'raced' image is merely an 'empty husk' for Hansen, it may have more to do with his acceptance of it as stereotype, than with its actual potential for progressive transformation and identification. It is true that a long history of racist portrayals has repressed human qualities in order to depict a given subject as a caricature or 'type' rather than as a unique individual.[25] For this reason, it is all the more important to attend to the ways that particular images perpetuate this tradition, and the ways in which other images work against it. As with semantic reversals of words, such as 'black', images that have served as tools of domination (i.e. racial stereotypes) have also been redeployed to serve a counter-hegemonic purpose.[26] Although Hansen's reading of Piper's work is clearly sympathetic, his insistence on the emptiness of the image in favour of the fullness of his own affective response obscures the deep, critical engagement with image culture that is its very basis.

The original installation of *Relocating the Remains* addressed the history of the African diaspora from the period of colonisation, through the Atlantic slave trade, to the migrations of the present. In one example, *Surveillances: Tagging the Other* (1992), Piper installed a row of four video screens on which a black male body is seen to be subject to the gaze of a variety of dominant surveillance technologies, from eugenics to criminology. Each screen shows a head and shoulders view – sometimes in profile like a mug shot, sometimes with a frontal view – framed by a map or landscape and a set of geometric diagrams, suggesting that he is both surveyed and silenced, both made to appear and prohibited from enunciation. When this piece was originally shown at the Institute of Contemporary Art in Boston, viewers were invited to activate the four screens by pointing an infrared gun and shooting at each image like a target. It was a decidedly unpleasant element of engagement.

What became clear immediately was that the work was not only about the body – or the face – as a target of racist violence but also about the responsibility one takes in relation to that body: the moment of pulling the artificial trigger became entwined with forms of physical assault in the culture at large; the violence necessary to activate the image in the space of the gallery invited comparisons with other forms of representational violence both in the history of art and in forms of museum display.

As with *Caught Like a Nigger in Cyberspace*, the digital interface had a powerful effect, but the image of the targeted subject was far from secondary; it was the very ground of the work's signification. The 'black' body is a signifier of critical importance, as an organising condition of possibility for historical subjectivity, as well as a locus for forms of subjection or subjugation. For Piper, visual images are not, or not only, always already corrupted signs participating in the spectacle that is capitalism; they can also be the site for significant identifications particularly for those subjects who are interpellated by them and can recognise themselves in specific histories of embodiment.

The face

Underlying Hansen's basic argument is a hopeful interest in the possibility that some kind of unprecedented ethical relation might emerge from the anonymity – the facelessness – of the internet and other forms of new media. He turns to the notions of the 'improper' and the 'whatever body' from the writings of Giorgio Agamben in order to argue for digital media's potential to produce the conditions for the emergence of an identity-less, subject-less singularity, citing the following passage from *The Coming Community*: 'if humans could, that is, not be-thus in this or that particular biography, but be only *the* thus, their singular exteriority and their face, then they would for the first time enter into a community without presuppositions and without subjects, into a communication without the incommunicable'.[27] Agamben suggests, in essence, the utopian possibility of human encounter that relies on a kind of purity of presence, where all else (history, memory, gender, race and class) falls away. Counter-intuitively, for Agamben 'the face' is not the human visage, in its material presence, but rather what he calls an opening to communicability. He writes, 'there is a face wherever something reaches the level of exposition and tries to grasp its own being exposed, wherever a being that appears sinks in that appearance and has to find a way out of it. (Thus art can give a face even to an inanimate object … and it may be that nowadays the entire Earth, which has been transformed into a desert by humankind's blind will, might become one single face.)'[28]

For Agamben, 'the face' is a restless power, a threshold, a simultaneity and being-together of the manifold 'visages' constituting it; it is the duality of communication and communicability, of potential and act. It seems, therefore, to be both the form and the function of signification. Yet it is also an ontological or existential state. He writes, 'in the face I exist with all of my properties (my being brown, tall, pale, proud, emotional …); but this happens without any of these properties essentially identifying me or belonging to me.'[29] Agamben wants us to be able to imagine the unique character of each human subject without limiting this uniqueness to surface representations, to the limits of particular resemblances between people, to the frameworks of socially defined characteristics. He not only wants us to be able to imagine this state but also to somehow voluntarily achieve it. He writes in the imperative: 'be only your face. Go to the threshold. Do not remain the subject of your properties or faculties, do not stay beneath them; rather, go with them, in them, beyond them.'[30]

Artist Nancy Burson's *Human Race Machine* (1999–) echoes Agamben's call, but replaces the universal singularity of the subject with universal sameness, emphasising the physical and racial properties of humans in an effort to precisely erase or transcend their significance. The artwork combines a complicated viewing-booth apparatus with a patented morphing technology that will transform a snapshot portrait of the user into a series of racially distinct replicas. A digital algorithm adjusts bone structure, skin tone, and eye shape, automatically reproducing the same face with a range of facial features, which is then displayed on the computer screen as a row of uncanny doppelgangers. Burson claims that the *Human Race Machine* is her 'prayer for racial equality' and suggests that, 'there is only one race, the human one.'[31] 'The more we recognize ourselves in others', Burson writes, 'the more we can connect to the human race.'[32] Her work adheres to the same conception of race as primarily a concern with visual appearance found in Hansen, but she reverses the importance of the image in the production of a universal subject. The power of visual representation, for Burson, lies in its ability to produce forms of cross-racial identification, whereas for Hansen visual representations of race are always already corrupted by their ideological history and therefore cannot be used productively as sites of identification.

Burson also claims that 'the *Human Race Machine* allows us to move beyond differences and arrive at sameness.'[33] Despite her progressive intentions, Burson's desire seems strangely undone by the artwork itself. Instead of promising greater human sameness, the *Human Race Machine* appears to offer a thinly veiled fantasy of *difference*. Presenting the argument that 'there is no gene for race', the *Human Race Machine* allows the user to engage in what Lisa Nakamura might call 'identity tourism'. As a form of temporary racial tourism, Burson's machine may make the process of cross-racial identification appear plausible, but its artificiality does nothing to reveal how people live their lives, or even how they engage with cyberspace.

To be more specific, the *Human Race Machine* does not offer users any insight into the privileges or discriminations that attend racial difference, such as the experience of being ignored by taxis or denied housing, being harassed by the police, receiving unfair legal representation, or having one's very life threatened. Instead, it offers users a kind of false promise of universality through the visual mechanics of race. By using the face as a device that is ultimately mutable and theoretically non-identitarian, she shows how any face (this time the actual visage) might become like any other face, any *whatever* face, and by doing so implies that the racial discourses attached to those signs will fall away. Like Agamben, Burson invites us to attend to our physical traits, our 'properties', in order that we might transcend them. Yet both fail to attend to the social and political constraints that might impede this transcendence.

In contrast, Franz Fanon has eloquently theorised the involuntary condition of *epidermalisation* that precisely interrupts the concrete possibility of being *only* one's 'face' (in Agamben's sense) because of one's racially defined, physical 'visage'.[34] Fanon describes the moment when he realised his own 'properties' were in fact created by others, writing: 'below the corporeal schema I had sketched a historico-racial schema. The elements that I used had been provided for me … by the other, the white man, who had woven me out of a thousand details, anecdotes, stories.'[35] As Delan Mahendran nicely summarises, for Fanon 'the racial-epidermal schema is the interior horizon of self and others in immediate perceptual experience of the world. The racial epidermal schema impacts a black person's tacit sense of self. The racial epidermal schema immediately in play is the phenomenon of appearing or showing up as black in an anti-black world.'[36]

When Agamben suggests that 'there is a face wherever something reaches the level of exposition and tries to grasp its own being exposed, wherever a being that appears sinks in that appearance and has to find a way out of it', he reveals the very fact of a subject who is undergoing the process of exposition, that is, of being defined, of being explained, framed, delimited and exposed as an *appearance*, and who is trying to grasp this exposition. One might say that this is an insightful description of the very process of racial formation, of epidermalisation, or of subjection per se. But for those human subjects who are constantly enclosed into these properties or faculties by *others*, Agamben's call to 'go with them, in them, beyond them' seems not only utopian (literally appropriate for a space that does not exist) but also blind to the conditions by which humans subjects are, indeed, produced through elaborately constructed discourses and relations with *other* humans. These discourses and relations are designed to prevent precisely this voluntary opening of 'the face', to prevent any movement beyond racial particularity. Perhaps this is why Agamben, to his credit, frames his argument as a conditional statement that marks the edge of the possible: if humans *could* be only 'their face' – that is, exist in a state of utter openness and non-identity – then they might for the first time enter into a 'community without presuppositions'. Agamben's approach to ethics is ultimately privileged in origin and messianic in structure, working toward a future point of unknowable possibility without attending in any depth to the material conditions of difference in the present.

Writing before Agamben, Emmanuel Levinas elaborated 'the face' as the critical site of human ethical encounter. For Levinas, the absolute infinity of the Other, legible in the physical presence of the face, simultaneously manages to appear within and exceed this material frame. Levinas foregrounds his ambivalence concerning visual knowledge by opening his discussion of 'Ethics and the face' in *Totality and Infinity* by stating, 'inasmuch as the access to beings concerns vision, it dominates those beings, exercises a power over them.'[37] He goes on to explain how the face is the condition for the visibility of the other *as* Other, and the origin for the opportunity to enter into speech and discourse. He writes, 'the idea of infinity is produced in the opposition of conversation, in sociality. The relation with the face, with the other absolutely other which I cannot contain, the other in this sense infinite, is nonetheless my Idea, a commerce.'[38] We can see clear parallels with Agamben's theorising of the face, which is clearly indebted to Levinas, but the latter seems to be more attuned to the involuntary nature of this coming into relation via the face-to-face encounter and to the responsibility and possible fraternity that emerges from this. He writes,

> one has to respond to one's right to be, not by referring to some abstract and anonymous law, or judicial entity, but because of one's fear for the Other. My being-in-the-world or my 'place in the sun', my being at home, have these not also been the usurpation of spaces belonging to the other man whom I have already oppressed or starved, or driven out into a third world; are they not acts of repulsing, excluding, exiling, stripping, killing?'[39]

Even given this sombre revelation that the encounter with the Other, with 'the face', is not a pure state of abstracted unity but also always grounded in the conditions of history and contingency, Levinas is not without hope that the radical and uncontainable Otherness that appears in face-to-face encounters can nevertheless be maintained 'without violence, in peace with this absolute alterity. The resistance of the other does not do violence to me, does not act negatively; it has a positive structure: ethical.'[40] While Agamben grounds the possibility of ethical encounters through an *erasure* of difference, Levinas grounds it *through* difference, since 'the face resists possession, resists my powers.'[41] It is this very resistance that allows us to recognise the infinity of the Other who always exists beyond, and in excess of, the mechanisms (whether visual or discursive, historical or taxonomic) which we might use to frame or delimit it. More to the point, our own historicity depends upon the Other, our

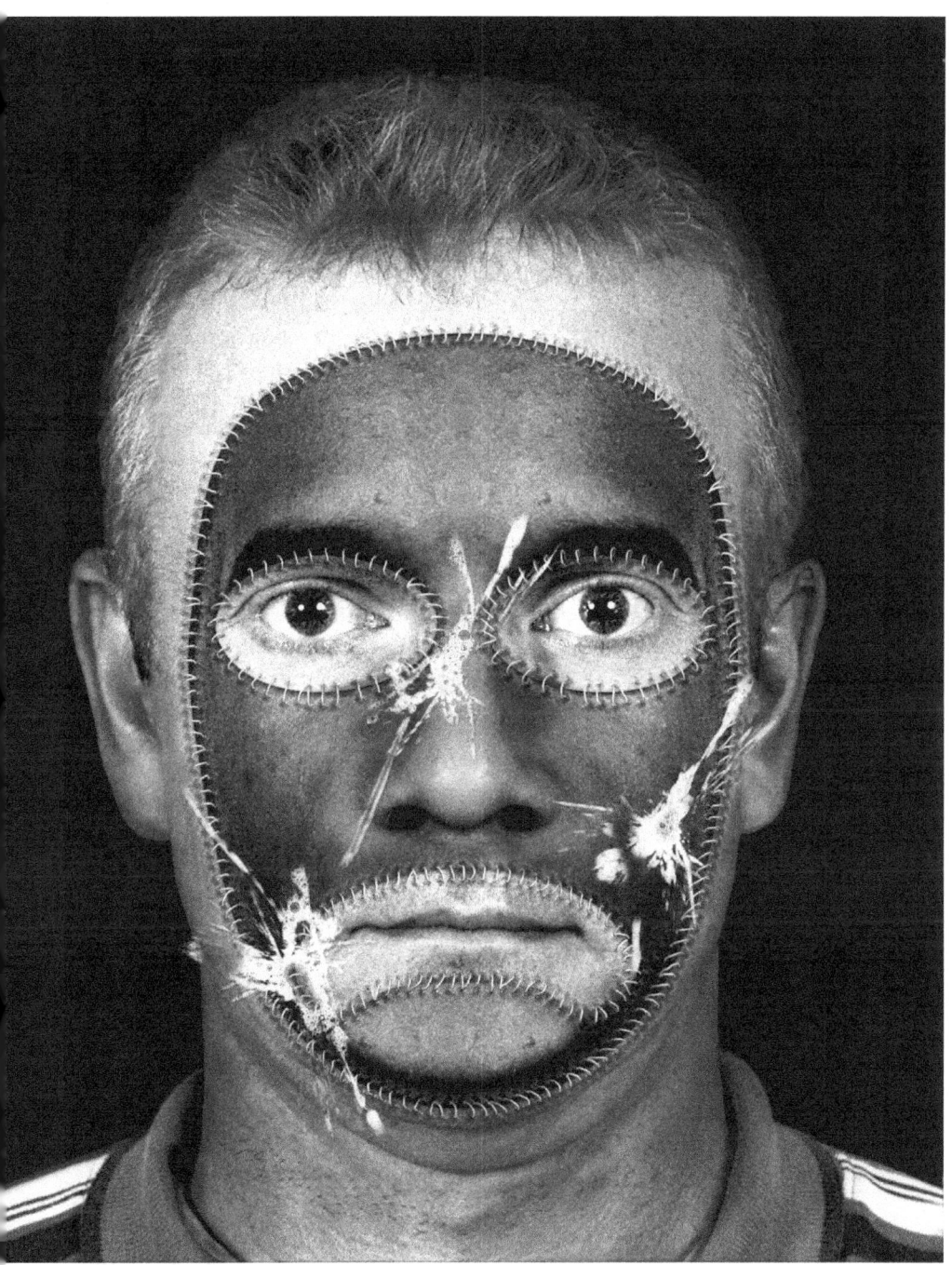

Mongrel, *Colour Separation*, 1997.   **10.2**

situatedness becomes defined by having to answer to, and for, histories which we may not have previously conceived as our own.

In contrast to Nancy Burson's *Human Race Machine*, which works to produce a form of seamless identification in her audience through the visual production of racial equivalence, the British-Jamaican artist collective Mongrel (Graham Harwood, Mervin Jarman, Matsuko Yokokoji, Richard Pierre Davis and Matthew Fuller) leverages the iconicity of the face to elicit a structure of ambivalence. Their print and online project *Colour Separation* (1997) offered users the opportunity to encounter masked subjects who signified as imaginary projections of racial types (figure 10.2). Each of the composite images consisted of a simple frontal head shot of a man or woman, upon which a smaller photographic mask of a different racial type was apparently sewn, revealing the eyes and mouth of the subject underneath. Produced with their own morphing software, strategically named 'Heritage Gold', the images were compiled from over one hundred photographs of people who were somehow connected to the core members of the art group into eight racial stereotypes. Echoing the processes of composite photography used in the early twentieth century to define criminal and racial types, these images emerged as the sign of the impossible referent – that is, they signified subjects who do not exist except in digital form, and in the imagination of those who created them. The phrase 'colour separation' also refers to an image processing technique that entails creating separate screens (magenta, cyan, black and yellow) for colour image printing – an artificial and mechanical process not unlike racial categorisation.

The layering of a racially distinct mask on top of the face implied not one but two subjects defined both by difference and intimacy, by their mutual interdependence and potential interchange. These double portraits reappeared in Mongrel's installation *National Heritage* (1999) with a dynamic, interactive element: by clicking on individual faces the user added another layer, of spit. These unexpected marks, not immediately legible as saliva, marred the surface of the face. At the same time, a voice recounted in some detail a personal narrative of everyday racial abuse, of which the spit was a visual sign. In drawing out the complexity of human race relations – its micro-violence and the inescapable complicity of every viewer – the work functions as a disruptive device in the ongoing experiments of race discourse. By naming its specialised morphing software Heritage Gold, Mongrel played off the rather insidious euphemistic term 'heritage', used in British culture typically to signify the preservation of a white, English patrimony. Rachel Green observes, 'based on the ubiquitous graphics software Adobe Photoshop, Heritage Gold replaces its banal tools and commands ("Enlarge", "Flatten") with terms pregnant with racial and class significance ("Define Breed", "Paste into Host Skin", "Rotate World View").[42] Pull-down menus allow users to transform photographic images according to racial types such as East Indian, Chinese and Caucasian.

Such designations reveal the strange equation of national identities with racial identities and seem to parallel the kind of morphing fantasies and identity tourism found in Nancy Burson's *Human Race Machine*. One crucial difference is that Heritage Gold is a free, unpatented, shareware that allows users to produce these visual manipulations and transformations themselves rather than imposing a homogenising algorithm on all participants. Both *Colour Separation* and the Heritage Gold software engage not merely the question of racism as a complex, multi-participant event without immediate remedy; both also emphasise the ways in which this condition is mediated by visibility and invisibility. As Graham Harwood writes, 'In this work as in the rest of society we perceive the demonic phantoms of other "races". But these characters never existed just like the nigger bogeyman never existed. But sometimes … reluctantly we have to depict the invisible in order to make it disappear.'[43]

In drawing out the impasses and intersections of human race relations, the work functions as a salutary disruptive device that more closely approximates a Levinasian ethics in which the resistance to possession takes place in the public domain of cyberspace. Common to all of these examples is the logic of the face as a visible threshold to the domain of communication, and ultimately to a practice of ethics. In the long tradition of portraiture, so thoroughly theorised in the history of art, the face is the object of public encounter, a device that mediates the historicity of the subject and its interior character. As many scholars have argued, the portrait and the face are primarily rhetorical, functioning like speech acts in both argument and address.[44] Sharing an etymology with façade, the face is architectural in its features, and potentially false in its design. This is the lure and disappointment of the face, both for the early twentieth-century eugenicist who hopes to discover in the features of the face the proof of racial superiority, and for the artist who hopes to capture in a glance or profile the essence of identity. At the bureaucratic level, however, the face guarantees legal status, defines passport control, and provides the focus of most surveillance and security technologies. As Sandy Nairne observes, 'In a future presumed by many thinkers to involve digital enhancement, electronic recording and constant surveillance, the technology of recognition (attributed to increased security pressures) promises to make the science of the face an arena for further work and development.'[45]

As the most reproduced visual sign on the internet, the face continues to operate as the threshold to public space. Facebook, the largest social networking site on the internet with more than 80 million registered members, has uploaded more than four billion images between 2003 and 2007.[46] Ninety per cent of the profiles on Facebook contain an image; most are faces. Each face is presented as one point in a nexus of other faces, each with its own extending network, creating vast pools of tenuous social links that grow exponentially. Unlike the portraits of previous eras, depicting wealth or fame, the faces on Facebook depict anyone who can follow the simple uploading directions on the website. More importantly, the face is no longer presented as singular and isolated, but becomes the ultimate origin of other faces; always defined by, surrounded by, and in some way guaranteed by the visual presence of others. The meaning of the Facebook face is not limited to facial features, to the façade, but extends to the other faces to which it is linked. Within multiple trajectories of signification, the face enlivens and mobilises social connections that become much more significant than the photographic representation of individuals. Yet race and class still play a role in the way Facebook and other sites, like MySpace, construct networks of inclusion and exclusion, such that membership and a sense of belonging are already circumscribed via categories existing in the culture at large.[47]

The public secret

The desire to locate a universal quality in human subjects or the allure of forms of universal address – the two are not the same, but the latter frequently presupposes the former – is probably tied to a will to eradicate not merely individual differences, but any difference that is believed to create an impediment to public action, public consensus, or communication. Race has traditionally been thought of as a 'quality' of individuals, therefore reducible by Agamben and other theorists, like Hansen, to a property or mere set of appearances that one can theoretically 'move beyond'. But race is not a *property*; it is a *relation of public encounter*.

In her book, *Publicity's Secret: How Technoculture Capitalizes on Democracy*, Jodi Dean observes that our widespread differences in culture, practice, language, information, race, status, religion and education in the world (and especially in online digital culture) preclude the possibility that 'the public' can refer to 'all of us'. Why, then, does the idea of 'the public' persist? For Dean 'the public' is symbolic; it may not exist in fact, but it still has real social effects both in political thought and in law. For these discourses, 'the public' is a central organising trope commonly contrasted with 'the private', such that the borders of this demarcation are the subject of theory, debate and controversy. Dean shifts this opposition by proposing another: that between 'the public' and 'the secret', and writes,

> few contemporary accounts of publicity acknowledge the secret. Instead they adopt a spatial model of a social world divided between public and private spheres. For the most part, the accounts claim either priority of the one or the

other ignoring the system of distrust, the circuit of concealment and revelation, that actively generates the public. To this extent they seem unable to theorize the power of publicity, the compulsion to disclose and the drive to survey.[48]

The 'other' of the public is not the private but the hidden, the unknown, even the unknowable. The secret is both the object of desire and fascination and the threat to the coherence of the public as homogeneous, open, knowable condition of universal participation.

Publicity requires secrets, for Dean, in so far as the secret maps the limit of public discourse. Secrecy is always a public fact. Revealing secrets is one of the goals of publicity, but producing secrets is another goal. Power resides in what people conceal as well as what they reveal, whether as part of the hegemony or the subaltern classes. Race and other forms of cultural difference have been historically presented as secret unknowns that require definition, mapping, measuring and legislating by those in power, in order to render them public. Race both constitutes and is constituted by the public. Race produces a form of resistance to ideals of the public because it stands as a marker of difference that stubbornly resists transformation or incorporation. Race serves as an aspect of secrecy in the logic of publicity, but as an already publicly constructed discourse, its secrets are plainly evident. This is its fundamental contradiction. As Homi Bhabha has observed

> the fetish of colonial discourse – what Fanon calls the epidermal schema – is not, like the sexual fetish, a secret. Skin, as the key signifier of cultural and racial difference in the stereotype is the most visible of fetishes, recognized as 'common knowledge' in a range of cultural, political and historical discourses, and plays a public part in the racial drama that is enacted every day in colonial societies.[49]

Racial schemas work to hide or mask not only individuals *as* individuals but also their real and imagined historical conditions.

If racial difference has frequently accompanied an emerging relation of imperial or colonial domination and violence, and a resulting economic and social asymmetry that profoundly mark our present moment, the humans living through this history have been, and continue to be, produced in radically different ways from each other and thus remain mysterious to each other. The sign of this mystery on the body, through the skin, elicits a general suspicion and curiosity. A fascination and compulsion to know or to reveal the mystery (which is the past), is countered by a simultaneous desire *not* to know this past. This ambivalent condition guards against the memory of the historical meaning of race. Hence, as David Marriot observes in his book, *Haunted Life*, the fearful projections accompanying the gaze that produces the raced subject are always haunted by the past, but 'what haunts is not so much the imago spun through with myths, anecdotes, stories, but the shadow or stain that is sensed behind it and that disturbs well-being'.[50]

The philosophical imperative for a homogeneous universal subject, without racial or cultural specificity, who might therefore properly participate in a 'neutral' public sphere can be seen as a demand for subjects not only to reveal their secrets, but to find ways to live without them; in other words, to find ways not to be *disturbing*. Jodi Dean argues that while the internet may, indeed, provide one site for democratic politics, it does not constitute a public sphere, particularly in the Habermasian sense of equal access and homogeneous participation. In fact, she suggests that the public sphere, with all of its structure of spectacle, suspicion, or celebrity, is the wrong model for understanding political process or democracy, especially within technoculture; rather, she suggests that we conceive of the web as an intersecting nexus of 'issue networks' that produce 'neo-democracies', borrowing these terms from Richard Rogers and Noorjte Marres.[51] For Dean, traditional 'public sphere' models rely on the nation as a site, consensus as a goal, rationality as a means, and individual actors as a vehicle, whereas the 'neo-democracy' model relies on the web as a kind neutral institution with contestation as a goal, networked conflict as a means, and the issues themselves (rather than individual actors) as a vehicle.

In different ways, Piper and Mongrel offer visions of race discourse as embedded in the domain of the public yet, like Dean, they eschew the ideal of a Habermasian public sphere. They instead examine the domain of technoculture with a healthy suspicion of the forms by which race discourse can be reproduced within it, particularly as a new form of capital or as an object of surveillance. For Piper, the public is an archive to be mapped, and an obstacle course to be run. For Mongrel, the public is an uneven terrain where unpredictable encounters can result in confrontation and transformation, but never final resolution. The kind of visual artefacts they produce offer alternatives to the hegemony of the images found elsewhere on the internet, and they participate in the kind of critical discourse important to any neo-democracy.

We can conclude that it is not yet possible to decouple race discourse as an oppressive regime from vision or the visible, and that visual culture (both on- and offline) is the very place where contemporary race discourse might be most powerfully critiqued and transformed. As Judith Butler has written,

> The media representations of the faces of the 'enemy' efface what is most human about the 'face' for Levinas. Through a cultural transposition of his philosophy, it is possible to see how dominant forms of representation can and must be disrupted for something about the precariousness of life to be apprehended. This has implications, once again, for the boundaries that constitute what will and will not appear within public life, the limits of a publicly

acknowledged field of appearance. Those who remain faceless or whose faces are presented to us as so many symbols of evil, authorize us to become sense-less before those lives we have eradicated, and whose grievability is indefinitely postponed. Certain faces must be admitted into public view, must be seen and heard for some keener sense of the value of life, all life, to take hold.[52]

The idea of a neo-democracy, with its emphasis on contestation and conflict centred on political issues rather than a consensus model addressing universal subjects might be a more appealing ideal, not only for the interactions of cyberspace, but also for the lived politics of our everyday lives.

Notes

This chapter was originally written for the journal *Camera Obscura*, 24: 1 (April 2009) and is excerpted here by permission. I would like to thank Wendy Chun, Lynn Joyrich, the students in the 2007–8 cohort of the Whitney Independent Study Program, and Jonathan Weiss for comments and responses to an early draft of this chapter.

1 Lisa Nakamura, *Cybertypes* (New York: Routledge, 2002), p. 57.
2 See Jennifer González, 'Electronic *habitus*: agit-prop in an imaginary world', in John R. Hall, Blake Stimson and Lisa Tamiris Becker (eds), *Visual Worlds* (New York: Routledge, 2005), pp. 117–38; 'Morphologies: race as visual technology', in Coco Fusco and Brian Wallis (eds), *Only Skin Deep: Changing Visions of the American Self* (New York: International Center of Photography, 2003), pp. 379–93; and 'The appended subject: race and identity as digital assemblage', in Beth Kolko, Lisa Nakamura, Gil Rodman (eds), *Race in Cyberspace* (New York: Routledge, 2000), pp. 27–50.
3 Franz Fanon, *Black Skin, White Masks*, trans. C. Lam Markmann (New York: Grove, 1967).
4 Mark Hansen, 'Digitizing the racialized body or the politics of universal address', *Substance*, 33 (2004), 107–33. All citations are from the revised version: 'Digitizing the racialized body, or the politics of common impropriety', in *Bodies in Code: Interfaces with Digital Media* (New York and London: Routledge, 2006), pp. 139–73. I include the title of the first essay because it indicates Hansen's emphasis on the ways in which the internet can serve as a site of 'universal' address or participation. Hansen's revised version of the essay offers a much more nuanced articulation of the way race discourse forms conditions for embodiment both on and offline.
5 Ibid., pp. 140–1.
6 Ibid., p. 144.
7 Ibid., p. 147.
8 Judith Butler, *Gender Trouble* (New York: Routledge, 1990), p. 25.
9 Nakamura, *Cybertypes*, p. 57.
10 Ibid., p. 57 (my emphasis).
11 Byron Burkhalter, 'Reading race online: discovering racial identity in usenet discussions', in Marc A. Smith and Peter Kollock (eds), *Communities in Cyberspace*

(New York: Routledge, 1999), p. 63.

12 See Marlon Riggs's film *Ethnic Notions*, 1987.

13 Stuart Hall, 'Subjects in history: making diasporic identities', in Wahneema Lubiano (ed.), *The House that Race Built* (New York: Vintage, 1998), pp. 289–99.

14 Fanon, *Black Skin*, p. 88.

15 Maria Fernandez, 'Cyberfeminism, racism, embodiment', in Maria Fernandez, Faith Wilding and Michelle M. Wright (eds), *Domain Errors: Cyberfeminist Practices* (Brooklyn: Autonomedia, 2002).

16 Michael Omi and Howard Winant, *Racial Formation in the United States: From the 1960s to the 1990s* (New York: Routledge, 1994), p. 60.

17 Hansen, 'Digitizing the racial body', p. 167.

18 Ibid.

19 Ibid., p. 172.

20 Ibid., p. 156

21 Ibid.

22 Ibid., p. 172.

23 Ibid.

24 Sara Ahmed, 'Collective feelings, or the impressions left by others', *Theory, Culture & Society*, 21:2 (2004), 39.

25 Henry Louis Gates Jr, 'The face and voice of blackness', in Christopher C. French (ed.), *Facing History: The Black Image in American Art 1710–1940* (San Francisco: Bedford Arts, 1990), pp. xxix–xliv.

26 There are many examples in the fine arts, but the work of Betye Saar (*Liberation of Aunt Jemima*, 1972) or Fred Wilson (*Mine/Yours*, 1995) come to mind.

27 Agamben, quoted in Hansen, 'Digitizing the racial body', p. 143.

28 Giorgio Agamben, 'The face', in *Means Without End: Notes on Politics*, trans. V. Binetti and C. Casarino (Minneapolis: University of Minnesota Press, 2000), p. 63.

29 Giorgio Agamben, 'Without classes', in *The Coming Community*, trans. Michael Hardt (Minneapolis: University of Minnesota Press, 1993), p. 98.

30 Ibid., p. 99.

31 Nancy Burson, www.nancyburson.com/human_fr.html (accessed March 21, 2008).

32 Ibid.

33 Ibid.

34 Fanon, *Black Skin*, p. 11.

35 Ibid., p. 111.

36 Delan Mahendran, 'The facticity of blackness', *Human Architecture: Journal of the Sociology of Self-Knowledge*, 5 (Summer, 2007), 198.

37 Emmanuel Levinas, *Totality and Infinity: an Essay on Exteriority*, trans. A. Lingis (Pittsburgh: Duquesne University Press, 1969), p. 194.

38 Ibid., p. 197.

39 Emmanuel Levinas, 'Ethics as first philosophy', in Seán Hand (ed.), *The Levinas Reader* (Oxford and Cambridge: Blackwell, 1989), p. 82.

40 Levinas, Totality and Infinity, p. 197.

41 Ibid., p. 193.

42 Rachel Green, 'Web work: A history of Internet art', *Artforum*, 9 (May 2000), 162–7, 190. www.articlearchives.com/computing/software-services-applications/836959 –1.html (accessed September 2008).

43 Harwood, www.mongrel.org.uk/colourseparation (accessed 31 March 2008).

44 Görel Gavalli-Björkman, *Face to Face: Portraits from Five Centuries* (Stockholm: National Museum, 2002), p. 141.

45 Sandy Nairne, 'Introduction', in Sandy Nairne and Sarah Howgate (eds), *The Portrait Now* (London: The National Portrait Gallery), p. 15.

46 Nicole B. Ellison, Charles Steinfield, Cliff Lampe, 'The benefits of Facebook friends: social capital and college students' use of online social network sites', *Journal of Computer-Mediated Communication*, 12 (2007), 1153.

47 Zeynep Tufekci, 'Grooming, gossip, facebook and Myspace: What can we learn about these sites from those who won't assimilate?' *Information, Communication & Society*, 11: 4 (June 2008), 544–64. See also Thomas Claburn, 'Migration from MySpace to Facebook shows class divide' www.informationweek.com/news/inter-net/showArticle.jhtml?articleID= 200000822 (accessed 18 December 2008).

48 Jodi Dean, *Publicity's Secret: How Technoculture Capitalizes on Democracy* (Ithaca: Cornell University Press, 2002), p. 44.

49 Homi Bhabha, *The Location of Culture* (London and New York: Routledge, 1994), p. 78.

50 David Marriot, *Haunted Life: Visual Culture and Black Modernity* (Piscataway: Rutgers University Press, 2007), p. 2.

51 Dean, *Publicity's Secret*, p. 170.

52 Judith Butler, *Precarious Life: The Powers of Mourning and Violence* (London: Verso, 2004), p. xviii.

Part III
Theorising participation

Anna Dezeuze

Transitional objects …

Spectator participation, for some artists working in the 1960s, emerged as
the privileged site for more general philosophical reflections on the relations
between subject and object, in particular, the ways in which, as human beings,
we structure our perception of the world. Both Fluxus artist George Brecht
and the Brazilian Hélio Oiticica, for example, were interested in Ernst Cassirer's idea, developed in the *Philosophy of Symbolic Forms*, that logical, scientific thought emerged from an original 'mythical' thought in which self and
other were not as clearly differentiated.[1] The term 'mythical' for both artists
seems removed from a specifically narrative or religious framework, and is
used primarily to describe a mode of perceiving and experiencing the world.
For Brecht, 'mythical' appears to designate a 'direct' way of structuring experience, in a manner distinct from discursive thought. In his notebooks, he listed
different objects to be included in such 'do-it-yourself' works as *The Dome*
or *The Case* (1959) (figure 3.2) in terms of whether they operate as symbols
(such as numbers, letters, words, pictures, signs, stamps or maps), or can be
considered 'things in their Suchness' (including a match, a stone, a glass chip,
a shell, a leaf, hair and a piece of cloth).[2] While Brecht encouraged participants in his works to engage in these two contrasting modes of structuring
experience, Oiticica seemed more concerned with foregrounding in his
'do-it-yourself' works a 'mythical' experience of subject–object relations, in
particular through his appeal to dance.[3] Dance was 'mythical', according to
him, because its immersive rhythms create 'a flux in which the intellect seems
obscured by' non-discursive forms of experience.[4] The *Parangolé* capes (see
figures 2.2 and 3.3), inspired by Oiticica's experience of samba dancing, can
thus be inscribed within this attempt 'to return to a creative state close to that
of myth': as wearers explore the stitched combination of fabrics, colours and
messages through their movements, they are invited to get a glimpse of this
flux.

Other artists were preoccupied by the ways in which the constructions that
human beings set up in order to make sense of the world can become objects

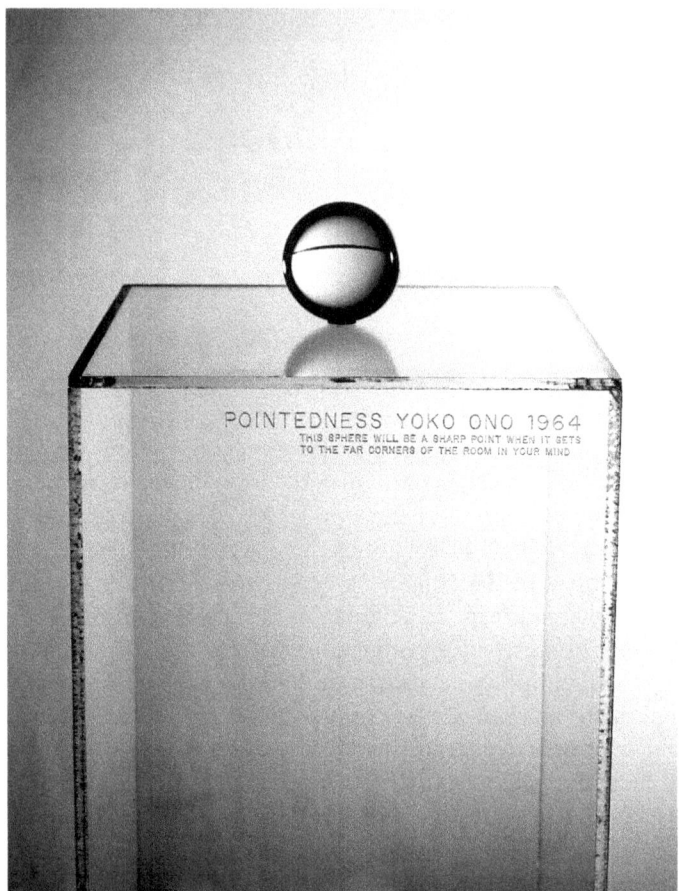

POINTEDNESS YOKO ONO 1964
THIS SPHERE WILL BE A SHARP POINT WHEN IT GETS
TO THE FAR CORNERS OF THE ROOM IN YOUR MIND

11.1   Yoko Ono, *Pointedness*, 1964/1966 (crystal sphere version).

in themselves. Yoko Ono, another Fluxus artist, was worried that the 'world of construction' that we elaborate to grapple with reality can 'appear' 'as equally real and valid as the law of nature'.[5] Brazilian artist Lygia Clark, a close friend of Oiticica's, addressed a similar problem when she wrote in a 1960 essay on the 'Death of the plane' that man uses concepts such as the picture plane or God to 'project' 'the transcendent part of himself' on an external support, which, in turn, becomes a false reality.[6] Both Clark and Ono shared the same desire to move from 'projection' – and 'placing too much emphasis on something outside you', in Ono's words – to 'introjection', or the 'need for poetry to be reintegrated as an indivisible part of [man's] own person', according to Clark.[7]

Ono explored these relations through what she called 'in-structures', defined as 'something just about to emerge – not quite structured – never quite structured … like an unfinished church with a sky ceiling'.[8] Many instruction pieces included in her book *Grapefruit* involve imaginary acts, such as the 1962 *Sun Piece*, which invites us to: 'Watch the sun until it becomes square.' At times, Ono combined instructions with objects, as in her 1964 *Pointedness* (figure 11.1), which consists of a small white marble sphere on a high Plexiglas pedestal bearing the instruction: 'This sphere will be a sharp point when it gets to the far corners of the room in your mind.'[9] The 'in-between' state of these 'in-structures' provided an arena in which participants are presented simultaneously with the reality of objects and the 'truth', 'fabricated' by the subject's consciousness.

Like Oiticica, Clark was more inclined towards creating works in which, 'There is no separation between subject–object.'[10] The 'death of the plane' enacted in her two-dimensional works of the late 1950s was further dramatised in the 'dialogue' set up between viewer and artwork in her hinged, manipulable sculptures known as *Bichos* (see figure 3.1). The 'fusion' that Clark was pursuing, however, did not occur until her 1963 *Caminhando* – a piece which invites participants to cut along a strip of paper looped into a Möbius strip. Because the work only exists when the participant cuts along the strip, Clark believed that subject and object are fused temporarily into 'a unique, total, existential reality'.[11]

In their shared interest in the human engagement with the world of things, Clark, Oiticica, Ono and Brecht created works that set up a new space of 'in-between-ness' – between subject and object, mind and matter, inside and outside. This in-between-ness, I would argue, can be usefully compared to the 'intermediate area of experience', 'between a subjective area and that which is objectively perceived', that was delineated by British psychoanalyst Donald W. Winnicott in his notion of the 'transitional object'.[12] Winnicott explained how a favourite toy, blanket or other object can play an important role in the process through which infants and small children gradually learn to differentiate themselves from their mothers' bodies, and to perceive themselves as separate human beings. The transitional object exists in an 'intermediate' area because it is conceived by the child simultaneously as two contradictory experiences. On the one hand, the transitional object appears to be totally controlled by the child, as in the infant's experience of being able to 'possess' and become one with the mother's breast when it cries out to be fed. On the other hand, it exists in itself, separately from the child who chose it, just like the mother who is gradually perceived as a different (and sometimes absent) person.

In this context, I would argue that comparing the do-it-yourself practices of Oiticica, Clark, and Fluxus artists including Ono and Brecht, to transitional objects, can shed light on two central defining features of 1960s participatory practices and the critical discourses surrounding them at the time: their consistent attack on the status of the art object as a commodity, and their political agendas of personal and social transformation. Following the concerns of these two groups of artists, I will account for the way in which a preoccupation with subject–object relations led to a definition of participatory artworks as play or ritual, before comparing the artists' political claims with New Left conceptions of activism and social change. The values and ambitions driving both these artistic and political types of project have since undergone a number of different critiques as well as revivals.[13] By offering a close reading of the artists' own statements, and situating their works more precisely within their contemporary discursive framework, I wish to retrieve the historical specificity of their dematerialising practices, and of their utopian claims for participation.

… v. fetishes

The transitional object can be related to another category of psychoanalytic object: the fetish. As Phyllis Greenacre has pointed out, both are inanimate objects used as 'security props serving to bring the current anxiety-provoking situation under the illusory control of the individual infant or man'.[14] According to the Freudian narrative of the fetish, the male child suffers a traumatic experience when he discovers that women have no penises, which triggers a fear of castration.[15] The fetish object, which often takes on the form of an object seen shortly before this vision (such as underwear or shoes), thus operates as a substitute – as a means of disavowing this traumatic lack, and protecting the subject against the threat of castration. Both the transitional object and the fetish, then, are invested with special value, and inhabit a shared space between reality and fantasy.

Before Freud adopted the word 'fetish' from Alfred Binet, the term had been in currency in different fields in the eighteenth and nineteenth centuries – including anthropology, sociology and philosophy, as well as psychology. According to William Pietz, what characterised most discourses about the fetish was, above all, a concern with the notion of value.[16] Psychology focused on the fetishist's obsessive investment of desire in a single shoe, while anthropologists puzzled over the ways in which a piece of wood could be worshipped for its magical properties. Most famously, Karl Marx used the term 'fetishism' to designate the aberrant character that 'attaches itself to the products of labour as soon as they are produced as commodities', that is, when they are produced for their exchange value (for money) rather than for their use value (to be used).[17] Crucially, discourses surrounding the fetish systematically criticised the values attached to the fetish as 'false objective values of a culture from which the speaker is personally distanced'.[18]

For Marx, the passage from 'use value' to 'exchange value' is problematic because it is concealed as an inevitable – and thus 'falsely' 'objective' – truth by a complex system that confirms and perpetrates it through repetition. Nowhere, perhaps, is this process more in evidence than in the circulation of artworks, which, as Yve-Alain Bois has suggested, may have served for Marx as a model of the ultimate commodity fetish. Not only have artworks in the modern era lost any collectively determined use; their exchange value itself is solely 'determined by the "psychological" mechanisms that are at the core of any monopoly system: rarity, authenticity, uniqueness, and the law of supply and demand'.[19] Where some avant-garde practices since the nineteenth century have turned to design as a means of reinserting their works within the category of functional artefacts, do-it-yourself artists in the 1960s aligned themselves with the discourse about fetishism in that they distanced themselves from, in order to critically explore, the very processes through which 'false objective values' transform the art object into a commodity fetish.

However, the attack on the commodity fetish by do-it-yourself artists did not involve a correlative celebration of fixed subject–object distinctions, which early critiques of fetishism conceived as the prerequisite for the rational logic that fetishist behaviour so obviously defied. On the contrary, the parallels between the pre-symbolic state inhabited by the transitional object, and the 'mythical' consciousness discussed by Cassirer and celebrated by Brecht and Oiticica, lie in the way both are, in fact, considered to be crucial milestones in the development of a logical consciousness – in a 'journey from the purely subjective to objectivity'.[20] Not only does this transitional space lie at the very 'root of symbolism',[21] it persists in the individual's later life, Cassirer and Winnicott agree, in the form of artistic and religious experience. Thus the explorations of the transitional space between object and subject in the work of Brecht, Oiticica, Ono or Clark are presented less as regressions to an infantile or 'primitive' stage (that would need to be surpassed), than as intermediate experiences that actively shape logical, discursive and rational forms of consciousness. Far from being an anti-art gesture, then, the do-it-yourself artwork as transitional object seeks to show what the artwork can be *before* it becomes a commodity fetish – namely, a 'potential' or 'transitional space' set apart, in the modern adult's life, to explore the processes of non-discursive thought. All artworks, in fact, are potentially transitional phenomena: this fundamental definition becomes distorted when they become commodities and take on the role of fetishes instead.

One of the key features of the transitional object, which sets it apart from the fetish, is the central role of play which, according to Winnicott, acts as a crucial link between transitional phenomena and art: 'There is a direct development from transitional phenomena to playing, and from playing to shared playing, and from this to cultural experiences.'[22] Winnicott's definition of play as inhabiting the same 'potential' arena of experience as the transitional object echoes those of other theorists such as Roger Caillois and Johan Huizinga, who both described play as a delimited space within the psychic and everyday life of the player.[23] All three theorists agree that play is 'an experience in the space-time continuum' – since it is performed in time and space like any other activity – and that it requires the complete absorption of the participant.[24]

These two characteristics have been further analysed, as features common to both play and ritual, by anthropologist Victor Turner.[25] In order to situate the shared space of play and ritual, Turner developed the concept of 'liminality', which describes the ambiguous phase, in rites of passage, between two moments in time, starting with the demarcation of a sacred space and the participants' temporary isolation from everyday life, and ending with the 'symbolic phenomena and actions which represent the return of the subjects to their new, relatively stable, well-defined position' in society.[26] This 'in-between' state is one of transition, where the given order of society can be subverted momentarily, where 'the social order may seem to have been turned upside down'.[27] To describe the state of absorption required by play and ritual, Turner used the term 'flow' and listed as its main characteristics: the experience of 'unified flowing from one moment to the next', as well as the erasure of distinctions 'between self and environment; between stimulus and response; or between past, present and future'.[28]

As I have suggested in Chapter 3, play is also a defining characteristic of many do-it-yourself artworks. While Fluxus scores can often be joke- or gag-like, many Fluxus objects look like games or toys. Brecht's series of *Games and Puzzles* (figure 11.2) designed and published by Fluxus impresario George Maciunas from 1964 onwards, often present themselves as riddles, or parodies of skill and intelligence games. *Inclined Plane Puzzle*, for example, requires us to place a ball on an inclined surface and 'observe it rolling downhill'. Takako Saito's reconfigured chess sets require players to identify each chess piece through a variety of non-visual sensory experiences (including smell and sound).[29] Critics Frederico Morais and Guy Brett have independently compared Oiticica's works to games as well as rituals,[30] while both Yoko Ono and Lygia Clark used the term 'ritual' when discussing their own work.[31]

Particularly striking are the kinds of 'flow' experiences often related to these game- and ritual-like works. The *Caminhando*, Clark wrote, was inspired by her experience of crossing the countryside by train, and suddenly perceiving 'each fragment of the landscape as a whole within time, making itself' in front of her eyes.[32] This, she argued, made her intensely aware of the 'immanence of the moment'. A similar train story was recounted by Fluxus artist Nam June Paik, as he recalled how while 'looking out of the window of the moving train', he 'realised for the first time the old Zen – [John] Cage thesis: "It is beautiful, not because it changes beautifully, but – simply – because it changes"'.[33] In both these instances, the participant's focus on an everyday activity led to a sudden immersion or absorption in a unique temporal experience. This temporal

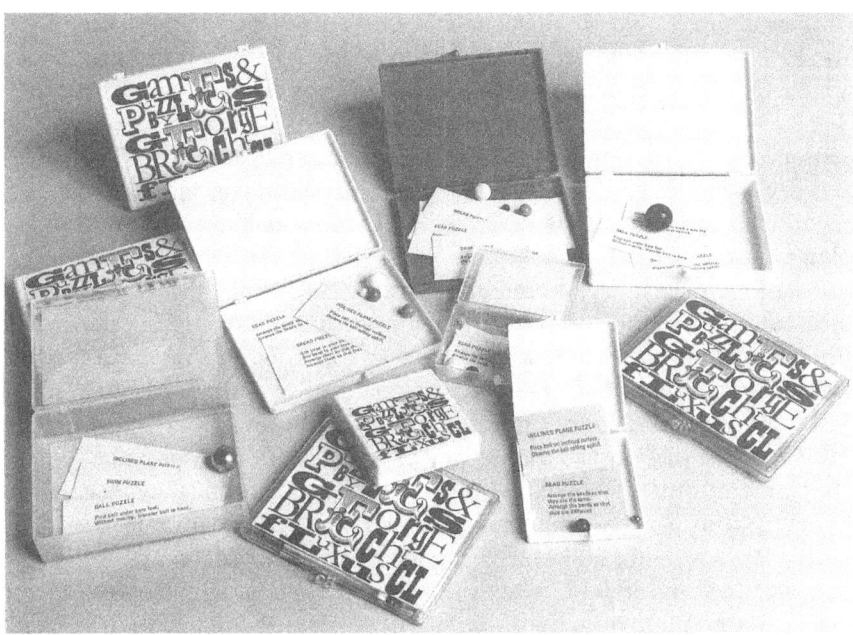

George Brecht, *Games and Puzzles*, 1964–early 1970s.   **11.2**

dimension is that of flow, in which past, present and future can be contained in a single moment that is experienced outside the continuity of everyday life, while at the same time heightening our consciousness of everyday life as if in a sudden illumination. Paik's reference to Zen is not coincidental. Alan Watts, one of the writers about Zen in America read by artists such as Brecht, explained how Zen experience is a state of mind that can be achieved in everyday life: 'if in something so simple and trivial as lighting a cigarette one is fully aware, seeing the flame, the curling smoke, and the regulation of the breath as the most important things in the universe, it will seem to an observer that the action has a ritualistic style'.[34] Both Clark and Ono related their own 'ritualistic' actions to similar activities – Clark described following the smoke of her cigarette 'ceaselessly forging its own path, annihilating itself and remaking itself continuously', while Ono's second husband remembers her repeatedly lighting matches and watching them go out.[35]

Early one morning in 1973, after reading Ono's book of scores, *Grapefruit*, Oiticica walked into the bathroom of his New York apartment. It was six o'clock, and looking at everything around him in the darkness, the everyday furnishings and familiar objects suddenly appeared 'like props to be shuffled by a magician, as if they had been freed from the definitions which limits them as objects'.[36] For Oiticica, Ono's scores questioned boundaries between subject and object by emphasising the relations between objects and imagination.

This awareness of the porous boundaries between self and other encouraged not only a sudden disorientation but also a new state of sensory perception, which Oiticica had defined in 1967 as the 'super-sensory' (*suprasensorial*). The super-sensory, according to Oiticica, involved a 'dilatation' of one's 'usual sensory capacities' comparable to a hallucinogenic experience.[37] The 'super-sensory' state was closely related to the artist's 'mythical experience' of dance, mentioned earlier – a state described by Oiticica as 'flux', a term obviously akin to Turner's 'flow'.

Clark's emphasis on the moment or 'instant' within this flow emerged gradually from her focus on the spectator's gestures, starting with the *Bichos*. The term 'ritual' makes its first appearance in Clark's writings at the time of the *Bichos*, as she argued that these new participatory works allowed her to transfer Jackson Pollock's 'ritual of the gesture' from a painting process experienced exclusively by the artist to the viewing experience of every spectator.[38] While the temporal dimension in do-it-yourself works by Clark and Oiticica emerged at the crossroads of painting, the sensory and the performative, Fluxus artists such as Brecht, Paik and Ono responded to a musical context. According to Paik, Cage introduced 'tediousness' or boredom as an alternative to the classical conception of composition as a narrative that culminates in a climax. For Paik, boredom allowed listeners to experience 'each single moment' independently, thus giving equal intensity to all moments. This uniform intensity can be found in spiritual experiences such as Zen meditation, which aim at 'a kind of calmness', 'without crescendo, climax, catharsis'.[39] Fluxus, according to Ina Blom, was characterised by such an '*immersive* ideal of art' in which 'cognitive boundaries dividing self and work or work and surroundings might, temporarily, fade out or be displaced'.[40] This 'immersive ideal' was achieved by Fluxus artists through two central devices: duration and attention. The experience of duration can be intensified by repeating an identical sound over and over again, or holding it for a long time; attention can be focused by inviting participants to listen out for existing sounds, including imperceptible sounds such as the earth turning (as in Ono's 1963 *Earth Piece*). In both cases, new states of consciousness are created, in which sound, space and listener temporarily converge within an intense, yet non-climactic, experience.

A similar shift in the spatial awareness of our bodies can also occur through mental exercises such as Brecht's, one of which asks readers to:

Determine the centre of an object or event.
Determine the centre more accurately.
Repeat, until further inaccuracy is impossible.

In the same way as viewers are asked to arrange and rearrange the objects in the *Case* or *Cabinet*, potentially ad infinitum, this *Exercise* explores the infinite connections between disparate objects and events through shifts of centres and borders. Clark's *Caminhando*, which is literally transformed and destroyed as it is made, enacts a similarly irreversible, unrepeatable process.[41] Both Brecht and Clark posit our relation to objects as a permanent renegotiation. As David Doris put it, Fluxus scores 'establish a shifting zone of impermanence, a *nomadism* in which the self is continually redefined in accord with the external force (for example, an event score, a performer, the weather) that is now asserting its momentary demands, and with which it now interacts'.[42] For Doris, this leads to a new conception of the self as 'whatever one happens to be doing at any given moment'. A new entity emerges which is 'neither subject nor object, and yet constituted by both'. This 'third entity', I would argue, is none other than the 'liminal' state described by both Turner and Winnicott.

'The precariousness of play', according to Winnicott, 'belongs to the fact that it is always on the theoretical line between the subjective and that which is objectively perceived.'[43] My contention here is that it is this very precariousness that distinguishes the transitional object from the fetish. Where the fetish remains evidence of a personal trauma that will affect the psychic life of the adult for the rest of his life, the transitional object exists in a temporal space of flow, and is always already on the verge of being abandoned. Another crucial feature of this precariousness is the reliance of play on a community of trust. Winnicott repeatedly emphasised how a climate of trust is essential to the formation of the transitional object and the potential space of play.[44] The child's carer, he argued, must play along with the illusion created through the transitional object, in order to let the child develop this space independently. Similarly, Huizinga has spoken of a 'play-community' characterised by 'the feeling of being "apart together" in an exceptional situation'.[45] Any 'spoilsport' who refuses to follow the rules shatters this illusion.

This ideal of a 'play community' is certainly present in many participatory artworks. The bags, fabrics, stones and elastic bands used by Clark and Oiticica rely on our willingness to play with them for their existence as artworks, while Fluxus scores emerged as implicit contracts between the artist and the performer who is made to take on individual responsibility for following the rules of the game. As Fluxus scores became distinct from traditional musical notation, trust and 'good will' came to replace the traditional relations binding composer and performer.[46] Performers/readers/viewers of Fluxus scores are invited to make more choices that affect the very nature of the composition, thus jeopardising criteria of value traditionally used to judge the end result.

Huizinga's notion of being 'apart together' in play was further defined by Victor Turner as '*communitas*' – 'an unmediated relationship between historical, idiosyncratic, concrete individuals', which can be experienced only briefly during certain 'liminal' experiences.[47] There is no doubt that this experience of *communitas* was what Oiticica encountered in his experience of samba dancing at Mangueira, and that it played a role in his conception of the *Parangolé*. Carnival, street celebrations, and dancing inhabit the same liminal space as ritual. Such practices of everyday life had been celebrated in the 1940s and 1950s by French philosopher Henri Lefebvre, who praised the ways in which they 'tightened social links': 'In celebrating, each member of the community went beyond himself.'[48] Echoing Lefebvre's descriptions of peasant festivals, Oiticica highlighted the way in which samba dancing produced a remarkable 'connection between the collective and the individual experience'.[49] As he started organising outdoor performances with other artists in Rio de Janeiro in 1967 and 1968, Oiticica moved from the *Parangolés* towards collective, festival-like works.

Like Lefebvre's Marxist philosophy of everyday life, the do-it-yourself artworks of Oiticica, Clark and Fluxus invoke ideals of immersion and *communitas* as an alternative to the fragmentation and alienation characteristic of industrial societies. As play and ritual, these participatory practices could thus be seen to alleviate the ills of capitalist society, in the same way as transitional objects work as 'security props' (as Greenacre put it) for the infant grappling with anxieties regarding the world of objects. Viewed from this perspective, do-it-yourself practices could be criticised on the same grounds as the object relations psychoanalysis founded by Winnicott: as normative and conservative strategies encouraging adaptation and acceptance, rather than subversion or critique.[50] While the appeal to immersive experiences and ritual communities certainly allowed do-it-yourself artists to resist the fetishisation of the art object, the transitional spaces set up by their participatory practices ran the risk of suspending the dialectic relation between illusion and reality, or between 'mythical' and critical states. The remainder of this chapter examines how these do-it-yourself artworks, operating as transitional phenomena, sought to negotiate these complex dynamics between escapism and critique, primitivism and activism.

'Imagine …' and 'do it!'

Clark was conscious of the dangers of operating within the liminal state of play; she wrote in 1971 of her fears that the contemporary artist may be employed by the state as an 'engineer of leisure activities'.[51] 'The only way for the artist to escape' this kind of 'recuperation', she concluded, was 'to seek to set off a general creativity without any psychological or social limits'.[52] Around that time, Clark was developing collective works involving two or more participants bound together by net bags, plastic tunnels and elastic bands, in order to create 'living architectures'. As the participants move, touch each other, stretch their arms, open and close their legs, these experiences operate as invasions of each participant's individual 'territory', revealing each person's level of tolerance to being touched by others, or touched by a stranger, and thus uncovering people's inhibitions. These experiences can be 'sexual, erotic or ludic'; they can, at times, turn out to be frightening.[53]

While play can be conceived as an activity consolidating the self in the Winnicottian sense, then, it can also be disturbing, as aggressive or violent feelings are revealed. By mobilising this darker side of play, Clark encouraged individuals to recover aspects of their own body and senses that are repressed in contemporary society. Significantly, Clark described her collective works as 'rituals without myths', deliberately refusing to impose on the participants any narrative structure or imagined tribal order.[54] Any such comforting form of organisation would only serve to substitute alternative 'psychological or social limits' for the old ones, thus forestalling 'general creativity'. Indeed, it is worth remembering that in the tribal societies described by Turner, the highly codified and controlled 'liminal' rituals tend to reinforce hierarchies and existing social structures.[55]

The potentially subversive aspects of play explored by Clark found their counterpart in Oiticica's unconditional celebration of anti-conformism and anarchism. Oiticica emphasised in his writings the violent potential of his brand of anarchism, linked to individual and collective revolts against established values and standards. Marginal criminals such as Cara de Cavalo – a bandit whom the artist had known before he was killed by the police – were, according to him, in a state of revolt, searching in their own way for a utopian happiness. 'All human aspirations to a "happy life" become realised only through great revolts or destructions ... The *Parangolé*'s programme is to give a helping hand to such manifestations.'[56] For Oiticica, the 'super-sensory' experiences found in samba, carnival and hallucinogenic states were all means to an end: to create a space where people can feel liberated from the rules and regulations of a repressive regime, and thus discover their capacity for revolt. The wearers of some *Parangolé* capes display mottos, written or stitched on the fabrics by the artist, like protest banners, thus proclaiming their (potential for) 'freedom' (see figure 2.2) or 'revolt' (see figure 3.3). Like Lefebvre, Oiticica believed that carnivals and popular festivals could offer a glimpse into alternative models of society: rather than a safety valve to contain society's excesses, as some have argued, the *carnaval* for Oiticica could operate as a way to momentarily liberate the participants from present reality so that they might be critical of that reality. As Clark put it: 'we use experience to incite awareness of the alienation in which one lives'[57] – a type of alienation held by many in the 1960s to be common to all subjects in late-capitalist societies, whether under the Brazilian dictatorship, or in democratic countries like France or the United States.

Both Oiticica and Clark agreed that forms of 'general creativity' were incompatible with the alienation of labour and the passive consumption characteristic of capitalism. In this sense, they aligned themselves with Guy Debord's contention that in the late-capitalist 'societé du spectacle', experience is absorbed passively through images, reducing man's capacity to act: 'The more he contemplates, the less he lives.'[58] The do-it-yourself artwork opposes this state by trying to stimulate lived experiences on the part of the viewer, and by refusing to be absorbed as yet another form of spectacle. No spectators were allowed in Clark's collective works; for Oiticica, the 'mythical' experience and *communitas* of the carnival were far more important than any visible spectacle that was produced. Oiticica directly addressed the threat of 'ultra-superficial' images when he was faced with the 'recuperation' of his 1967 *Tropicália* environment by Brazilian popular culture.[59] This work, which involved shelter-like constructions on a mixture of sand and gravel, interspersed with potted tropical plants and live parrots (figure 11.3), was embraced as a reference for a new fashion in Brazilian popular culture.[60] For Oiticica, this reading ignored 'the existential lived experience' encountered in the environment, as participants walk around barefoot, reading some texts written on scattered pieces of paper, touching and feeling with their hands and feet, listening to the sound of parrots, until they reach the second, darkened tent-like structure, which contains a switched-on television set. As both Clark and Oiticica turned to lived experience as a means of resisting spectacularisation, transitional phenomena emerged once again as an alternative to the commodity. It is partly because they are less reliant on visual systems than the fetish that transitional phenomena such as play and ritual were perceived as effective means of escaping the all-powerful scopic regime of the *société du spectacle*.

As Hannah Higgins has demonstrated, Fluxus was also fundamentally concerned with non-visual modes of experience, which encouraged the kind of 'general creativity' wished for by Clark.[61] For the group's self-appointed theorist, George Maciunas, Fluxus's attack on the art object as a commodity and art as a profession was part of wider project to teach 'people the needlessness [*sic*] of art, including the eventual needlessness of Fluxus itself'.[62] This is why, Maciunas explained, Fluxus artists should not themselves work as professional artists, but have a 'socially constructive and useful' day job to earn a living, and spend their evenings 'propagandizing' the Fluxus 'way of life among other idle artists and art collectors and fighting them'.[63] Thus Maciunas clearly positioned Fluxus within the very space allocated to leisure activities – where the artist could potentially be assimilated as a provider of entertainment and escapism – but only in order to transform the very definition of leisure and the role of the artist.

For Maciunas, play or 'Fluxus-art-amusement' as he termed it, had to be used to debunk the claims of 'serious' culture, to accelerate the disappearance of the artist, and to encourage people to create their own, potentially subversive activities. One of Maciunas's models was Brecht's score for *Word Event*, which simply reads 'exit'. Since this activity, Maciunas explained, 'happens daily without any "special" performance of it', Brecht's score clearly demonstrates that Fluxus performances and publications can eventually 'eliminate themselves'.[64] Neither Brecht nor most other Fluxus artists actually envisaged this disappearance of art and artists realistically, let alone, as Maciunas hoped, 'in a few years'. The possibility of this disappearance, however vague, is nevertheless implied by Fluxus works, as it is in Clark's and Oiticica's. Strikingly, Maciunas repeatedly used the term 'transitional' to describe Fluxus activities: just as the child, according to Winnicott, gradually grows out of the transitional object, do-it-yourself artworks were often conceived as temporary solutions. This is why Maciunas defined Fluxus as largely a 'propagandizing' activity, why Clark defined the artist's role as a 'proposer',[65] and Oiticica as an 'impresario' or an 'educator'.[66]

Henry Flynt's concept of 'brend', first developed in the early 1960s and outlined in an essay published by Fluxus in 1968, can be read as a concrete extension of Maciunas's ideal of a 'transitional' art. Brend, according to Flynt, involves 'just-likings' – 'everything you do just because you like it', rather than because you need to.[67] 'Spontaneous self-amusement or play' should be privileged, but there is no 'interpersonal example' of 'brend' because 'just-likings' are inseparable from individual experiences. Thus, the Fluxus score or object can serve as a basis for people to explore their 'just-likings', but are ultimately deemed entirely dispensable by Flynt. Like many in the 1960s, Flynt dreamt of a society in which the distinction between work and leisure could be abolished (and thus, presumably, people would not have to do anything that was *not* a 'just liking'); in the meantime, however, the artist would have to settle with

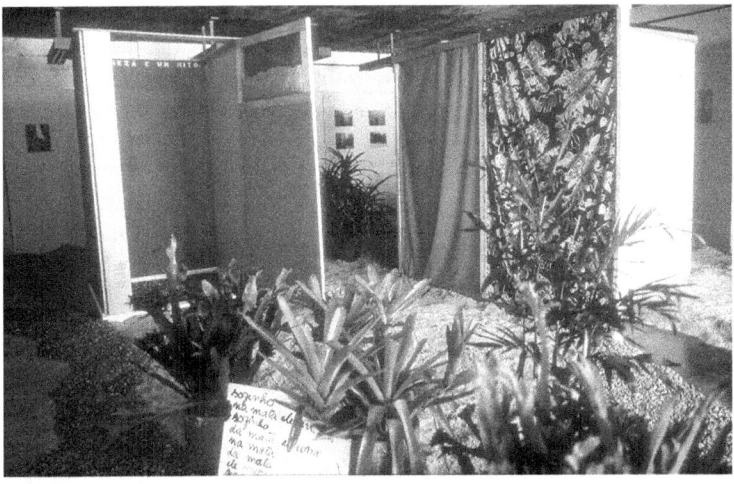

Hélio Oiticica, *Tropicália: Penetrables PN2 and PN3*, 1967.   **11.3**

giving to 'whoever can grasp it the realisation that the experience beyond art' – the 'general creativity' aspired to by Clark – 'already occurs in his life – but is totally suppressed by the general repressiveness [*sic*] of society'.[68] This kind of suppression was also singled out by French critic Jean Clay when he wrote, in 1971, that Clark's and Oiticica's practices offered 'a model which allows us to glimpse fragmentarily at the type of human relations which could be possible in a society which would not be subjected to alienation, separation and taboos'.[69]

Do-it-yourself artists thus tried to maintain a dialectic movement between reality and utopia by combining both within the space of the transitional space. In this sense, do-it-yourself artworks as transitional phenomena are conceived not only as material enactments of a possible transition towards the disappearance of art and artists: they were also seen to embody a wider transition towards a new, freer, non-alienated, society. According to Winnicott, the central feature of the transitional object is its existence in a space of conscious illusion or suspension of disbelief – since the infant can simultaneously believe and not believe that his object is autonomous. By emphasising their transitional nature, do-it-yourself artworks can thus be seen to dramatise the dialectic of reality and fantasy at the heart of utopia. If either term is privileged, the work loses its transitional status and risks falling into either conformism or escapism.

This dialectic of reality and fantasy is inscribed within the dynamic modes of participation offered by such do-it-yourself artworks, as they mobilise both action and imagination in the participant's experience. Ono's scores most clearly stretch the viewer's/reader's imaginary participation, whether by asking us to transform 'a sphere into a sharp point' in *Pointedness* or by asking us, in her earlier *Painting to Construct in your Head no. 5* to 'observe three paintings carefully' and then 'mix them well' in our heads. According to Ono, the *Paintings to Construct in your Head* were inspired by her childhood experience, in Japan during the Second World War, of imagining menus with her brother when they had no food to eat.[70] In Ono's childhood story, an imagined reality is clearly a substitute for an absent reality; but this dialectical movement can be mobilised within broader utopian projects as well. Ono herself, in collaboration with John Lennon, would dramatically appeal to the power of the imagination in the 1971 billboards proclaiming 'War is Over!' and, in smaller print, 'if you want it'. Lennon's invitation to 'imagine' another world in his famous song would bring this utopian drive to the attention of an even wider audience.

'Imagining', and other terms used by do-it-yourself artists such as 'inciting awareness' or 'setting off general creativity', also point to a relation with more direct political actions akin, for example, to Jerry Rubin's exhortation to all young Americans to 'do it!' as a generic call to rebel against the state of things.[71] Oiticica read Rubin's 1970 *Do It! Scenarios of the Revolution* when he moved to New York, and Stewart Home has pointed out some of the interrelations between Fluxus and 'freak-style agitators' such as Rubin's 'youth international party' known as Yippies. For example, Home explained that Maciunas's development of communal artists' studios in New York's SoHo in the 1970s may have contributed to SoHo's central role in the East Coast hippie scene, while the 'freak life-style also left its mark on Fluxus' in their move away from formal public presentations such as concerts towards collective events at the end of the 1960s.[72] (Events such as the Fluxfeasts, Fluxwedding or Fluxmass served primarily to create and consolidate a sense of community.)[73] Clark and Oiticica were more explicit in their alignment with contemporary protests in Brazil, the United States and Europe. 'These young people', explained Clark speaking of the protesters, 'have the same existential attitude as we do, they unleash processes whose end they don't know, they open a path whose exit is unknown.'[74] In the same way as Oiticica celebrated criminals like Cara de Cavalo as the heroes of a resistance to repressive society, Clark believed that the young revolutionaries were less 'domesticated' than artists in trying to 'unleash' or 'set off' their own creativity, and that of others.

Indeed, there seems to have been a remarkable convergence between participatory practices in the 1960s and the new activist tactics of the New Left in that period. (Rubin's 'Yippies' defined themselves as a 'hybrid mixture of New Left and hippie'.)[75] This convergence operated on two general levels. At the level of tactics, the New Left privileged action over political programmes, and 'extraordinary' rather than 'normal' (electoral) politics, encouraging community projects, direct action and symbolic demonstrations such as sit-ins and teach-ins.[76] Disruption was perceived as the only fruitful platform for a new political dialogue with authority, and punctual interventions were preferred to systematic projects. These shifts were perceived by many commentators as encouraging an unprecedented 'interplay between politics and culture', which was introducing a new 'aesthetic component' into politics.[77] Like do-it-yourself artworks, new forms of agitation sought to present 'both cultural and political alternatives to capitalist domination',[78] and to enact them through organised actions and performances. They did not only foreground values of freedom and equality, but also such ideals as a 'belief in creativity' and a 'wish for community and communal values'.[79]

One premise in particular of this new aesthetic turn in politics resonates strongly with do-it-yourself practices. Having moved away from Marxist attempts to locate the agents of change within a specific constituency – such as workers' unions or farm movements – the New Left started from the belief that all people can be politicised. On this belief hinged two core principles of New Left activism: first, the ideal of 'participatory democracy', which privileges issues of self-determination over economic struggles,[80] and second, the attempt to involve people who were hitherto 'politically apathetic'.[81] It is difficult not to recall the rhetoric of spectator participation when reading the conclusion to a 1968 statement by activist Carl Oglesby, the former president of the Students for a Democratic Society (SDS), as he invited his audience to 'go inside' themselves 'to rediscover the feeling of' their 'own possible freedom, and from there to the feeling of the possible freedom of others'.[82] Oglesby's statement is premised on the very same set of beliefs as do-it-yourself artworks by Fluxus, Clark or Oiticica: the idea that individuals need to be encouraged to rediscover their own potential – for freedom, creativity, self-determination – and to imagine alternative modes of living and engaging with others outside current power structures, as well as the notion that individual experience can constitute the starting point for collective actions. The role of the activist, like that of the artist according to Clark, Oiticica and some Fluxus artists, was thus to find new means of raising this consciousness.

The precise nature of the passage from personal, individual consciousness to wider changes within society can be better understood through the image of the 'breach', borrowed from Herbert Marcuse by student protester Rudi Dutschke. However small, these breaches in what was termed a 'false consciousness' were considered as a 'starting point' for 'emancipation' – their proliferation could lead to a veritable 'transformation of the world'.[83] It has been shown how the fetish, according to Marx, encourages a 'false consciousness' to the extent that it masks the mechanisms that determined its value. The 'false consciousness' discussed by Marcuse and New Left thinkers was seen as pervading all spheres of human existence in the late-capitalist *societé du spectacle* – including leisure, pleasure and human relations. By demystifying the 'false consciousness' at the heart of fetishised subject–object relations, do-it-yourself artworks sought to create 'breaches' in which participants could find their own 'personal freedom' and catch a glimpse of what society could be like outside such all-pervasive repression and alienation. By mobilising play more particularly, do-it-yourself artworks invested and transformed the fraught terrain of the work/leisure separation that had precisely contributed to this 'false consciousness'. And by acting in the transitional space of play and rituals, they clearly aspired to act as so many places, 'however small', between imagination and reality, which could hold utopian promises for the transformation of society.[84] New playful and pleasurable 'rituals without myths', the artists believed, could offer models of experience in which the participants' bodies and minds could be fully liberated, and non-alienated forms of community could take shape. For a short time in the late 1960s and early 1970s, such 'breaches' did indeed seem to be proliferating across the world, through protests and counter-culture as well as participatory art practices. Whether, and how, they succeeded in 'transforming the world', is, of course, another question.

Notes

My thanks to Frazer Ward and Aris Sarafianos for their comments on this chapter.

1 George Brecht read and followed a course about Ernst Cassirer's *Philosophy of Symbolic Forms* in 1958. His notes are included in his notebooks: *Notebook II, October 1958–April 1959* and *Notebook III, April 1959–August 1959* (Cologne: Walther König, 1991). Hélio Oiticica quotes the same book by Cassirer in his 'Amilcar de Castro', *Habitat* (May–June 1965), in Alberto Tassinari (ed.), *Amilcar de Castro* (São Paulo: Cosac & Naify, 1997), p. 154. (Unless otherwise stated, all translations from the Portuguese or the French in this chapter are mine.) Both Cassirer and Cassirer's main disciple in the United States, Suzanne Langer, had been mentioned in the 1959 manifesto of the Neoconcrete movement, which Oiticica joined in 1960. (For more information about Neoconcretism, see Chapter 3.)

2 Brecht, *Notebook III*, p. 148.

3 Hélio Oiticica, 'A dança na minha experiência, 12 de novembro de 1965', in Luciano Figueiredo, Lygia Pape and Waly Salomão (eds), *Aspiro ao grande labirinto: textos de Hélio Oiticica (1954–1969)* (Rio de Janeiro: Rocco, 1986), pp. 72–5.

4 Ibid., p. 73.

5 Yoko Ono's 'The word of a fabricator' was originally published in Japanese in *SAC Journal*, 24 (May 1962). A translation by Ono was published in Jon Hendricks and Alexandra Munroe (eds), *Yes Yoko Ono* (New York: Japan Society and Harry N. Abrahams, 2000), p. 285.

6 Lygia Clark, 'A morte do plano', in Guy Brett et al., *Lygia Clark* (Marseilles: MAC, galeries contemporaines des Musées de Marseille, 1998), p. 117. I am referring here to the original Portuguese essays; all translations are mine.

7 Yoko Ono, 'The poetry of the personal: Gray Watson and Rob La Frenais in conversation with Yoko Ono', *Performance*, 63 (March 1991), 13; Clark, 'A morte do plano', p. 117.

8 Yoko Ono, 'To the Wesleyan people who attended the meeting, a footnote to my lecture of January 13, 1966', in *Grapefruit: A Book of Instructions by Yoko Ono* (New York: Simon & Schuster, 2nd edn, 2000), n. p.

9 The ball in *Pointedness* was initially made of white marble but was remade by Ono in crystal in 1966.

10 Lygia Clark, '*Caminhando*', in Guy Brett et al., *Lygia Clark*, p. 151.

11 Clark, '*Caminhando*', p. 151.

12 Donald W. Winnicott, 'Transitional objects and transitional phenomena', *International Journal of Psychoanalysis*, 34:2 (1953), in *Playing and Reality* (London: Tavistock Publications, 1971), p. 3. The notion of the 'transitional object' was developed by Winnicott from 1951.

13 For instances of art historical critiques, see Chapters 1, 12 and 13. For a recent revival of the anti-fetish revolutionary discourse, see John Holloway, *Change the World Without Taking Power: The Meaning of Revolution Today* (Ann Arbor: Pluto Press, 2002).

14 Phyllis Greenacre, 'The fetish and the transitional object', *The Psychoanalytic Study of the Child*, 24 (1969), 150.

15 See Sigmund Freud, 'Fetishism' (1927), in *The Standard Edition of the Complete Psychological Works of Sigmund Freud*, vol. 21, ed. and trans. James Strachey (London: The Hogarth Press, 1961), pp. 152–7.

16 William Pietz, 'The problem of the fetish, part I', *Res*, 9 (Spring 1985), 9.

17 See Karl Marx, *Capital: a Critique of Political Economy, vol. 1* (1867), trans. B. Fowkes (London, Penguin, 1976), p. 165.

18 Pietz, 'The problem of the fetish', 14.

19 Yve-Alain Bois, 'Painting: the task of mourning' (1986), in *Painting as Model* (Cambridge: MIT Press, 1990), p. 237.

20 Winnicott, 'Transitional objects', p. 6.

21 Ibid.

22 Donald W. Winnicott, 'Playing: a theoretical statement', in *Playing and Reality*, p. 51.

23 Roger Caillois, *Les Jeux et les hommes: le masque et le vertige* (Paris: Gallimard, 2nd edn, 1967); Johan Huizinga, *Homo Ludens* (1944), trans. R.F. Carrington Hull (London, Henley and Boston: Routledge & Kegan, 1949).

24 Winnicott, 'Playing', p. 50.

25 Victor Turner, *From Ritual to Theatre: The Human Consciousness of Play* (New York: Performing Arts Journal Publications, 1982).

26 Ibid., p. 24.

27 Ibid., p. 27.

28 Ibid., p. 56.

29 For more about Fluxus games, see Ina Cozen (ed.), *Art Games: Die Schachteln der Fluxus Künstler (Sohm Dossier 1)* (Stuttgart: Staatsgalerie, 1997).

30 Guy Brett [untitled text], in *Hélio Oiticica* (London: Whitechapel Gallery, 1969), n. p. Frederico Morais, 'Arte na rua: jôgo, rito e participação', second supplement of the *Diário de Notícias* (4 July 1968), p. 1.

31 Lygia Clark, 'A propósito da magia do objeto' (1965), in Brett et al., *Lygia Clark*, p. 152; Ono, 'The word of a fabricator', p. 285.

32 Clark, '*Caminhando*', p. 152.

33 Nam June Paik, 'To the "symphony for 2000 rooms"', in La Monte Young (ed.), *An Anthology …* (New York: Heiner Friedrich, 1970), n. p. For information about Fluxus's relation to John Cage, see Chapter 3.

34 Alan W. Watts, *The Way of Zen* (London: Thames & Hudson, 1957), p. 158.

35 Clark, '*Caminhando*', p. 152; Anthony Cox, 'Instructive auto-destruction: Yoko Ono leads in a direction that might be called concept-art', *Art and Artists*, 1:5 (August 1966), 17. This experience, argues Cox, inspired Ono to write her 1955 *Lighting Piece* which invites readers to 'light a match and watch it until it goes out'.

36 Hélio Oiticica, unpublished *Notebook, 22 Junho 1973*, p. 50. Hélio Oiticica Archives, Rio de Janeiro, Projeto Hélio Oiticica, Notebook 2/13.

37 'O aparecimento do suprasensorial na arte brasileria (Novembro–Dezembro 1967)', *Revista GAM*, 13 (1968), in Guy Brett et al., *Hélio Oiticica* (Paris: Galerie nationale du Jeu de Paume, 1992), p. 128. (My translation from the Portuguese)

38 Lygia Clark, 'Do ritual' (1960), in Guy Brett et al., *Lygia Clark*, pp. 122–3.

39 Paik, 'To the "symphony for 2000 rooms"', n. p.

40 Ina Blom, 'Boredom and oblivion', in Ken Friedman (ed.), *The Fluxus Reader* (London: Academy Editions, 1998), p. 63.

41 On the entropic qualities of the *Caminhando*, see Yve-Alain Bois 'Water Closet', in Yve-Alain Bois and Rosalind Krauss, *Formless: A User's Guide* (New York: Zone Books, 1997), pp. 204–14.

42 David T. Doris, 'Zen vaudeville: a medi(t)ation in the margins of Fluxus', in Friedman (ed.), *The Fluxus Reader*, p. 125.

43 Winnicott, 'Transitional objects', p. 3.

44 See Winnicott, 'Playing', p. 48.

45 Huizinga, *Homo Ludens*, p. 12.

46 Dick Higgins mentions 'good will' in his 'Preface to *Saint Joan at Beaurevoir*' (1959), in *FOEW & OMBWHNW: A Grammar of the Mind and a Phenomenology of Love and a Science of the Arts as Seen by a Stalker of the Wild Mushroom* (New York, Barton, Cologne: Something Else Press, 1969), p. 178.

47 Turner, *From Ritual to Theatre*, p. 45.

48 Henri Lefebvre, *Critique of Everyday Life* (1947), trans. J. Moore (London: Verso, 1991), p. 202.

49 Hélio Oiticica, 'A dança', p. 73.

50 The criticism has been most clearly voiced against the American school of object relations including Erik H. Erikson. See Anthony Elliott, *Psychoanalytic Theory: An Introduction* (Oxford and Cambridge: Blackwells 1994), chapters 3 and 5.

51 Lygia Clark, 'L'Homme, structure vivante d'une architecture biologique et cellulaire', *Robho*, 5–6 (n. d. [April 1971]), in Brett et al., *Lygia Clark*, p. 248.

52 Ibid.

53 Bruno Paraiso, 'Lygia Clark: a coragem e a magia de ser contemporâneo', supplement of the *Correio da Manhã* (10 November 1971), p. 2.

54 Ibid.

55 This is why Turner distinguishes between such 'liminal' states and the 'liminoid' experiences to be found in industrial societies. Turner, *From Ritual to Theatre*, pp. 33 ff.

56 Hélio Oiticica, 'Parangolé: da antiarte às apropiações ambientais de Oiticica: posição e programa', *Revista GAM* (July 1966), in Figueiredo et al., *Aspiro ao grande labirinto*, p. 81.

57 Lygia Clark, 'Nós recusamos' (1966), in Brett et al., *Lygia Clark*, p. 211.

58 Guy Debord, *La Société du spectacle* (1967) (Paris: Editions du Champ Libre, 1971), p. 19.

59 Hélio Oiticica, 'Tropicália, 4 de Março de 1968', in Brett et al., *Hélio Oiticica*, p. 125.

60 For more on this debate, see Carlos Basualdo (ed.), *Tropicália: a Revolution in Brazilian Culture* (São Paulo: Cosac & Naify, 2005).

61 See Hannah Higgins, *The Fluxus Experience* (Berkeley: University of California Press, 2002). Unlike Higgins's comprehensive account, my focused reading of Fluxus will not address the debates within the group regarding the different means of obtaining such 'general creativity'.

62 See George Maciunas, 'Letter to Tomas Schmit, January 1964', in Emmett Williams and Ann Nöel (eds), *Mr. Fluxus: a Collective Portrait of George Maciunas, 1931–1978* (London: Thames & Hudson, 1997), p. 104.

63 Ibid., p. 105.

64 Ibid.

65 See Lygia Clark, 'Nós somos os propositores' (1968), in Brett et al., *Lygia Clark*, p. 233.

66 Hélio Oiticica, 'Esquema geral da nova objetividade', in *Nova Objetividade Brasileira* (1967), in Brett et al., *Hélio Oiticica*, p. 118.

67 Henry Flynt, 'Down with Art!/Art or Brend?' (New York: Flux Press, 1968), in Stewart Home (ed.), *Art Strike Handbook* (London: Sabotage Editions, 1989), p. 19.

68 Ibid.

69 Jean Clay, 'Unité du champ perceptif', *Robho*, 5–6 (n. d. [April 1971]), 11.

70 Ono, 'To the Wesleyan people', n. p.

71 Jerry Rubin, *Do It! Scenarios for the Revolution* (London: Jonathan Cape, 1970).

72 Stewart Home, *The Assault on Culture: Utopian Currents from Lettrisme to Class War* (Stirling: AK Press, 1991), p. 59.

73 See Kristine Stiles, 'Between water and stone: Fluxus performance, a metaphysics of acts', in Elizabeth Armstrong and Joan Rothfuss (eds), *In the Spirit of Fluxus* (Minneapolis: Walker Art Center, 1994), p. 90 ff.

74 Clark, 'Estamos domesticados?' (1968), in Brett et al., *Lygia Clark*, p. 233.

75 Rubin, *Do It!*, p. 82.

76 See Matthew Stolz, 'Introduction', in Stolz (ed.), *Politics of the New Left* (Beverly Hills: Glencoe Press, 1971), pp. vii–xii.

77 Ibid., p. viii.

78 Home, *The Assault on Culture*, p. 68.

79 Theodor Roszak, *The Making of a Counter Culture* (1969), quoted by Stolz, 'Introduction', pp. viii–ix.

80 See Richard Flacks, 'On the uses of participatory democracy' (1969), in Stolz (ed.), *Politics of the New Left*, pp. 27–35.

81 Arthur Waskow, 'The meaning of creative disorder' (1966), in ibid., p. 61.

82 Carl Oglesby, 'An open letter to McCarthy supporters', in ibid., p. 81.

83 This is a paraphrase of Marcuse's ideas by student protest-leader Rudi Dutschke, which is quoted by Jean Clay, 'Quelques aspects de l'art bourgeois: la non-intervention', *Robho*, 5–6 (n. d. [April 1971]), 39.

84 Ibid.

Exchange rate: on obligation and reciprocity in some art of the 1960s and after

Miwon Kwon

In the face of a plethora of visual art experiments of the late 1960s – all tamed by now into discrete categories, such as conceptual art, land art, happenings, performance, process art, activist art – the influential art historian and critic Lucy Lippard proposed the overarching concept of 'dematerialisation' as a means to understand their collective motivation. She predicted in her 1968 essay 'The dematerialization of art':

> As more and more work is designed in the studio but executed elsewhere by professional craftsmen, as the object becomes merely the end product, a number of artists are losing interest in the physical evolution of the work of art. The studio is again becoming a study. Such a trend appears to be provoking a profound dematerialization of art, especially art as object, and if it continues to prevail, it may result in the object's becoming wholly obsolete.[1]

Listing an eclectic array of what she called 'post-aesthetic' works from this period, including Robert Rauschenberg's erasure of a Willem de Kooning drawing, Yves Klein's 'empty gallery' show in Paris, On Kawara's daily date paintings, Joseph Kosuth's photostat *Art as Idea as Idea*, Christine Kozlov's open film canister with a reel of transparent film inside, Hans Haacke's condensation and frost sculptures, Robert Smithson's maps and earthworks, Ed Ruscha's books, George Brecht's 'events', and Ray Johnson's mailings, among numerous other examples, Lippard acknowledged the moment as indicating a major art historical shift[2] – away from art as product to art as idea or art as action, she declared.

Reflecting back on this moment in the introduction to the 1997 reissue of her book *Six Years: The Dematerialization of the Art Object from 1966–1972*, in which a wider range and a longer list of art projects and publications are inventoried, Lippard elaborated further on the dematerialisation principle, emphasising its political significance.[3] Partly quoting herself from 1969, she wrote:

> Anti-establishment fervor in the 1960s focused on the de-mythologization and de-commodification of art, on the need for an independent (or 'alternative') art

that could not be bought and sold by the greedy sector that owned everything that was exploiting the world and promoting the Vietnam War. 'The artists who are trying to do non-object art are introducing a drastic solution to the problems of artists being bought and sold so easily, along with their art.'[4]

Which is to say, dematerialised art, in which the 'idea is paramount and the material form is secondary, lightweight, ephemeral, cheap, unpretentious,'[5] is viewed as a strategic subversion of the commercialisation of art and the commodification of the art object. In 1968, Lippard had reasoned that 'since dealers cannot sell art-as-idea, economic materialism is denied along with physical materialism.'[6]

Such a claim, energising and generation-defining at the time, seems poignantly utopian now. Clearly, dealers *have* figured out how to sell art-as-idea or art-as-action. The reconstitution of art that seemed dematerialised in the late 1960s via what Lippard called its 'epilogue', the residual materials that physically evidence the idea or action in the form of a proposal, instruction, 'score', relic, souvenir, or documentation, is a commonplace in today's art market.[7] The very nature of the market economy has also shifted since the late 1960s so that immaterial, invisible aspects, such as services, information and 'experience', are now quantifiable units of measure to gauge economic productivity, growth, and profit.[8] Ideas and actions do not debilitate or escape the market system because they are 'dematerialised'; they drive it precisely because so. Despite these profoundly changed realities, however, which inevitably recast the wisdom of certain political ambitions of 1960s and 1970s art, the presumption that dematerialisation = anti-commodity still persists in structuring contemporary art discourse. This is not to cast the past investment in 'dematerialisation' as a historical mistake on the grounds that it failed to escape the commodity system or did not understand it well enough. Rather, given the conceptual impasse of the equation – denial of physical materialism = denial of economic materialism – and changed historical circumstances, we might reapproach the art of the 1960s and 1970s with a different set of questions or frames of reference.

In concert with the exhibition *Work Ethic*'s ambition to present a major reconsideration of the art of this period, specifically through the lens of the changing status of work and artistic labour, this essay sketches some issues pertaining to a related problematic, the nature of exchange. My working hypothesis is as follows. Much of so-called dematerialised art may have complicated the conventional methods of buying and selling art by not conforming to an agreeable and readily exchangeable commodity form. But the radicality, or the intelligence, of such art lies not merely in its non-object status. The negation of the object form is not an automatic challenge to the abstraction of commodity exchange. I would argue that of greater significance is the fact that many works from the 1960s–1970s and later – art as idea, art as action, conceptual art, performance art, happenings, and so on – attempt to install alternative models of exchange that counter, complicate, or parody the dominant market- and profit-based system of exchange.[9] In fact, many of them engage the logic of the gift economy as one such alternative. By this I mean that the artwork in such cases functions as a mechanism to

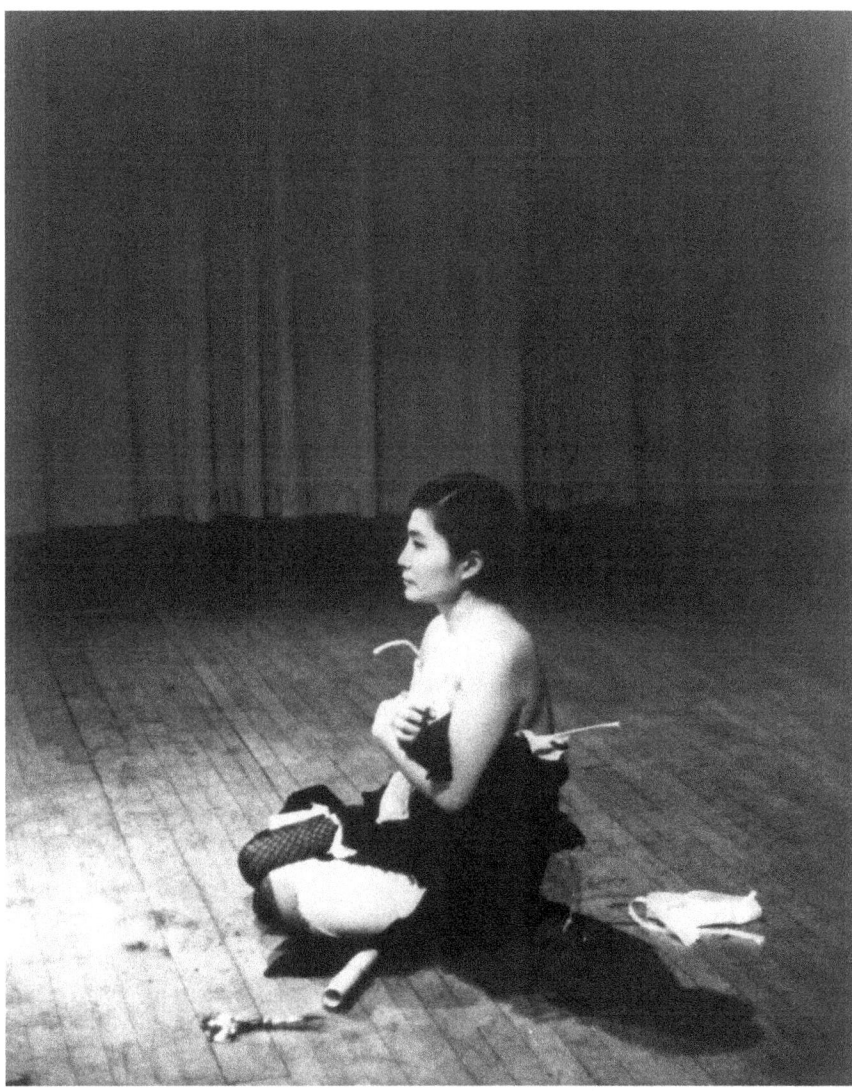

Yoko Ono performing *Cut Piece*, Carnegie Recital Hall, New York, 21 March 1965.   **12.1**

instigate social exchanges or interactions that specifically put into motion a circuit of obligation and reciprocity, typically involved in giving, receiving or accepting, and giving in return.[10] Furthermore, in addition to reorganising the position and relationship of the art maker and audience in a general sense, such an artwork, through the process of exchange, tests each person's sense of honour and dishonour, shame, power, risk, fear, status, humiliation and prestige.

> [The] giver's undeclared calculation has to reckon with the receiver's undeclared calculation, and hence satisfy his expectation without appearing to know what they are. (Pierre Bourdieu)

Let us consider the following works drawn from the *Work Ethic* exhibition. On a typewritten piece of paper, Alison Knowles humbly suggests (or sternly demands, depending on how one interprets the statement), 'Make a salad.' Piero Manzoni builds a pedestal for viewers to stand on so that they can be transformed into works of art. Yoko Ono instructs her audience members to cut off pieces of her dress and take the scraps away with them (figure 12.1). Eleanor Antin notarises her plan to immediately leave a group meeting if she fails to address certain persons from behind them. Valie Export bares her breasts inside a modified cardboard box, to be touched, though not seen, by random people on the street. Edward Kienholz proposes in writing several different versions of a 'concept tableau' to suit a potential patron's preference and/or pocket book. Lee Lozano demands of herself that she not participate in any art-related events or activities starting on 8 February 1969.

Claiming that artworks such as these engage the logic of the gift is not to say that they are literally gifts. Few of them may indeed appear to satisfy the conventional definition of the gift as a voluntary act of generosity, even a sacrificial offering, that harbours no expectation of a return in kind or of personal gain on the part of the giver (i.e., Export, Ono).[11] But by invoking the gift economy here, I mean to call attention to the more complex ways in which artworks such as those mentioned above operate like gifts, presenting explicit and implicit demands, challenges, invitations, and dares that create an obligation to reciprocate with a suitable response. As we know from the work of Marcel Mauss, the French sociologist and author of the hugely influential 'Essai sur le don' ('The gift', 1924), as well as subsequent theories of the gift, there is no such thing as a free gift or entirely disinterested, uncalculated giving.[12] And, as recently summarised by anthropologist Maurice Godelier, Mauss teaches us that 'the interest of giving-while-appearing-disinterested resides ultimately in one fundamental characteristic of gift-giving, which is that … what *creates the obligation to give is that giving creates obligations*'.[13]

So the question remains: What kind of obligation do artworks of this kind impose upon their audience? How are we to 'reciprocate'?

Sometimes, as in the examples of Antin, Lozano and Kienholz, artists give instructions that obligate them to fulfil their own challenges. These cases present a self-enclosed circuit of obligation and reciprocity which is beyond the scope of this chapter. In other instances, as in the cases of Manzoni, Knowles, Ono and Export, the viewer/audience is put in an 'indebted' position, obligated to respond to the artistic instruction or offering via the avenues prescribed by the works themselves – that is, engagement, interaction, participation. This kind of situation, in which the audience is given the opportunity to 'complete' the work, is usually described as resulting from an artist's self-abnegation. The artist ostensibly gives up to the audience, as if a gift, his or her authority of creative authorship.

This displacement, often loosely associated with Roland Barthes's well-known notion of 'death of the author' (and the 'birth of the reader'), is commonly viewed as a critique of exclusive and elitist cultural values upheld by the art market and mainstream art institutions. Moreover, to borrow Lippard's words, it is generally considered an 'attack on the notion of originality … an attack on the genius theory, the hitherto most cherished aspect of patriarchal, ruling-class art'.[14] But if we accept this act of relinquishing the privileged right or ownership of artistic authorship as indeed an act of critical generosity, even as an effort to democratise art, as some have argued,[15] then we have to also attend to the full extent of the paradoxical condition that this act actualises.

Consider the following passage from Maurice Godelier's book *The Enigma of the Gift*, substituting the author's use of the terms 'giver', 'receiver', and 'gift' with artist, audience, and artwork, respectively.

> The act of giving seems to create simultaneously a twofold relationship between the giver and receiver. A relationship of *solidarity* because the giver shares what he has, or what he is, with the receiver; and a relationship of *superiority* because the one who receives the gift and accepts it places himself in the debt of the one who has given it, thereby becoming indebted to the giver and to a certain extent becoming his 'dependant', at least for as long as he has not 'given back' what he was given.
>
> Giving thus seems to establish a difference and an inequality of status between donor and recipient, which can in certain instances become a hierarchy: if this hierarchy already exists, then the gift expresses and legitimizes it. Two opposite movements are thus contained in a single act. The gift decreases the distance between the protagonists because it is a form of sharing, and it increases the social distance between them because one is now indebted to the other.[16]

Following this insight, we can confirm that the gift of sharing the authorial role of the artist, rendering the audiences into active participants or partners to complete the work, registers the artist's desire for solidarity or equality with his or her audience while at the same time reaffirming the artist's superior position.

The work of Brazilian artist Lygia Clark from the 1960s and 1970s is a paradigmatic example of this power dynamic. Like many artists of her generation, she rejected ego-centred art production. Her work – from simple objects and contraptions to more elaborate group events – elicited direct physical participation from audiences usually more accustomed to passive, distanced and exclusively visual appreciation of art.[17] But if Clark was 'content to simply propose to others to be themselves', as critic Guy Brett claims, then it is equally true that she imagined her audience as unable, lacking the means and knowledge, to 'be themselves' without her particular artistic intervention.[18] Clark presupposed that people generally suffer from fragmentation of body and mind, from alienation from self and others, and that basic multi-sensory engagement with objects and/or other people would stimulate repressed aspects of their perceptual capacities, encouraging them to regain a holistic and renewed sense of self. It is no coincidence that Clark eventually came to think of her audience as 'patients' and her art as a form of unorthodox psycho-therapy – that is, as a form of healing. In her case, the sharing of creative or authorial power between artist and audience constitutes nothing short of a gift of life, the reinstatement of a full subjecthood.

While Clark's practice represents an extreme case of art as gift and artist as gift-giver, more recent works mobilise, if less explicitly, a similar economy of exchange in which the artwork functions as an invitation or a challenge that provokes the audience into active participatory roles. Erwin Wurm's *One Minute Sculptures*, for instance, provide instructions for, potentially, anyone to become a work of art, however briefly. As a seemingly light-hearted and simple project that belies a complex engagement with distinctions of media and the function of time in the constitution of a work of art, *One Minute Sculptures* are initiated in the form of drawings and written propositions that diagram variously humorous, provocative and nonsensical actions.[19] Wurm suggests: holding one's breath while thinking of Spinoza, balancing a roll of toilet paper on one's back while forwardly bent over, propping up a line of balls and buckets against a wall with one's head, lying on tennis balls without letting one's body touch the floor, putting on a pair of pants over one's head as if it were a sweater. Although *One Minute Sculptures* are usually exhibited as already accomplished deeds, as already reciprocated 'gifts', through photographic and video documentation, any future viewer's attempt to fulfil Wurm's challenging propositions (with built-in failure) will result, in principle, in another unique 'sculpture'. Thus, the work sustains itself as an open-ended invitation that has the potential to obligate respondents continuously, converting artistic reception into artistic production any time and anywhere.

Gabriel Orozco's *Mesa de ping-pong con estanque (Ping Pond Table)* (1998) likewise offers its audience an opportunity to 'complete' or become a work of art. In Orozco's case, the 'gift' is an unexpected group interaction based in play. His eccentrically reconfigured ping-pong table, now extended and four sided with a square, lily-filled 'pond' in the middle, recalls Arte Povera's prevalent use of natural elements as sculptural material on the one hand and Claude Monet's famous Impressionist lilies on the other. More important than such art-historical references, however, is the way the work brings into the museum space, which traditionally demands quiet secular reverence, a 'low' recreational sport that can transform it into a spirited site of social exchange. Whether seen as a critique of institutional conventions, exposing what is normally repressed by them, or seen as a capitulation to the rising tendency toward entertainment-oriented programming among museums, *Ping Pond Table* leaves up to its audience the rules of engagement and potential competition. The work's status as a sculptural object or a performance prop also depends entirely on the reaction of the people gathered around the work at any one time, on their inclination or aversion to interact with others, possibly strangers. Orozco's distorted game of ping-pong, in other words, offers its audience the capacity to determine its meaning and purpose.

This kind of authorial generosity, however, also maintains a distance between artist and audience, securing the 'superior' position of the former, as noted earlier. The hierarchy of relations between the artist as creative thinker/maker and the viewer as disciplined consumer/receiver is not ultimately negated or refuted, as is often claimed. It is rather expressed and legitimised in the very gesture of giving away the ownership of the creative act.[20] Giving things away is tied up with ego-consolidation. Abdication of one's authority asserts one's superiority. This is a point that many critics, especially those who champion 'interactive' and participatory art generally, such as museum educators, public art sponsors and internet enthusiasts, continue to miss.

But what of the gift that is refused or otherwise unacknowledged? A dinner party to which no one comes? An instruction that goes ignored? As much as the accepting of a gift puts one in debt, in an inferior position to the giver until the debt is cleared through reciprocation, the refusal of a gift functions as a rejection of both the giver's superiority and his or her invitation to solidarity. Consequently, there is always the risk of personal humiliation and the possibility of a breach in social relations involved with gift-giving. The dreadfulness of this breach was brought home to me during a visit to the 1995 Guggenheim Museum retrospective of works by Felix Gonzalez-Torres, an artist noted for translating so many lessons from the art of the 1960s and 1970s.[21] Of great popularity in the exhibition were his well-known paper stacks and candy piles, which invite viewers to not only touch the art but also to take pieces of it with them (see figure 12.2). The large number of museum visitors, cheerfully collecting sheets of paper and grabbing handfuls of candy as they moved through the spiralling exhibition, seemed to bear out the observation of many critics and curators that these works are acts of unusual generosity. And the thought of Gonzalez-Torres's work being distributed around the world through the movement of his audience (rather than through the standard art market as a precious and expensive commodity) heartened me as to how modestly yet effectively art can enter the spaces of people's daily lives.

Even before leaving the museum, however, I was shocked by the sight of overstuffed garbage cans in the lobby, jammed with rolled and scrunched sheets of paper from Gonzalez-Torres's stacks. Outside the museum, too, Fifth Avenue waste bins were filled to capacity with what were, only few yards away inside the museum, 'works of art'. Granted, one can argue that the brilliance of Gonzalez-Torres's work lies in making evident precisely this kind of categorical slippage. But the ungracious scene of the audience's hoarding and then trashing of Gonzalez-Torres's 'gift' threw into harsh relief another fact: the thinness of the line separating honour and humiliation and the tenuousness of the very notion of the gift. The 'repudiation of artistic control' in Gonzalez-Torres's giveaway works, as in other works of the past and present that offer authorship privileges to the audience (many included in *Work Ethic*), may continue to bring high esteem to the artist as a generous gift-giver. But this esteem is predicated on the belief that anonymous recipients for whom the work is intended accept the 'gift of the artist' unconditionally and properly.

If we take stock of the gift's rejection, however – or, in Gonzalez-Torres's case its apparent acceptance at the outset followed by its quick disposal as trash – the artist's standing seems to diminish dramatically and become vulnerable,

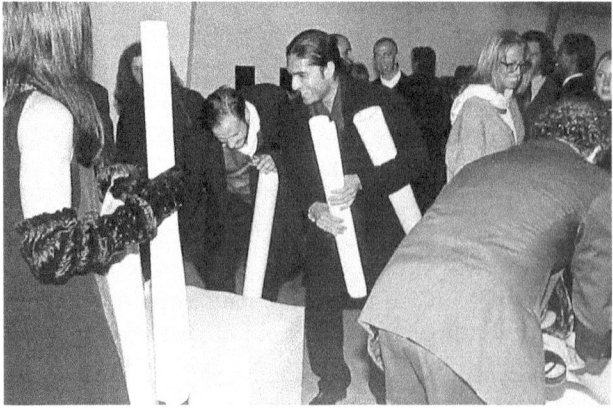

12.2   Opening reception for the *Ross Bleckner* and *Felix Gonzalez-Torres* exhibitions, Solomon R. Guggenheim Museum, New York, 2 March 1995. Visitors helping themselves to paper posters from Gonzalez-Torres's *Untitled (Republican Years)*,

as though he were a victim of a brutally hurtful personal rebuff. (How sad and truly exposed would Yoko Ono have appeared if her instruction to her audience in *Cut Piece* had been met with no response – utter silence, inaction and indifference?) The throwing away of the gift/work may be an unpremeditated or uneducated act, thus of little consequence to the meaning of the work, but that would render the taking of the gift/work all the more significant as potentially an act of thoughtlessness instead of interaction. The trashing of the gift is akin to the rejection of the solidarity that the artist/artwork proposes. Through the repudiation of a work's (and by extension, an institution's) generosity, the audience/receiver can assert its 'superior' position.[22]

As French sociologist Pierre Bourdieu has noted, an 'inaugural act that institutes communication (by addressing words, offering a gift, issuing an invitation or a challenge, etc.)', like so many of the dematerialised artworks under consideration here that propose an action or expect a response, 'always entails a kind of intrusion or even a calling into question … [that] inevitably contains the potentiality of a bond, an obligation'.[23] This possibility of a bond, an ongoing relationship of mutuality and exchange – between artist and audience, between persons – is at the heart of the anti-commodification efforts. For if the economy and moral code of commodity exchange is based on alienable objects and alienated subjects, whose ties of dependence to one another are cancelled at the moment of exchange, the economy and moral code of gift-giving asserts the impossibility of that cancellation. Just as the acceptance of a gift immediately puts one in debt to the gift-giver, a debt that must be repaid in an appropriate and timely manner following certain cultural rules in order that one should not lose face or insult the gift-giver, these artworks place on their addressees – upon us, even many years hence – a burden to answer their call for solidarity and communality.

But such art, as I have tried to show, also hazards the possibility of legitimising and reinforcing existing hierarchical power relations (the giver/artist maintains superiority). It can also reveal the impotence of generosity, especially when the gift is rejected, when there is no counter-gift or riposte, when the call goes unheeded. Again, Bourdieu says: 'It is true that … one can always choose not to reply to the interpellation, invitation, or challenge or not to reply immediately, to defer and to leave the other party in expectation. But non-response is still a response, and it is not so easy to shrug off the initial calling into question, which acts as a kind of *fatum*, a destiny.'[24] This resonates with the particular temporality of the artworks considered in this essay. Like the temporality of the gift, each work anticipates a social process and a future. The articulation of as-yet-unrealised possibilities of social interaction and relations *is* the work. This is why when these works are exhibited only through object residues, they seem so inadequate: the immediacy of 'presence' is missing, of course, but in addition, the *promise* of potential actions and relations – of mutual dependence, reciprocity and solidarity – is denied.

A final thought: On certain occasions when one receives or accepts a gift, the obligation is not to reciprocate with a comparable counter-gift but to hold on to the original one. Continuity of social relations is secured not always in the moment of taking or receiving a gift but in keeping it over time.[25] As implied in the Gonzalez-Torres incident, it takes a certain commitment and vigilance to abide by the obligation to *keep* a gift, to withhold it from dominant modes of circulation and exchange, to protect it from becoming alienable. The weight of *this* obligation seems more ambiguous and heavier than the obligation to reciprocate. For once this kind of gift is accepted, we are beholden to continuously imagine different destinies for art.

Notes

This chapter was originally published in Helen Molesworth (ed.), *Work Ethic* (Baltimore: The Baltimore Museum of Art, 2003), pp. 83–97. This edited reprint contains additional endnotes.

1 Lucy Lippard and John Chandler, 'The dematerialisation of art', *Art International*, 12:2 (February 1968), in Lucy Lippard, *Changing: Essays in Art Criticism* (New York: Dutton, 1971), p. 255.

2 Lippard heeds Joseph Schillinger's evolutionary mapping of artistic development in his 1948 book *The Mathematical Basis of the Arts*, which posits the eventual 'disintegration of art' and the 'abstraction and liberation of the idea'. While she argues for this moment as almost a historical inevitability, Lippard claims Dada and Surrealism as precedents for the 'post-aesthetic' dematerialisation of art that she sees around her. Marcel Duchamp is championed above all as the forerunner, the model of the artist as thinker rather than the artist as maker. Ibid., pp. 258, 268–70.

3 Lucy Lippard, 'Escape attempts', in *Six Years: The Dematerialization of the Art Object from 1966 to 1972* (New York: Praeger, 1973; Berkeley: University of California Press, 1997), pp. vii–xxii.

4 Ibid., p. xiv. The quotation from 1969 concludes, 'The people who buy a work of art they can't hang up or have in their garden are less interested in possession. They are patrons rather than collectors.'

5 Ibid., p. xiii.

6 Lippard and Chandler, 'The dematerialization of art', p. 270.

7 See, for instance, Paul Schimmel (ed.), *Out of Actions* (Los Angeles: Museum of Contemporary Art, 2000).

8 See my *One Place after Another: Site-specific Art and Locational Identity* (Cambridge: MIT Press, 2002).

9 Random examples include Edward Kienholz's watercolours that depict the object or monetary sum to be bartered with the painting, David Hammons's Dada-esque sale of different sizes of snowballs on a New York City street corner, and David Avalos's distribution of a National Endowment for the Arts grant to undocumented workers in the San Diego/Tijuana area as a tax 'rebate'.

10 Janet Kraynak first made the connection between participation and gift giving in her 1998 essay on 'Tiravanija's liability', reprinted in this volume (Chapter 9).

11 For a reading of Yoko Ono's *Cut Piece* in relation to the gift, see Julia Bryan-Wilson, 'Remembering Yoko Ono's *Cut Piece*', *Oxford Art Journal*, 26 (Spring 2003), 99–123.

12 Marcel Mauss, *The Gift: The Form and Reason for Exchange in Archaic Societies*, trans. W.D. Hall (New York: W.W. Norton, 1990). Recent publications on the gift include Alan D. Schrift (ed.), *The Logic of the Gift: Toward an Ethic of Generosity* (New York: Routledge, 1997), Maurice Godelier, *The Enigma of the Gift* (Chicago: University of Chicago Press, 1999), Jacques Derrida, *The Gift of Death*, trans. D. Wills (Chicago: University of Chicago Press, 1995).

13 Godelier, *The Enigma of the Gift*, p. 15 (emphasis in the original).

14 Lippard, 'Escape attempts', p. xv.

15 See, for instance, the rhetoric around 'new genre public art' described in Suzanne Lacy (ed.), *Mapping the Terrain* (Seattle: Bay Press, 1995). See also Chapter 13 in this volume.

16 Godelier, *The Enigma of the Gift*, p. 12.

17 See Chapters 2, 3 and 11.

18 As noted by critic Guy Brett, Clark's eccentric goggles, gloves, bags, masks, suits, restraints, elastic netting and 'biological architecture', all emphasising tactility and bodily engagement over opticality, allowed those 'who had been art's spectator … [to] rediscover his or her own poetics (expressivity, creativity) in themselves and come to be the subject of their own experience'. Guy Brett, 'Lygia Clark: six cells', in Guy Brett et al., *Lygia Clark* (Barcelona: Fundació Antoni Tàpies, 1998), p. 18.

19 For an insightful analysis of the various manifestations of Erwin Wurm's *One Minute Sculptures* (i.e., drawing, performance, photography, video), see Michael Newman, 'Photography and video as sculpture in the work of Erwin Wurm', in *Erwin Wurm* (London: The Photographer's Gallery, 2000), pp. 4–8.

20 In Lygia Clark's case, her generosity secures the 'superior' position of the artist as the healer/therapist in relation to a pathologised audience's state of debilitation and lack. Interestingly, it seems Clark was quite aware of the paradoxical nature of this kind of generosity: 'my self-centeredness which being so great made me give everything to the other, even the authorship of the work'. Brett, 'Lygia Clark', p. 18.

21 See Nancy Spector, *Felix Gonzalez-Torres* (New York: Solomon R. Guggenheim Museum, 1995).

22 Felix Gonzalez-Torres was contrarily very specific about the responsibilities and 'rights' of those who would come to own the paper stack and candy pile pieces as 'works', be they individual collectors or museums. He made a distinction between ownership and participation. On the complexities of Gonzalez-Torres's certificate of authenticity and the issues that they raise for authorship, ownership and the question of what constitutes a 'work', see David Deitcher, 'Contradictions and containment', in *Felix Gonzalez-Torres* (Ostfildern-Ruit: Cantz, 1997), pp. 104–9.

23 Pierre Bourdieu, 'Marginalia: some additional notes on the gift', in Schrift (ed.), *The Logic of the Gift*, p. 238.

24 Ibid., p. 238.

25 See Annette Weiner, *Inalienable Possessions: The Paradox of Keeping-while-Giving* (Berkeley and Los Angeles: University of California Press, 1992).

13 Working on the community: models of participatory practice

Christian Kravagna

There is today a widespread feeling of political impotence. The possibilities that unions, citizens' groups, workers' councils and other subordinated levels have to influence the political process appear to be constantly dwindling. Even politicians argue more and more frequently that their decisions depend on higher instances such as the European Union. Finally, many refer to the powerlessness of politics in comparison with the economy. Regardless of whether one believes in the omnipotence of globalisation or regards it as a simple economic excuse, it seems that many have given up on the prospect of any effective political engagement from below. Moreover, the presence and fear of unemployment seem to encourage a focus on economic survival.

On the other hand, there are proposals to merge both the unused potential for engagement, and the newly unemployed workforce, into a meaningful third term. Under the provocative title 'The soul of democracy', sociologist Ulrich Beck recently argued for his concept of 'citizens' labour'.[1] Instead of 'financing the idleness of several million people at the cost of billions', the unemployed should be integrated (voluntarily) within a framework of organised social engagement under the leadership of 'public good enterprises', ranging from palliative care and care of the homeless to 'art and culture'. 'Citizens' labour will not be remunerated, but rewarded. And specifically in an immaterial manner, for example … with distinctions.' According to this notion of work in exchange for social assistance, this would mean 'building up an engaged civil society that takes care of public concerns and stimulates the community with its initiatives'. The reduced possibilities of political participation are thus to be compensated with work. The state saves money and the citizens are meaningfully occupied. They are even 'rewarded' for this, so they have no reason to be restless.

This is the background against which I discuss a number of participatory practices in this chapter. Also in the background is the question: to what extent is 'social action' political, and to what extent does a social interest take the place of a political one? The following examples are taken from very different contexts, but I have omitted, however, a whole group from the spectre of artistic practices that make use of participatory methods. This is the fashion-able approach of 'working with others' that is so popular among the young, dynamic curators of mainstream exhibitions, because it allows for the incor-poration of 'the social' in small bites that are aesthetically easily digestible, but do not require any further reflection.[2]

At least in terms of its intention, the concept of a participatory practice is to be distinguished from two others: from interactivity, and from collective action. Interactivity goes beyond a purely perceptual proposition in that it allows for one or more reactions to affect the work – usually in a momentary, reversible and repeatable manner – in its appearance, but without fundamen-tally changing or co-determining its structure. Collective practice describes the conception, production and implementation of works or actions by several people with no principal differentiation among them, in terms of status. Participation, on the other hand, is initially based on a differentiation between producers and recipients, and focuses on the participation of the latter by turning over a substantial portion of the work to them, either at the point of conception or at a later stage in the work. Whereas interactive situations are usually addressed to an individual, participatory approaches take place mostly in group situations. There are, of course, combinations of all three; the boundaries are permeable, and rigid categorisations are not useful.

'Participation' as a practice or postulate is (almost) always mobilised in the art of the twentieth century when the definition of art, the role of the author or the distance between art and 'life' or society are called into question. The activation and participation of the audience aims at transforming the relationship between producers and recipients exemplified in the traditional artwork–viewer relationship. The traditional artwork's one-dimensional, hierarchical 'communication structure' produces a consumerist, distanced observer, representing a 'school of asocial behaviour', as Varvara Stepanova wrote in 1921.[3] The intention to resolve this situation through a dynamic of reciprocity develops in parallel with a criticism of purely visual experience and is frequently aimed at an activation of the body as a precondition for participation. This physical involvement can have phenomenological bases, as they are described by El Lissitzky in his *Demonstration Rooms* (1926): 'Our construction/design shall make the man active. This is the function of our room. … With each movement of the viewer in space the perception of the wall changes … The viewer is physically engaged in an interaction with the object on display.'[4]

However, participation can also be initiated, as with the Dadaists, through acts of provocation. The beginnings of a 'history of participation' as a sub-history of the avant-garde should probably be looked for in the 'proto-participatory' tendencies of both Dada and Russian Constructivism and Productivism. In the Soviet press, according to Sergei Tretyakov, 'the difference between the author and the audience begins … to disappear. There the reader is ready to become a writer … at any time'.[5] Depending on its ideological foundation, different claims to change are combined with participation as a programme: whether revolutionary ('dissolution of art in the praxis of life'), reformative ('democratisation of art') or – less politically – playful and/or didactic, perception- and consciousness-altering.

After the Second World War, many practices using participatory methods initially seemed to develop from the Cage school, whether Fluxus, happenings, or the work of Robert Rauschenberg. In music, John Cage fulfilled a wish that Walter Benjamin had already ascribed to Hanns Eisler, namely that of 'eliminating the opposition between performers and listeners'.[6] *4'33"* (1952) consists of nothing other than the noises in the concert hall. Although the audience essentially produces these noises, it is not yet really *active*. This is also true for Robert Rauschenberg's *White Paintings* created at the same time, which reflect nothing but the movements of the viewers. In contrast, Rauschenberg's later *Black Market* (1961) actually calls for the audience to take action. Objects are to be taken out of a case and replaced with others. The boundary between art and life is to be bridged by turning the recipients into co-performers.[7]

The neo-avant-gardes of the 1950s were obsessed with 'reality'.[8] Following the integration of surrounding noises in music and of objects in images, happenings and Events involved 'real-time' processes. The 'blurring of art and life' strove for a 'concrete art' located in or even dissolving into 'real life'. Allan Kaprow, influenced by John Dewey's *Art as Experience*, defined aesthetic experience as participation. Taking action becomes a condition for experience, because otherwise no happening can take place. The kind of action is taken from everyday routines that are imbued with a new aesthetic quality through collective, mostly playful, practices. The final outcome involves carrying these newly valued actions back into everyday life: 'Doing life, consciously.'[9] For George Maciunas, who refers to both Dada and the Russian Productivists, artists have acquired an elitist, parasitic status in society. It is therefore up to the 'anti-professional' Fluxus artist to demonstrate the disposability of artists by showing 'that everything can be art and everyone can practice it'.[10] What begins as participation within the framework of art should thus be fulfilled in a general aesthetic (life) praxis. This is a programme of democratisation, whose failure hinges on the artist's role as an authoriser of lay participation. In the Beuysian variation, it certainly acquires a connection to real politics, but this does not change the fact that everything is called into question but the status of the artist.

Alongside these open, chance-oriented, anarcho-poetic and sometimes even destructive (in the case of Wolf Vostell's work) practices, another direction in 1960s art existed that is more strongly didactic in its orientation and is more reliant on objects. These kinds of practices attempted to replace the concept of the artwork with new 'communication' or 'action' objects, which suggested a more or less clearly defined use. Based on a critique of everyday behaviours conditioned by the consumer industry and social constraints, these kinds of objects, which were not subject to any previously ritualised mode of use, were designed to enable immediate, basic experiences through processes of encounter and experimental use. A position of this kind, embodied by Franz Erhard Walther for example, replaces observation with action, and at times also introduces collective action. Yet by opposing 'alienated' experience with 'genuine' experience, it remains indebted to an aesthetic of autonomous art that suggests alternatives without opening up sites of resistance.

Heal the world: the rhetoric of the NGPA

The context in which participatory art has been most prominently discussed in recent years is that of the conglomerate of heterogeneous practices that has come to be labelled 'New Genre Public Art' (NGPA). The terms 'community-based art' and 'art in the public interest' are also used to describe this trend. As even its proponents note, this 'new genre' describes less a set of really 'new' practices than a kind of practice that has been pursued since the 1970s, but which has been largely marginalised by an elitist and object-fixated art world. Their time is said to have now come, as these different practices can be discussed as a category of 'public art', in the framework of which they first become a kind of movement, and in which they mark a change of paradigm. This new paradigm sketches out, briefly summarised, the following history of 'Public Art': after public places were initially rather randomly beautified with autonomous artworks, the next step led to site-specific artistic interventions within architectonic, spatial situations. After the work and the place, the focus has now shifted, in a further step, to the social, a local population (group), minority or 'community'.

The NGPA is first and primarily concerned with defining its audience. Alongside individual concerns, there are at least two objective reasons for this move. First, many of the (older) socially and politically engaged artists were marginalised for so long by the dominant art system that they were forced to open up other fields of work outside institutions. Second, local resistance to 'art in public spaces' and the ensuing debates (exemplified by the controversy surrounding Richard Serra's *Tilted Arc*) clearly showed that the question of the audience had not been taken seriously enough by conventional public art programmes. A practice that starts from locally defined, relatively manageable publics and that usually has a clearly defined time limit as well, seemed to offer a welcome solution to official programmes for public art.

Every criticism of the NGPA finds itself confronted with the problem of whether to address single artistic projects or the strategic discourse, the identity produced by the label. All too often the practices subsumed under the term differ from one another, and thus the practice also often diverges from its theorisation. The 'compendium' of over eighty artists and groups that Suzanne Lacy appends to her discourse-defining book *Mapping the Terrain: New Genre Public Art* ranges from Vito Acconci and the Border Art Workshop, through Group Material and Jenny Holzer, to Paper Tiger TV and Fred Wilson, from identity politics through media activism to institutional critique. A lowest common denominator is hard to find. In contrast, there is a strong tendency to discursive homogenisation, which can probably only be explained by the need to identify a 'movement' and a 'change of paradigm'. If I choose to deal with the rhetoric of the NGPA specifically in the following, it is because I value its role within the current redefinition of art more highly than that of its practices. If we assume that central points of this artistic self-understanding include shifting from the symbolic level to the 'real', and putting social practices in the place of the interpretation and critique of social issues, then it is primarily the rhetoric of this pragmatic attitude that can provide insights into its underlying worldview.

Mary Jane Jacob, a curator of community-oriented projects who has acted, alongside Suzanne Lacy, as one of the most important mentors of 'new public art', outlines its historical place in the following way: 'If, in the 1970s, we were extending the definition of who the artist is along lines of nationality or ethnicity, gender and sexual orientation; and in the 1980s the place of exhibitions expanded to include any imaginable venue … then in the 1990s we are grappling with broadening the definition of who is the audience for contemporary art.'[11] 'Widening' the audience means here, above all, differentiating the audience. From *one* anonymous art audience emerge specified publics, so to speak, which are constituted as such through direct contact with the artist, which differ from one project to the next, and which are frequently included in the realisation of works: 'This work activates the viewer – creating a participant, even a collaborator.'[12] It is through the 'dialogical structure' of the integration of the community in the creative process that the work must derive its relevance for the community itself.

What is noticeable about the programmatic writings of Lacy and Jacob, and also of Lucy Lippard, Suzi Gablik and Arlene Raven, is that political analysis is largely missing, even though there is much talk of social change. This political deficit is compensated by an inventory of concepts that clearly exhibits pastoral features: 'To search for the good and make it matter: this is the real challenge for the artist', is printed in large letters on the cover of Lacy's book. Starting from the diagnosis of an elitist, self-absorbed art business on the one hand, and a whole series of 'social ills' on the other,[13] 'connective aesthetics' (as Gablik calls them) are intended to be a bridge between art and 'real people'. In order to build this bridge by means of a 'dialogical structure', the two sides that are to be linked must first of all be separated: on the one hand the artists, whose engagement is motivated by a 'longing for the Other'[14] or 'desire for connection'[15] and on the other, the 'real people' in 'real neighborhoods'[16] which actually tends to refer to (generally non-white) working class or generally poorer sections of the population.

The rhetoric of the NGPA barely obscures the process of 'othering', the construction of an 'other' as a condition for further projections. The 'others' are not only poor and disadvantaged, they are also representatives of what is genuine and real, so that they are at once both needy and a source of inspiration.[17] The NGPA's relation to art is similarly ambivalent. Considered aloof, bourgeois and decadent in its institutionalised form, it nevertheless represents a reservoir of creativity without which the life of the 'others' could not be enriched: 'The community-based art ... can not only expose the energy and depth of ordinary people but also help these people develop their human potential in individual and communal acts.'[18] For Gablik, 'care and compassion' are the central values of 'connective aesthetics', which are defined as 'feminine'; Lacy and Lippard emphasise a 'capacity for empathy'.

Although they do not refer to it explicitly, these authors' gender-specific attributions of moral attitudes seem in tune with Nancy Chodorow's and Carol Gilligan's conclusion that the social behaviour of women, characterised by care and empathy, differs fundamentally from the male orientation towards law and justice.[19] This schematic logic of difference corresponds to the rigid dichotomy between an individualistic 'museum art' and a collaborative NGPA – an opposition asserted by the latter by denying any fluid passages, even within its own ranks. The fact that women are, in fact, comparatively very well represented in this 'genre', however, is less a proof of its gender-specific social character than of the familiar power relations in the institutional art field.

Yet for art to actually fulfil, in the process of social interaction, the 'healing function' of which all the authors speak, it requires, in addition, an educational dimension. In order to be able to 'heal a society that has been alienated from its life forces'[20] – Jacob brings the figure of the shaman again into play – 'the unique perceptions and creative mechanisms of artists' must be passed on to the non-artist participants.[21] The pastoral mixture of care and education explains some of the pseudo-religious features of the NGPA, such as the spiritually inflected invocations of community, as well as certain tendencies to bind communities through traditionalist rituals such as 'parades'. The critique of individualism and the search for a communal foundation for aesthetic action, for a 'reconciliation' of social spheres, for civil participation in the processes of meaning production – all testify to a close proximity between connective aesthetics and the social theory of communitarianism.[22]

We should remember, however, that a homogenising discourse is being applied here to extremely different practices. Its traditionalist, essen-tialist, moralising and mystifying (see Gablik's 're-enchantment of art') elements should therefore not be taken as a basis for evaluating individual artistic processes. It is, nevertheless, necessary to recognise the conserva-tive tendencies of the NGPA, because they threaten to illegitimately co-opt a spectrum of approaches which are, in part, much more productive and progressive.

Get down and party. Together.

Adrian Piper's *Funk Lessons* (1982–84) (figure 13.1) follow an understanding of participation that is in stark contrast with the pastoral type. The collective dance performances combine political subject matter with pleasurable experiences. Unlike the ideal step-by-step model of the NGPA – illness diagnosis, therapy plan, healing – the *Funk Lessons* have an explicitly experimental character ('A collaborative experiment in cross-cultural transfusion'). The unpredict-ability already begins with the way the participants arrive, in response to an offer, rather than being defined beforehand according to certain categories like 'community' or 'the others' (workers, old people, homeless, etc.). Community emerges, if at all, in the course of the event; it makes no claim to permanence; there is nothing essential about it.

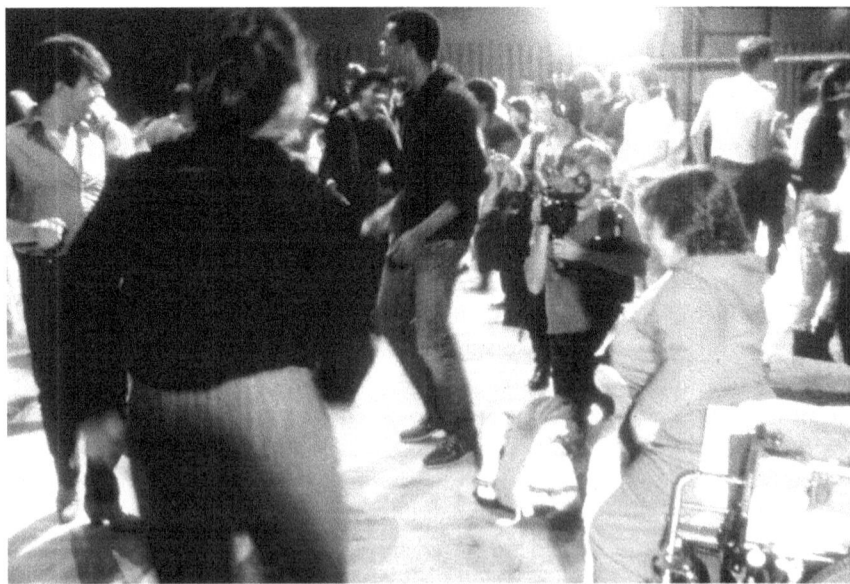

13.1   Adrian Piper, *Funk Lessons*, 1983, 00:15.17.

Starting from the widespread racist rejection by the white middle class of the funk idiom as 'black working-class culture', Piper didactically employs funk as a 'collective medium of self-transgression' in order to 'overcome cultural and racist barriers'. She explains funk's music and dance basics, its cultural backgrounds and relationships to 'white' music. What starts as learning-by-doing then develops according to how deep-seated rejections, fears, insecurities or enthusiasm and curiosity are expressed in the participants' reactions, and how counter-reactions set off a polyvocal dialogue, which transforms the original 'learning situation' into an open discussion that can become quite vehement. Participation in this kind of process is less about taking part in a vague feeling of community than it is about entering into a confrontation that touches on the boundaries of politics and personality. Involving the participants within an ambivalent situation of gifts (of aesthetic experience, of information) and obligations (an articulation of their resistances, and a co-responsibility for the collective process) means, from the standpoint of the artist, proposing a risky scenario with an open end.

What sets Piper's *Funk Lessons* apart from all the well-intentioned 'pastoral' tendencies is perhaps her openly articulated self-interest: 'My motivation in doing the *Funk Lessons* performances also has a very large self-interested component (of course). The ignorance and xenophobia that surround the aesthetic idiom of black working-class culture have affected the audience's comprehension of my performance work since 1972.'[23] To be able to continue to use this idiom as part of her personal identity, it seemed necessary to attempt to share it in some form with her predominantly white middle-class audience. To emphasise this aspect of the work, which is certainly not the most important, seems appropriate here because it is so diametrically different from the NGPA's rhetoric of improving the world, manifest in one of Suzanne Lacy's 'acknowledgments': 'Most important to me are the many invisible communities … who have inspired my work over the years, those who suffer various forms of discrimination, violence, and injustice.'[24]

Radical democracy …

Since the late 1980s, Michael Clegg and Martin Guttmann have been working on artistic projects in public spaces, for which the active participation of the local population is a prerequisite. A first attempt of this kind, *A Model for an Open Public Library* (1987), involved placing a bookshelf, stocked by the artists, in various places in New Jersey. The disconcerting appearance of a bookshelf in open spaces, especially empty or infrequently visited places, had poetic, almost surreal features, which probably worked better in the documentary context of subsequent gallery displays. In a short text, 'Proposal for an "open-air" library', published in 1990, Clegg and Guttmann already formulated the basic ideas for their *Open Public Library* later set up in Graz and Hamburg:

> A library without librarians and without surveillance, the stock of which is determined by the users themselves through a system of exchange, according to which every borrowed book is to be replaced by another chosen at will by the user. As an institution, a library of this kind could contribute to the self-definition of a community ... and would thus be a kind of portrait of the community.[25]

On the one hand, the *Open Public Library* was thus conceived as a 'social sculpture', which is constituted as such, and acquires a specific function, only through the intensity and the concrete process of the audience's interaction. On the other hand, the conception of the work as a 'portrait' of a community is derived from the artists' earlier photographic works based on an expanded concept of the portrait. Although the idea of the social portrait is important for the *Open Public Library*, and the problems it raises remain to be discussed, it appears of secondary interest in the context of our discussion here. More relevant to the question of the background and potential for participatory experience is the way in which it works as a test model for a type of cultural institution that largely dispenses with hierarchies, control mechanisms and bureaucratic regulations.

Following a first version of the *Open Public Library* in 1991 in Graz and a model for a freely accessible tool repository in Toronto that same year, which operated according to the same principle, the Hamburg version of the *Open Public Library*, implemented in autumn 1993, represented its first fully mature variation (see figures 13.2–13.3 for a subsequent version in Mainz, in 1994). In three demographically different districts of the city, the circuit boxes of electrical companies were equipped with shelves and glass doors and thus turned into public, freely accessible libraries. Prior to the project, local residents were informed about the concept and asked for book donations. Only one minimal rule for using the library was given in writing on location: 'Please take the books of your choice and bring them back within an appropriate period of time. Additions to the stock of books are welcome.' The lack of further regulations and instances of surveillance transferred the responsibility for the functioning and fate of the installation to the users. In this Clegg and Guttmann see 'an experiment with a radically democratic institution.'[26]

The political dimension of such an 'experimental set-up' lies in the provocation of a self-determined collective action characterised by an absence of rules that is highly unusual in our institutionally administered society. Questions raised by this challenge were formulated by Clegg and Guttmann in conjunction with their Graz project: 'What happens when you leave books

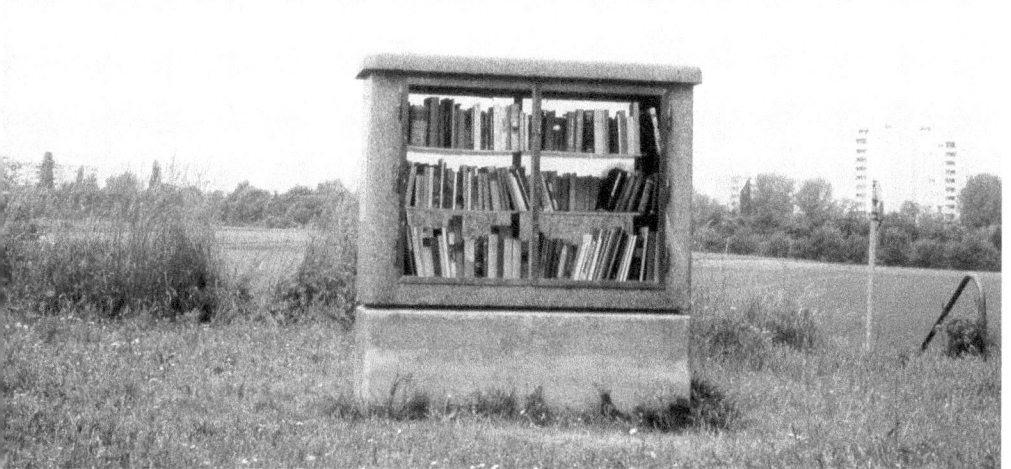

Clegg & Guttmann, *Open Public Library*, Mainz, 1994.   **13.2**

unprotected by guards or librarians? How will people react to such a utopian proposition? People are very opinionated about questions like that. But they have no data to rely on. We wanted to find out what the real situation was.'[27] The sociological studies that accompanied the project indicated a high degree of participation, which was manifested by the almost complete renewal of the library stock in the course of the project, among other things, as well as a fundamentally positive reaction to the 'utopian proposition': 'Reasons given for the attractiveness of the project referred primarily to the display of trust, the possibilities for communication that it opened up, and an increased solidarity based on exchange relationships.'[28] Even though participation in the project varied from one district to another and ultimately had a broad span 'ranging from vandalism to support through citizens' initiatives',[29] the resulting communicative situations and social relationships as a whole indicate a structure of needs that provides a real foundation for the 'utopian' dimension of a radically democratic institution. This is what also makes it possible to ultimately overlook the somewhat exaggerated rhetoric with which Clegg and Guttmann position their practice within the traditional claims of the historical avant-garde when they use the well-known motto 'breaking down the boundaries to life'.

Although Clegg and Guttmann's work has long been firmly anchored in the commercial art world and they do not hesitate to make use of this background for 'art-external projects',[30] its theoretical foundation is derived from an idiosyncratic reading of Peter Bürger's *Theorie der Avantgarde*. Clegg and Guttmann take up the historical avant-garde's desire to transfer art to life praxis discussed by Bürger, but ignore Bürger's conclusion that historically this transfer did not take place and that it 'probably cannot take place within bourgeois society'.[31] According to Bürger, 'the means with which the avant-gardists hoped to effect the dissolution of art have in the meantime acquired the status of artwork', which is why 'their application can no longer legitimately be tied to any claim to a renewal of life praxis'.

For Bürger the neo-avant-garde institutionalises *the avant-garde as art*, thus negating its 'genuinely avant-gardist intentions'.[32] With reference to Bürger, it does in fact seem to be a 'very particular interpretation' to maintain an avant-gardist rhetoric and combine it with a 'position of leadership'.[33] Nevertheless, this interpretation of avant-garde history as 'an inspiration for a process of democratizing institutions'[34] indicates a way of departing from the grand narrative of a revolutionary 'avant-garde' without relinquishing its potential for social critique. Indeed, works like the *Open Public Library* promise to

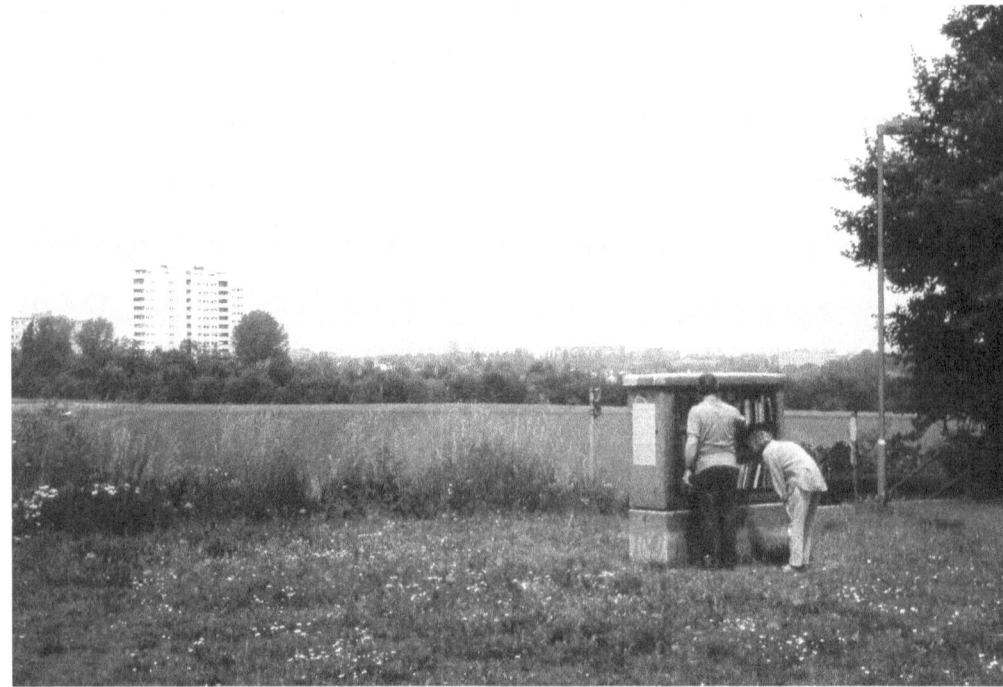

13.3   Clegg & Guttmann, *Open Public Library*, Mainz, 1994.

honour some of the historical avant-garde's claims summarised by Bürger, such as 'suspending the opposition between producers and recipients',[35] collective types of reception, or the notion that 'art and life praxis form a unit if the praxis is aesthetic and the art is practical'.[36]

How effective these kinds of practices can be in terms of the democratisation of art as an institution is an open question. The more interesting question would be, however, what it means for the emancipatory symbolic power of an undoubtedly astonishingly well-functioning radical democratic experimental set-up, if it turns out – as it did in Hamburg – that an installation like this is most successful among the population with the greatest economic and educational capital. That is precisely the population group that participates most in the democratic process (e.g. elections) under normal circumstances as well.[37] The problematic aspect of the 'portrait of a community' should then also be discussed in this context, if it threatens to portray nothing other than the somewhat stereotypical notion that the aptitude for democracy is determined by social factors.

… and counter-consciousness

Clegg and Guttmann's projects, and the *Open Public Library* in particular, are undoubtedly characterised by a high degree of conceptual reflection and precision in their practical implementation. In this way, they differ from a number of other projects that do not go beyond a rhetorically playful level. However, the construction of a singular position, as it is undertaken in the discussion of this work again and again, is somewhat problematic. The abstract, generalising reference to participatory approaches in the art of the 1960s and 1970s, which are largely regarded as having 'failed', ultimately only serves here to mark Clegg and Guttmann's historically specific position. The artists themselves stress that they do not 'consider the project' 'as a revival of the (somewhat naive) works of the 1960s'.[38] And Michael Lingner, who deals specifically with the art-historical dimension of the *Open Public Library*, radically distinguishes the way it works from earlier attempts to transfer the responsibility to act to the audience. There have been 'diverse attempts to include the public in an artistically productive way' but for Lingner the '1960s artistic conceptions of actions aimed at the audience's self-determination' have not been 'put into practice until now' as they have been 'merely presented and received as ideas.'[39] It is only because Lingner's main point of reference is the *Handlungsobjekte* (*Performance Objects*) by Franz Erhard Walther that he can claim that Clegg and Guttmann's effort to set up a 'self-determined involvement on the part of the public' in concrete and practical ways, 'instead of confining their realisation to the restricted context of art', is the key to their 'fundamentally distinct position within history'.[40]

Indeed, these 'fundamental' differences become much less clear when one turns to historical models that are, in fact, closer to that of the *Open Public Library*. As one of the most elaborate concepts of participatory art practice, which can also be traced consistently over a long period of time, I would like to turn to the projects that Stephen Willats has carried out since the 1960s. Willats's work typically demonstrates that the generalising references to the 'naivety' or the merely idealist nature of older models of participatory practice are not justified. In the early 1960s, Willats had been producing kinetic objects and plastic constructions that are partly oriented to interactivity with the audience. Critical reflections on the elitist character of the museum and the exclusive structure of the art system, however, very soon led Willats to develop new working methods, which build on the 'communicative' properties of the earlier objects, but which shift the emphasis from the relationship between people and objects to inter-subjective, social relationships. Art considered as a form of communication should not be reduced to the communicative relationship between artist and audience, but can also be invested in existing social spaces and their relationships. The term that is central for Willats in this respect is 'self-organisation', which means establishing or intensifying the social relationships within a group of participants involved in an aesthetic creative process: 'I consider that the audience of the work of art is as important as the artist, and that the active involvement of people in the origination of [the] art work is an essential part of the process of generating interventions in the social process of culture.'[41]

Willats's understanding of participation is characterised by two specific features. First, the 'audience' (now, in fact, co-producers) is already integrated in the *origination* of the artwork, not just in the actuation of a given score as in other models, such as that of Fluxus, or in the implementation of one of several given possibilities. Second, the projects are conceived as 'interventions in the social process': the scope of action extends beyond the art context itself. Willats's projects are thus less concerned with the abstract idea of 'participation' as some kind of logical consequence of the 'death of the author', but are instead oriented from the start towards the concrete everyday context of the people who take part, and always aim to change these conditions: 'From the outset it became obvious that a model of practice would be required that would bind it to the context in which the artwork was to be presented, and which could embody the priorities, languages and behaviours of the audience.'[42]

The redefinition of the relation between art and its public at stake here does not involve merely expanding an existing artist–viewer circle, familiar with the conventions and criteria of art, in order to include an uncertain factor – the ordinary citizen who would be able to actively participate in the creative and aesthetic values of art. What is characteristic of Willats's model is, rather, the focus on a different, yet very specific, audience, which is from the start more or less identical with the circle of participants in each project. Willats is not just interested in cancelling the separation between producers and audience: the groups he works with also become the theme, the subject matter of the work.

The social-critique position from which Willats cooperates with each specific audience is based on an insight into the institutional constraints of modern living conditions, the social norms and culturally predominant codes that dominate the everyday life, behaviours and perceptions of human beings. Willats finds an exemplary embodiment of these repressive structures in the characteristic council flat buildings of post-war modernism, which impact on the mental and social life of their inhabitants – to the point of creating a contradictory 'community of the isolated'. The projects that Willats develops with the residents are intended to set in motion processes of perception, which are designed to lead to the analysis, and possible change, of both the individual relationships to the environment and the social relationships between inhabitants. In this respect, Willats presumes a latent 'counter-consciousness', which he feels is manifested in the subversive recoding of signs, and through actions ranging from graffiti and vandalism to the 'improper' use of public spaces. Part of the work consists in articulating different forms of counter-consciousness, and extending them from the individual to the communal level through confrontations with others.

Willats's model of a participatory practice is illustrated in a project such as *Vertical Living* (1978). The choice of a typical example of council housing, Skeffington Court in West London, was followed by initial contacts with the caretaker, and with a friend's mother who lived in the building, to talk freely about the idea of a collaboration with the residents, and to let potential participants introduce themselves. Following the constitution of a larger group of participants, Willats conducted individual conversations over the course of three months, which explored the relations between the building, daily habits, leisure time and social contacts. The recordings of the collected conversations revealed a set of common problems, which could serve as the basis for further more specific discussions about certain problems. Finally, picture panels were prepared, each by one resident in cooperation with the artist, which addressed certain circumstances, a problem, a deficit or an expectation, through photos and texts. The panels were set up in the hall next to the elevator; new panels were placed two floors higher at regular intervals, thus reflecting the architectonic structure of the building. Feedback forms, distributed so that other tenants could suggest solutions to the problems, were collected and publicly presented, in turn.

In addition to requiring the participants' physical movements within the building, the project generated, above all, a momentum of communication, which resulted in a network of social relationships. These have been found so productive that the tenants continue to develop similar structures themselves after the end of the project. Even though Willats starts from a concept of art as a socially relevant practice, his purpose is not an immediate 'improvement' of social situations. The respective interventions simply open up a new framework of action that enables long-lasting changes if it is accepted or pursued.

The individual tendencies of participatory art – the playful and/or didactic, the 'pastoral' and the 'sociological' – have at least one thing in common: the background of institutional critique, the critique of the socially exclusionary character of art as an institution, which they counter with 'inclusive' practices. For all of them, 'participation' means more than just expanding the circle of recipients. The form of participation and the participants themselves become constitutive elements in terms of content, method and aesthetic. These tendencies differ significantly, however, in their ideas of 'community' and their criteria for social relevance. Some understand the community as pre-existent and, therefore, tend to attribute a (fixed) identity to it. For others, community is a temporary phenomenon with a potential for development that emerges in the course of the project.

In the end, it seems that it is possible to assess the value or success of participatory practices neither by evaluating the scope for action that they offer the participants, nor by trying to measure any 'concrete change'. Scepticism seems advisable in particular with regards to the recurrent issue of usefulness. Where it once appeared necessary to defend art's usefulness in society by insisting on the possibility of its 'real' impact, the situation is different when, increasingly, it is political institutions that call for engagement, solidarity and civil participation. In some circumstances, social (artistic) actions become useful to a state that can no longer help its citizens, and exhorts them to self-help. The concept of 'citizen's work' mentioned in the introduction is only one instance of such a plan to replace possibilities of political involvement with the idea of 'social practice'. Under such conditions, it seems justified to ask whether changes that 'only' take place at the symbolic, rather than the 'concrete', level – as proposed by certain models of participatory practice – must be re-evaluated. In many cases, these are the practices that retain at least the ideal of potential political action. This is not least because they dwell, first, on the political consciousness and foundations of participation, without immediately committing themselves to the pragmatism of problem solving.

Notes

This is a version of Aileen Derieg's translation, substantially revised by Anna Dezeuze, of my essay 'Arbeit an der Gemeinschaft: Modelle partizipatorischer Praxis', first published in republicart.net, special issue on 'The Author as Producer', in 2004. See http://eipcp.net/transversal/1204/kravagna/en (accessed 18 May 2009). The original German version was first published in Marius Babias and Achim

Könneke (eds), *Die Kunst des Öffentlichen* (Dresden: Verlag der Kunst, 1998). Since the publication of this essay, a number of authors have addressed similar themes, including in particular Grant Kester, whose book *Conversation Pieces: Community and Communication in Modern Art* (Berkeley and London: University of California Press, 2004) addresses similar issues of participation, community and the New Genre Public Art, as well as discussing some of the artists mentioned here, such as Suzanne Lacy, Adrian Piper and Stephen Willats.

1 Ulrich Beck, 'Die Seele der Demokratie', *Die Zeit*, 49:28 (November 1997), 7–8.
2 For instance Rirkrit Tiravanija, Christine and Irene Hohenbüchler or Jens Haaning might be named as representatives of this kind of socio-chic. In their criticism of these kinds of methods, to which they ascribe a 'marked exploitation character', Alice Creischer and Andreas Siekmann use the term 'sub-enterprise'. This outsources production, but profits from the added value. See Alice Creischer and Andreas Siekmann, 'Reformmodelle', *springer*, III:2 (1997), 17–23. For the variation that remains limited to the social-communicative relationships between artists and exhibition visitors, Nicolas Bourriaud initially coined the term 'relational aesthetics' for the exhibition *Traffic* that he curated, and went on to develop it in his 1998 book *Esthétique relationelle*. For a discussion of 'relational aesthetics', see Chapter 14.
3 Quoted by Benjamin Buchloh, 'From faktura to factography', *October*, 30 (Autumn 1984), 91.
4 Lissitzky, quoted in ibid., 92–3.
5 Quoted by Walter Benjamin, 'Der Autor als Produzent', in *Gesammelte Schriften*, vol. II:2 (Frankfurt: Suhrkamp, 1991), p. 688.
6 Ibid., p. 694.
7 For a discussion of spectator participation in *Black Market*, see Lars Blunck, *Between Object and Event: Partizipationskunst Zwischen Mythos und Teilhabe* (Bonn: VG Kunst, 2001), pp. 86–92.
8 For a discussion of this turn to the 'concrete' and to the everyday, see Chapters 3 and 4.
9 Allan Kaprow, *Essays on The Blurring of Art and Life* (Berkeley and London: University of California Press, 1993), p. 195.
10 George Maciunas, 'Fluxus Manifesto' (1965), quoted by Estera Milman, 'Historical precedents, trans-historical strategies, and the myth of democratisation', in *FLUXUS: A Conceptual Country*, special issue of *Visible Language*, 26:1/2 (Winter/ Spring 1992), 31. For more about Fluxus, see Chapters 3 and 11.
11 Mary Jane Jacob, 'Outside the loop', in Michael Brenson et al., *Culture in Action* (Seattle: Bay Press, 1995), p. 52.
12 Suzanne Lacy, 'Cultural pilgrimages and metaphoric journeys', in Lacy (ed.), *Mapping the Terrain: New Genre Public Art* (Seattle and Washington: Bay Press, 1995), p. 37.
13 Ibid., p. 32.
14 Ibid., p. 36.
15 Ibid.
16 Michael Brenson, 'Healing in time', in Brenson et al., *Culture in Action*, p. 21.
17 In her text 'Won't play other to your same' in *Texte zur Kunst*, 3 (1991), Renée Green noted that the construction of the 'other' can involve the attribution of a state that

can also serve to affirm 'sameness' as the norm.

18 Brenson, 'Healing in time', p. 27.

19 See Seyla Benhabib, 'Ein Blick zurück auf die Debatte über "Frauen und Moraltheorie"', in *Selbst im Kontext: Kommunikative Ethik im Spannungsfeld von Feminismus, Kommunitarismus, und Post-Moderne* (Frankfurt: Suhrkamp, 1995), pp. 161–220.

20 Lucy Lippard, 'Looking around: where we are, where we could be', in Lacy (ed.), *Mapping the Terrain*, p. 126.

21 Jacob, 'Outside the loop', p. 56.

22 For a criticism that deals more with the problematic 'effects' than the ideological backgrounds, see Christian Höller, 'Störungsdienste', *springer*, I:1 (1995), 20–6, and Miwon Kwon, 'Im Interesse der Öffentlichkeit ...', *springer*, II:4 (1996/97), 30–5. Ulf Wuggenig conversely criticises the 'elitist and individualistically oriented' art world's repulsion of the 'populist community orientation' of the NGPA. Ulf Wuggening, 'Kunst im öffentlichen Raum und ästhetischer Kommunitarismus', in Achim Könneke (ed.), *Christian Philipp Müller: Kunst auf Schritt und Tritt* (Hamburg: Kellner, 1997), p. 88 ff.

23 Adrian Piper, 'Notes on Funk I–IV', in *Out of Order, Out of Sight, Vol. I: Selected Writings in Meta-Art 1968–1992* (Cambridge and London: MIT Press, 1996), p. 201.

24 Lacy, 'Cultural pilgrimages', p. 16.

25 Clegg and Guttmann, 'Entwurf für eine "Open Air" Bibliothek', *Durch*, 6/7 (1990), 136.

26 Claus Friede, 'Interview mit Clegg & Guttmann', in Achim Könneke (ed.), *Clegg & Guttmann: Die Offene Bibliothek* (Hamburg and Ostfildern: Cantz, 1994), p. 18.

27 Clegg and Guttmann, *Breaking Down the Boundaries to Life: Avantgarde Practice and Democratic Theory* (Vienna: AKKU, 1995), p. 57.

28 Ulf Wuggenig, Vera Kockot und Kathrin Symens, 'Die Plurifunktionalität der Offenen Bibliothek. Beobachtungen aus soziologischer Perspektive', in Könneke (ed.), *Clegg & Guttmann*, p. 88.

29 Ibid., p. 85.

30 Friede, 'Interview mit Clegg & Guttmann', p. 20.

31 Peter Bürger, *Theorie der Avantgarde* (Frankfurt: Suhrkamp, 1981), p. 72.

32 Ibid., p. 80.

33 Clegg and Guttmann, *Breaking Down the Boundaries*, p. 43.

34 Ibid., p. 35.

35 Bürger, *Theorie der Avantgarde*, p. 72.

36 Ibid., p. 69.

37 See the results of the sociological study in Wuggenig et al., 'Die Plurifunktionalität der Offenen Bibliothek', p. 84.

38 Clegg and Guttmann, 'Entwurf für eine "Open Air" Bibliothek', 136.

39 Michael Lingner, 'Ermöglichung des Unwahrscheinlichen. Von der Idee zur Praxis ästhetischen Handelns bei Clegg & Guttmanns Offener Bibliothek', in Könneke (ed.) *Clegg & Guttmann*, p. 50.

40 Ibid.

41 Stephen Willats, *Between Buildings and People* (London: Academy Editions, 1996), p. 7.

42 Ibid., p. 8.

Antagonism and relational aesthetics 14

Claire Bishop

Relational aesthetics

Esthétique Relationnelle is the title of art critic and curator Nicolas Bourriaud's 1998 collection of essays, in which he attempts to characterise artistic practice of the 1990s. Since there have been very few attempts to provide an overview of 1990s art, particularly in Britain where discussion has myopically revolved around the Young British Artists (YBA) phenomenon, Bourriaud's book is an important first step in identifying recent tendencies in contemporary art. It also comes at a time when many academics in Britain and the United States seem reluctant to move on from the politicised agendas and intellectual battles of 1980s art (indeed, for many, of 1960s art), and condemn everything from installation art to ironic painting as a depoliticised celebration of surface, complicitous with consumer spectacle. Bourriaud's book, written with the hands-on insight of a curator, promises to redefine the agenda of contemporary art criticism, since his starting point is that we can no longer approach these works from behind the 'shelter' of 1960s art history and its values. Bourriaud seeks to offer more appropriate criteria by which to approach these often rather opaque works of art, while also claiming that they are no less politicised than their 1960s precursors.[1]

Nicolas Bourriaud argues that art of the 1990s takes as its theoretical horizon 'the realm of human interactions and its social context, rather than the assertion of an independent and *private* symbolic space' (*Relational Aesthetics* [*RA*], p. 14). In other words, relational artworks seek to establish inter-ubjective encounters (be these literal or potential) in which meaning is elaborated *collectively* (*RA*, p. 18) rather than in the privatised space of individual consumption. The implication is that this work inverses the goals of Greenbergian modernism.[2] Rather than a discrete, portable, autonomous work of art that transcends its context, relational art is entirely beholden to the contingencies of its environment and audience. Moreover, this audience is envisaged as a community: rather than a one-to-one relationship between work of art and viewer, relational art sets up situations in which viewers are not just addressed as a collective, social entity, but are actually given the wherewithal to create a community, however temporary or utopian this might be.

It is important to emphasise, however, that Bourriaud does not regard relational aesthetics to be simply a theory of interactive art. He considers it to be a means of locating contemporary practice within the culture at large: relational art is seen as a direct response to the shift from a goods- to a service-based economy.[3] It is also seen as a response to the virtual relationships of the internet and globalisation, which, on the one hand, have prompted a desire for more physical and face-to-face interaction between people, while on the other have inspired artists to adopt a do-it-yourself approach and model their own 'possible universes' (*RA*, p. 13). This emphasis on immediacy is of course familiar to us from the 1960s, recalling the premium placed by performance art on the authenticity of our first-hand encounter with the artist's body. But Bourriaud is at pains to distance contemporary work from that of previous generations. The main difference, as he sees it, is the shift in attitude towards social change: instead of having a 'utopian' agenda, today's artists seek only to find provisional solutions in the here and now; instead of trying to change their environment, artists today are simply 'learning to inhabit the world in a better way'; instead of looking forward to a future utopia, this art sets up functioning 'microtopias' in the present (*RA*, p. 13). Bourriaud summarises this new attitude vividly in one sentence: 'it seems more pressing to invent possible relations with our neighbours in the present than to bet on happier tomorrows' (*RA*, p. 45). This do-it-yourself, microtopian ethos is what Bourriaud perceives to be the core political significance of relational aesthetics.

Bourriaud names many artists in his book, most of whom are European, and many of whom were featured in his seminal exhibition *Traffic* at the CAPC-Musée d'Art Contemporain de Bordeaux in 1996. Certain artists are mentioned with metronomic regularity: Liam Gillick, Rirkrit Tiravanija, Phillippe Parreno, Pierre Huyghe, Carsten Höller, Christine Hill, Vanessa Beecroft, Maurizio Cattelan and Jorge Pardo, names that will be familiar to anyone who has attended the many international biennials, triennials and *Manifestas* that have proliferated since the 1990s. The work of these artists is rather low-impact in appearance, including photography, video, wall texts, books, objects to be used and leftovers from the aftermath of an opening event. It is essentially installation art in format, but this is a term that many of its practitioners would resist. Rather than forming a coherent and distinctive transformation of space (in the manner of Ilya Kabakov's 'total installation', a theatrical *mise-en-scène*), relational artworks insist upon *use* rather than contemplation. I now wish to focus on the work of these two artists in particular, Tiravanija and Gillick, since Bourriaud deems them both to be paradigmatic of 'relational aesthetics'.

Rirkrit Tiravanija is a New York-based artist, born in Buenos Aires in 1961 to Thai parents and raised in Thailand, Ethiopia and Canada. He is best known

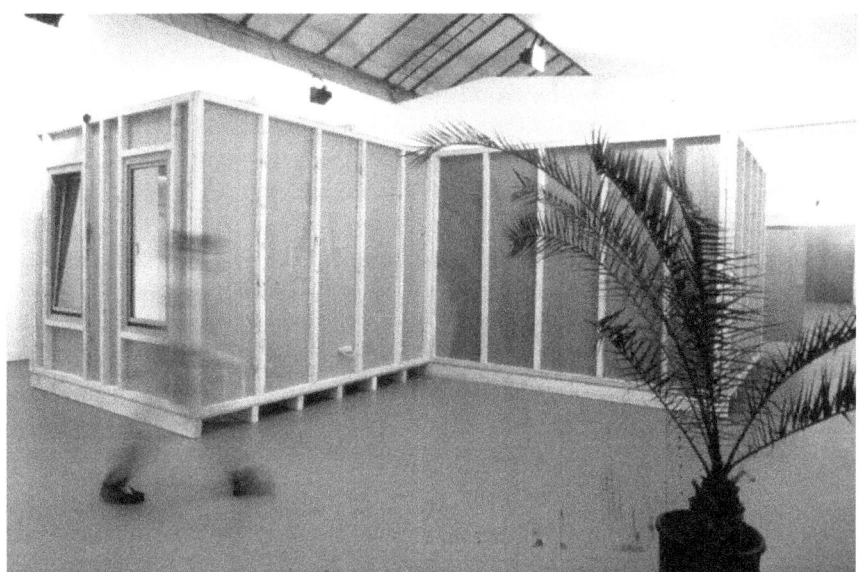

Rirkrit Tiravanija, *Untitled 1996 (Tomorrow Is Another Day)*, Kölnischer Kunstverein,   **14.1**
Cologne, 1996.

for hybrid installation-performances in which he cooks vegetable curry or pad thai for people attending the museum or gallery where he has been invited to work. In *Untitled (Free)* (1992) at 303 Gallery, New York, Tiravanija moved everything he found in the gallery office and storeroom into the main exhibition space, including the director, who was obliged to work in public, among cooking smells and diners. In the storeroom he set up what was described by one critic as a 'makeshift refugee kitchen', with paper plates, plastic knives and forks, gas burners, kitchen utensils, two folding tables and some folding stools.[4] In the gallery he cooked curries for visitors, and the detritus, utensils and food packets became the art exhibit whenever the artist was not there. Several critics, and Tiravanija himself, have observed that this involvement of the audience is the main focus of his work: the food is but a means to allow a convivial relationship between audience and artist to develop.[5]

Underlying much of Tiravanija's practice is a desire not just to erode the distinction between institutional and social space, but between artist and viewer; the phrase 'lots of people' regularly appears in his lists of materials. In the late 1990s, Tiravanija focused increasingly on creating situations where the audience could produce its own work. A more elaborate version of the 303 Gallery installation/performance was undertaken in *Untitled 1996* (*Tomorrow is Another Day*) (1996) at the Kölnischer Kunstverein (figure 14.1). Here, Tiravanija built a wooden reconstruction of his New York apartment, which was made open to the public twenty-four hours a day. People could use the kitchen to make food, wash themselves in his bathroom, sleep in the bedroom, or hang out and chat in the living room. The catalogue accompanying the Kunstverein project quotes a selection of newspaper articles and reviews, all of which reiterate the curator's assertion that 'this unique combination of art and life offered an impressive experience of togetherness to everybody'.[6] Although the materials of Tiravanija's work have become more diverse, the emphasis remains on use over contemplation. As Janet Kraynak has written, although Tiravanija's dematerialised projects revive strategies of critique from the 1960s and 1970s, it is arguable that in the context of today's dominant economic model of globalisation, Tiravanija's itinerant ubiquity does not self-reflexively question this logic, but merely reproduces it.[7] He is one of the most established, influential and omnipresent figures on the international art circuit, and his work has been crucial to the emergence of relational aesthetics as a theory.

My second example is the British artist Liam Gillick, born in 1964. Gillick's output is interdisciplinary: his heavily theorised interests are disseminated in sculpture, installation, graphic design, curating, art criticism and novellas. A prevailing theme throughout his work in all media is the production of relationships (particularly social relationships) through our environment. His early work investigated the space between sculpture and functional design. Examples include his *Pinboard Project* (1992), a bulletin board containing instructions for use, potential items for inclusion on the board, and a recommendation to subscribe to a limited number of specialist journals; and *Prototype Erasmus Table #2* (1994), a table 'designed to nearly fill a room' and conceived as 'a working place where it might be possible to finish working on the book *Erasmus is Late*' (Gillick's publication of 1995), but which is also available for use by other people 'for the storage and exhibition of work on, under or around it'.[8]

Since the mid-1990s, Gillick has become best known for his three-dimensional design work: screens and suspended platforms made of aluminium and coloured Plexiglas, which are often displayed alongside texts and geometrical designs painted directly onto a wall. Gillick's descriptions of these works emphasise their potential use value, but in a way that carefully denies them any specific agency: each object's meaning is so overdetermined that it seems to parody both claims made for modernist design and the language of management consulting. His 120 × 120 cm open-topped Plexiglas cube *Discussion Island: Projected Think Tank* (1997) is described as a work that 'may be used as an object that might signify an enclosed zone for the consideration of exchange, information transfer and strategy', while the *Big Conference Centre Legislation Screen* (1998), a 3 × 2 m coloured Plexiglas screen (similar to figure 14.2), 'helps to define a location where individual actions are limited by rules imposed by the community as a whole'.[9]

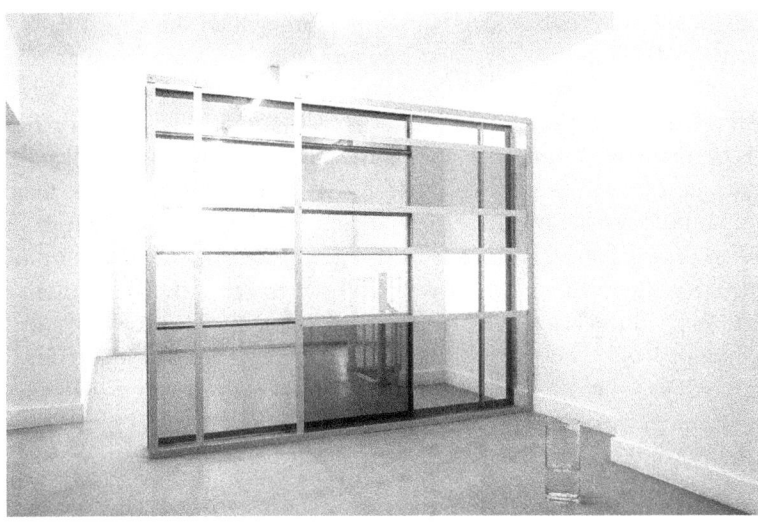

Liam Gillick, *Big Conference Centre Limitation Screen*, 1998. **14.2**

Gillick's design structures have been described as constructions having 'a spatial resemblance to office spaces, bus shelters, meeting rooms and canteens', but they also take up the legacy of Minimalist sculpture and post-Minimalist installation art (Donald Judd and Dan Graham immediately come to mind).[10] Yet Gillick's work differs from that of his art historical precursors: whereas Judd's modular boxes made the viewer aware of his/her physical movement around the work, while also drawing attention to the space in which these were exhibited, Gillick is happy for viewers to 'just stand with their backs to the work and talk to each other'.[11] Rather than having the viewer 'complete' the work, in the manner of Bruce Nauman's corridors or Dan Graham's video installations of the 1970s, Gillick seeks a perpetual open-endedness in which his art is a backdrop to activity: 'It doesn't necessarily function best as an object for consideration alone', he says. 'It is sometimes a backdrop or décor rather than a pure content provider.'[12]

I have chosen the examples of Gillick and Tiravanija because they seem to me the clearest expression of Bourriaud's argument that relational art privileges inter-subjective relations over detached opticality. Tiravanija insists that the viewer be physically present in a particular situation at a particular time – eating the food that he cooks, alongside other visitors in a communal situation. Gillick alludes to more hypothetical relations, which in many cases do not even need to exist, but he still insists that the presence of visitors is an essential component of his art: 'My work is like the light in the fridge', he says. 'It only works when there are people there to open the fridge door. Without people, it's not art – it's something else – stuff in a room.'[13] This interest in the contingencies of a 'relationship between' – rather than the object itself – is a hallmark of Gillick's work, and of his interest in collaborative practice as a whole.

This idea of considering the work of art as a potential trigger for participation is hardly new – think of happenings, Fluxus instructions, 1970s performance art, and Joseph Beuys's declaration that 'everyone is an artist'. Each was accompanied by a rhetoric of democracy and emancipation that is very similar to Bourriaud's defence of relational aesthetics.[14] The theoretical underpinnings of this desire to activate the viewer are easy to reel off: Walter Benjamin's 'Author as producer' (1934), Roland Barthes's 'Death of the author' and 'birth of the reader' (1968) and – most importantly for this context – Umberto Eco's *The Open Work* (1962). Writing on what he perceived to be the open and aleatory character of modernist literature, music and art, Eco summarises his discussion of James Joyce, Luciano Berio and Alexander Calder in terms that cannot help but evoke Bourriaud's optimism:

> The poetics of the 'work in movement' (and partly that of the 'open' work) sets in motion a new cycle of relations between the artist and his audience, a new mechanics of aesthetic perception, a different status for the artistic product in contemporary society. It poses new practical problems by organising new communicative situations. In short, it installs a new relationship between the *contemplation* and the *utilisation* of a work of art.[15]

Analogies with Tiravanija and Gillick are evident in Eco's privileging of use-value and the development of 'communicative situations'. But Bourriaud's position differs from Eco's in one important respect: Eco regarded the work of art as a *reflection* of the conditions of our existence (a fragmented modern culture), while Bourriaud sees the work of art *producing* these conditions. The interactivity of relational art is therefore superior to optical contemplation of an object, which is assumed to be passive and disengaged, because the work of art is a 'social form' capable of producing positive human relationships. As a consequence, the work is automatically political in implication and emancipatory in effect.

Aesthetic judgement

When confronted by a relational artwork, Bourriaud suggests that we ask the following questions: 'does this work permit me to enter into dialogue? Could I exist, and how, in the space it defines?' (*RA*, p. 109). He refers to these questions, which we should ask in front of any aesthetic product, as 'criteria of co-existence' (*RA*, p. 109). The problem that arises with Bourriaud's notion of 'structure' is that it has an erratic relationship to the work's ostensible subject matter, or content. For example, what Tiravanija cooks, how and for whom, is less important to Bourriaud than the fact that he gives away the results of his cooking for free.

Gillick's bulletin boards can be similarly questioned: Bourriaud does not discuss the texts or images referred to on the individual clippings pinned to the boards, nor the formal arrangement and juxtaposition of these clippings, but only Gillick's democratisation of material and flexible format. (The owner is at liberty to modify these various elements at any given time according to personal tastes and current events.) For Bourriaud, the structure *is* the subject matter – and in this he is far more formalist than he acknowledges.[16] Although the works claim to defer to their context, they do not question their imbrication within it. Gillick's pinboards are embraced as democratic in structure – but only those who own them may interact with their arrangement. We need to ask, as Group Material did in the 1980s, 'Who is the public? How is a culture made, and who is it for?'

I am not suggesting that relational artworks need to develop a greater social conscience – by making pinboard works about international terrorism, or giving free curries to refugees. I am simply wondering how we decide what the 'structure' of a relational artwork comprises, and whether this is so detachable from the work's ostensible subject matter, or so permeable with its context. Bourriaud wants to equate aesthetic judgement with an ethico-political judgement on the relationships produced by a work of art. But how do we measure or compare these relationships? The quality of the relationships in 'relational aesthetics' are never examined or called into question. When Bourriaud argues that 'encounters are more important than the individuals who compose them',[17] I sense that this question is (for him) unnecessary: all relations that permit 'dialogue' are automatically assumed to be democratic and therefore good. But what does 'democracy' really mean in this context? If relational art produces human relations, then the next logical question to ask is what *types* of relations are being produced, for whom, and why?

Antagonism

Rosalyn Deutsche has argued that the public sphere remains democratic only in so far as its naturalised exclusions are taken into account and made open to contestation: 'Conflict, division, and instability, then, do not ruin the democratic public sphere; they are conditions of its existence.'[18] Deutsche takes her lead from Ernesto Laclau and Chantal Mouffe's *Hegemony and Social Strategy: Towards a Radical Democratic Politics*. Published in 1985, Laclau and Mouffe's *Hegemony* is one of the first books to reconsider Leftist political theory through the lens of post-structuralism, following what the authors perceived to be an impasse of Marxist theorisation in the 1970s. Their text is a rereading of Marx through Gramsci's theory of hegemony and through

Lacan's understanding of subjectivity as split and decentred. Several of the ideas that Laclau and Mouffe put forward help us to reconsider Bourriaud's claims for the politics of relational aesthetics in a more critical light.

The first of these ideas is the concept of antagonism. Laclau and Mouffe argue that a fully functioning democratic society is not one in which all antagonisms have disappeared, but one in which new political frontiers are constantly being drawn and brought into debate – in other words, a democratic society is one in which relations of conflict are *sustained*, not erased. Without antagonism there is only the imposed consensus of authoritarian order – a total suppression of debate and discussion, which is inimical to democracy. It is important to stress right away that the idea of antagonism is not understood by Laclau and Mouffe to be a pessimistic acceptance of political deadlock; antagonism does not signal 'the expulsion of utopia from the field of the political'.[19] On the contrary, they maintain that without the concept of utopia there is no possibility of a radical imaginary. The task is to balance the tension between imaginary ideal and pragmatic management of a social positivity without lapsing into the totalitarian.

This understanding of antagonism is founded in Laclau and Mouffe's theory of subjectivity. Following Lacan, they argue that subjectivity is not a self-transparent and rational pure presence, but is irremediably decentred and incomplete.[20] However, surely there is a conflict between a concept of the subject as decentred and the idea of political agency? 'Decentring' implies the lack of a unified subject, while 'agency' implies a fully present, autonomous subject of political will and self-determination. Laclau argues that this conflict is false, because the subject is neither entirely decentred (which would imply psychosis) nor entirely unified (i.e. the absolute subject). Following Lacan, he argues that we have a failed structural identity, and are therefore dependent on identification in order to proceed.[21] Because subjectivity *is* this process of identification, we are necessarily incomplete entities. Antagonism, therefore, is the relationship that emerges between such incomplete entities.

Laclau contrasts this to the relationships that emerge between complete entities, such as contradiction (A-not A) or 'real difference' (A-B). We all hold a number of mutually contradictory belief systems (for example, there are materialists who read horoscopes, and psychoanalysts who send Christmas cards) but this does not result in antagonism. Nor is 'real difference' (A-B) equal to antagonism; because it concerns full identities, it results in collision – like a car crash, or 'the war against terrorism'. In the case of antagonism, argue Laclau and Mouffe, 'we are confronted with a different situation: the presence of the "Other" prevents me from being totally myself. The relation arises not from full totalities, but from the impossibility of their constitution.'[22] In other words, the presence of what is not me renders my identity precarious and vulnerable, and the threat that the other represents transforms my *own* sense of self into something questionable. When played out on a social level, antagonism can be viewed as the limits of society's ability to fully constitute itself. Whatever is at the boundary of the social (and of identity), seeking to *define* it also *destroys* its ambition to constitute a full presence: 'As conditions of possibility for the existence of a pluralist democracy, conflicts and antagonisms constitute at the same time the condition of impossibility of its final achievement.'[23]

I dwell on this theory in order to suggest that the relations set up by relational aesthetics are not intrinsically democratic, as Bourriaud suggests, since they rest too comfortably within an ideal of subjectivity as whole, and of community as immanent togetherness. There is debate and dialogue in a Tiravanija cooking piece, to be sure, but there is no inherent friction since the situation is what Bourriaud calls 'microtopian': it produces a community whose members identify with each other, because they have something in common. The only substantial account that I can find of Tiravanija's first solo exhibition at 303 Gallery is by Jerry Saltz in *Art in America*:

> At 303 Gallery I regularly sat with or was joined by stranger, and it was nice. The gallery became a place for sharing, jocularity and frank talk. I had an amazing run of meals with art dealers. Once I ate with Paula Cooper who recounted a long, complicated bit of professional gossip. Another day, Lisa Spellman related in hilarious detail a story of intrigue about a fellow dealer trying, unsuccessfully, to woo one of her artists. … Later in the show's run, I was joined by an unidentified woman and a curious flirtation filled the air. Another time I chatted with a young artist who lived in Brooklyn who had real insights about the shows he'd just seen.[24]

The informal chattiness of this account clearly indicates what kind of problems face those who wish to know more about such work: the review only tells us that Tiravanija's intervention is considered good because it permits networking among a group of art dealers and like-minded art lovers, and because it evokes the atmosphere of a late-night bar. Everyone has a common interest in art, and the result is art-world gossip, exhibition reviews and flirtation. Such communication is fine to an extent, but it is not in and of itself emblematic of 'democracy'. To be fair, I think that Bourriaud recognises this problem – but he does not raise it in relation to the artists he promotes: 'Connecting people, creating interactive, communicative experience', he says. 'What for? If you forget the "what for?" I'm afraid you're left with simple Nokia art – producing interpersonal relations for their own sake and never addressing their political aspects.'[25]

I would argue that Tiravanija's art, at least as presented by Bourriaud, falls short of addressing the political aspect of communication – even while certain of his projects do at first glance appear to address it in a dissonant fashion.

Returning to accounts of Tiravanija's Cologne project, *Untitled (Tomorrow Is Another Day)*, I have already quoted curator Udo Kittelmann's comment that the installation offered 'an impressive experience of togetherness to everybody'. He continues: 'Groups of people prepared meals and talked, took a bath or occupied the bed. Our fear that the art-living-space might be vandalised did not come true … The art space lost its institutional function and finally turned into a free social space.'[26] The *Kölnischer Stadt-Anzeiger* concurred that the work offered 'a kind of "asylum" for everyone'.[27] But who is the 'everyone' here? This may be a microtopia, but – like utopia – it is still predicated on the exclusion of those who hinder or prevent its realisation. (It is tempting to consider what might have happened if Tiravanija's space had been invaded by those seeking genuine 'asylum'.)[28] His installations reflect Bourriaud's understanding of the relations produced by relational artworks as fundamentally harmonious, because they are addressed to a community of viewing subjects with something in common.[29] This is why Tiravanija's works are political only in the loosest sense of advocating dialogue over monologue (the one-way communication equated with spectacle by the Situationists). The content of this dialogue is not in itself democratic, since all questions return to the hackneyed non-issue of 'is it art?'[30]

Despite Tiravanija's rhetoric of open-endedness and viewer emancipation, the structure of his work circumscribes the outcome in advance, and relies on its presence within a gallery to differentiate it from entertainment. Tiravanija's microtopia gives up on the idea of transformation in public culture and reduces its scope to the pleasures of a private group who identify with each other as gallery-goers.[31]

Gillick's position on the question of dialogue and democracy is more ambiguous. At first glance he appears to support Laclau and Mouffe's antagonism thesis:

> While I admire artists who construct 'better' visions of how things might be, the middle-ground, negotiated territories I am interested in always carry the possibility of moments where idealism is unclear. There are as many demonstrations of compromise, strategy, and collapse in my work as there are clear recipes for how our environment can be better.[32]

However, when one looks for 'clear recipes' in Gillick's work, few if any are to be found. 'I'm working in a nebulous cloud of ideas', he says, 'which are somewhat partial or parallel rather than didactic'.[33] Unwilling to state what ideals there are to be compromised, Gillick trades on the credibility of referencing architecture (its engagement with concrete social situations) while remaining abstract on the issue of articulating a specific position. The *Discussion Platforms*, for example, do not point to any particular change, just change in general – a 'scenario' in which potential 'narratives' may or may not emerge. Gillick's position is slippery, and ultimately he seems to argue for compromise and negotiation as recipes for improvement. Logically, this pragmatism is tantamount to an abandonment or failure of ideals: his work is the demonstration of a compromise, rather than an articulation of a problem.[34]

By contrast, Laclau and Mouffe's theory of democracy as antagonism can be seen in the work of two artists conspicuously ignored by Bourriaud in *Relational Aesthetics* and *Postproduction*: the Swiss artist Thomas Hirschhorn and the Spanish artist Santiago Sierra.[35] These artists set up 'relationships' that emphasise the role of dialogue and negotiation in their art, but do so without collapsing these relationships into the work's content. The relations produced by their performances and installations are marked by sensations of unease and discomfort rather than belonging, because the work acknowledges the impossibility of a 'microtopia' and instead *sustains* a tension between viewers, participants and context. An integral part of this tension is the introduction of collaborators from diverse economic backgrounds, which in turn serves to disrupt contemporary art's self-perception as a domain that embraces other social and political structures.

Non-identification and autonomy

The work of Santiago Sierra (born in 1966), like that of Tiravanija, involves the literal setting-up of relations between people: the artist, the participants in his work, and the audience. But since the late 1990s Sierra's 'actions' have been organised around relations that are more complicated – and more controversial – than those produced by the artists associated with relational aesthetics. Sierra has attracted tabloid attention and belligerent criticism for some of his more extreme actions, such as *160 cm Line Tattooed on Four People* (2000), *A Person Paid for 360 Continuous Working Hours* (2000), and *Ten People Paid to Masturbate* (2000). These ephemeral actions are documented in casual black-and-white photographs, a short text and occasionally video. This mode of documentation appears be a legacy of 1970s conceptual and body art – Chris Burden and Marina Abramović spring to mind – but Sierra's work significantly develops this tradition in the use of other people as performers, and in the emphasis on their remuneration. While Tiravanija celebrates the gift, Sierra knows that there is no such thing as a free meal: everything and everyone has a price. His work can be seen as a grim meditation on the social and political conditions that permit disparities in people's 'prices' to emerge. Now regularly commissioned to make work in galleries throughout Europe and the Americas, Sierra creates a kind of ethnographic realism, in which the outcome or unfolding of his action forms an indexical trace of the economic and social reality of the place in which he works.

Interpreting Sierra's practice in this way runs counter to dominant readings of his work, which present it as a nihilistic reflection on Marx's theory of the exchange value of labour. (Marx argued that the worker's labour time is worth less to the capitalist than its subsequent exchange value in the form of a commodity produced by this labour.) The tasks that Sierra requires of his collaborators – which are invariably useless, physically demanding, and on occasion leave permanent scars – are seen as amplifications of the status quo in order to expose its ready abuse of those who will do even the most humiliating or pointless job in return for money. Because Sierra receives payment for his actions – as an artist – and is the first to admit the contradictions of his situation, his detractors argue that he is stating the pessimistic obvious: capitalism exploits. Moreover, this is a system from which nobody is exempt: Sierra pays others to do work for which he gets paid, and in turn he is exploited by galleries, dealers and collectors. Sierra himself does little to contradict this view when he opines, 'I can't change anything. There is no possibility that we can change anything with our artistic work. We do our work because we are making art, and because we believe art should be something, something that follows reality. But I don't believe in the possibility of change.'[36]

Sierra's apparent complicity with the status quo does raise the question of how his work differs from that of Tiravanija. It is worth bearing in mind that, since the 1970s, older avant-garde rhetorics of opposition and transformation have been frequently replaced by strategies of complicity; what matters is not the complicity, but how we receive it. If Tiravanija's work is experienced in a major key, then Sierra's is most definitely minor. What follows is an attempt to read the latter's work through the dual lenses of *Relational Aesthetics* and *Hegemony* in order to tease out these differences further.

It has already been noted that Sierra documents his actions and thereby ensures that we know what he considers their 'structure' to be. Take, for example, *The Wall of a Gallery Pulled Out, Inclined Sixty Degrees from the Ground and Sustained by Five People*, Mexico City (2000). Unlike Tiravanija and Gillick, who embrace an idea of open-endedness, Sierra delimits from the outset his choice of invited participants and the context in which the event takes place. 'Context' is a key word for Gillick and Tiravanija, yet their work does little to address the problem of what a context actually comprises. (One has the impression that it exists as undifferentiated infinity, like cyberspace.) Laclau and Mouffe argue that for a context to be constituted and identified as such, it must demarcate certain limits; it is from the exclusions engendered by this demarcation that antagonism occurs. It is precisely this act of exclusion that is disavowed in relational art's preference for 'open-endedness'.[37] Sierra's actions, by contrast, embed themselves into other 'institutions' (such as immigration, the minimum wage, traffic congestion, illegal street commerce, homelessness) in order to highlight the divisions enforced by these contexts. Crucially, however, Sierra neither presents these divisions as reconciled (in the way Tiravanija elides the museum with the café or apartment), nor as entirely separate spheres: the fact that his works are realised moves them into the terrain of antagonism (rather than the 'car crash' model of collision between full identities) and hints that these boundaries are both unstable and open to change.

In a work for the 2001 Venice Biennale, *Persons Paid to Have Their Hair Dyed Blond*, Sierra invited illegal street vendors, most of whom came from southern Italy or were immigrants from Senegal, China and Bangladesh, to have their hair dyed blond in return for 120,000 lire ($60). The only condition to their participation was that their hair be naturally dark. Sierra's description of the work does not document the impact of his action on the days that followed the mass bleaching, but this aftermath was an integral aspect of the work.[38] During the Venice Biennale, the street vendors – who hover on street corners selling fake designer handbags – are usually the social group most obviously excluded from the glitzy opening; their newly bleached hair literally highlighted their presence in the city. This was coupled by a gesture inside the Biennale proper, where Sierra gave over his allocated exhibition space in the Arsenale to a handful of the vendors, who used it to sell their fake Fendi handbags on a groundsheet, just as they did on the street. Sierra's gesture prompted a wry analogy between art and commerce, in the style of 1970s

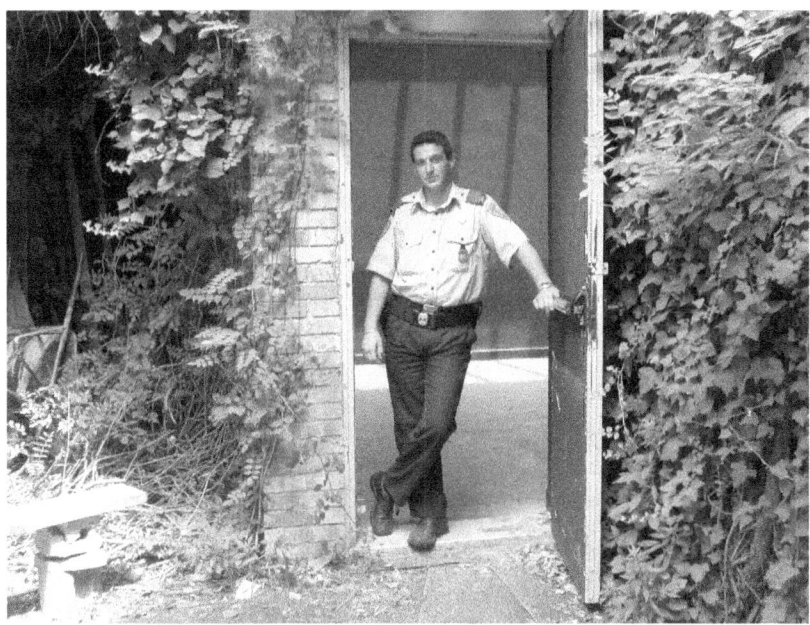

Santiago Sierra, *Wall Enclosing a Space*, Spanish Pavilion, Venice Biennale, 2003.   **14.3**

institutional critique, but moved substantially beyond this since vendors and exhibition were mutually estranged by the confrontation. Instead of aggressively hailing passers by with their trade, as they did on the street, the vendors were subdued. This made my own encounter with them disarming in a way that only subsequently revealed to me my own anxieties about feeling 'included' in the Biennale. Surely these guys were actors? Had they crept in here for a joke? Foregrounding a moment of mutual non-identification, Sierra's action disrupted the art audience's sense of identity, which is founded precisely on unspoken racial and class exclusions, as well as veiling blatant commerce. It is important that Sierra's work did not achieve a harmonious reconciliation between the two systems, but sustained the tension between them.

Sierra's return to the Venice Biennale in 2003 comprised a major performance/installation for the Spanish pavilion (figure 14.3). *Wall Enclosing a Space* involved sealing off the pavilion's interior with concrete blocks from floor to ceiling. On entering the building, viewers were confronted by a hastily constructed yet impregnable wall that rendered the galleries inaccessible. Visitors carrying a Spanish passport were invited to enter the space via the back of the building, where two immigration officers were inspecting passports. All non-Spanish nationals, however, were denied entry to the pavilion, whose interior contained nothing but grey paint peeling from the walls, left over from the previous year's exhibition. The work was 'relational' in Bourriaud's sense, but problematised any idea of these relations being fluid and unconstrained by exposing how all our interactions are, like public space, riven with social and legal exclusions.[39]

The work of Thomas Hirschhorn (b. 1957) often addresses similar issues. His practice is conventionally read in terms of its contribution to sculptural tradition – his work is said to reinvent the monument, the pavilion and the altar by immersing the viewer in an overload of found images, videos and photocopies, bound together in cheap, perishable materials such as cardboard, brown tape and tinfoil. Beyond occasional references to the tendency of his work to get vandalised or looted when situated outside the gallery, the role of the viewer is rarely addressed in writing on his art.[40] Hirschhorn is well known for his assertion that he does not make political art, but makes art politically. Significantly, this political commitment does not take the form of literally activating the viewer in a space: 'I do not want to invite or oblige viewers to become interactive with what I do; I do not want to activate the public. I want to give of myself, to engage myself to such a degree that viewers confronted with the work can take part and become involved, but not as actors.'[41]

Hirschhorn represents an important shift in the way that contemporary art conceives of its viewer, one that is matched by his assertion of art's autonomy. One of the presumptions underlying *Relational Aesthetics* is the idea – introduced by the historical avant-garde and reiterated ever since – that art should not be a privileged and independent sphere, but instead fused with 'life'. Today, when art has become all too subsumed into everyday life – as leisure, entertainment and business – artists such as Hirschhorn are reasserting the autonomy of artistic activity. As a consequence, Hirschhorn does not regard his work to be 'open-ended' or to require completion by the viewer, since the politics of his practice derive instead from *how* the work is made: 'To make art politically means to choose materials that do not intimidate, a format that doesn't dominate, a device that does not seduce. To make art politically is not to submit to an ideology or to denounce the system, in opposition to so-called "political art". It is to work with the fullest energy against the principle of "quality".'[42]

A rhetoric of democracy pervades Hirschhorn's work, but it is not manifest in the viewer's literal activation; rather, it appears in decisions regarding format, materials and location, such as his 'altars' that emulate the ad hoc memorials of flowers and toys at accident sites, and which are located in peripheral locations around a city. In these works – as in the installations *Pole-Self* and *Laundrette* (both 2001) – found images, texts, adverts and photocopies are juxtaposed to contextualise consumer banality with political and military atrocities.

Many of Hirschhorn's concerns came together in the *Bataille Monument* (2002), made for *Documenta XI* (figure 14.4). Located in Nordstadt, a suburb of Kassel several miles away from the main *Documenta* venues, the *Monument* comprised three installations in large makeshift shacks, a bar run by a local family, and a sculpture of a tree, all erected on a lawn surrounded by two

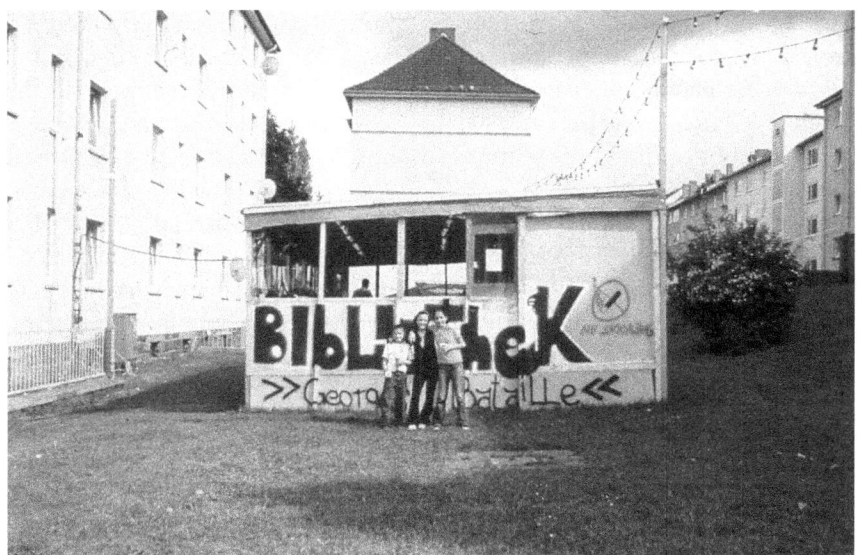

Thomas Hirschhorn, *Bataille Monument*, at *Documenta XI*, Kassel, 2002.   **14.4**

housing projects. The shacks were constructed from Hirschhorn's signature materials: cheap timber, foil, plastic sheeting and brown tape. The first housed a library of books and videos grouped around five Bataillean themes: word, image, art, sex and sport. Several worn sofas, a television and video were also provided, and the whole installation was designed to facilitate familiarisation with the philosopher, of whom Hirschhorn claims to be a 'fan'. The two other shacks housed a television studio and an installation of information about Georges Bataille's life and work. To reach the *Bataille Monument*, visitors had to participate in a further aspect of the work: securing a lift from a Turkish cab company who were contracted to ferry *Documenta* visitors to and from the site. Viewers were then stranded at the *Monument* until a return cab became available, during which time they would inevitably make use of the bar.

In locating the *Monument* in the middle of a community whose ethnic and economic status did not mark it as a target audience for *Documenta*, Hirschhorn contrived a curious rapprochement between the influx of art tourists and the area's residents. Rather than make the local populace subject to what he calls the 'zoo effect', Hirschhorn's project made visitors feel like hapless intruders. Even more disruptively, in light of the international art world's intellectual pretensions, Hirschhorn's *Monument* took the local inhabitants seriously as potential Bataille readers. This gesture induced a range of emotive responses among visitors, including accusations that Hirschhorn's gesture was inappropriate and patronising. This unease revealed the fragile conditioning of the art world's self-constructed identity. The complicated play of identificatory and dis-identificatory mechanisms at work in the content, construction and location of the *Bataille Monument* were radically and disruptively thought-provoking: the 'zoo effect' worked two ways. Rather than offering, as the *Documenta* handbook claims, a reflection on 'communal commitment', the *Bataille Monument* served to destabilise (and, therefore, potentially liberate) any notion of community identity, or what it might mean to be a 'fan' of art and philosophy.

A work like the *Bataille Monument* depends on its context for impact, but it could theoretically be restaged elsewhere, in comparable circumstances. Significantly, the viewer is no longer required to participate literally (i.e. to eat noodles, or to activate a sculpture), but is asked only to be a thoughtful and reflective visitor: 'I do not want to do an interactive work. I want to do an active work. To me, the most important activity that an artwork can provoke is the activity of thinking. Andy Warhol's *Big Electric Chair* (1967) makes me think, but it is a painting on a museum wall. An active work requires that I first give of myself.'[43] The independent stance that Hirschhorn asserts in his work – though produced collaboratively, his art is the product of a single artist's vision – implies the readmittance of a degree of autonomy to art. Likewise, the viewer is no longer coerced into fulfilling the artist's interactive requirements but is presupposed as a subject of independent thought, which is the essential prerequisite for political action: 'having reflections and critical thoughts is to get active, posing questions is to come to life'.[44] The *Bataille Monument* shows how installation and performance art now find themselves at a significant distance from the historic avant-garde calls to collapse art and life.

Relational antagonism

My interest in the work of Thomas Hirschhorn and Santiago Sierra derives from their tougher, more disruptive approach to 'relations' than that proposed by Bourriaud, but also from their remoteness from the socially engaged public art projects that have sprung up since the 1980s under the aegis of 'new genre public art'. But does the fact that the work of Sierra and Hirschhorn demonstrates better democracy mean that it is better art? For many critics, this question would be obvious: of course it does! The fact that this question arises is itself symptomatic of wider trends in contemporary art criticism: today, political, moral and ethical judgements have come to fill the vacuum of aesthetic judgement in a way that was unthinkable forty years ago. This is partly because post-modernism has attacked the very notion of aesthetic judgement, and partly because contemporary art solicits the viewer's literal interaction in ever more elaborate ways. Yet the 'birth of the viewer' (and the ecstatic promises of emancipation that accompany it) has not halted appeals to higher criteria, which have simply returned in other guises.

This is not an issue that can be adequately dealt with here. I would point out that if the work Bourriaud considers exemplary of 'relational aesthetics' wishes to be considered politically, then we must address this proposition seriously. There is now a long tradition of viewer participation and activated spectatorship in works of art across many media – from experimental German theatre of the 1920s to new-wave film and the *nouveau roman* of the 1960s, from Minimalist sculpture to post-Minimalist installation art in the 1970s, from Beuys's social sculpture to 1980s socially engaged performance art. It is no longer enough to say that activating the viewer *tout court* is a democratic act, for every artwork – even the most 'open-ended' – determines in advance the depth of participation that the viewer may have with it.[45] Hirschhorn would argue that such pretences to emancipation are no longer necessary: all art – whether immersive or not – can be a critical force that appropriates and reassigns value, distancing our thoughts from the predominant and pre-existing consensus. The task facing us today is to analyse how contemporary art addresses the viewer, and to assess the quality of the audience relations it produces: the subject position that any work presupposes, the democratic notions it upholds, and how these are manifested in our experience of the work.

It can be argued that the works of Hirschhorn and Sierra, as I have presented them, are no longer tied to the direct activation of the viewer, or to their literal participation in the work. This is not to say that this work signifies a return to the kind of high-modernist autonomy advocated by Clement Greenberg, but rather to a more complicated imbrication of the social and the aesthetic. In this model, the kernel of impossible resolution on which antagonism depends is mirrored in the tension between art and society conceived of as mutually exclusive spheres – a self-reflexive tension that the work of Sierra and Hirschhorn fully acknowledges.

In this light, the motif of obstruction or blockade so frequently found in Sierra's works is less a return to modernist refusal as advocated by Theodor Adorno than an expression of the boundaries of both the social and the aesthetic after a century of attempting to fuse them.[46] In his exhibition at Kunst-Werke in Berlin, viewers were confronted with a series of makeshift cardboard boxes, each of which concealed a Chechen refugee seeking asylum in Germany.[47] The boxes were an Arte Povera take on Tony Smith's celebrated 6 × 6 ft sculpture *Die* (1962), the work that Michael Fried famously described as exerting the same effect on the viewer as 'the silent presence of another person'.[48] In Sierra's piece, this silent presence was literal: since it is against the law in Germany for immigrants to be paid for work, the refugees' status could not be announced by the gallery. Their silence was exaggerated and exacerbated by their literal invisibility beneath the cardboard boxes. In such works, Sierra seems to argue that the phenomenological body of Minimalism is politicised precisely through the quality of its relationship – or lack of relationship – to other people. Our response to witnessing the participants in Sierra's actions – be they facing the wall, sitting under boxes, or tattooed with a line – is quite different from the 'togetherness' of relational aesthetics. The work does not offer an experience of transcendent human empathy that smoothes over the awkward situation before us, but a pointed racial and economic non-identification: 'This is not me.' The persistence of this friction, its awkwardness and discomfort, alerts us to the relational antagonism of Sierra's work.

The works of Hirschhorn and Sierra stand against Bourriaud's claims for relational aesthetics, the microtopian communities of Tiravanija and the scenario formalism of Gillick. The feel-good positions adopted by Tiravanija and Gillick are reflected in their ubiquitous presence on the international art scene, and their status as perennial favourites of a few curators who have become known for promoting their preferred selection of artists (and thereby becoming touring stars in their own right). In such a cosy situation, art does not feel the need to defend itself, and it collapses into compensatory (and self-congratulatory) entertainment. The work of Hirschhorn and Sierra is better art not simply for being better politics (although both of these artists now have equally high visibility on the blockbuster art circuit). Their work acknowledges the limitations of what is possible as art ('I am not an animator, teacher or social-worker', says Hirschhorn) and subjects to scrutiny all easy claims for a transitive relationship between art and society. The model of subjectivity that underpins their practice is not the fictitious whole subject of harmonious community, but a divided subject of partial identifications open to constant flux. If relational aesthetics requires a unified subject as a prerequisite for community as togetherness, then Hirschhorn and Sierra provide a mode of artistic experience more adequate to the divided and incomplete subject of today. This relational antagonism would be predicated not on social harmony, but on exposing that which is repressed in sustaining the semblance of this harmony. It would thereby provide a more concrete and polemical grounds for rethinking our relationship to the world and to one other.

Postscript: the aesthetics of 'relational antagonism'

(extracts from an exchange between Claire Bishop, Walid Raad and Alan Gilbert about the original essay)[49]

Walid Raad and Alan Gilbert: … [You argue that in 'relational antagonism,'] the tension between art and viewer allows the latter to maintain the independent position and critical thinking necessary for political action. As a result, 'relational antagonism' entails the work of art acquiring a certain degree of autonomy. … [Do you not fear that] the call for the work of art's autonomy may be the beginning of its de-politicisation and transcendence of the social?

Claire Bishop: [I agree with] Jacques Rancière [that] good art exists between two vanishing points: 'art becoming mere life or art becoming mere art'.[50] Pushed to an extreme, each of these scenarios entails its own entropy, its own end of art. The task is to sustain a tension between the two. Without this antinomy, art risks being subsumed into the means-ends rationality of political praxis, or into the comfortable irrelevance of art for art's sake.

WR/AG: In describing the effects of Santiago Sierra and Thomas Hirschhorn's work on both yourself personally and on art world audiences generally, you use words such as 'anxiety', 'unease', and 'discomfort'. … What is gained by this emotional/affective component? …

CB: The emotional/affective component is constitutive of aesthetic judgement. Without taking into account the emotional/affective component, we judge works of art as if they were scientific concepts, political gestures, legal documents, advertising etc. The emotional/affective impact of a work is precisely what allows us to suspect that Santiago Sierra's works are not simply replicating the everyday exploitation of manual labour, but providing a disgusted critique of this. So, rather than signalling a retreat to the merely subjective, the emotional/affective is a specific mode of knowledge that must be factored into any analysis of a work of art. ...

WR/AG: ... You argue that Hirschhorn's *Documenta XI* installation *Bataille Monument* took 'seriously as potential Bataille readers' the mostly Turkish residents of a local housing project. Does it matter how and in what manner the local inhabitants in question actually became readers of Bataille and what this reading might have meant to them? ...

CB: This is a good question. But it misleadingly focuses on the *Bataille Monument*'s outcome or result, rather than on its significance in presenting a particular knot of problematic relationships, which is what I was addressing in Bourriaud's writings. It doesn't matter how and in what manner the local inhabitants of the *Bataille Monument* – or its visitors for that matter – became readers of Bataille. The work isn't about education, but the creation of a situation that allows certain difficult relationships to emerge. Within this situation, a knowledge of Bataille *may* or *may not* be an outcome, just as a knowledge of TV production or of making a sculpture or of a porn video in the library might equally be an outcome.

... [The *Bataille Monument*] foregrounded the inevitability of a disjunction between participants and viewers, staging a division between them; as on a revolving stage, both groups of performers – local residents and art visitors – were uneasy about how they should be interacting, never fully able to know what the other was experiencing. It would be misleading to say that Bataille was just a pretext for this staging, but his status as a dissident Surrealist is not inappropriate for Hirschhorn's provocation.

Notes

This is an abridged and revised version of an essay originally published in *October*, 110 (Autumn 2004), 51–79. A response from Liam Gillick was published, along with my reply, in *October*, 115 (Winter 2006), 95–107.

1 'Contemporary art is definitely developing a political project when it endeavours to move into the relational realm by turning it into an issue.' Nicolas Bourriaud, *Relational Aesthetics*, trans. S. Pleasance and F. Woods (Dijon: Les Presses du Réel, 2002), p. 17. Hereafter cited in the text as *RA*.

2 This change in mode of address from 'private' to 'public' has for some time been associated with a decisive break with modernism; see Rosalind Krauss, 'Sense and sensibility', *Artforum* (November 1973), 43–53, and 'Double negative: a new syntax for sculpture', in *Passages in Modern Sculpture* (London: Thames & Hudson, 1977).

3 This is reflected in the number of artists whose practice takes the form of offering a 'service', such as the Berlin-based American artist Christine Hill, who offered back and shoulder massages to exhibition visitors, and who later went on to set up a fully functioning second-hand clothes shop, the *Volksboutique*, in Berlin and at *Documenta X* (1997).

4 Jerry Saltz, 'A short history of Rirkrit Tiravanija', *Art in America* (February 1996), 106.

5 If one wanted to identify historical precursors for this type of art, there are ample names to cite: Michael Asher's untitled installation at the Clare Copley Gallery, Los Angeles, in 1974, in which he removed the partition between exhibition space and gallery office, or Gordon Matta-Clark's restaurant *Food*, opened with his artist colleagues in the early 1970s. *Food* was a collective project that enabled artists to earn a small living and fund their art practice without succumbing to the ideologically compromising demands of the art market. Other artists who present the consumption of food and drink as art in the 1960s and early 1970s include Allan Ruppersberg, Tom Marioni, Daniel Spoerri and the Fluxus group.

6 Udo Kittelmann, 'Preface', in Kittelmann (ed.), *Rirkrit Tiravanija: Untitled, 1996* (*Tomorrow Is Another Day*) (Cologne: Salon Verlag and Kölnischer Kunstverein, 1996), n. p. As Janet Kraynak has noted, Tiravanija's work has occasioned some of the most idealised and euphoric art criticism of recent times: his work is heralded not just as an emancipatory site, free of constraints, but also as a critique of commodification and as a celebration of cultural identity – to the point where these imperatives ultimately collapse, in the institutional embrace of Tiravanija's persona as commodity. Janet Kraynak, 'Tiravanija's liability', *Documents*, 13 (Autumn 1998), 26–40 (also reproduced in this volume, Chapter 9).

7 Kraynak, 'Tiravanija's liability', 39–40.

8 Gillick, cited in Susanne Gaensheimer and Nicolaus Schafhausen (eds), *Liam Gillick* (Cologne: Oktagon, 2000), p. 36.

9 Gillick, in ibid., pp. 56, 81.

10 Mike Dawson, 'Liam Gillick', *Flux* (August–September 2002), 63.

11 Gillick, in Liam Gillick and Catsou Roberts, *Renovation Filter: Recent Past and Near Future* (Bristol: Arnolfini, 2000), p. 16.

12 Gillick, in Daniel Birnbaum et al., *Liam Gillick: The Wood Way* (London: Whitechapel Gallery, 2002), p. 84.

13 Gillick, in Gillick and Roberts, *Renovation Filter*, p. 16.

14 Beuys is mentioned infrequently in *Relational Aesthetics*, and on one occasion is specifically invoked to sever any connection between 'social sculpture' and relational aesthetics. Bourriaud, *Relational Aesthetics*, p. 70.

15 Umberto Eco, 'The poetics of the open work' (1962), in *The Open Work* trans. A. Cancogni (Cambridge: Harvard University Press, 1989), pp. 22–3. For more about the relation between participation and the open work, see Chapter 3.

16 This is reflected in Bourriaud's discussion of Felix Gonzalez-Torres, an artist whose work he considers to be a crucial forerunner of relational aesthetics. Before his death from Aids in 1996, Gonzalez-Torres gained recognition for his emotive reworkings of Minimalist sculpture using piles of sweets and stacks of paper, to which visitors are encouraged to help themselves. Through this work, Gonzalez-Torres made subtle allusions to politically charged issues such as the Aids crisis (a pile of sweets matched the weight of his partner Ross, who died in 1991), urban violence (handgun laws in *Untitled* (*NRA*), 1991) and homosexuality (*Perfect Lovers*, 1991). Bourriaud, however, demotes this aspect of Gonzalez-Torres's practice in favour of its 'structure' – its literal generosity towards the viewer.

17 Nicolas Bourriaud, *Postproduction*, trans. J. Herman (New York: Lucas & Stern-berg, 2002), p. 43.

18 Rosalyn Deutsche, *Evictions* (Cambridge: MIT Press, 1996), p. 289.

19 Ernesto Laclau and Chantal Mouffe, *Hegemony and Socialist Strategy: Towards a Radical Democratic Politics* (London: Verso, 1985), p. 190.

20 For Lacan, the subject is not equivalent to a conscious sense of agency: 'Lacan's "subject" is the subject of the unconscious … inescapably divided, castrated, split' as a result of his/her entry into language. See Dylan Evans, *An Introductory Dictionary of Lacanian Psychoanalysis* (London: Routledge, 1996), pp. 195–6.

21 'the subject is partially self-determined. However, as this self-determination is not the expression of what the subject *already* is but the result of its lack of being instead, self-determination can only proceed through processes of *identification*.' Laclau, *New Reflections on the Revolution of Our Time* (1990), quoted in Mouffe (ed.), *Deconstruction and Pragmatism* (London: Routledge, 1996), p. 55.

22 Laclau and Mouffe, *Hegemony*, p. 125.

23 Chantal Mouffe, 'Introduction', in Mouffe (ed.), *Deconstruction and Pragmatism*, p. 11.

24 Jerry Saltz, 'A short history', 107.

25 Bourriaud, in 'Public relations: Bennet Simpson talks with Nicolas Bourriaud', *Artforum* (April 2001), 48.

26 Kittelmann, 'Preface', n. p.

27 *Kölner Stadt-Anzeiger* (3 January 1997), cited in Kittelmann (ed.), *Rirkrit Tiravanija*, n. p.

28 Saltz muses on this question in a wonderfully blinkered fashion: 'theoretically anyone can come in [to an art gallery]. How come they don't? Somehow the art world seems to secrete an invisible enzyme that repels outsiders. What would happen if the next time Tiravanija set up a kitchen in an art gallery, a bunch of homeless people turned up daily for lunch? What would the Walker Art Centre do if a certain homeless man scraped up the price of admission to the museum, and chose to sleep on Tiravanija's cot all day, every day? … In his own quiet way, Tiravanija forces these questions to the forefront, and jimmies the lock (so efficiently left bolted by much so-called political art) on the door that separates the art world from everything else.' The 'invisible enzyme' that Saltz refers to should alert him precisely to the limitations of Tiravanija's work and its non-antagonistic approach to issues of public space. Saltz, 'A short history', 106.

29 Jean-Luc Nancy's critique of the Marxist idea of community as communion in *The Inoperative Community* (Minneapolis: University of Minnesota Press, 1991) has been crucial to my consideration of a counter-model to relational aesthetics. Since the mid-1990s, Nancy's text has become an increasingly important reference point for writers on contemporary art, as seen in Deutsche, *Evictions* (chapter four), Pamela M Lee's *Object to be Destroyed: The Work of Gordon Matta-Clark* (Cambridge: MIT Press, 2000), George Baker, 'Relations and counter-relations: an open letter to Nicolas Bourriaud', in Yilmaz Dziewior (ed.), *Zusammenhänge herstellen/Contextualise* (Cologne: Dumont, 2002), and Jessica Morgan (ed.), *Common Wealth* (London: Tate, 2003). See also Chapter 7.

30 'No subject is given, yet the artistic context automatically leads all discussions back to the question about the function of art.' Christoph Blase, *Frankfurter Allgemeine Zeitung* (19 December 1996), cited in Kittelmann (ed.), *Rirkrit Tiravanija*, n. p. He continues: 'Whether this discourse is read on a naïve or a context-educated level – the intermediate level would be the obligatory reference to Duchamp – is a matter of chance and depends on the respective participants. Anyway, the fact that communication in general and a discussion on art in particular takes place, gains a positive value as smallest denominator.'

31 Essentially, there is no difference between utopia (societal perfection) and the microtopia, which is just personal perfection to the power of ten (or twenty, or however many participants are present). Both are predicated on exclusion of that which hinders or threatens the harmonious order. This is seen throughout More's description of Utopia. Describing a troublesome Christian zealot who condemned other religions, the traveller Raphael recounts: 'When he'd been going on like this for some time, he was arrested and charged, not with blasphemy, but with disturbance of the peace. He was duly convicted and sentenced to exile – for one of the most ancient principles of their constitution is religious toleration.' Thomas More, *Utopia* (London: Penguin Books, 1965), p. 119.

32 Gillick, in Birnbaum et al., *Liam Gillick*, pp. 81–2.

33 Gillick, in Gillick and Roberts, *Renovation Filter*, p. 20.

34 We could even say that in Gillick's microtopia, devotion to compromise *is* the ideal: an intriguing but untenable hypothesis, and ultimately less a democratic microtopia than a form of 'third way' politics.

35 However, Hirschhorn was included in the exhibition *GNS* and Sierra in *Hardcore*, both held at the Palais de Tokyo in Paris, then directed by Bourriaud, in 2003. See also Bourriaud's discussion of Sierra in 'Est-il bon? Est-il méchant?' *Beaux Arts*, 228 (May 2003), 41.

36 Sierra, cited in Katya García-Antón (ed.), *Santiago Sierra: Works 2002–1990* (Birmingham: Ikon Gallery, 2002), p. 15.

37 As Laclau argues, it is this 'radical undecidability', and the decision that has to be taken within this, that is constitutive of a political society. Laclau, *Emancipation(s)* (London: Verso, 1996), pp. 52–3.

38 Sierra, cited in García-Antón (ed.), *Santiago Sierra*, p. 46.

39 As Laclau and Mouffe conclude, politics should not found itself on postulating an '"essence of the social" but, on the contrary, on affirmation of the contingency and ambiguity of every "essence" and on the constitutive character of social division and antagonism'. Laclau and Mouffe, *Hegemony*, p. 193.

40 The most substantial example of this approach is Benjamin Buchloh, 'Cargo and cult: the displays of Thomas Hirschhorn', *Artforum*, 40:3 (November 2001), 108–15, 172–3. The peripheral location of Hirschhorn's sculptures has on occasion meant that their contents have been stolen, most notably in Glasgow, 2000, before the exhibition had even opened.

41 Hirschhorn, interview with Okwui Enwezor, in Enwezor et al., *Thomas Hirschhorn: Jumbo Spoons and Big Cake* (Chicago: Art Institute and Renaissance Society, 2000), p. 27.

42 Ibid., p. 29. Hirschhorn is here referring to the idea of quality espoused by Clement Greenberg, Michael Fried and other critics as a criterion of aesthetic judgement. I should like to distance my use of 'quality' (as in 'the *quality* of the relationships in relational aesthetics') from that alluded to by Hirschhorn.

43 Thomas Hirschhorn, in Morgan (ed.), *Common Wealth*, p. 63.

44 Ibid., p. 62.

45 I am reminded of Walter Benjamin's praise of newspapers because they solicit opinions from their reader (via the letters page) and thereby elevate him/her to the status of a collaborator: 'The reader is at all times ready to become a writer', he says, 'that is, a describer, but also a prescriber … he gains access to authorship'. Walter Benjamin, 'The author as producer', in Benjamin, *Reflections*, trans. E. Jephcott (New York: Harcourt Brace Jovanovich Inc., 1978), p. 225. Even so, the newspaper retains an editor, and the letters page is but one among many other authored pages beneath the remit of this editor.

46 The blockade or impasse is a recurrent motif in Sierra's work, such as *68 People Paid to Block the Entrance to Pusan's Museum of Contemporary Art, Korea* (2000) or *465 People Paid to Stand in a Room at the Museo Rufino Tamayo, Mexico City* (1999).

47 *Workers Who Cannot be Paid, Remunerated to Remain Inside Cardboard Boxes*, Kunst-Werke, Berlin (September 2000). Six workers remained inside the boxes for four hours a day for six weeks.

48 Michael Fried, 'Art and objecthood', *Artforum* (Summer 1967), reproduced in Gregory Battcock (ed.), *Minimal Art* (Berkeley and Los Angeles: University of California Press, 1995), p. 128.

49 This exchange took place at the symposium *Viewing Acts: A Panel and Discussion on Contemporary Art and Audience Relations*, New School for Social Research, New York, 5 May 2005.

50 Jacques Rancière, 'The aesthetic revolution and its outcomes', *New Left Review* (March–April 2002), 150.

What kind of participative system? 15
Critical vocabularies from new media art

Beryl Graham

From Cycloramas to VR [virtual reality] (via the tradition of urban panoramas in painting and photography), the 'surround view' has been a recurring element of urban and cinematic manifestos. Of course, the city surrounds us already. Here we just connect the dots, and look again. (Ashok Sukumaran)[1]

Ashok Sukumaran makes artworks using invisible systems – those of electrical or computer networks. The media that he uses are not discrete physical media in the art-historical sense of paint, photography or film, but draw on some of the ubiquitous networks of 'new media' that surround us. His *Glow Positioning System* (2005), for example, makes reference to the global positioning systems (GPS) originally developed for US military use, which tell us where we are on the globe, via invisible satellite connections. This artwork, however, uses the more low-tech existing array of Christmas, Diwali and decorative lights at the busy Kabutarkhana intersection in Mumbai, India, and connects them into a 1,000-ft long panorama. A hand-crank mounted on the pavement, and connected to electronics, provides a way for the audience to 'scroll' this landscape, turning the lights on and off in a wave that moves in the direction of the cranking (figure 15.1). 'It allows the physical length of the view to become a chronological one – to be viewed at a speed determined by the user … The crank mechanism itself refers to not only its specific history in the moving panorama, but also a general history of the moving image: as a driver for cinema.' The artist is here 'connecting the dots' of old and new systems, popular and art media, and he is, above all, aware of how the audience connects with the artwork. As he points out, the fact that the audience can control the work makes for an essentially different experience to that of watching cinema, or a light spectacle. Even though the artwork reacts to the audience in a relatively simple way, there is the physical 'promise of a haptic journey',[2] and the control of time and space, which makes an audience member an active 'user'. Like many of Sukumaran's street installations, no instructions are given for using the work – the audience can, and do, figure out the cause and effect for themselves by drawing on their existing knowledge of technological systems. Neither literacy nor an art education are necessary in order to be an active user and reader of the artwork.

Other artworks by Sukumaran have explored the economic control of electricity or other networks, and have played with disrupting the audience's expectations of what happens when a switch is pressed. Sometimes he reconnects existing computer network systems in unexpected ways: *Sideways* (2006), installed in a gallery in Bangalore, included a networked computer that the audience could use to explore images and texts on screen. If they were observant, they would notice that computer screens near the windows of the office block across the alley were showing enlarged sections of the actions on their own screen. In both of these works, the artist is highly aware of the exact positioning of the audience as user, as voyeur, as controller, or as participant, and audience members discover for themselves their own position in

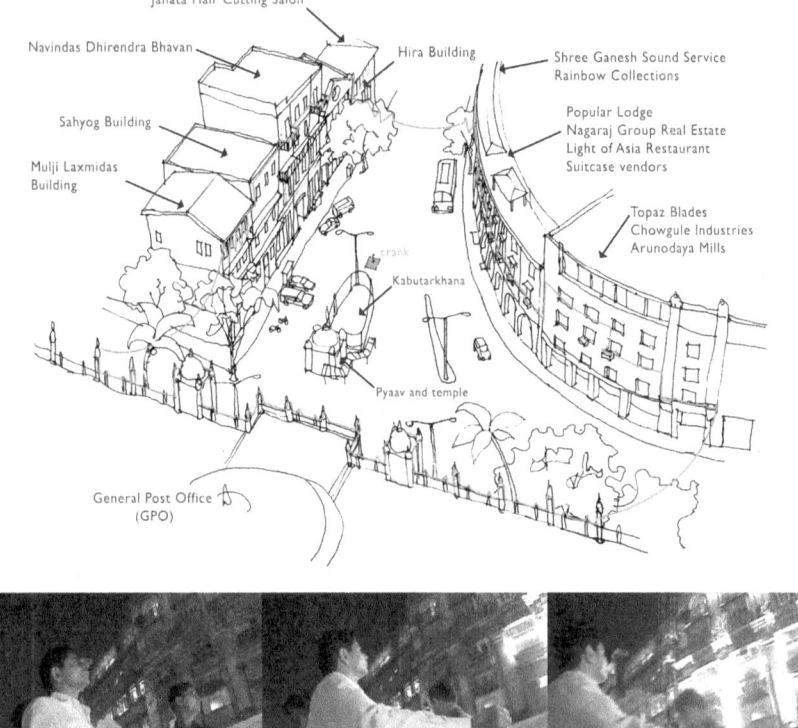

15.1   Ashok Sukumaran, *Glow Positioning System*, 2005. Top: diagram showing installation plan. Bottom: stills from video documentation showing crank in use.

'the system' through their physical and conceptual journey. The artwork is not an object, but a process. Art has, of course, been dealing with issues of immateriality, virtuality, mechanical reproduction, conceptualism, time and audience participation for some time, but the notable thing about new media art is that these factors have been inherent starting points for the work, from which further critical distinctions have been made – for each instance of a participatory system, there has been the question of *how* participatory, and *what kind* of system?

This chapter offers up to the wider field of contemporary art the critical vocabularies resulting from this awareness of different kinds of participatory system. These vocabularies have not, of course, sprung fully formed from the thigh of a computer programmer, but have been informed by previous art histories, including those of conceptual art, activist art and performance art.[3] They are offered, therefore, not in the first flush of the technological 'hype cycle', but in the light of post-utopian experience. It is notable how the rhetoric of both 'audience participation' and of new technologies has tended towards hyperbole: the inventions of the railways, electricity, the internet, trade unions and quilting bees share certain vocabularies of connecting people, sharing knowledge, and somehow bringing light to the world. In Victorian England the new railway lines were promising, in a poem in the *Illustrated London News*, to 'Link town to town; unite with iron bands/ The long estranged and oft embattled lands.'[4] Because new media art draws from histories of technology and of popular culture as well as art, then practitioners are less inclined to think that any technology, information superhighways included, is likely to unite embattled lands, or that audience participation is inherently better or more empowering than other forms of reception.

'New media' is in itself a particularly ungainly term for a wide range of emerging media and communication tools. It encompasses not only digital versions of media such as video, but media which behave in significantly different ways, including computer networks, the internet, software viruses and global positioning systems. The complex networks of new media have found themselves in a 'post-medium' condition where the exact techno-logical medium is not as important as the way it which it 'behaves'. In 2003 Guggenheim curator Jon Ippolito and others considered the challenges of conserving a range of contemporary art including Felix Gonzalez-Torres's *Public Opinion* and Mark Napier's *Net Flag*, and came to the conclusion that it was the 'medium-independent behaviours' of the work, such as interactivity, that demanded the most rigorous language of documentation and curation.[5]

In 1999 curator Steve Dietz described the characteristics of net art as those of interactivity, connectivity and computability: 'interactivity' is an inherent characteristic of computer software as further defined later in this chapter; 'connectivity' characterises the *live* connections and links of the internet, which mean that net art would not function properly if disconnected; 'computability' means that software is a set of logarithmic instructions which once started off, may evolve over time with a degree of autonomy.[6] These characteristics may be present together or separately in new media art. The internet, for example, can behave like broadcast, like a telephone, like publishing, like a bulletin board, or can facilitate less familiar behaviours, as with wikis, where several users can simultaneously edit the same online 'document'.[7]

Alex Galloway, in his 2004 book *Protocol*, gives perhaps the clearest schema of differences between kinds of networked computer system, and the kinds of behaviour that they afford, naming them as: centralised networks (one to many), decentralised networks (several to many), and the rhizome-like distributed networks (many to many) (see figure 15.2). Broadcast media can be seen as a centralised network, whereas the distributed network of the internet works in a way that is fundamentally different in terms of understandings of distribution, and of audience participation. Galloway goes on to further differentiate levels of control within distributed networks by describing the system of 'protocol', the 'management style' of which can be hierarchical or can distribute control.[8] New media vocabularies have to be very specific about the control of what connects with what. The points where the lines of communication in a network meet are called 'nodes', and nodes where many lines converge become 'hubs', so that actually, some nodes can be more important than others, even in a rhizomic network. Vocabularies of 'behaviour' are thus emerging which are proving more useful than attempting to describe artworks by specific medium.

Because new media can involve computer software that, once programmed, can carry out instructions with a degree of autonomy, there are additional questions about authorship in particular.[9] In 1997 Cornelia Sollfrank, for example, worked with computer programmers to create *Net Art Generator*. The generator searches the internet in response to keywords entered by any user, to automatically collage images and code into 'artworks'. These works were submitted under various female pseudonyms in response to a German museum's call for submissions to a web art competition.[10] While there have been previous examples of artist challenging the craft values of the 'artist's hand' by using chance, or by making 'art machines', computer software offers more layers of autonomy, and hence authorship: If Sollfrank works with programmers, then who is the author of the work? If the users type in the keywords, then are they the authors? If the software is exercising autonomy and 'learning' over time from previous keyword searches or other stimuli and this effects the selection of images to collage, then is the software programmer still the author? All of these questions present challenges to art institutions' notions of author and art object; Sollfrank pointed out how, as early as 1997, art institutions were 'already starting to force the new art form into traditional categories of "work" and "author", which many net artists had dreamt of escaping'.[11]

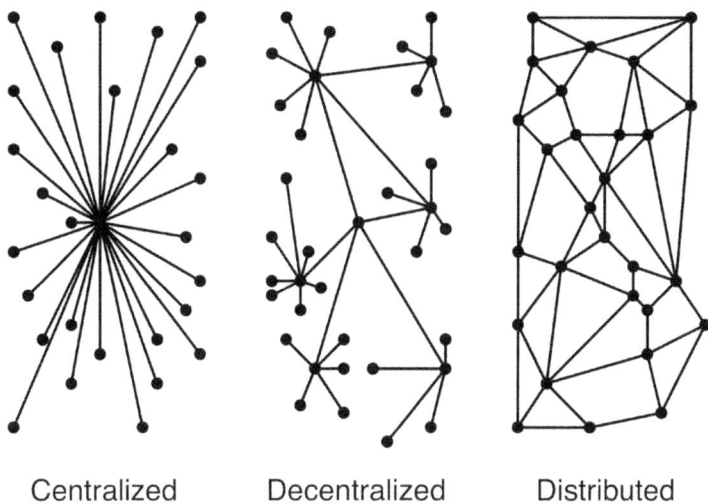

Centralized   Decentralized   Distributed

Diagram of centralised, decentralised and distributed networks, drawn by Beryl   **15.2**
Graham based on Paul Baran's *On Distributed Communications Memorandum RM–3420–PR*, published by the RAND Corporation in August 1964.

New media artists tend to take the active reader as a given starting point, and work with layers of activity beyond a conceptual understanding of activity. The particular characteristics of new media, with the ability to cut and paste, copy, manipulate and morph any media in digital form, adds a layer of active readership that is literal rather than metaphorical, and inherently offers the opportunity for the reader to become an author. The rhetoric around this opportunity has the tendency to become dominated by the commercial new media of internet shopping, narrowcasting by streaming video on the web, and rather lame 'interactive television'. To use the vocabulary of computer networks, these are not, however, distributed many-to-many systems of 'user-generated content' where the audience may also be the author, but rather hyped-up centralised systems. Those working with new media art are, there-fore, necessarily critical of the many levels of activity possible within reader-ship and authorship.

Using the terminologies of behaviours and systems already introduced, these vocabularies are described under three headings, which are in current usage in contemporary art discourse, but which are notoriously loosely used – those of interactivity, participation and collaboration.

Interactivity

> as far as we're concerned, many of the works we make (whether online or in the gallery) are not interactive in the purest sense but are navigable bodies of data. (Thomson and Craighead)[12]

Interactive literally means 'acting upon each other'. Taken literally or physically, very little art, including new media art, is actually interactive. Sukumaran's *Glow Positioning System*, for example, physically reacts to the input of the audience (via a turning crank), but does not physically act upon the audience in return. Such works are currently more usually described as 'reactive'. Even with a relatively simple reactive artwork, however, the nature of the reading changes considerably. As Sukumaran has already illustrated, audience 'control' of time and space makes for significantly different kinds of readings. The critical repercussions of the computer affordance of hypertext – where links offer branching choices rather than a linear narrative – have been well described and discussed, including the obvious limitations of the approach. As long ago as 1991, Ann Sargent Wooster was pointing out that:

> The current romance of interactivity promises such things as being a better or more democratic art form and/or the art form of the future. Many of these siren songs are based on a false understanding of the term interactivity. The word interactive sounds like it will alleviate the alienation of modern life by generating a dynamic alliance between artists and their audiences, joining them together in a splendid waltz that lets viewers become equal partners with artists in creating art. Yet interactive videodisks do not empower the viewer to create a wholly new work with the materials they are given, and they only appear to eliminate the alienation of the artist and viewer present in most avant-garde art.[13]

New media artists have had to be very clear about using the correct terms for their artwork. The artists Thomson and Craighead, for example, whilst exhibiting at the San Francisco Museum of Modern Art, state explicitly (in the quote above) that their work is not interactive or empowering, but uses systems of 'navigable bodies of data'. This navigation of a database structure, where items relate to each other (and to items in other databases, as in a 'relational database') harks back to the vocabulary of rhizomes, and Galloway's typology of networks. Because most new media is inherently reactive in some way, those using the media have necessarily had to map in more detail different kinds of reactivity or interactivity: the audience being in control of the pace and timing of an artwork is different from watching a broadcast or video installation; choosing options to navigate a body of data is different from being able to have creative input. Those using computers in particular need to be clear about what is interacting with what: humans may interact with each other, computers may interact with each other, but human computer interaction (HCI) has been a field of particular study owing to the inherent difficulties of this feat, and exact vocabularies have necessarily been developed.

In 1973, Stroud Cornock and Ernest Edmonds, for example, subdivided their typology of 'Art and Interaction' into dynamic, reciprocal, participatory or interactive.[14] They stated that 'An "interactive" art system has within it an artefact so organized as to be able to sustain a conversation with the user approaching the kind of conversation we witness between people.' They acknowledged that 'approaching' was perhaps the nearest to strictly defined interaction that computer-based media could offer. Computers can afford a very elaborate series of reactions, but no computer program has yet passed the Turing Test for artificial intelligence, where a human judge must decide whether their typed dialogue is with a human or a computer.[15] Those working with HCI have developed some highly critical definitions of conversation. Alluquère Rosanne Stone, for example, in describing some corollaries of Andy Lippman's definition of interaction and conversation, lists mutual interruptibility, graceful degradation and limited look-ahead as just some of the conversational skills that computer program find particularly tricky. 'Thus interactivity implies two conscious agencies in conversation, playfully and spontaneously developing mutual discourse, taking clues and suggestions from each other as they proceed.'[16]

Computer program may be poor playful conversationalists, but can be quite good at chess, with its more limited set of logical rules for interaction. The vocabulary of computer-based games can, therefore, be an additional differentiation of different kinds of systems, from the simple reaction and navigation of 'shoot-em up' games, to collaborative construction games, or where the game is a platform for competition between humans.[17] New media vocabularies of interaction have, therefore, been necessarily accurate about levels and behaviours of interaction, independent of the hype which may surround individual media: virtual reality systems, for example, may be very 'immersive' and have sophisticated input devices such as movement-sensitive helmets, but on the scale of interaction, they show a simple 'reactive' behaviour to human input, similar to Sukumaran's hand crank.

New media art, therefore, cannot offer a full conversation between a machine and a person, but it can offer a platform for conversation between people, and can act as a 'host' to facilitate this. The skill of the artist lies in understanding the 'behaviours' of both the new media, and of people, without lapsing into a prescriptive 'behaviouralist' approach. Rafael Lozano-Hemmer's *Body Movies, Relational Architecture No. 6* (2001–) is a huge installation in outdoor plazas and public squares, and offers users the opportunity to make giant shadows with their bodies (figure 15.3). The work actually enables at least two kinds of reaction or interaction. First, there are projected photographic images of people, which the audience can see properly only when they cover the photographs with their own shadow – they may find themselves copying the body shape of someone of a different gender or race. If individuals in the audience collaborate to cover all of the photographs at the same time, then the computer program reacts by projecting a new crop of photographs. Audience readings of the artwork may, therefore, be complex, but here the computer program is simply reacting to their movements. Second, the audience can freely improvise with the huge shadows to interact with each other. The kinds of interaction encouraged are, therefore, very varied, and work differently for groups or individuals: those who just like to stand and look at things will be satisfied; the shyer person may like to be 'introduced' to the party by covering the photographs; while the extroverts will do their own thing with the shadows, or one person may move through all three states. Here, the new media art is reacting to the audience, and acting as a good 'host' for full inter-action between humans.

The skills of hosting such interaction are often underestimated, and demand a particular approach: 'Dependency on participation is a humbling affair. My pieces do not exist unless someone dedicates some time to them. Most people, with the exception of children, will opt not to participate in an installation in a public space, which may seem strange considering that we live in the age of reality TV and the society of the spectacle.'[18] The limited nature of programmed reaction can here serve to host the much wider range of human interaction. There is room for creative input here, and for any kind of interaction between people, including conflict. Huge shadows might squish smaller shadows between their fingers, and there is the obvious oppor-tunity for sexual shadow play and exhibitionism. The artist has described, however, that trust should be placed in the participants to deal with this in a way appropriate to their own culture – night-time revellers in Liver-pool apparently showed a tendency to act out shadow stripping, while the participants in Madrid, for example, showed a marked territorial respect for the shadows of other people. Those in Rotterdam brought along props for visual performances. Humorous shadow violence and sex were accepted, and people discovered that participants who got too dominant or brainlessly violent could be removed from the limelight if others stood together in front of the spotlights.[19] If the audience are to participate fully then the host can only start off the participatory system, and trust the audience to do the rest. Lozano-Hemmer vouches that: 'Successful pieces that feature "interactivity for groups" are usually out-of-control.'[20]

Vocabularies of interaction help to define who is interacting with what, and the sub-divisions of levels of reaction. The amount of 'control' for the user or audience play an important part in defining these levels, but full inter-activity between users will always be 'out of control' to an extent. New media has a particular relationship with 'control': although certain forms such as virtual reality, GPS and the internet were all developed for 'command and control' military systems, the distributed network of the internet was designed to function even if several 'nodes' were destroyed, which means that the internet can never be 'under control', however hard organisations or govern-ments might try. Hackers and artists will usually resist control systems, and theorist Lev Manovich has described the heaving, out-of-control mass of data on the internet as being of such enormous dimensions that it is 'sublime'.[21] The vocabulary of new media tools being able to form a platform to 'host' interaction between people has obvious parallels with other participative contemporary art forms. Rirkrit Tiravanija's reconstruction of his New York flat at the Serpentine Gallery in London plays very deliberately as his real-world role of host, and the 'platforms' and 'stations' for audience interaction which increasingly feature in arts festivals.[22]

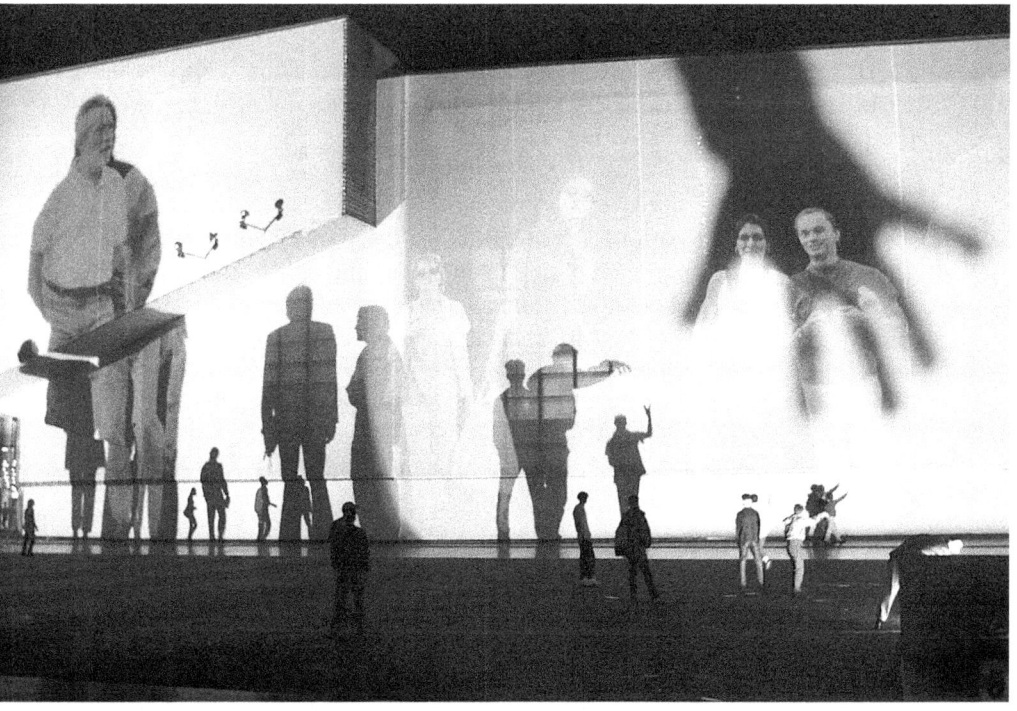

Rafael Lozano-Hemmer, *Body Movies, Relational Architecture No. 6*, Rotterdam, 2001.   **15.3**

Participation

> BONANNO (THE YES MEN) … Right now, we could organise a flash mob
> over the internet that could maybe get a couple of thousand people to show up
> at an instant to do something ridiculous at any given place. The internet creates
> a context for social networks, but it doesn't actually make them. … I think this
> is the critical issue, what kind of networks are those and are they temporary or
> are they more sustaining?[23]

Participation – to have a share in or take part in – is the kind of idea that
sounds good to certain curators and politicians alike: to encourage stake-
holders, audience participants, to go beyond reactive button-pressing and join
Wooster's 'splendid waltz' between artist and audience … However, there is a
range of levels of participation: political participation can mean simply voting
once every few years or changing policy; artistic participation can mean just
showing up (or logging in) or having real creative input. The history of new
media art, and net art in particular, has a strongly activist history – those who
once used 'telephone trees' to notify networks of individuals about protest
gatherings now use email or mobile phones to create 'flash mobs'. The Yes
Men quoted above use a wide range of 'tactical media', and famously created
a web page parodying Dow Chemicals, which has been mistaken for the real
thing.[24]

Those who have defined types of participation most sharply have,
unsurprisingly, often been from socio-political fields, with experience of
the power relationships within systems designed by the powerful. Sherry
Arnstein, for example, uses examples from city planning to describe eight
rungs on the 'ladder of citizen participation', ranging from manipulation and
therapy (non-participation), through informing, consultation and placa-
tion (tokenism), to partnership, delegated power and citizen control (citizen
power).[25] The path to full citizen control is obviously a steep and rugged one,
and those who have worked in 'socially engaged art' or projects involving
audience participation, may recognise ruefully that therapy or tokenism are
more often achieved than the higher rungs of the ladder.[26] Coinciding with the
vocabulary of conversation from the field of new media is the vocabulary of
dialogue from socially engaged art: Suzi Gablik, in 1995, placed her 'connective aesthetics' in contrast to the individual artist as author, and talked of 'a
new kind of dialogical structure'.[27] Grant Kester's book *Conversation Pieces:
Community And Communication In Modern Art* explicitly makes conversation
a metaphor for describing the behaviours of socially engaged art.[28]

Many participatory art projects, where creative input is possible, whether
new media or not, tend to hover around Arnstein's 'delegated power' rung
rather than full 'citizen control'. The audience is participating in a 'system'
designed by someone else, artist or otherwise, and they may be contributing a

square to a larger quilt project, or making a small ceramic figure for Anthony Gormley's *Field for the British Isles* (1993). There may be tighter or looser parameters to the systems: for example, *Learning to Love You More* (2002–), a project by Harrell Fletcher and Miranda July, allows anyone to send in an artistic response to various directive yet open 'assignments', and the result is a web site containing many high-quality responses. In this case, the artists can filter the responses before they go online, which goes some way towards addressing the concerns that traditional arts institutions may have about artistic 'authorship' and control issues over open audience participation – the work was selected for the 2004 Whitney Biennial.[29]

Ever since the internet ceased to be solely for military access, however, the system has been one of 'user-generated content' and, in theory at least, of 'citizen control' (subject to economic access, of course). Anyone can put material on the internet, the audience can be the author, and the recent excitement around 'Web 2.0' is merely due to the fact that it is now easier to put more kinds of media online with less technical knowledge. Commercial iterations of Web 2.0 such as YouTube, where anyone can put a video online, have raised questions about commercial control of the means of distribution. Beyond the obvious questions of copyright, there are the more subtle questions of how the audience (who may also be the participants) navigate and filter the content: like an 'open submission' exhibition, there are those who act as filters for this mass participation, by selecting 'favourites' in a curatorial manner (the differentiation of these kinds of filtering are explored further in the next section on collaboration).

New media, therefore, offer particular kinds of mass participation, afforded by Dietz's characteristics of 'interactivity', 'connectivity' and 'computivity'. Both socially engaged art and new media art can offer 'platforms' for interactive, communicative experience. The difference here is that new media (or any connective communications media) can offer this interaction remotely or at a distance. Annmarie Chandler and Norie Neumark identify 'distance' as a common factor in fax art, certain conceptual art and net art.[30] Just as technologies of connection such as railways or the telegraph were met with deep suspicion as well as the utopian rhetoric mentioned earlier, the issue of 'distance' has been problematic for those involved in socially engaged art, as it connotes distance from audience, from responsibility and from face-to-face feedback. Those with a background in public art or community art are often disturbed by the 'distance' of connectivity and scorn the ersatz nature of 'online communities', even though the internet may appeal to internationalist leanings. The opening quote from the Yes Men concerning flash mobs was a response to Lucy Lippard's concerns that human contact was being somehow replaced: 'what kind of community access do we have now? Was the organizing all done on the internet? No more getting small groups together and getting them to go out and have more meetings …?'[31] However, as the Yes Men state, those using new media seriously for participation do not see them as a utopian replacement for human contact, but as just one of the 'necessary media' for connection and interaction.[32]

This hybridity between 'distance' and site-specificity is often found in participative projects. *Learning to Love You More*, for example, involved many physical workshops, and the direct contact of an existing network of physical personal exchanges, as well as purely online 'open submissions'. What the Yes Men also stress is the importance of a critical differentiation of how the various kinds of new media function in time, space and social context: 'flash mobs' are a quick means of contacting networks of mobile people at a distance and getting them to gather in a physical place – useful for a fast political response to, say, nuclear waste transportations, or having a party, but less useful for sustaining knowledge or debate, which may happen better on web sites. Heath Bunting's net art project *BorderXing Guide* (2002–2003), for example, maps on a web site various accessible European border crossing points, with a little help from GPS and physical hiking on the ground, and encourages others to share their knowledge.

Those using new media, therefore, have a highly developed awareness of the vocabulary and etiquette of participation 'at a distance': online discussion lists, for example, have formal rules similar to those of political meetings to try to avoid the online equivalent of shouting matches, cliques and walk-outs. They work more slowly over time, compared, for example, to live 'chat rooms', and are consequently more suitable for a deeper level of debate, and a 'sustaining' network. Discussion lists archives can be searched, and, therefore, form a 'published' record which can be used for academic research. Discussion lists can involve large numbers of participants over time, whereas chat rooms tend to be small-scale social spaces. These differences of function and scale have been critically examined by many in HCI and new media, as computer software can offer tools for mapping and visualising the recurring vocabularies and themes from the vast amounts of text produced by online discussion. In his work on 'Very Large-Scale Conversations', Warren Sack is keen for example to make parallels with other fields of study:

> Just as physical architecture facilitates certain activities and inhibits others (compare, for instance, the exchanges supported by amphitheatres versus those supported by cafes), so do system architectures facilitate certain types of conversations. For example, media architectures like television broadcasting facilitate one-to-many exchanges, but do not directly support a democratic, many-to-many exchange between people[33]

A major challenge for those working with audience participation in contemporary art is that much of the knowledge about the difficult task of achieving meaningful participation comes from the fields of design, architecture, socially-engaged art or social systems, rather than from art. As with the difficulty of achieving full 'interaction' between the audience and an artwork, it is easy to drastically underestimate the skills needed to achieve the higher levels of participation, especially in an art context. In 1972, the artist Joseph Beuys was writing reports on each day's proceedings at his *Bureau for Direct Democracy*, a room installation a *Documenta 5* where the artist sat for 100 days in order to develop discussion. As he rather endearingly reveals, sometimes this did not even get to the first rung of the ladder: '11:00 a.m. Until now about eighty visitors in the office. Half, however, remain standing in the doorway and look around, others walk past the blackboards, and then remain longer in the office. Some only come to the door and leave in fright, as if they had come into the wrong restroom.'[34]

Beuys is not alone in finding it difficult to set up an art platform for meaningful participation. Many art projects have built web sites for user-generated content and participation, only to find that nobody participated. Hosting participation is a delicate skill, and the participatory system must be clear, yet flexible, and the authorship must be at least partially 'decentralised'. Here again, the language of network systems is useful: an immaculately designed distributed system can quickly become a centralised system if nobody participates and one person ends up creating the content, and a conversation can become a monolog.

Collaboration

> Many of today's collaborations in art contexts operate horizontally and consist of agents from different fields; very often these collaborations lie on the border between activist, artistic and curatorial activities and they tend to be self-organised. (Maria Lind)[35]

If interaction and participation in the relationship between artwork and audience are more often claimed than achieved, then collaboration is an even rarer beast. Full collaboration – 'working jointly with' – implies the production of something with a degree of equality between the participants, rather than participating within a system designed by somebody else: something 'self-organised' in the words of Maria Lind, 'Citizen Control' in the words of Shelly Arnstein, or perhaps Wooster's 'splendid waltz that lets viewers become equal partners with artists in creating art'. In practice, collaboration rarely takes place between viewers and artists, but more often between artists and others, in small production teams, and often, as Lind mentions, blurs the roles between artists, activists and curators. This collaborative approach to production is often confused with the idea of collaboration between artist and audience: Sukumaran's *Glow Positioning System* for example, could be claimed to be collaborative in production because he worked with lighting designers, technicians and the owners of existing domestic and shop lights, even though they were working under his direction. However, he would never claim that he was collaborating with the audience.

There are useful vocabularies of collaboration available from histories of 'community art' and media workshops, where, for example, artists might work with non-artists on a video project, and be able to access the recurring debates of who has control over storyboarding, directing, producing, or the means of distribution. There are also differentiations available from the history of 'artist-run spaces', as to whether an organisation is a collective, a cooperative or an agency. What new media offers in addition, however, is a particular understanding of online systems of collaboration, and of Open Source production methods.

Computer-based tools for collaborative practice are of great commercial interest, and have been researched extensively since the 1980s under the acronym of CSCW (Computer Supported Cooperative Work). Artists have

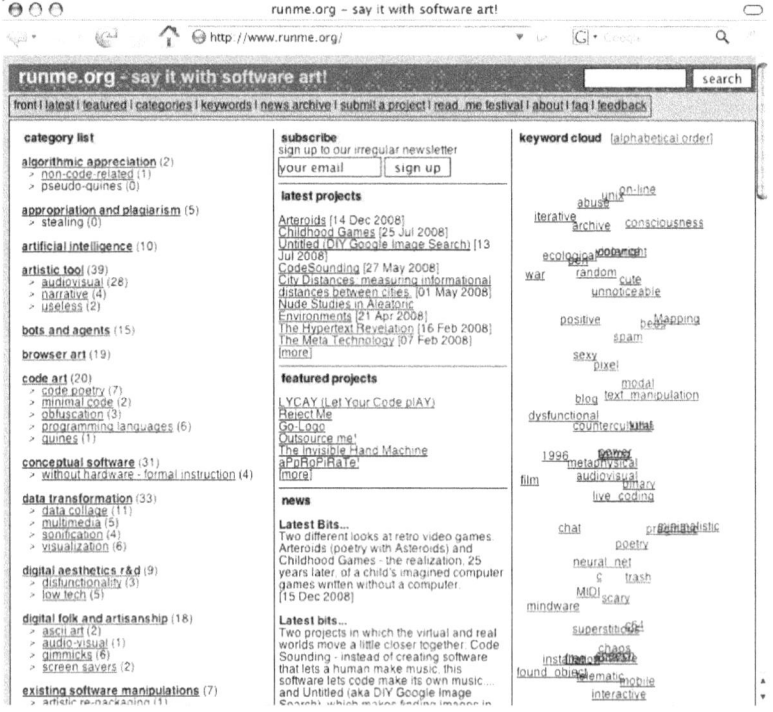

15.4   *Runme*, software art website (www.runme.org/), 2003 – . Screenshot showing keyword cloud (accessed 2 February 2009).

also been very interested in the field, and organisations with an interest in cross-disciplinary new media production have helped develop the vocabulary of artistic collaboration using teleconferencing, online textual tools or any combination of useful media. Sara Diamond, for example, in her quest for 'The Beauty of Collaboration', has questioned whether the creative input of individuals function in a 'parallel' or 'conjoined' way, and she has experimented with collaborative tactics gathered from fields as diverse as online performance and wearable technology, even going so far as to lock individuals from different disciplines in a room for some time, and filming what happens.[36] As with discussion lists and chat rooms, different new media work in different ways. Wikis, for example, enable several people to edit the same online text over a period of time, but exactly how this works out depends on the system and the people. Those with most experience of using these tools tend to develop their own critical view of the affordances of the tools. Tactical media activist Geert Lovink, for example, was of the opinion that wikis work best in combination with frequent cigarette breaks away from the screen, and that they 'reflect a culture of pragmatic non-commitment'.[37] The structure of new media collaborative systems can reflect any of the beauties and pitfalls of collaboration that human flesh is heir to, but there are, nevertheless, certain new media characteristics that make a difference in the understanding of collaboration. The arts group Furtherfield in London, for example, were able to collaboratively curate the project *Do It With Others* (DIWO) with other people online and in the physical gallery space. Anyone subscribing to their discussion list could join in. Artworks were viewed using a webcam, and reviewed and selected by live text 'chat'. The artworks were moved around the physical gallery space by collective decision, again observed by webcam. This experimental and hybrid approach was in line with the organisation's experience of collaborative projects, and what they learnt from the process was shared online via discussion lists and blogs.[38]

In 1996, museum theorist Friedrich Kittler argued that beyond the obviously active nature of reading hypertext, the databases of museum collections offered not only active reading and navigation, but active sorting and curating: 'Visitors too – they especially – should be given access not just to lovingly presorted information but to all available information.'[39] Software can offer various means by which the audience may sort masses of information themselves. YouTube, for example, is a large online database of visual material, from which users can 'tag' their own favourites into a 'collection'. If you liked one video clip in an individual's collection, then you might like another clip. Software also tracks the popularity of items, so that you can, if you wish, look at what most other people are looking at. Beyond these simple mechanisms, however, the user can have more control over the ways in which the data is searched and arranged. The runme.org web site for example, is an open submission collection of software art (figure 15.4). As there is no established taxonomy of different kinds of software art, the artists who submit their work can 'tag' their submission with keywords of their choice. Those who search the site also have their keywords recorded. On the web site, a 'keyword cloud' visually maps central or more peripheral keywords. Recurring keywords get used more, and gradually change the way the collection is arranged by category. These are called 'folksonomies', and function bottom-up from the audience rather than top-down as taxonomies from the curator. The audience is here not collaborating in artistic production, but is arguably collaborating in 'curatorial' production. If a participant is someone who participates in a system designed by others, then certain new media characteristics can offer something closer to the user being able to change the system, even if only in subtle ways.

'Open Source' is the other new media vocabulary which may be useful to those considering types of collaborative production. The source code for Open Source software is made 'open' to other programmers. It is made open primarily by not copyrighting and restricting it as with proprietary software, and also by making its working structure obvious to other programmers, and open to modification. The system varies over space and time – many individual programmers may be working on the same software at the same time but in different places, or they may be working in teams to evolve software into different 'versions' (version 2.0, for example), which develop over time. The term has been picked up and used rather loosely, but as Felix Stalder explains, it is actually a specific means of software production which, like Galloway's 'protocol', may have a hierarchical structure: 'The openness in open source is often misunderstood as egalitarian collaboration.'[40] Applications made with Open Source software may be bought and sold, and may be produced in hierarchical teams indistinguishable from corporate structures – the bottom line is simply that the code is open to view and change. Where a political position of free software is intended, then the term used is FLOSS (Free/Libre and Open Source Software), and where the 'operating system' of a computer is FLOSS, such as Linux, then this enables users to escape the control systems, limited metaphors and great expense of Macintosh or Microsoft. In 2006, the Brazilian government announced that most software used by most public institutions in Brazil should be Open Source, so the position has significant real-world repercussions, but as Stalder states, this does not mean that everyone can participate in changing the software. The software can be more accessible, and adapted and evolved for specific local needs, but participants still need to be programmers in order to change the system. Open Source, therefore, is not the same as an open work, or an open system: to apply the term to a non-new-media example, if an artist cooks a meal for a group of people and encourages people to interact, then, that is a participatory system; if he gives people the recipe and the project manager's notes, and tells them to adapt the idea for their own contexts (assuming that they have the skills), then that would be Open Source.

Vocabularies of collaboration in new media, therefore, concern production and authorship, and differ depending on 'the system'. If collaborative authorship is to be achieved, then online tools and a distributed network can help people do this at a distance, but these tools do have pre-existing face-to-face equivalents. If the system is to be changed collaboratively, then online tagging methods such as folksonomies can help to change the ways in which data is navigated, but this is acknowledged to be only a partial change in a system. If the way in which a system works is to be changed collaboratively, then the source code must be available for modification, and the knowledge available to the collaborators.

Critical vocabularies for an audience of beasts

> The trouble with participation, it seems, is that apart from making us forget what art's all about, and inducing the very restlessness of mind which it's supposed to ease, it makes people behave like wild beasts. (Michael Shepherd of *The Sunday Telegraph*, on the 1971 Robert Morris exhibition)[41]

In 1971, the artist Robert Morris had a retrospective exhibition at the Tate, London, where the public could physically interact with large sculptural forms. The exhibition received scathing press headlines and was closed after five days, when audience injuries were reported.[42] Steve Dietz's 2004 article traces how the show was reinstalled as hands-off sculpture, and how the 'dangerous' participative elements were safely confined to art objecthood via a film wherein a naked woman moved among the sculptures. Dietz jokingly blames Robert Morris for all subsequent institutional fear of physical interaction. The perceived 'dangers' of participation are, however, not so much practical as psychological, and concern some deeply held value judgements.

There are several layers to the perceived incompatibilities between the value systems of fine art and those of participation. The first layer of issues concern a basic Cartesian distain for bodily interaction – the devalued half of the mind/body split – those bestial parts of us which so disturb *The Sunday Telegraph* critic quoted above. The very idea of touching and changing art rubs up against much curatorial training in conserving and theorising about art. However distanced new media may appear at first sight, it crucially places the body and hapticity of at the centre of the debate. Rather than 'othering' the body in terms of race, gender, sexuality or abjection as in fine art, new media has tended to focus on the relations between body and identity in 'virtual space'.[43]

The second layer is related, but concerns the political position of the audience. An individual audience member as a disembodied eye in solitary contemplation is one thing; the undifferentiated mob of wild beasts wanting to touch and participate is quite another. As critic Hal Foster commented pithily in 2006: 'This is where I side with Sartre on a bad day: often in galleries and museums, hell is other people.'[44] Much of the history of contemporary art has been based on shocking, resisting or challenging 'the audience', and yet participation might involve the audience challenging the artist, curator or institution. The vocabulary of art museums in relation to audience has been driven by interpretation, accessibility and demographic target groups, and haunted by the spectre of 'dumbing down', rather than by consideration of what systems might be needed for different levels of participation.[45] The vocabulary of HCI or interface design necessarily writes the human user into the equation of the system, rather than considering them as beasts howling at the gates. Members of the audience are not an audience in this vocabulary – they are always a user, and the system must always react to the user, and may be more or less open to user-generated content. If audience members are interacting with each other as well as participating in an artwork, they might even form a pack of beasts – the very word 'flash mob' is likely to make the hierarchical art critic think of the guillotine. If the masses are interacting with each other as well as with the artwork, then this is always going to be outside the control of the artist, curator or gallery. As Lozano-Hemmer states, this is going to be a humbling affair, demanding trust in the audience, rather than the assumption of bestial behaviour. Those working in public places, with public participation, or with participative new media art, have critical knowledge of different systems of control, but eventually have to be able to deal with the 'out-of-control'. It could be argued that those who work with new media art, with its platforms for human interaction, Open Source production, distributed networks, flash mobs and the fluid, changing, 'sublime' masses of data with broken links and glitches galore, are particularly well equipped to deal with and relish the out-of-control.

A third layer of incompatibility concerns the meaning of the technologies of connection and communication between people. Technologies such as mobile phones, chat rooms or wifi are now identified strongly as popular culture for children and young people – lightweight, fast and shallow. In 1970, Jack Burnham curated the exhibition *Software* in New York, and commented on the press reaction that

> As a result of training and personality, many art critics consider themselves 'humanists' with strong feelings concerning the encroachments of technology on nature and cultural traditions … most critics instinctively realize that it would damage their art world credibility if they became serious advocates of hard technology as an aesthetic life-style.[46]

Times have changed since 1970, but perhaps not substantially for art critics. If critics do not use the media themselves for serious ends, then they are unlikely to be aware of the content carried by connective media. The vocabulary of new media is sometimes found in the mouths of contemporary critics, but is frequently associating new media with the 'shallow' technology of flash mobs or chat rooms, regardless of the content of the mob or chat. Critics may compare examples of new media unfavourably with participative art but, unfortunately, they rarely compare examples of new media *art*. Nicolas Bourriaud has commented pejoratively on 'Nokia art – producing interpersonal relations for their own sake and never addressing their political aspects',[47] whereas there are many examples of artists using these technologies where the political content is the point of the artwork – this is not 'Nokia art' any more than Rirkrit Tiravanija makes 'restaurant art'. Like most art, it is the content and intent of the work that is important, rather than the media used. As critics and curators become more aware of how new media art works, however, there is more evidence of using vocabulary from the field, even if only as a metaphor for a way of working. To quote Nicolas Bourriaud again: 'I prefer a "collaborative" approach, on conditions of availability of powerful ideas, I hope … First of all, I need to have a general conception. Then a discussion starts out. I am more concerned not with creation of works, but with, I would say, a program, I would compare it with a computer program, with the same degree of flexibility.'[48]

How then, beyond the basic questioning of vocabularies of audience and authorship, can the critical vocabularies from new media art (and from political fields) be most usefully applied to defining kinds of audience participation in contemporary art contexts? Firstly, using the vocabulary of 'behaviours' rather than media helps to identify what the art does rather than what it is, and is suitable for art based on process rather than object. Dietz's vocabulary of interactivity, connectivity and computability helps to identify for arts workers and audiences alike what they might need to consider when exhibiting, and how the art may behave in time and space. In avoiding media-specific terminologies, not only is the press hype around specifically 'new' media such as virtual reality circumvented, but also the critical knee-jerk question of how the 'media' of a urinal, a Thai meal, video tape, or a wiki can possibly be art. The vocabulary of 'systems' also usefully describes the ways in which things work, and Galloway's 'protocols' of centralised, decentralised and distributed networks form some of the more simple new media vocabularies which may be usefully applied to participative art systems.

The words interaction, participation and collaboration are particularly differentiated in new media, both because they are different 'systems' and because of the question applicable to all three terms – 'between what/whom'? The behaviours are very different, dependent upon whether the action takes place between people, between human and computer/programmed artwork, or between machines. In contemporary art discourse, there tends to be less clarity: in Bourriaud's *Relational Aesthetics*, for example, it is unclear whether the 'relations' are between artwork and context, between teams of artists in production, between artwork and audience, or between audience members. The terms interaction, participation and collaboration may also be elided, or elevated a rung or two on the ladder. As a starting point, a critical resistance to the tendency to use a term that claims to be several 'rungs' above the actuality is a step towards a more accurate vocabulary, and away from hyperbole. Within each category of interaction, participation and collaboration there is a ladder of levels, with the top rungs of each being very difficult to fully achieve (even for Joseph Beuys). A reactive artwork is not interactive; consultation is not citizen power. Those seeking to criticise participative art should therefore be able to describe different kinds of participative intent, and in recognising the difficulties of the higher levels, a respect for the artistic skills needed to reach even the middling rungs might be developed.

Within all three areas of interaction, participation and collaboration, new media vocabularies offer descriptions of the different behaviours afforded by the different media, and different levels of 'control' for the audience. Both political and new media practices have useful vocabularies for describing systems in terms of hierarchies, including Arnstein's ladder of participation. Galloway has acknowledged the hierarchy or 'protocol' behind computer systems, and importantly has described computer systems in terms of networks rather than ladders. The three kinds of network of centralised, decentralised, or distributed/rhizomic, work in very different ways in terms of power relationships between the 'nodes' in the network. If the audience or participants are considered as nodes, then it becomes easier to map exactly what kind of 'level of control' and hierarchical position they occupy. Whether or not a system itself can be changed is an important question for both new media and for politics – user-generated content is one kind of participation, the ability to change the taxonomy of the way in which information is displayed is a more sophisticated effect upon the system, but the control of a system (a 'sysadmin' in computer parlance) still demands particular access and skills.

For all three areas of interaction, participation and collaboration, there is also a recurring vocabulary of 'conversation'. Used critically, this vocabulary helps to clarify the relationships between artist, artwork and audience: there can be no literal full conversation between artwork and human, but an artwork can provide a platform for conversation between people. An artwork may, therefore, be critically judged on the quality of that platform. There are also critical way-stations on the path *towards* a conversation between artwork and audience: an artwork may simply be dynamic in reaction to an audience, or simple dialogue-like exchanges may be possible with a certain amount of elaboration on either side. Conversation has both common-language and technical levels of critical use, but has the advantage of having a pre-existing critical structure even in popular culture: formulaic dialogue greetings exchanged with strangers are different from conversations with friends, chat is different from discussion (both online and off) and the 'choices' of automated telephone lines are justifiably loathed for their lack of human conversational skill. In software fields conversation is highly defined in terms of reciprocity, mutual interruptibility, graceful degradation and limited look-ahead, and so the shortfall in human-computer interaction can be mapped against this. Those in socially-engaged art and political practices have been using conversational terms for art for some time, and can differentiate call-and-response from therapeutic monologue, or consultation from the conversation between citizens. 'Games' form another set of critical vocabularies, where different kinds of games can be differentiated by the relationships between the players and the game, from 'single-player shooter' to cooperative production. Both common-language and technical definitions of conversation can help to puncture hyperbole about the 'democratic' potential of participation in general, and can help form a more realistic judgement of whereabouts on the ladder (or in the network) the art project actually sits.

When it comes to 'hosting' participation, some artists or curators are very much better at this than others. Participative systems challenge not only the role of the artist but that of the curator – if artists are making 'platforms' for interaction, or if the audience are sorting artworks into folksonomies, then what is the role of the curator? The kinds of skills needed come from a wide variety of disciplines: an understanding of audience, social systems, conversational patterns, cultural contexts and media systems are needed. New media systems are only one example of a network of systems available – they are not an ersatz for face-to-face participation, but just one of the 'necessary media'. In considering 'generosity and exchange' in art including new media art, Ted Purves argues that, 'The cultural context that they are made "as" is less interesting as a central point of discussion than a consideration of what they "do". By moving action and project based art practice into the world, it opens such work to be considered simply as an act placed in a world of acts, alongside good neighbor days, telemarketing drives and acts of petty theft.'[49]

New media can, therefore, offer a certain vocabulary of systems, but the parting proviso to this offering is that the best way of understanding how systems work tends to be using and pushing the system, rather than the tradition of distanced, perception-based art criticism. Those who use the systems tend to end up with a more accurate and more critical vocabulary. Christiane Paul, for example, a curator at the Whitney Museum of American Art with a particular interest in new media art, offers a useful warning within the critical structure of systems in art:

it is important to avoid falling back into the trap of systems utopianism – the belief that 'systems', depending on their degree of openness, can produce better conditions. Perhaps the term 'open system' itself needs to be avoided since it inherently promises what it can never deliver. Each and every system and project needs to be investigated in terms of its framework and ask questions about the degree of openness and constraint it is based upon …[50]

Notes

1 Ashok Sukumaran, 'Glow Positioning System' http://out.in/GPS/ (accessed 9 March 2009).
2 Ibid.
3 The relationships and differences between new media art and other art forms, with particular reference to issues of immateriality, audience, and participative systems, are discussed at more length in Beryl Graham and Sarah Cook, *Rethinking Curating: Art after New Media* (Cambridge: MIT Press, 2010).
4 Simon Penny, 'Consumer culture and the technological imperative: the artist in dataspace', in Simon Penny (ed.), *Critical Issues in Electronic Media* (New York: State University New York, 1995), p. 62.
5 Jon Ippolito, 'Accommodating the unpredictable: the variable media questionnaire', in Alain Depocas, Jon Ippolito and Caitlin Jones (eds), *Permanence Through Change: The Variable Media Approach* (New York: Guggenheim Museum, 2003), pp. 47–54. Also available on: www.variablemedia.net/e/preserving/html/var_pub_index.html.
6 Steve Dietz, 'Why have there been no great net artists?' (1999), www.voyd.com/ttlg/textual/dietz.htm (accessed 9 March 2009).
7 This chapter forms part of the ongoing research work of CRUMB, the resource for curators of new media art: www.crumbweb.org. Therefore, the quotes here are often directly from practising artists and curators, including material from discussion lists and forums, as well as from published works.
8 Protocol is a term of some complexity, and may present difficulties to traditional cultural or linguistic analysis in that it resists 'interpretation'. As Galloway states: 'Protocol is a circuit, not a sentence.' Alex Galloway, *Protocol: How Control Exists after Decentralization* (Cambridge: MIT Press, 2004), p. 53.
9 Edmond Couchot defines two levels of autonomy: 'The term "low autonomy" (or also "low self-organisation") concerns systems whose "performances are realised thanks to changes in the connections that were not explicitly programmed", and "high self-organisation", systems that accomplish tasks that "emerge from the way the machine itself evolves".' Edmond Couchot, 'The automatization of figurative techniques: toward the autonomous image', in Oliver Grau (ed.), *MediaArtHistories* (Cambridge: MIT Press, 2007), pp. 181–92.
10 This *Female Extension* project led to the museum proudly announcing how many responses the call had generated and how interesting it was that so many were from women artists. On the day the winners were announced (all men), Sollfrank revealed her intervention.

11 Cornelia Sollfrank, *net.art generator* (Nurenberg: Verlag Fur Moderne Kunst Nurenberg, 2004).

12 Kathleen Forde, 'You have just entered room "010101 Round Table"', in *Open: The magazine of SFMOMA*, 4 (Winter/Spring 2001), 35.

13 Ann-Sargent Wooster, 'Reach out and touch someone: the romance of interactivity', in Doug Hall and Sally Jo Fifer (eds), *Illuminating Video* (New York: Aperture, 1991), p. 294.

14 Cornock and Edmonds also acknowledge that, within 'interactive', interactions are more or less complicated depending on whether the interaction involves an individual, a small group or a culture, or is cross-cultural. Stroud Cornock and Ernest Edmonds, 'The creative process where the artist is amplified or superseded by the computer', *Leonardo*, 6:11 (1973), 11–15. Definitions of kinds of interactivity for new media art are an area of some complexity and debate and are further explored in Graham and Cook, *Rethinking Curating*. More recently, Nathan Shedroff has described 'continuums of interactivity' which are differentiated by 'the amount of control the audience has over the tools, pace or content; the amount of choice this control offers; and the ability to use the tool or content to be productive or to create'. Nathan Shedroff, 'Information interaction design: A unified field theory of design', 2002, www.nathan.com/thoughts/unified/index.html (accessed 9 March 2009).

15 The Loebner Prize Competition, in which computer programs undergo a version of the Turing Test, has a website that documents transcripts of the 'conversations'. No program has yet passed the Test, but the prize is awarded for the best attempt. See www.loebner.net/Prizef/loebner-prize.html (accessed 14 April 2009). According to Louise Poissant, the word 'interactive' in French dictionaries 'is defined as a term from the field of computing: *Which allows* [one] *to use a conversational mode*.' Louise Poissant, 'The passage from material to interface', in Grau (ed.), *MediaArtHistories*, pp. 229–50.

16 Alluquère Rosanne Stone, *The War of Desire and Technology* (Cambridge: MIT Press, 1995), pp. 10–11.

17 An accessible overview of games is outlined in Katie Salen and Eric Zimmerman (eds), *The Game Design Reader* (Cambridge: MIT Press, 2005); Alexander R. Galloway, *Gaming: Essays on Algorithmic Culture* (Minneapolis: University of Minnesota Press, 2006).

18 Heimo Ranzenbacher, 'Metaphors of participation: Rafael Lozano-Hemmer interviewed by Heimo Ranzenbacher', *Ars Electronica Festival 2001*, http://90.146.8.18/en/archives/festival_archive/festival_catalogs/festival_artikel.asp?iProjectID=8231 (accessed 14 April 2009).

19 Ibid.; and Joyce Hor-Chung Lau, 'Now in Hong Kong, an interactive display by Rafael Lozano-Hemmer', *International Herald Tribune*, 15 November 2005. www.iht.com/articles/2006/11/15/opinion/HKART.php (accessed 9 March 2009).

20 Rafael Lozano-Hemmer, 'Too interactive (belated)', *New-Media-Curating Discussion List*, 6 December 2001, www.jiscmail.ac.uk/lists/new-media-curating.html (accessed 09 March 2009).

21 Lev Manovich, 'Data visualisation, new media, and anti-sublime.' Lecture at the

Fruitmarket Gallery, Edinburgh, 18 November 2002. Manovich was referring to Lisa Jevbratt's artwork *1:1* (1999–) http://jevbratt.com/, where each of thousands of pixels maps on to an internet location.

22 The 'platforms' of *Documenta 11* spring to mind and the *Utopia Stations* project at the Venice Biennale. See Molly Nesbit, Hans-Ulrich Obrist and Rirkrit Tiravanija, 'What is a Station?' (2003), reprinted in Claire Bishop (ed.), *Participation* (Cambridge and London: MIT Press and Whitechapel Gallery, 2006), pp. 184–9.

23 The Yes Men in Melanie Franklin Cohn (ed.), *Who Cares* (New York: Creative Time Books, 2006), p. 33.

24 http://theyesmen.org/hijinks/bbcbhopal (accessed 9 March 2009).

25 Sherry R. Arnstein, 'A ladder of citizen participation', *Journal of the American Planning Association*, 35:4 (July 1969), pp. 216–24. http://lithgow-schmidt.dk/sherry-arnstein/ladder-of-citizen-participation.html (accessed 9 March 2009).

26 'Socially engaged art' is here used as a term to encompass practices such as community art, art in the public interest, or social sculpture, where the audience may be non-traditional, and may participate in, or be consulted about, art production. This discussion has been informed in part by Ele Carpenter's research work on comparisons between the two fields: Ele Carpenter, 'Politicized Socially Engaged Art and New Media Art' (PhD thesis, University of Sunderland, 2008).

27 Suzy Gablik 'Connective aesthetics: art after individualism', in Suzanne Lacy (ed.), *Mapping the Terrain: New Genre Public Art* (Seattle: WA Bay Press, 1995), p. 76.

28 Grant Kester, *Conversation Pieces* (Berkeley: University of California Press, 2004). Kester includes references to Homi K. Bhabha's 'conversational art', Tom Finkelpearl's 'dialogue-based public art', and Mikhail Bakhtin's concept of 'dialogical' systems (although Bakhtin used it in a much more technical sense – concerning the development of language – than the common use of the word). See also Beryl Graham, 'A dialogue with an idiot? Some interactive computer-based art', in Finn Bostad, Craig Brandist, Lars Sigfred Evensen, Hege Charlotte Faber (eds), *Bakhtinian Perspectives on Language and Culture: Meaning in Language, Art and New Media* (London: Macmillan, 1995), pp. 217–32.

29 These issues are further explored in Graham and Cook, *Rethinking Curating*.

30 Annmarie Chandler and Norie Neumark (eds), *At a Distance: Precursors to Art and Activism on the internet* (Cambridge: MIT Press, 2005).

31 Franklin Cohn (ed.), *Who Cares*, p. 33.

32 Ele Carpenter, 'Gregory Sholette and Nato Thompson', *CRUMB* (2004), www.crumbweb.org/getInterviewDetail.php?id=26 (accessed 9 March 2009).

33 Warren Sack, 'Discourse architecture and very large-scale conversations', in Robert Latham and Saskia Sassen (eds), *Digital Formations* (Princeton: Princeton University Press, 2005). hybrid.ucsc.edu/SocialComputingLab/Publications/wsack-discourse-paper.doc (accessed 9 March 2009).

34 Joseph Beuys and Dirk Schwarze 'Report on a day's proceedings at the Bureau for Direct Democracy' (1972), in Bishop (ed.), *Participation*, pp. 120–4.

35 Maria Lind, 'The collaborative turn', in Johanna Billing, Maria Lind and Lars Nilsson (eds), *Taking the Matter into Common Hands: On Contemporary Art and Collaborative Practices* (London: Black Dog Publishing, 2007), pp. 15–31.

36 Sara Diamond, 'Introduction' to *Summit: Participate/Collaborate: Reciprocity,*

Design and Social Networks, conference, Banff: Banff Centre for the Arts, Banff New Media Institute, 30 September–3 October 2004; Sara Diamond, 'Aesthetics of Collaboration', panel at *ISEA04,* conference, Tallinn, 17 August 2004; Anne Nigten, *Tunnels and Collisions*, 2004, http://archive.v2.nl/v2_events/2004/papers/Nigten-tunnels-connect-2004.pdf (accessed 09 March 2009).

37 Geert Lovink, 'Theses on wiki politics: an exchange with Pavlos Hatzopoulos for Re-public', www.re-public.gr/en/?p=39 (accessed 9 March 2009).

38 See http://blog.furtherfield.org/?q=node/96 (accessed 9 March 2009). This project, and the collaboratively structured NODE.London festival are discussed by Graham and Cook, *Rethinking Curating.*

39 Friedrich Kittler, 'Museums on the digital frontier', in John Hanhardt (ed.), *The End(s) of the Museum* (Barcelona: Fundació Antoni Tàpies, 1996), p. 73.

40 Felix Stalder, 'On the difference between Open Source and Open Culture', in Marina Vishmidt, with Mary Anne Francis, Jo Walsh and Lewis Sykes (eds), *Media Mutandis: a NODE.London reader. Surveying Art, Technologies and Politics* (London: NODE/Mute, 2006), p. 194.

41 Quoted in Jon Bird, 'Minding the body: Robert Morris's 1971 Tate Gallery retrospective', in Michael Newman and Jon Bird (eds), *Rewriting Conceptual Art* (London: Reaktion Books, 2000), p. 88. On this exhibition, see Chapter 6 in this volume.

42 The headlines included 'Visitors Play Role in Funfair Art', 'Assault Course at Tate Gallery' and 'The have-a-go show'; Steve Dietz, 'Is it all Robert Morris's fault?' *Yproductions: WebWalkAbout* (19 December 2004) www.yproductions.com/WebWalkAbout/archives/is_it_all_robert_morriss_fault.html (accessed 9 March 2009).

43 See Michele White, *The Body and the Screen: Theories of internet Spectatorship* (Cambridge: MIT Press, 2006).

44 Hal Foster, 'Chat rooms' (2004), reprinted in Bishop (ed.), *Participation*, p. 194.

45 The issue of 'audience studies' in relation to participative systems is discussed in Graham and Cook, *Rethinking Curating.*

46 Jack Burnham, 'Art and technology: the panacea that failed', in Kathleen Woodward (ed.), *The Myths of Information: Technology and Post-Industrial Culture* (Bloomington: Indiana University Press, 1980), pp. 206–7.

47 Claire Bishop, 'Antagonism and relational aesthetics', *October,* 110 (Autumn 2004), 43. A revised version of this essay is reproduced in this volume (Chapter 14).

48 Miroslav Kulchitsky, 'Interview of Miroslav Kulchitsky with Nicolas Bourriaud', *Boiler,* 1 (1999), www.nyu.edu/tisch/preservation/program/student_work/2006 spring/06s_1806_campbell.pdf (accessed 14 April 2009).

49 Ted Purves, response to Dilettante Ventures, 'Maria Lind – tactical/agnostic artist – Ted Purves', *Leisurearts* (26 April 2006), http://leisurearts.blogspot.com/2006/04/maria-lind-tacticalagnostic-artist-ted.html (accessed 9 March 2009).

50 Christiane Paul, 'Public forum and openness', *Tate Online Events: CodE of practice: Online Panel Discussion June 13 – July 18, 2005* (23 June 2005) www.tate.org.uk/forums/thread.jspa?threadID=2932&start=15&tstart=0 (accessed 9 March 2009).

Index

Note: Page numbers in italic refer to illustrations; 'n' after a page reference indicates the number of a note on that page.

EU authorised representative for GPSR:
Easy Access System Europe, Mustamäe tee 50,
10621 Tallinn, Estonia
gpsr.requests@easproject.com

www.ingramcontent.com/pod-product-compliance
Lightning Source LLC
Chambersburg PA
CBHW072130170526
45158CB00004BA/1316